EDWIN LONGSDEN LONG RA

Mark Bills

with essays by Juliet Kinchin and Simon Olding

Foreword by Sir Philip Dowson, CBE,
President of the Royal Academy

cygnus arts

London **Cygnus Arts**
Madison & Teaneck **Fairleigh Dickinson University Press**

PUBLISHED IN THE UNITED KINGDOM BY
Cygnus Arts, a division of Golden Cockerel Press
16 Barter Street
London
WC1A 2AH

PUBLISHED IN THE UNITED STATES OF AMERICA BY
Fairleigh Dickinson University Press
440 Forsgate Drive
Cranbury
NJ 08512

First published 1998

ISBN 1 900541 55 6
ISBN 0 8386 3821 X

CATALOGUING-IN-PUBLICATION DATA
Catalogue records are available from the British Library
and the Library of Congress

PRINTED BY GORENJSKI TISK IN KRANJ, SLOVENIA

CONTENTS

LIST OF ILLUSTRATIONS

Page references to illustrations of works by Edwin Long are listed under the artist's name in the index on page 184.

FOREWORD

by Sir Philip Dowson CBE, President, Royal Academy of Arts

ACCLAIMED DURING HIS LIFETIME, but sadly neglected over recent years, Edwin Long RA was a prime example of a Victorian artist who used the Royal Academy of Arts as the institution through which he gained artistic, commercial and social success. From 1855 he exhibited at the Royal Academy's annual summer exhibition, to the plaudits of critics and public alike. Indeed, it was the exceptional reception accorded his monumental *Babylonian Marriage Market* that ensured Long's election as Associate Member of the Royal Academy. Five years later he achieved full Academician status, depositing for posterity of his proficiency as a painter, a study of a female oriental water carrier, *Nouzhatoul âouadat.* Yet Long's association with the Royal Academy extended beyond the field of painting; like his fellow Academicians, Luke Fildes and G. F. Watts, he commissioned the architect Norman Shaw RA to design not one, but two grand studios.

In keeping with his peers such as Frederic, Lord Leighton PRA and Sir Edward Poynter PRA, Edwin Long viewed his association with the Royal Academy as confirmation of his own artistic abilities. It was this sanction of artistic status which recommended their works to a powerful group of new collectors such as Sir Merton Russell-Cotes. Acceptance by the Royal Academy was a guarantee of quality and aesthetic distinction.

This book provides a succinct overview of the work of a long neglected Royal Academician and describes the relationship between Victorian artist and Victorian patron. It is to be most warmly welcomed.

PREFACE

by Mark Bills

EDWIN LONG IS A NAME that has become obscured by his more famous contemporaries. In his day, however, Long was a well-known, respected, and above all successful and popular artist. Although the criterion of the public and critics is clearly different today, Long's paintings and the context within which they were created remain important, informing us of an significant artist at the heart of the Victorian art world.

When I began working at the Russell-Cotes Art Gallery and Museum, Bournemouth, I was fascinated with the large period works by Long in the collection and even more surprised that so little was known about this important figure. Relegated to the ranks of the lesser Victorian Olympians, research has been unjustly meagre, a point this book aims to redress. The book includes a biography of this very private artist and a catalogue of known works. The gathering of research and the compilation of the catalogue has been an enormous task. I have brought together the majority of his completed oils of which all his major works are included. Due to Long's prolific output in often catering to a demanding public, I have not included the hundreds of smaller oil studies that exist. I am sure that several works, particularly before 1857, are still extant. However, that is the nature of such a task and it is my hope that publication will bring to light many missing and previously unknown works.

In the ranks of the Academicians Long was a respected figure. His paintings reveal a range and interest that informs us that he was not a mere follower but an artist who made a unique contribution to British nineteenth century art. As the *Art Journal* wrote in their obituary of Long in 1891:

to the large mass of the populace he was a great artist . . . and in spite of his wrapping up his subject in a vast amount of erudition, his work almost always contained a keynote of interest, which not only fastened itself on the memory, but sometimes even engrossed attention to an altogether unexpected extent.

ACKNOWLEDGEMENTS

Researching the life and works of Edwin Long has been an enormous task and I am indebted to those who have helped me to complete this book. The real starting point of the work was the collection at the Russell-Cotes Art Gallery Museum and in the compilation of the catalogue I am grateful to the work of the gallery's previous curators, in particular to the late Richard Quick, whose *Life and Works of Edwin Long R.A.* has been for a long time the only booklet on Long, and to Penny Thompson who worked on the early stages of compiling information on Long. I would also like to thank the research work of Chris Batty carried out whilst on placement from the Winchester School of Art at the Russell-Cotes, and to Jane Audas, Sally Bills, Susan Buck, Paul Houston and Virginia Woodcock.

I would also like to thank all of the curators who have responded to requests for information about their collections. I would like to thank Dr Catherine Gordon in particular as well as other members of staff at the Witt Library. I am grateful too, to all the other libraries and archives that were extremely helpful in my research and all the individuals who offered useful advice. I am grateful to Dr Jody Lamb whose information was extremely helpful.

Private collectors have been of enormous help in compiling this catalogue and I would like to specially thank Dr Chan Cheng and Irene Matlin for allowing me to visit their homes once owned by Long. I would like to acknowledge the help of all the auction houses, particularly Agnew's who had many dealings with Long, without whom the catalogue could not exist, and to Sotheby's and to Christie's and their invaluable archives.

In addition I would like to thank Natwest Bank who gave financial support in the early stages of research and to the late Doris Heading whose generous bequest made much of this work possible.

EDWIN LONGSDEN LONG RA

CHRONOLOGY

1829 Edwin Longsden Long born on 16 July in Bath, the son of James Long, a Congregationalist Dissenter, whose family home is in Kelston, Somerset.

late 1830s–1845 Educated at Dr. Charles William Viners Academy, 15 Edward Street, Bath.

1846 Enrols as at student at James Matthew Leigh's School of Art, Maddox Street, London, despite objections from his family and friends. Among his contemporaries there are the painters P. H. Calderon and J. B. Burgess.

c. 1847–49 Twice attempts to enter the Royal Academy and, although he is accepted as a 'probationer' on both occasions, he fails to secure a place as a student.

c. 1848 Continues his art studies with a visit to Italy.

c. 1849 Sets up as a portrait painter in Bath at 15 Old Bond Street. He paints the portraits of local dignitaries including several of Bath's mayors. The first painting that brought him to repute is his portrait of *Sir Hugh Gough* which was made into a lithograph in 1850.

1853 In March, Long marries Margaret Jemima Aiton, of 31 Via Condotti, at the British Consulate in Rome. Her father, William Aiton, is a surgeon at the Navy and MD. On his return Long moves to a new studio at 28 River Street, Bath.

1855 Three of his portraits are accepted at the Royal Academy Exhibition. All three receive favourable mentions in the *Art Journal*.

1856 Commissioned to paint portraits of important figures including Lord Ellesmere and Lord Robert Grosvenor.

1857 Attends classes at the studio of John 'Spanish' Phillip. They travel together to Spain where he his encouraged to copy and learn from the example of Velasquez and Murillo. On his visit to Madrid and Seville in this year Long painted his first Spanish subject, *Un ochativo por el amor de Dios*, of a congretation leaving a church in Seville which he titled. After this visit Long travelled to Spain regularly between 1857 and 1873

1858 Permanent move to London, beginning at 53 Upper Berkeley Street West. He exhibits *Un ochativo por el amor de Dios* to great success at the British Institution.

1859 Exhibits his first Spanish subject at the Royal Academy, *Bravo El Toro!* Experiences failure in exhibiting his Spanish pictures at Wallis's where he fails to sell any.

1860 Visits Burgos in Spain. On 10th May, he is one of 119 men who enrolled in the Corps of Artist Volunteers set up from the fear of a French invasion. The Artists Rifles, officially 38th Middlesex (Artists)

Rifle Volunteers, included Morris, Millais and Rossetti under their CO Leighton. Moves to 33 Ovington Square, London.

1862 *Dialogus Diversus* exhibited at the British Institution, later bought by Sir Merton Russell-Cotes who mistakes it for a John Phillip. As well as painting Spanish genre scenes Long paints his first large scale biblical subject, *Jairus' Daughter*.

c. 1866 Extended visit to Andalucia, where, according to Spielmann, he lives with shepherds in the mountains.

1867 Travels to Rome, a visit which results in three important genre scenes, *The Catechism, Begging for the Monastery* and *St. Anthony's Day*, the last two being exhibited at the Royal Academy of this year. *St. Anthony's Day* receives critical acclaim in *The Times* and *Art Journal*.

1868 *1st Earl of Ellesmere* exhibited at the National Portrait Gallery. The Doré Gallery, Fairless and Beeforth proprietors, opens at 35 New Bond Street.

1870 *A Question of Propriety* and *Lazarillo and the Blind Beggar* exhibited at the Royal Academy.

1871 Studies portraits of Phillip II and his Queen in Madrid in preparation for *The Suppliants*.

1872 *The Suppliants* exhibited at Burlington House.

1873 *The Moorish Proselytes of Archbishop Ximenes, Granada, 1500*, Long's last grand Spanish history painting, completed. A print is produced from it in the *Illustrated London News*.

1874 Makes an extensive tour of Egypt and Syria.

c. 1874–75 George Clausen studies at his studio and carries out pictorial research for him. On Long's advice Clausen visits Belgium and Holland.

1875 Visits Cairo and paints the place and its inhabitants. *The Babylonian Marriage Market*, commissioned by Edward Hermon MP for a reputed £1,700, is exhibited at Burlington House. On the strength of this work and the unanimous critical acclaim he receives, he is elected Associate of the Royal Academy. Long moves to 19 Marlborough Hill, where his garden pavilion studio at 1a Carlton Hill is called 'Long's Den' after his middle name.

1876–61 Fitzjohn's Avenue is commissioned by Long from the architect Richard Norman Shaw.

1877 *An Egyptian Feast* is exhibited at the Royal Academy. Long paints this as a sequel to *The Babylonian Marriage Market* using the same source, Swayne's *History of Herodotus*.

1878 On 13 April, Long is commissioned by Taddy Thomas to produce a copy of *Esther*. In the summer, Long visits Paris in an unsuccessful attempt to find an authority on the costume of Persian women. *The Gods and their Makers* is exhibited at Burlington House.

1879 Long and his family joins the yacht *Walrus* at Weymouth for a

Mediterranean cruise organised by the Baroness Burdett-Coutts (one of Long's chief patrons). The party includes the Baroness and Henry Irving. The Baroness commissions several portraits by Long including herself, Hannah Brown and several of Irving. *The Late Hannah Brown, the Lifelong Friend of Baroness Burdett-Coutts* is exhibited at the Royal Academy.

1880 In March, Long moves into 61 Fitzjohn's Avenue which he names 'Kelston' after his family home in Somerset. Due to its design he refers to it as 'The Labyrinth'. *Henry Irving as Hamlet* is exhibited at the Royal Academy.

1881 The Graphic Gallery, at 190 Strand, exhibits *Mrs Patrick Campbell in Balkan Dress,* in their exhibition 'Types of Beauty'. A double-page engraving of this appears in *The Graphic* as 'Types of Beauty, No. IV', on 23 July. *Diana or Christ?* is exhibited at Burlington House. Long is elected as a full Royal Academician. His diploma painting is *Nouzhatoul-âouadat* (*The Delight of the Home*).

1882 *The Babylonian Marriage Market* achieves an auction house record when it is sold at Christie's on 13 May for £6,615 (including copyright).

1883 In January, Gustave Doré dies. Fairless and Beeforth, the fine art publishers of the Doré Gallery, commission Long to paint *Anno Domini. Merab* and *Michal* are exhibited at the Royal Academy.

1884 The Galleries (also named The Lawrence Gallery) opens at 168 New Bond Street, with Fairless and Beeforth as the proprietors. *Anno Domini* is exhibited there from January 1884. The gallery remains open until 1889.

1885 His companion paintings *Zeuxis at Crotona* and *Merab* and *Michal* are exhibited at The Galleries.

1886 Long is commissioned by Thomas Agnew & Sons to paint a series of national beauties. His series of three paintings *Jephthah's Vow* is completed.

1887 The *Daughters of Our Empire* series is exhibited at Thomas Agnew & Sons. The twenty national beauties include five of England and fifteen of other countries in the British Empire. Long commissions another studio house from Richard Norman Shaw. For this one, Long designs the entrance doors, using beaten brass with mediaeval knights and horses in armour. There are also Roman and Spanish mosaics included in the building's interior. The Manchester Jubilee Exhibition includes eight of Long's most important pictures.

1888 Moves into the new 'Kelston' at 42 Netherhall Gardens. Spielmann interviews Long for his series in The Graphic, *Artists in their Studios.* He is drawn by Paul Renouard working on *The Crown of Justification* in his new studio for *The Graphic.*

1889 *Alethe* is exhibited at Burlington House. *Propitiating the Deity* is commissioned by Agnews.

CHRONOLOGY

1890 The Galleries, 168 New Bond Street closes.

1891 Long completes his last painting, *The Parable of the Sower*. He refuses 5,000 guineas for it and it is left to his widow on his death. Sir Merton Russell-Cotes visits Long in his studio and sees the painting. Long's work continues to be exhibited at the Doré Gallery. *Alethe* sells at auction for 700 guineas. On 15 May, Long dies of influenza. His funeral is held at St Augustine's on Kilburn Park Road. The funeral includes a full choral mass and is attended by fellow Academicians and eminent figures. He is buried at Hampstead West Cemetery. His financial success is reflected in his will in which he leaves £1,750 per annum to be divided between his three children for life. His eldest child, Ethel contests the codicil and remains estranged from her mother for the rest of their lives.

1892 On 23 September, Long's eldest son dies in a railway accident at Burgos, Spain. In December, the Doré Gallery is renamed the Sacred Art Gallery by its owners Fairless and Beeforth. It exhibits a large number of Long's religious paintings including *Anno Domini, Diana or Christ?* and *The Story of Jephthah*. It stays open until 1896.

1893 The Edwin Long Gallery opens at 25 Old Bond Street. The gallery shows work exclusively by Long, mainly from the collection of his widow including *The Parable of the Sower*. The venture is short-lived, closing early in 1894. Fairless and Beeforth open other premises at 128 New Bond Street, which remain open for two years.

1897 The Sacred Art Gallery closes.

1906 *The Parable of the Sower* is exhibited under its subtitle *Christ Preaching on the Shores of Galilee* at the Royal Society of Artists exhibition, New Street, Birmingham.

1907 Long's widow Margaret Jemima dies on 27th January. Long's studio effects are sold on 24th October.

1908 On 1 February, Margaret's collection of Long's paintings is sold at Christie's at a fraction of their value when Long was alive. *The Parable of the Sower* sells for £131 and 5s. 'Kelston' is put on the market.

1912 On 1 January, Alice and Edward Elgar move into their new home at 42 Netherhall Gardens and rename it 'Severn House'.

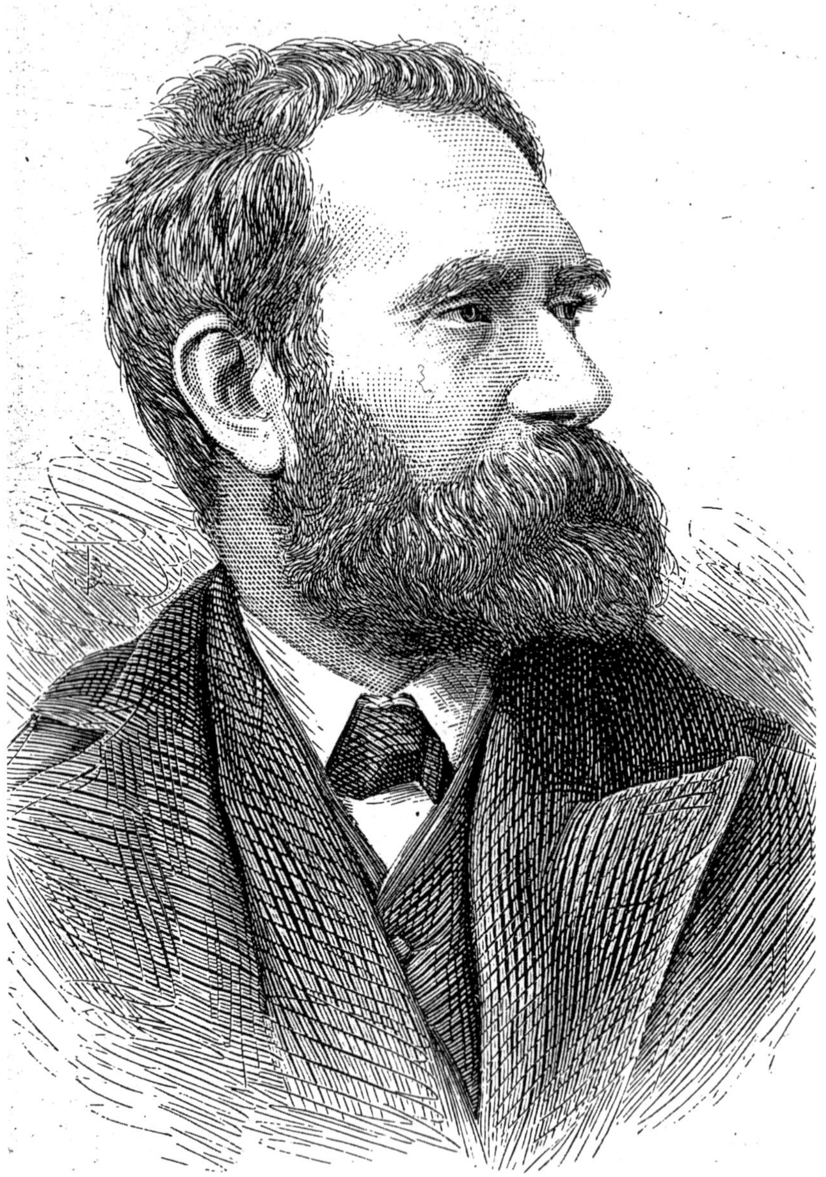

Fig. 1. 'The Late Edwin Long, R.A.' From *The Illustrated London News*, 1891.

THE LIFE AND WORKS *of* EDWIN LONGSDEN LONG RA (1829–1891)

Mark Bills

EDWIN LONGSDEN LONG was an artist who lived at a time when it was possible, through artistic endeavour, to gain the highest benefits that society had to over. It was possible to gain material riches and unprecedented social status. Like many other artists of the Victorian period Long rose in society and wealth, but, unlike many, he died before the golden period had faded. On his death Long left a personal estate of around £120,000, a phenomenal amount that is a testament to the success and popularity of his art. But by the turn of the century, Britain's love affair with its art and artists had diminished. On the death of his wife in 1907, the value of Long's paintings had plummeted to less than a tenth of their value on his own death in 1891. One of the Victorian art world's important figures had drifted into relative obscurity. The throngs of visitors who went to see his work at Burlington House and Bond Street had disappeared, his auction house record dismissed as an isolated sensation.[1] The aesthetic backlash against the Victorians in the new century had a complete and damning effect on him. In the contemporary critics' eyes he was the worst possible thing – an artist supremely popular with the Victorian public. In 1961, Gerald Reitlinger wrote that "a dingy Phillip or an anaemic Alma-Tadema will often be found to bear Long's signature in exceptionally large letters."[2] Such criticism was typical of an attitude that swept away a fascinating period of British art history. It is only in the last ten years that this critical attitude has been replaced with a growing interest in the paragons of Victorian art. Edwin Long's history is that of a quintessential Victorian artist, an artist who reveals to us today the popular tastes, interests, ambitions and prejudices of the period.

The details of Long's early life remain sketchy. As *The Illustrated London News* noted: "Mr. Long has so persistently refused to give any information respecting himself to biographers that it would be indecorous for us to attempt to penetrate the veil which he thought fit to throw over his earlier years."[3] The reasons for this may stem from his wish to keep secret his family, his early religious convictions and his two failed attempts to become a student at the Royal Academy.[4]

Edwin Longsden Long was born in Bath on 16 July 1829 into a middle class family. The

1. *The Babylonian Marriage Market* achieved an auction house record when it was bought for the highest price paid for the work of a living British artist at that time (see p. 14 below).
2. Gerald Reitlinger, *The Economics of Taste*, vol. 1, *The Rise and Fall of Picture Prices, 1760–1960* (London: Barrie and Rockliff, 1961), p. 160.
3. Obituary of Edwin Long, RA, in the *Illustrated London News*, 1891.
4. Long must not be confused with Edwin Williams Long, an artist who was accepted at the Royal Academy as a painting student on 19 December 1849. E. W. Long received a silver medal for drawing from the antique in 1852 which was wrongly attributed in the *Bath Chronicle* to Edwin Longsden Long.

occupation of his father, James Long, is listed on Edwin's marriage certificate as a gentleman although many later biographers contradict this and refer to his profession as either a hairdresser or artist.[5] He was educated in accordance with his class at the Academy of Dr Charles William Viner at 15 Edward Street, Bath. It is unknown where Long's desire to be a painter stems from but his determination to be one went against the advice of family and friends.[6] His family did not consider painting to be a suitable pursuit for their son. Long struggled to establish himself as an artist though his religious background was a source of inspiration for his work. In particular his religious upbringing as a congregational dissenter and follower of the Reverend William Jay, a charismatic preacher based at the Argyle Chapel, Bath, was to have clear ramifications in his work. Religion, in diverse ways, is a dominant theme in the majority of his paintings. The early genre paintings of Spanish subjects, for example, often involved depictions of religious ritual and devotion, as we shall see. In his final years his work became increasingly religious and pious. As his station in life improved so he moved towards greater orthodoxy and seriousness, but even in these later paintings there still appears a conviction led not by orthodoxy but by the early charismatic and evangelical zeal of his early Christian upbringing.

In 1846 Long moved to London to study art. At the time there were only two private art schools in existence – Sass's Academy (later Cary's), and Leigh's School of Art (later Heatherley's). Long entered Leigh's which had just been established in 1845 at Dickenson's Drawing Gallery at 18 Maddox Street. It was named after its principal, James Matthew Leigh (1808–60), a history and portrait painter, known as 'Dagger' Leigh due to his rapier-like criticism. The novelist William Thackeray was a student at the school and satirised it as Gandish's in his novel *The Newcomes*: "Not a successful painter, Mr. Gandish was an excellent master, and regarding all artists, save one, a good critic."[7] Thackeray describes in detail the large antique gallery that was an essential element in Leigh's training and the studio system he adopted. He also describes the competition that existed between Leigh's and Sass's art schools:

Nigh to Gandish's was, and perhaps is, another establishment for teaching the art of design-Barker's, which had the additional dignity of a life and costume academy . . . Between these and the Barkerites there was a constant rivalry and emulation . . . Gandish sent more pupils to the Royal Academy; Gandish had brought up three medallists; and the last R.A. student sent to Rome was a Gandishite.[8]

While a student at Leigh's, Long attempted to rise to studentship at the Royal Academy and, although he was twice accepted as a probationer, he was refused both times as he was unable to produce "the drawings necessary to qualify him admission as a student."[9] Clearly this was a blow to Long who desperately wanted the prestige of the Academy and was probably the root of

5. Quick and others seem to make the mistake of assuming a James Long, whose hairdressing practise was on the same street as Edwin's portrait business (Old Bond Street, Bath) was his father. The Bath census proves otherwise.
6. *Illustrated London News*, 6 May 1876, 'Recently Elected Associates to the Royal Academy', notes that "his resolution was strongly opposed by his parents and friends".
7. William Thackeray, *The Newcomes* (London: Penguin, 1996), p. 176. First published in serial form between 1853 and 1855.
8. Ibid., p. 180.
9. *Illustrated London News*, 6 May 1876.

an insecurity that dogged him all his life. He remained bitter about the critics' refusal to acknowledge his technical ability even though they often praised his work. He claimed that this was due to his "never having conciliated the press."[10] It is interesting to note that so few of Long's drawings have failed to survive. Long appears to have considered his drawing weak and tended to sketch in oils which, unlike his drawings, survive in their hundreds. Writing on Long's working methods in *The Graphic*, Spielmann noted that, after making many rough sketches (he does not specify in which medium), "without waiting to make a 'finished sketch' as is the case nine out of ten with his compeers, he straightaway draws the picture upon his canvas, and proceeds with his work."[11]

Leigh's system of teaching was inspired by continental models that he had learnt in his travels. He adopted the French-inspired open *atelier* system which meant on the one hand that it included very little individual tuition, but on the other that it was reasonably priced and did not require matriculation. This might account for its attraction to Long and also for his efforts while there to become a student at the Royal Academy. In *The Newcomes*, Mr Gandish continually talks of " 'Igh Art", meaning history painting over portraiture, and there seems little doubt that is where Long's ambitions ultimately lay, although his rejection from the Royal Academy meant that he was forced to begin his professional life as a portrait painter.

Art schools have always been a place that lifetime friendships and influences are formed and Leigh's school was no exception. Long's contemporaries included P. H. Calderon and J. B. Burgess, both of whom were to attend his funeral. John Bagnold Burgess in particular became a close friend of Long's and they travelled to Spain together in the 1860s.

The exact length of time that Long spent at Leigh's academy is not known. By 1850 he had returned to Bath and at sometime during the intervening period he had travelled to Italy to study art.[12] The impact of Italy on Long's art is almost impossible to assess as so little work survives from this period of Long's life. The work that has survived comprises the few portraits that have been retained through public collections. The earliest of these are military commissions. They did not fulfil his burgeoning ambition but they did provide an income and the beginnings of a reputation for portraiture. These military commissions are varied in quality and indicate that the start of his professional career was a struggle. This is reflected in his acceptance of a commission to make three large-scale copies of a miniature of Sir Edward Charles Whinyates painted by Mrs Robertson in 1827. If this was a commission that Long was compelled to accept, his portrait of Sir Hugh Gough of about 1849 was of altogether a different order. The work was made into a lithograph by H. Squire, and its reputation, helped by the status of the sitter, was to significantly aid Long's career. The head and shoulders portrait was one of the first opportunities for him to display his ability to paint the face.[13] Like most of his portraits at this time it focuses primarily on the sitter's face and includes little background, costume or figure drawing. An exception to this is his rather clumsy full-length portrait of Lieutenant-Colonel G. J. M. MacDowell which reveals Long's inexperience in painting from the figure.

10. Long quoted in an undated *Bath Journal* obituary in Bath Reference Library.
11. M. H. Spielmann, 'Painters in Their Studios, II. – Mr. Edwin Long R.A', *The Graphic* (9 June 1888), p. 612.
12. According to his niece, Mrs H. F. Ostler, he left home "to study art in Italy at the age of nineteen or twenty". *The Bath Chronicle*, 28 July 1934.
13. Throughout his career Long was a prolific painter of heads. His studio at Netherhall Gardens had more than sixty hanging on the walls, and at the Edwin Long Gallery between 1893 and 1894 more than a hundred were exhibited.

By 1853, although he was still struggling, his income was such that he was able to marry Margaret Jemima Aiton, the daughter of a Naval surgeon, who he had met on a visit to Italy. They were married in March of that year at the British Consulate in Rome. On their return to Bath they moved to new premises at 28 River Street. While Long's portraiture became increasingly accomplished, he continued to paint in a somewhat old-fashioned style. Living away from London, Long seems to have been influenced by earlier modes of portraiture rather than the brighter and crisper, and more fashionable painting which characterised the 1850s.

In 1855 he succeeded in having his first pictures accepted at the Royal Academy. The achievement of having the works exhibited was compounded when the *Art Journal* chose to mention all three in favourable terms. In particular it noted of his portrait of his father in law, Dr William Aiton: "The unobtrusive bearing and sedate tone of this impersonation would suggest one of the doctors of the Sorbonne. It is a daring essay to paint, in these days, a portrait so low in tone as this."[14]

"From 1847 to 1858", wrote Margaret Long in a letter to *The Times*, "Mr. Long painted portraits only".[15] His skill in portraiture not only admitted him to exhibition at the Royal Academy but also brought him to the attention of the art press. It also brought him important commissions from aristocratic clients and his portraits of 1856 include Lord Ellesmere and Lord Robert Grosvenor. The provincialism of Bath, however, had little to offer an ambitious painter. Seeking greater success in the art world inevitably led him to London. In 1857, an important year for Long, none of his pictures were to be found on the walls of the Royal Academy for during this time he was seeking out the art world of London that he had left seven years before. His stay in the city at this stage was temporary and it was not until the following year that he fully committed himself to finding a studio in London. In 1857 it seems likely that he renewed old acquaintances and was introduced to artistic circles that included Burgess and Phillip. His meeting with John Phillip was a turning point in Long's career and he attended lessons in Phillip's studio, then at 38 Gloucester Road. Phillip, named 'Spanish' Phillip by some critics, was a Scottish artist who had moved to London in 1846 and established himself as a painter of Spanish genre subjects. The recently elected ARA clearly favoured Long and he encouraged him to visit Spain with him.[16]

The visit to Spain, which included visits to Madrid and Seville, made an enormous impact on Long. Phillip introduced Long to the painters that had influenced him, particularly Velasquez and Murillo, and to the land and people that provided him with the subject of his paintings. Long learnt a great deal from the study of Spanish painting and copied two paintings by Velasquez from the Prado, Madrid, *The Surrender of Breda* and *Las Hilanderas*.[17] There is little doubt, particularly when one considers the significant technical achievement in his copy of *Las Hilanderas*, that Long's ability to draw the figure was primarily learnt from Spanish masters. The influence of Murillo can be noted not only in the copies he made after the Spanish master but also in his own paintings such as *Ustred Gustra?*. If Long advanced his ability in painting through example, his turn to Spain as a subject for his own painting was achieved in Seville. Long remembered clearly the scene that had convinced him to paint Spain, a significant moment in his career, later recorded by his wife and the critic M. H. Spielmann:

14. *Art Journal*, 1855, p. 177.
15. Margaret Long, letter to *The Times*, 1 November 1892, p. 7.
16. The association between Long and Phillip can been seen in the portrait of Velasquez by Long that was owned by Phillip, and in the portrait that Long painted of Phillip.
17. Long's copy of *Las Hilanderas* (undated) is in the collection of the Royal Academy.

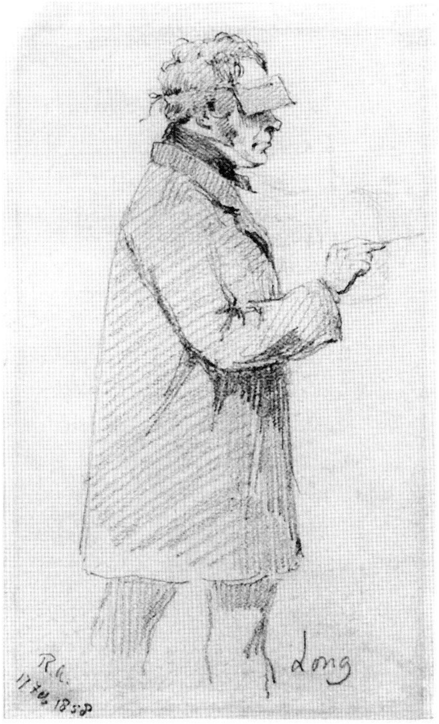

Fig. 2. Edwin Long, 17 February 1858. Drawing by Charles Bell Birch. COURTESY OF THE NATIONAL PORTRAIT GALLERY, LONDON.

He then determined to wait and see the religious ceremonies which were just about to begin. This decision really settled his career, for the very next day he perceived a beggar in front of a church holding aside a curtain for a lady and child to pass, and so picturesque was all the group, after the manner of Spanish beggars and ladies, that on returning to his studio he made a sketch of the scene.[18]

Long, "struck by the picturesque people",[19] turned his sketch into a painting titled *Leaving Church* first exhibited with its Spanish title *Un ochativo por el amos de Dios.* The character of such genre scenes was appealing to the art-going public and its success at the British Institution must have tightened Long's resolve to be a painter of picturesque Spanish scenes. The work was exhibited at the British Institution in 1858 still bearing Long's Bath address, but for the last time. The painting was sold for £35 before the exhibition had opened on private view day and, according to Spielmann, was "well criticised in the papers. All this success simply staggered the artist".[20]

In the same year as the success of his first Spanish subject, Long, his wife Margaret and young daughter Ethel, moved to London and took up residence at 53 Upper Berkeley Street, West, near Marble Arch. This was a temporary arrangement as the property was situated away from the main artistic centres that existed in London at the time. Such a move, however, indicated Long's growing confidence in his ability as an artist and in his ability to provide for his young family. Further, he had found a subject beyond portraiture, a subject that appealed to him artistically as well as being commercially viable. The success of *Leaving Church* was followed with *Agua Santa* (1859) a similarly Spanish religious scene set in Burgos, which illustrated an

18. Spielmann, 'Painters in Their Studios', p. 612.
19. Margaret Long, letter to *The Times*, 1 November 1892, p. 7.
20. Spielmann, 'Painters in Their Studios', p. 612.

enchanting ritual of passing holy water allowing lovers' hands to touch. It was exhibited at the British Institution of 1859 where it was sold for £100, and Long made a copy of the work a year later. The popularity of the painting is further emphasised by the fact that it was engraved for a periodical.[21] His Spanish period was not without its failures, however, as Spielmann was later to recount concerning Long's second visit to Spain: "He went again to Spain, and returned with a harvest of pictures, some of which were duly exhibited, chiefly at Wallis's Gallery; but the whole thing turned to failure, for he did not sell a single one of them."[22]

Unperturbed by this failure and the critical indifference of the art press at his first exhibition of Spanish subjects at the Royal Academy, Long continued to paint Spain. His portraiture was still well regarded and it provided a continuous and important source of income. Even in later life when he no longer needed the financial security that it brought "he never refused a portrait if he liked the subject, as he found it a rest for his prolific brain."[23] Long's infatuation with Spain, initiated by John Phillip, showed too the influence of that artist in his use of colour, light and shade. On many occasions in the art press he was dismissed as a mere follower of Phillip. Why then did an ambitious artist like Long continue to paint in the manner of Phillip? Spain for Long may indeed have been initially seen through the eyes of Phillip, but he began to find in that country the opportunity of widening his own artistic *œuvre.* He had genuinely found the place picturesque and as time progressed he learnt of the lucrative rewards that pleasant genre scenes could bring. Many of the pictures that survive do not reveal any greater ambition than this. It is important to remember, however, that he had faced failure and struggled on a number of occasions, and that a step forward to him must have been seen as a risk to his reputation as an artist as well as to his livelihood.

Despite this he still retained the ambition of becoming a high artist tempered by the need for the affirmation of popularity. Spain, which allowed him to widen his range of subject, was well within the realm of popular painting. Even within the most typical of his genre scenes he was able to introduce themes that he would explore on a much deeper level in his later works.

In his time at 53 Upper Berkeley Square Long had renewed contacts and developed new ones. In 1860 he was able to move to 33 Ovington Square where he was to live for fifteen years. It was situated on the outskirts of the Chelsea artists' community and near to the developing sites of South Kensington. He was also nearer to the studios of John Phillip and John Bagnold Burgess. His connections also grew with a wider artistic circle as he joined the 38 Middlesex (Artists) Rifle Volunteers. On 10 May 1860, 119 men enrolled including Long, Watts, Poynter, Millais, Holiday and Leighton who was to become their Commander-in-Chief.

Long's paintings in the next two years were predominantly Spanish genre scenes. If they revealed anything about Long himself, it was his strong interest in religion and ritual and the depiction of female beauty. Paintings like *Dialogus Diversus* contained many of the elements that characterised his Spanish period – the priests, lovers, fruit-sellers revealing a diversity of colourful Spanish costume. The religious devotion of young women is a frequent subject in his work in such paintings as *At Mass* and *An Easter Vigil.* In 1862 the range of his work was broadened by his taking on of bigger narrative subjects – in the painting *Jarius' Daughter*, based on a story in the New Testament, and a large scale depiction of a scene from Cervantes' *Don Quixote.*

21. Unattributed engraving of *Agua Santa*, in Bath Reference Library.
22. Spielmann, 'Painters in Their Studios', p. 612.
23. Margaret Long, letter to *The Times*, 1 November 1892, p. 7.

In around 1866, Long took his interest in Spain to new heights by living amongst the shepherds of Andalucia:

Whilst painting he bribed one of the uncouth shepherds of Andalusia to sit to him and, struck by the enthusiasm he roused in the man to whom he paid a peseta, actually allowed himself to be persuaded to join the man and his companions, and live with them for a month or more upon the mountains far away in the heart of the country, and this in spite of the warnings with which he was hotly plied by the English Consul. He was the first Englishman who had ever left the beaten path, but the result vindicated his courage and his faith in the shepherds, who, he was firmly convinced, were all 'good fellows,' and as a result laid the foundation of his later success, 'The Siege of Cadiz' was the outcome – a large picture full of small figures, and tiny but very carefully-painted heads. The picture was skied at the Academy . . . [24]

The painting, *During the Armistice,* painted in 1867 and exhibited at Burlington House in 1869, depicts the siege of the fortress on the Bay of Cadiz. It was his first real essay in historical painting and is in many ways an ambitious painting of transition. *The Times,* in its review of the work, found that it lacked a greater cohesion: "the picture sins . . . by a want of concentration and a profusion of episode which fatigues and distracts. That 'half is more than the whole' is truer of nothing than of his pictures."[25] The painting seems to use the genre vignettes that he had developed in a wholly different context. In this sense his depiction of picturesque figures does not live up to the painting's grander ambitions. It is nevertheless an important painting in prefiguring the later and more successful Spanish history paintings.

In 1867 Long returned to Italy and to Rome where he had married in 1853. The paintings he produced as a result of the visit echoed the subjects and treatment as his Spanish paintings. He focused on what had made his other paintings so popular and saleable – religious ritual and the charm and apparent simplicity of peasant life. He appears to have been incredulous at the wealth of Italian painting that he must have seen on his visit. There is a possibility that the grandeur of many of the works he would have seen there may have influenced him in attempting the grander subject of the siege of Cadiz even if he did not yet have the individuality and technique to carry it off convincingly.

Perhaps his first wholly successful painting on an ambitious scale is *A Question of Propriety* of 1870. It is important in many ways. Before beginning the work, Long carried out extensive historical research. Copyright in the work was sold separately to the painting itself to James L. Fairless of the Doré Gallery in 1873, an important publisher in Long's career. Furthermore, the demand for the painting induced Long to make two replicas of the painting. In this painting, Long achieves a cohesive composition and style that is suited to the painting; and lastly, that it is a convincing prelude to *The Suppliants.* Long's ambitions for this painting, which depicts a gypsy woman dancing before the inquisition, are made clear in a letter from Alfred Thomas Taddy who wrote "He thinks it would ensure his election to the honours of associateship."[26] Unfortunately for Long, it did not achieve this but it did receive favourable

24. Spielmann, 'Painters in Their Studios', p. 612. 'Skied' is an expression that refers to paintings which were hung very high on the walls at the time when pictures were hung one on top of the other.

25. *The Times,* 1 May 1869, p. 12.

26. Letter, dated c. August 1870, by Alfred Thomas Taddy, in the archive of the National Gallery of Victoria.

reviews in the journals, in particular the *Art Journal* which noted that "E. Long improves though we shall expect still better work than this".[27]

1871 saw yet another visit to Spain, this time with the intention of researching an even more ambitious work. He longed for associateship to the Academy, and the grand painting that he looked forward to producing required an even greater amount of research. For his subject he returned to the writings of Pachecho which he had used in *A Question of Propriety*. The documents of the inquisition, preserved at the archives at Simancas, informed Long of Phillip II's proposal to expel the gypsies from Spain. Long visited the Prado in Madrid to sketch the portraits of Phillip, his Queen and Cardinal. The setting for the painting was Santa Annunciata, a church at Valladolid where he painted as well as made studies of the gypsies' descendants still living in Spain. The painting was completed in 1872 and exhibited at the Royal Academy exhibition of that year.

Titled *The Suppliants: Expulsion of the Gypsies from Spain*, it depicts the moment the edict was about to be executed. In Long's own words "it attempts to represent when the King and the Cardinal [Gonzales] were descending the steps of the Santa Annunciata in Valladolid, and for the compassionate intervention of the young queen, who may be seen in the corridor above."[28] In technique, composition and the characterisation of the scene, Long had achieved a major success. He effectively severed his stylistic ties with Phillip and produced on a grand scale a picture that was critically acclaimed as high art. *The Times* noted that "No painter of the year has made a more decided advance than Mr. Long."[29] It was the *Art Journal* however that recognised its true significance as a "manifestation of the new that is rising in English Art . . . a picture of very high class, painted by E. Long who could not have produced a composition like this without having already shown tokens of being on the road to high achievement; and so we have predicted of this rising painter."[30]

Long's reaction to such praise was characteristically cautious and in the following year, instead of attempting to surpass the achievements of *The Suppliants*, he aimed to repeat it in *The Moorish Proselytes of Archbishop Ximenes, Granada, 1500*. The result was a painting which was clearly accomplished yet which failed to show the concentration charactersitic of *The Suppliants*. The critics responded favourably but he did not achieve associateship to the Academy or any greater praise than the previous year. Long's yearning for the honours and benefits that the Royal Academy might one day bestow manifested itself not only in a further Spanish history painting but another painting which attempted to escape these confines. It was becoming increasingly clear to Long, no doubt aided by the criticism of the *Moorish Proselytes* that he had exhausted the subject of Spain as the main subject of his paintings. The first indication of a major change of focus appeared in a work which was in essence experimental.

A Dorcas Meeting in the 6th Century, painted between 1873 and 1877, was Long's first real attempt at painting a classical subject. As Long himself noted, it was a transitional work: "It was my very first attempt at anything like a classic subject, a sort of transition picture between modern Spanish and the Antique and I am sorry to say it was considered a dead picture when shown for a few weeks at Wallis's."[31] For Long to achieve a convincing move to the 'Antique', he

27. *Art Journal*, 1871, p. 150.
28. Letter from Long to Thomas Holloway, dated 1 June 1882, in the Royal Holloway Archives.
29. *The Times*, 4 May 1872, p. 5.
30. *Art Journal*. 1872, p. 149.
31. Letter from Long, dated 11th July 1889, in the collection of the Art Gallery of New South Wales.

required a more focused approach stimulated by experience of real places and objects. The *Dorcas Meeting* owes too much to Spain to be antique in the sense that Long wished, and he appears to have found difficulty in casting aside the hard lessons he had learnt in painting Spanish history. The real breakthrough was achieved in 1874 when he went on an extensive tour of Egypt and Syria.

By 1875 British artists had long since discovered ancient Egypt as a subject for paintings. The public's fascination with Egypt was reflected in the widespread popularity of exhibitions of Egyptian artefacts from, for example, the archaeological excavations from Thebes exhibited in London in 1862. The art periodicals such as the *Art Journal* carried numerous well-illustrated articles on Egyptology and Sir Edward J. Poynter's enormous pictorial reconstruction of ancient Egypt, *Israel in Egypt*, had made a huge impact when it was exhibited at the 1867 Royal Academy exhibition.

Long's decision to visit Egypt and Syria reflected this general interest. The deep impression that his extended visit made upon him cannot be understated. Long entered his new subject with great enthusiasm and took, as he had done in Spain, to reading contemporary accounts of the ancient civilisation's history. The source material for Long's antique paintings can be located in books and articles of archaeology, through visits to museums, particularly the British Museum, to draw artefacts directly and through his visits to the Middle East.[32] The subjects for the paintings, in the main, are derived from contemporary accounts, biblical stories and fictitious reconstructions expanded upon with a wealth of archaeological detail.

In ancient Egypt and Babylon, Long found a subject where he could explore in a new way his painterly concerns. The ever present themes of his Spanish works, of religious conviction and female beauty, remained. What Egypt provided was a new arena in which to explore them. His interest in history and pictorial historical accuracy could be developed to new heights through the numerous studies of ancient archaeology and rich visual resource of artefacts. As Spielmann noted, Long's ambitions to produce paintings of a higher order and grander scale could be achieved through his new subject.

Fired in his imagination by the types to which he had been devoting himself, and ambitious of producing a work more important than he had yet painted, he set about the study of ancient history, so that he might combine Art and Archaeology in a more thorough manner than he or others were at the time attempting.[33]

According to Spielmann, Long had begun to read Herodotus in 1873 before his visit to the sites described in the book.[34] His visit occupied all his time and energies, and his contribution to the Academy of 1874 was only one modest painting, *M'liss*, a pleasant yet undistinguished depiction of a heroine from a Francis Bret Harte novelette of the same name.

Long's energies were focused on a passage from Herodotus which he struggled to represent in paint. "This subject, hitherto pictorially untouched was difficult of realisation. It was so full of

32. In particular, George Rawlinson, *The Five Ancient Monarchies of the Ancient World; or The History of Chaldea, Assyria, Babylon, Media and Persia*, four vols. (London, 1862–67), and Sir John Gardner Wilkinson, *Manners and Customs of the Ancient Egyptians*, 6 vols. (London, 1837).
33. Spielmann, 'Painters in Their Studios', p. 612.
34. Ibid.

promise that the artist clung to it for a couple of years or so without being able all the time to realise the composition of the scene."[35] The passage was Herodotus's account of an ancient Babylonian custom which involved the auctioning of women for marriage, the most being paid for those considered more beautiful and a dowry coming with those considered most ugly. Such a subject could only have fired the imagination of a Victorian artist like Long who could use such an account to display a technical prowess in scale, composition and treatment, and to explore his own somewhat narrow conception of beauty and present it as historically accurate. Long had successfully managed to concentrate all his energies on one major painting, and the concentrated effort required is quite apparent. His experience of the Middle East and absorption of archaeological sources is combined in a painting that was original, in its research and subject, as well as accomplished in composition and technique. Long exhibited the completed work, which he had been involved with for nearly three years, at the Royal Academy exhibition of 1875, where his ambitions for the painting were more than fulfilled.

Its appearance at Burlington House raised high criticism for the work, amongst them the voice of John Ruskin. Ruskin saw the work's importance as primarily historical, recommending it as "well deserving purchase by the Anthropological Society", but also found its painting of a high standard noting that "as a mere piece of painting the work is remarkable, in the modern school, for its absence of affectation: there is no insolently indulged indolence nor vulgarity asserted dexterity – the painting is good throughout, and unobtrusively powerful."[36] Ruskin was not alone in his praise of the work, the Art Journal commenting that "The picture, in our eyes, is historic in the best sense, and does honour to the British School."[37]

More important to Long than the praise which had established him as worthy of serious criticism was that, on the strength of it, he was made an Associate Royal Academician. He had finally broken all links with John Phillip and Spain and found his own voice. This assertion of individuality was clearly recognised in his own time but is less recognised in the twentieth century where his works have until recently been seen as mere imitations of other greater Victorian Olympians. What Long had achieved was to establish a name that from now on would be synonymous with archaeology. However Victorian we now find these visions of ancient civilisations, he was seen (as Ruskin had seen him) as an artist who went to the greatest lengths to achieve an historical accuracy.

He had also found a public and Long straddled what he had hoped to achieve – serious criticism and popular acclaim, two things, which he was later to discover to his cost, that did not always sit easily together. *The Times* reviewed his painting and noted the fine line that he walked between popular subject and serious treatment: "the painter has hit a popular subject which a less restrained–or what French critics would be apt to call prudish -taste in treatment might have easily made cynical in the worst sense of the word."[38] The painting was popular with the art-going public and huge crowds came to see it. If he had pleased both critics and public alike in this painting he was not to do so in many of his works where he was often accused of pandering to the common sentiment of the populace.

To paint the work Long had needed a larger studio and as a rising star among historical and

35. Spielmann, 'Painters in Their Studios', p. 612.
36. John Ruskin, *Academy Notes*, 1875, 1902 complete edition, pp. 233–35.
37. *Art Journal*, 1875, p. 250.
38. *The Times*, 24 May 1875, p. 5.

genre painters, he felt the need to move closer to the hub of this group. 33 Ovington Square was no longer a fitting residence for him and in 1875 he moved to 19 Marlborough Hill, St. Johns Wood.[39] The house, now destroyed, was renovated by Long who added a garden studio that could be entered from the side and bore a separate address, 1a Carlton Hill. He even named the studio *Long's Den* after his middle name Longsden. Despite his own involvement in creating his studio in St. John's Wood, Marlborough Hill was not an ideal location or an ideal building. Julian Hawthorne remembered visiting the studio to see the *Babylonian Marriage Market* with Frederick Leighton and emphasised the reputation that Long was quickly gaining for studious archaeological research:

One afternoon, a little before Academy Day, Long asked some of us to his big studio to see his picture for that year – 'The Babylonian Slave Market.' Long was a thin, unobtrusive man, with a brown beard, gentle of speech, with a kindling of ideality in his modest eyes. I should have expected him to paint little cabinet pieces, refined, but in the minute Dutch style, correct values, unobtrusive in tone. But he brought us up against an enormous canvas . . . The drawing of the figures was unexceptionable, the design of the whole was clever, but the archaeology stood out. One thought of studious hours spent over learned folios; an almost painful effort to reproduce the atmosphere of 3,000 years ago. Those draperies! that architecture and furnishings; those dozen or twenty types of exotic girl beauty! . . . I was standing at Fred Leighton's elbow, and I whispered to him: 'You should have painted that!' He shook his hyacinthine curls; but it was a safe thing to say, and my technical ignorance wouldn't allow me to venture further.

And there stood little Long, not actually blushing, but with a blushing expression. 'Great oaks from little acorns grow,' says the proverb.[40]

Long's residency at Marlborough Hill was short-lived and the success of the 1875 Academy allowed him to make grander plans for his studio home. In 1876, Long, boosted by his artistic and financial success, commissioned the then very fashionable architect Richard Norman Shaw to design a studio house for him in South Hampstead. The house took several years to design and build and in the meantime Long continued large scale works in his garden den. 1876 saw a first attempt since *Jairus' Daughter* to paint a biblical subject (his biblically inspired *A Dorcas Meeting* was still in progress at this time). Exhibited as his only work for Burlington House that year, *Bethesda* received favourable reviews but failed in many critics' eyes to live up to the promise recognised in his Academy works of the previous year. *The Times* believed that it would "hardly disturb the recollection of his 'Babylonian Marriage Market.'" praising however its "unhackneyed treatment of an often painted subject. . . . "[41] The *Magazine of Art* in retrospect, however, found the work a key point in Long's career.[42] As the first biblical painting after Long had found his own voice, it is clearly an important landmark in the career of an artist in which religion played an important part.

In 1877 the walls of Burlington House displayed three paintings by Long. Of the three the largest and most important was *An Egyptian Feast.* In subject and scale it had clear parallels

39. During this period George Clausen was a student of Long's.
40. Julian Hawthorne, *Shapes That Pass* (London: John Murray, 1928) pp. 251–52.
41. *The Times*, 8 May 1876, p. 9.
42. *Magazine of Art*, July 1891, p. xl.

with *The Babylonian Marriage Market* and was aimed at repeating its success. For his subject he had returned to Herodotus for his depiction of an ancient Egyptian custom where at the end of the meal guests would view a wooden bier which was passed around to remind them of their own mortality. The archaeological detail of Babylon was certainly rivalled in this depiction of ancient Egypt. Spielmann wrote of the picture that:

In this work, rising higher than had hitherto touched, he carried his antiquarian research to its furthermost point. Indeed, the artist went so far as to introduce a pineapple in the feast on the authority of a recent traveller, who had discovered modelled representations of the fruit in recently-unearthed tombs, which proved them to have been not unknown at the period of the picture.[43]

The Times claimed that it would be the picture of the year and rank with the pictorial merits of a *Babylonian Marriage Market.*[44] The picture shows a wealth of archaeological detail in its murals, architecture and its mass of artefacts. Its grand composition is imposing and sustains the gravitas befitting the subject showing it to be a fit successor in ancient Egypt to his Babylon of 1875.

Long was to use Egypt as a subject the following year, but this time with a difference. Long's obvious delight in charming genre scenes, particularly those of religious devotion, was evident in his Spanish period. *An Ancient Custom* of 1876 had displayed that smaller scale genre scenes, this time in his mature style taking ancient history as their backdrop, still interested him. In *The Gods and Their Makers* he developed his interest for charming genre scenes on a larger scale. Furthermore it was also in this picture that he revealed his growing interest in contrasting Christianity with earlier pantheistic religions. It stemmed from his low Church background in criticising false idolatry, a theme he would develop to its furthest point in *Anno Domini. The Gods and Their Makers* contained an implied amusement at the idolatry of Catholicism. The idea "had its origins in the sight of one of the many shops that swarm in the neighbourhood of St. Sulpice in Paris, displaying for sale the plaster figures of the Saints. Catching sight of the manufactory beyond, his mind, now imbued with Egyptian lore, transferred the scene in the imagination to the banks of the Nile . . . "[45] His fascination with the rituals of Catholicism became increasingly serious. His development of the Christian/Pagan themes in later paintings used the fictional writings of mainly Catholic writers.[46] Long's move towards orthodoxy and ritual in religious matters made him far more sympathetic to Catholicism and although he never made the complete transition to Catholicism he did become an Anglo-Catholic.

Despite its frivolous treatment, *The Gods and Their Makers* reveals important religious undertones and contained serious archaeological research. It also displays the development of Long's significant technical abilities and contains painting of a high order, a point noted by critics. The painting depicts a studio producing idols and takes the subtitle from Sir Frederick Pollock's translation of Juvenal telling of ancient Egypt's zoomorphic worship. The light and pleasing appearance of the work, its depiction of exotic female beauty enhanced by a myriad of archaeological detail is exquisitely painted. Long proved in this work that his painting of the

43. Spielmann, 'Painters in Their Studios', p. 612.
44. "In this room is what will no doubt be picture of the year – E. Long's 'Egyptian Feast', worthy for dimensions and pictorial merits to rank with his Babylonian slave market . . . " *The Times*, 5 May 1877, p. 12.
45. Spielmann, 'Painters in Their Studios', p. 612., p. 612.
46. Cardinals Newman and Wiseman (see p. 21 below).

figure could be masterly. The *Art Journal* found it the "finest we think that Mr. Long has yet painted",[47] and the *Magazine of Art* that "his power of drawing and modelling . . . has gained greatly in sureness. The extreme refinement in colour . . . is very pleasing."[48]

Long's more serious religious feelings found their expression in a pair of companion paintings painted between 1877 and 1879. Within them he successfully combined his interests in religion, archaeological research and depiction of female beauty. *Esther* and *Vashti* were exhibited at Burlington House in 1879 although for some unknown reason they did not appear side by side.[49] Both paintings were derived from the Book of Esther and both depict the two queens awaiting the consequences of the momentous decisions that they have made.[50] Long took over two years to complete the works, a fact which indicates their importance to him. In one sense they are the opposite of each other – one an established and majestic queen, the other about to become queen, courageous and hesitant. One is fair, the other is dark. They are almost identical companions in scale and composition. They are identical too in the dignity that they both express. The degree and subtlety of expression that Long achieved in the faces of his subjects is particularly noteworthy; as the *Magazine of Art* wrote, "Both pictures are eminently attractive studies of feminine beauty, with which is combined much emotional expression. Esther is the more solemnly heroic, Vashti the more majestic".[51]

In archaeological detail both are derived from Rawlinson's *Five Great Monarchies*[52] guided by the descriptions contained in the Bible. Accuracy was undoubtedly an important intention of the picture and Long's combination of interests sit together comfortably. What is apparent is that Long's interest in exotic beauty and archaeological detail still maintained the upper hand with regard to his growing religious concerns. At this point in his career he still had much to achieve, particularly full Academician status, which meant that his growing reputation depended on his skills as a painter as well as his handling of subject. In these two paintings Long had achieved his mature painterly technique which involved the use of quite thin paint. In his description of the process involved in painting Esther's head and body he explains how he firstly painted the flesh in light, warm grey impasto. The colours and tints of the flesh are then added thinly afterwards to allow the initial painting to show through.[53] The weakness of this method has been noticed mostly as a result of time. It is moreover a technique that is most suited to large scale works and is evident in his larger canvases.

While working on the large scale paintings like *Esther* and *Vashti*, Long continued to paint portraits, and also to move in increasingly important circles. The most important of his new clients was the Baroness Burdett-Coutts (1814–1906), the wealthy philanthropist. In 1879 she organised an extended Mediterranean cruise, and Long and his wife were among the guests.

47. *Art Journal*, 1878, p. 147.
48. *Magazine of Art*, 1878, p. 43.
49. "These important pictures in which there is much dignity and beauty of design should be examined together. It is to be regretted they are not in the same gallery." *Academy Notes*, 1879, p. 62.
50. Vashti had refused the King's summons and Esther had entered his chamber uninvited; the consequences of both actions were potentially severe.
51. *Magazine of Art*, 1879, p. 127.
52. Rawlinson, *Five Ancient Monarchies.*
53. Long's notes for *Esther* for the 1879 Royal Academy Exhibition: "solid impasto on the flesh, prepared light warm grey afterwards finished with all colours laid on thinly so as to let the first painting through." Royal Academy Library.

Together with the Baroness' other guests, which included the actor Henry Irving, they visited Spain, Greece and Italy. The Baroness commissioned Long over a period of years to paint several portraits for her including one of herself and one of her lifelong friend and helper, Hannah Brown, which was exhibited at the 1879 Royal Academy Exhibition. The most interesting paintings that she commissioned from Long, however, were a series of three paintings of Henry Irving portrayed in different roles for which he had become renowned – Hamlet, Richard III and Vanderdecken. During this period, Long established further influential clients. In order to provide a fitting house and studio more in keeping with his rising career, he built a new home at Fitzjohn's Avenue.

When Edwin Long moved into 'Kelston', 61 Fitzjohn's Avenue, in March 1880 at the age of fifty, he had nearly achieved all his major artistic ambitions. While resident there, he succeeded in reaching full Academician status (in 1881) and achieved unprecedented success in the commercial art world. The 'Labyrinth', as Long came to call it, was a fitting home for an artist of growing status. It established a family seat that never was – a seat to entertain and to show the world that this was an artist who was worth investing in. The scale and siting of the house was impressive yet retaining a personal aspect of homeliness. The interior of the house was grand and imposing, the studio was described by the *Architect* as, at first sight, looking "like a church".[54] Certainly the addition of a organ raised above an inglenook fireplace gave the studio sacred connotations. The studio having a pseudo-religious backdrop was certainly in keeping with his work of this period, particularly if one thinks of his huge painting of the flight into Egypt, *Anno Domini,* which was painted in this studio.

Entertaining potential clients in the studio house was an important aspect of an artist's life at this time. Long was well aware of this function and went to elaborate lengths to provide a welcome that was grand and that reflected the exotic nature of his works. In April 1882, on a show day when artists privately displayed their work that would shortly be exhibited at Burlington House, he invited the famous surgeon Sir Spencer Wells and Frank Archer who later recorded their visit. Long was displaying *The New Fugue,* a portrait incorporating the studio's organ, a portrait of *Sir Stavord Northcote,* the exotic Eastern and biblical *Why Tarry the Wheels of his Chariot?* and his diploma work *Nouzhatoul-âouadat* (*The Delight of the Home*):

One show-day in April 1882 the great surgeon asked my wife and myself to join him and his daughters to go and see Edwin Long's Academy pictures, on view at his house in Fitzjohn's Avenue. We were received by a splendid Nubian, who ushered in the visitors. He was draped, beturbined, and with his fine eyes and thick lips looked every inch a denizen of the East. He came forward to take our names.[55]

In the following month, *The Babylonian Marriage Market* achieved an auction house record that was not to be broken until after Long's death in 1892. On 13 May 1882, the sale of works belonging to Edward Hermon MP was held at Christie's. Lot no. 66, *The Babylonian Marriage Market,* sold for an astounding £6,615 to Martin on behalf of Thomas Holloway. This was the highest price to have been paid for a painting by a living artist. It is important to note that the price of the work included copyright as further profit could be, and was, derived from the

54. *The Architect,* vol. 22 (15 November 1879), p. 286.
55. Frank Archer, *An Actor's Notebooks* (London: Stanley Paul & Co., 1912), pp. 241–42.

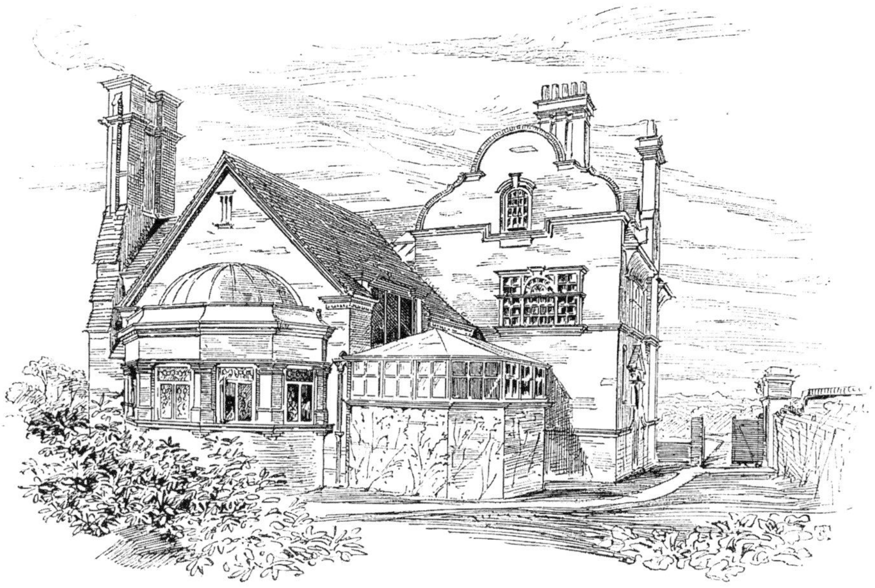

The House of Mr. Edwin Long, A.R.A., at Hampstead.

Fig. 3. 'The House of Mr. Edwin Long A.R.A.' From *The Art Journal*, 1881.

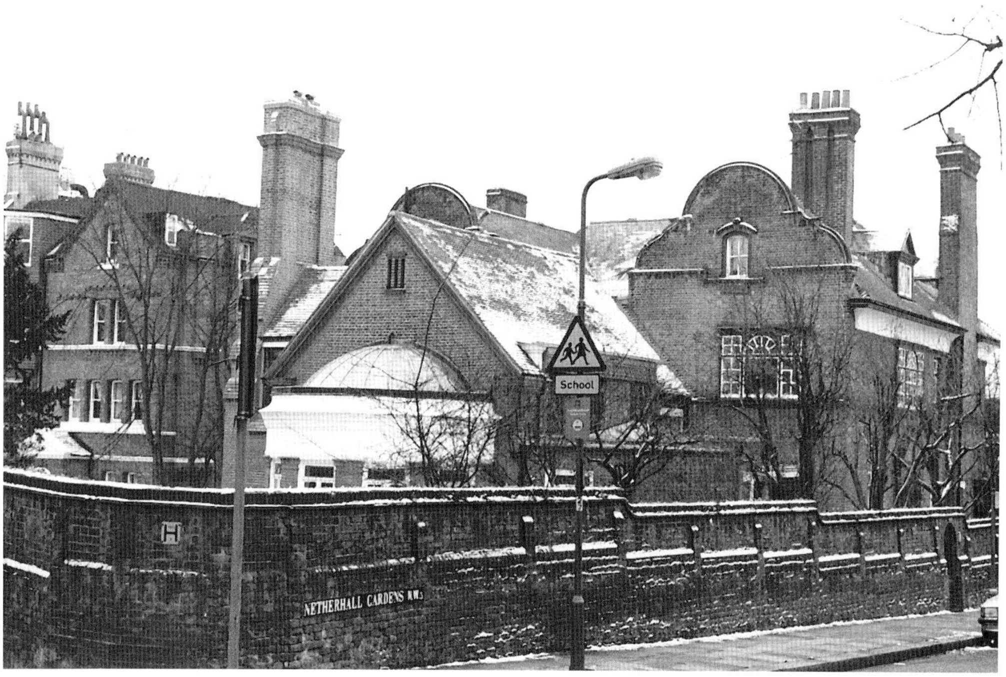

Fig. 4. 61 Fitzjohn's Avenue in 1996. PHOTOGRAPH BY SHAUN GARNER.

purchase of this painting. In an age that produced so many eminent painters, it is surprising that it was Edwin Long, a name that has become neglected in the twentieth century, who should have achieved this distinction. This significant commercial success was followed by a long series of commissions through the 1880s from Bond Street galleries by Thomas Agnew's and by Messrs Lawrence and Beeforth.

Another turning point in Long's commercial success came as a result of the death of another artist in 1883. Since 1868, there had been a gallery, set up by the fine art publishers Fairless and Beeforth at 35 New Bond Street, exclusively devoted to the work of Gustave Doré. The Doré Gallery was successful in its permanent exhibition of works solely by the artist, charging a shilling entry and selling prints after the paintings. Doré's sudden death in Paris on 6 January 1883 was a setback to the publishers who regularly showed his immense religious canvases at the gallery. Their replacement for Doré effectively came in the form of Long, as the *Magazine of Art* noted in retrospect:

When Gustave Doré died, the caterers for that devout and sentimental portion of the public who took unctuous delight in the wonders of the Doré Gallery could find in England no worthier heir to his mantle than Mr. Long, who exerted himself considerably in their behalf, and produced a number of gently inspired and scriptural paintings."[56]

Although the Doré Gallery continued to display the work of its namesake for several years after his death, until it became transformed into the Gallery of Sacred Art (which displayed many of Long's works), the Lawrence Gallery, set up by Fairless and Beeforth, was used to exclusively display the work of Edwin Long (see Appendix II). Long had been chosen, if not for exhibition at the same gallery, as a replacement for Doré, a decision that must have been influenced by the similar scale, subject and popularity of his work. In its summation of Long's career, *Bryan's Dictionary* notes that Long was

partial to large pictures, and endeavoured to rival Doré, an artist for whom he had a profound admiration, not only in the subject of his paintings, but in their gigantic size. His work appealed strongly to the religious sensibilities of his day, and was sufficiently sentimental and poetic to be considered devout.[57]

Long was commissioned by Fairless and Beeforth sometime in 1883 to produce large scale works for the Lawrence Gallery. The extent to which the publishers determined the commissioned work is not clear but Long's status in 1883 seems to indicate that he remained reasonably independent in determining the nature of the work. One might fairly assume that the work was to be of a Christian subject although the two works he added to *Anno Domini* at the Lawrence Gallery in 1885 were not at all religious in character and dealt instead with an exploration of female beauty.[58]

The success of the venture was reliant on the sale of large numbers of prints to an audience that found the work accessible, attractive and which appealed to their religious sensibility. Prints were sold at a variety of prices which ranged from two to ten guineas depending on whether

56. *Magazine of Art*, 1891, p. xl.
57. *Bryan's Dictionary of Painters and Engravers* (London: George Bell & Sons, 1903–05, 7th edn.), vol. III, p. 242.
58. The companion paintings *Zeuxis at Crotona, The Search for Beauty* and *The Chosen Five.*

they were proofs and on the quality of paper on which they were printed. Sir Merton Russell-Cotes, who later purchased *Anno Domini* and other works exhibited at the Lawrence and Beeforth galleries,[59] remembered the system adopted by the publishers:

Mr. Beeforth, whom I knew intimately, was a very wealthy art collector and connoisseur. He became enamoured of the works of that great French artist Gustave Doré, and decided to project a gallery in London to exhibit this artist's work exclusively . . . Eventually, however, the public demanded a new sensation, and after serious consideration induced Long to paint a series of pictures . . . the commission to be paid half in cash and half out of receipts. The results was a series of exceptionally marvellous subjects superbly painted which caused the Doré Gallery to become a still more popular resort. A gentleman named Cadham was engaged to tour the country to obtain subscriptions for the engraved reproductions of these works, the receipts from which soon became a gold mine. These subscriptions ranged from two guineas for an ordinary print to ten guineas for an artist's signed proof on India paper."[60]

The first painting that Long completed for the Lawrence Gallery was *Anno Domini*, a depiction of the Flight into Egypt which caused a sensation. Widely and favourably reviewed in the periodicals, the *Art Journal* devoted a page to its exposition. The painting was to be on exhibition for the next ten years and attracted regular and devoted visitors over that period including Lewis Carroll.[61] Within this painting Long gave his most ambitious and sustained depiction of his own religious beliefs, producing a work that encompasses his painterly interests on a unique scale and in an altogether new way. The setting for *Anno Domini* is the heart of Egypt amongst its temples at dusk, lit by the rosy light of evening. In the background the pyramids are faintly outlined in the evening glow. A long procession leads from the pyramids to the front right of the painting overseen by the Roman guards. In the foreground, moving from left to right, the Holy Family are the largest and tonally brightest figures.

The painting's title gives us an important indication to the nature and ambition of this particular *Flight into Egypt* which depicts the beginning of a new age and religion. The Holy Family are humble, poor in dress, constructed of softer lines and are represented as the spiritual embodiment of the new and true religion. In stark contrast to this he presents the old dying religion of Ancient Egypt as idolatrous, brazen and sexual. The costumes are rich and the crowds are in awe of the ancient gilded icons of their pantheistic faith. The whole of the picture is based upon the marked contrast that he had explored, albeit less ambitiously, in *Diana or Christ?*:

The prominent and all-pervading idea of the 'Flight into Egypt', is to indicate by direct pictorial contrast, by the arrival of the Holy Child and His parents in a country reeking of idolatry, the ensuing contact of the old and new faiths, and to imply the conflict, which, ere long, must inevitably arise between paganism and Christianity.[62]

Within *Anno Domini* there are two contrasting Victorian pictures combined to create one rich

59. *The Story of Jephthah* (a series of three paintings), *The Chosen Five* and *Anno Domini*.
60. Sir Merton Russell-Cotes, *Home and Abroad* (Bournemouth: privately printed, 1921) p. 709–10.
61. Lewis Carroll's diary entries note that he saw *Anno Domini* on four occasions between 1884 and 1893: 27 May 1884; 18 March, 3 April, 28 June 1893.
62. G. A. Sala, *Anno Domini* (London: Lawrence Gallery, 1885).

image. A grand archaeological reconstruction of Ancient Egypt and an intimate Flight into Egypt. Both are linked by their move towards some kind of realism but arise from different genres. This new and unorthodox treatment was noted by the *Art Journal*:

The Flight into Egypt has been painted from two points of view, one in which the actors themselves receive primary treatment, the other where they are accessory figures in the landscape. Mr. Long's conception cannot be classed in either category. With great skill and sound judgement he has contrived to render the travellers from Judea of first importance in his composition, and has done this in spite of the dangerous competition of the elaborate procession of various important adjacent groups.'[63]

It was more typical of the period to link large scale ancient scenes with the Old Testament rather than the New. This is the whole key to the painting – two startlingly contrasted images linked by Long's realism. The pictorial linking of the Holy Family and the background is primarily achieved through the similar hues that Long adopts and the eye contact that exists between the painting's leading protagonists. There is a precedence in Long's picture *Diana or Christ?* painted two years earlier in his church-like studio, but this was a wholly more coherent image and although the contrast of the early church and ancient religions inspired Long's choice of subject it did not present such a marked dichotomy of imagery. It is surprising that, in a sketch for the painting, Long outlined a halo on the baby Christ which seems to move against the clearly contrasting images of the painting and his own wavering religious beliefs. As one review pointed out: "Mr. Long has wisely disregarded the use of the nimbus around the virgin and child, and, in portraying actual facts, his work gains rather than suffers by the absence of that which can be alone suitable to the idealistic."[64] The use of the nimbus would create an unwanted link between the golden imagery of Egypt with the humble Holy Family. The whole of the painting relies on that contrast of material richness and poverty, spiritual wealth and empty religious idolatry. The decision not to include the nimbus was also, as most commentators were keen to point out, evidence of a move towards a greater realism: " . . . The nimbus round the head has been judiciously omitted. It has been evidently the design of the painter to present, without the faintest suggestion of the supernatural, such a scene that might really have occurred in Egypt, *Anno Domini I.*"[65]

Although the realism of the painting was emphasised by the commentators of the day, in many aspects it appears unconvincing today. The ethnic origin of many of the painting's figures is not convincing and they look to be rather of European origin. Furthermore the realism of the work, so carefully staged, is overtly theatrical. This is not to underestimate the research that Long undertook nor the powerful impression that it made on visitors to Bond Street. It is a powerful and unique picture which explored Long's religious and painterly concerns in a new way. It was also a commercial success in its appeal to a public who were given a glimpse into what many believed was an accurate portrayal of religious history.

Anno Domini was the first of several works purchased by Fairless and Beeforth for their Bond Street galleries and many followed throughout Long's life. The majority were of a reli-

63. *Art Journal*, 1884, p. 59.
64. Catalogue to an exhibition at the Lawrence Gallery, 1885, p. 25. Hereafter referred to as 'LG, 1885'.
65. Ibid., p. 15.

gious character although there were others like the companion paintings *Zeuxis of Crotona* which explored the depiction of female beauty.[66] Long's commercial endeavours were not limited to Fairless and Beeforth, however, and throughout this period he maintained a long and close relationship with Agnew's. Writing from Fitzjohn's Avenue on Christmas Day Long wrote to William Agnew after completing *Anno Domini:*

My Dear Agnew

Now that my big picture is done with I shall be delighted to do anything I can for you, the only thing is I am anxious to be strong at the Academy this time.

When you are in this direction I should be glad to show you what I am up to and then we can decide which of the paintings you would like me to finish first.

With compliments of the season.

Believe me Yours most truly

Edwin Long.[67]

Agnew's purchasing and commissioning from Long significantly increased in the 1880s where pictures like *Why Tarry the Wheels of his Chariot?, Love's Labour Lost* and *Thisbe* passed through their hands. The most ambitious number of commissions from Long were a series of twenty three-quarter length portraits exhibited at Agnew's in 1887 under the title of the *Daughters of Our Empire.* The series and subject had its precedents in other suites of paintings, usually by renowned artists, that focused on different types of beauty. These were predominantly depictions of young women who were seen to typify a certain look or historical period. Long himself had been involved in a similar project for *The Graphic* which had commissioned him, and many other artists including Leighton, Alma Tadema and Calderon, to produce a painting for their exhibition 'Types of Beauty' at the Graphic Gallery in 1881. Many of the exhibits, including Long's, were engraved for this popular periodical over several years.

What was notable about the *Daughters of Our Empire* series was that they were all executed by Long and each took as its subject a country within the realms of the British empire. Like other series they explored types of beauty, but the picture book encyclopaedic approach was clearly developed to have a popular appeal. The series included *Jamaica, Wales, India* and five of *England* which each had a separate subtitle. The importance that he placed on representing England, predictable in a commercial and patriotic sense, reflected the importance of the country at the heart of the empire. Indeed, *England, the Rose* was a portrait of the Princess May of Teck and was the most symbolic work of the series. Each of the paintings illustrates the background of the country from which the subjects hails; in appropriate national dress, accompanied by a poem written, probably by Long or his son Maurice, for the works.[68] The constrained and commercially contrived conception, perhaps predictably, could not be sustained successfully through twenty works, and although the core of the series contains several distinguished portraits, many are flawed artistically. Despite Long's attempts to illustrate women representative of these countries around the globe, he clearly only uses European models, giving a homogeneous represen-

66. Other religious paintings commissioned or purchased by Fairless and Beeforth include *The Story of Jephthah* and *Merab* and *Michal.*

67. Letter from Long to William Agnew, 1883, in the National Art Library, Victoria & Albert Museum.

68. Maurice St. Clair Long wrote the poem for Long's painting *Love's Labour Lost.*

tation of a diverse empire. This appealed to a public which comfortably saw a convincingly united empire despite its divergent breadth. As Austin Chester wrote in his 1908 article on Long: "people sought eagerly to buy them, that they might 'command the view of so many Imperial faces'".[69]

Even though the *Daughters* series, which were clearly aimed at a popular market achieved popularity, his more ambitious paintings which contained a greater artistic integrity were more popular still. The *Daughters* were produced on the whole for collectors of domestic scale works, whereas the large scale works were not only for purchase by collectors but were even more important for the copyright and the profits that could be gained in selling prints made after them. Agnew's owned the copyright of many of Long's paintings and published prints which were typically advertised in one of their catalogues as:

New Publications.
'Diana or Christ' 'Let her cast but one grain , and she is free'
Painted by Edwin Long R.A.
(Recently exhibited at the Royal Jubilee Exhibition, Manchester)
Messrs Thos, Agnew & Sons have the honour to announce the publication of an important Photogravure after this picture.
19 x 33 inches
Artists Proof £8.8.0 India Prints £3.3.0
Proof before letters £5.5.0 Plain Prints £2.2.0[70]

The subjects that so fascinated Long were explored within this public arena of commercial demands. Furthermore his choice of subject was often guided by popular taste, as his decision to continue to paint Spanish scenes had been in many respects a commercial one.

To see Long as merely a slave to the taste of the Victorian picture and print buying public, however, would be unjust. Long aimed to be popular, he also wished for the material rewards that his art would bring, but he wished above and beyond this to be recognised as an artist who produced works which would be regarded as the highest art. He wished for recognition from the Academy, from the important art periodicals and from his fellow artists. Within the realm of popular painting where he found success, he strove to explore those subjects that remained important to him. In Spain, as well as continuing his genre scenes, he had been able to expand the range of his art. His later successes gave him an unprecedented financial independence which allowed him greater freedoms, ones on the whole he chose to ignore as he never lost contact with his audience. The greatest expression of this freedom manifested itself much later, in the last year of his life, when he painted a religious painting, *The Parable of the Sower*, on an unprecedented scale and for which he refused 5,000 guineas (see p. 25 below).

The commercial excesses of the *Daughters* series had allowed some exploration of his depiction of female beauty. What was evident from this and many of his other paintings was that it was a very limited vision. His wife Margaret wrote after his death of him that "No one ever rendered female beauty more successfully"[71] and it was clearly an important aspect of Long's work. There is an apocryphal tale that claims that Long only ever painted the body and face of

69. Austin Chester, 'The Art of Edwin Long, R.A.', *Windsor Magazine*, February 1908, p. 349.
70. Agnew's sale catalogue, 1888, p. 33.
71. Mrs Margaret Jemima Long, letter to *The Times*, 1 November 1892, p. 7.

his wife.[72] Indeed the same dark-haired, dark- skinned models appear again and again in his work. Although they are clearly based on different models Long does in fact appear to be repeatedly painting the same face. In the *Babylonian Marriage Market*, he portrayed gradations of beauty that displayed his own rather narrow ideal. In presenting a picture of Ancient Babylon, which so many critics had found convincing, he had laid down a very Victorian hierarchy of shape, features and skin. His ideal of beauty is revealed as a westernised representation of an Eastern woman, and ugliness is all those features that ran contrary to that idea.

The pursuit of this timeless ideal was explored by Long, most seriously in two companion paintings titled *Zeuxis at Crotona*. The two paintings are taken from passages by Cicero and Pliny the Younger which tell of the artist Zeuxis's preparation and painting of Helen, the epitome of classical beauty. The first of the two, *The Search for Beauty,* shows Zeuxis choosing his five models from the women of Crotona. The second, *The Chosen Five,* shows Zeuxis in his studio painting the five nude models for his composite painting of Helen. The subject, despite having a clear sexual and voyeuristic aspect, is nevertheless strangely unsenuous. Every critic of these paintings emphasised the fact that, in the face of temptation to let such a subject descend into immodesty, Long had shown restraint and refinement in his treatment. *The World* noted that "the academic atmosphere throws, as it were, a veil over those undisguised humanities which should, I think, tend to keep them in the pure mind of Mrs. Boyn from the category of 'hussies'."[73] Long had found an acceptable way to present his depiction of beauty and display of flesh, though the double standards are clear to us today. The depiction of a painting with such an overtly sexual aspect was deemed acceptable within a certain code of academic representation. In Long, however, the sensuousness present in many other artists' work, is often missing and they often give the appearance of a rather dry academic exercise.

The other subject that preoccupied Long was religion. This was expressed through large biblical scenes from the Old Testament like his series on *Jephthah's Vow,* but more interestingly through his exploration of the contrast between Christianity and pantheistic religions. *Diana or Christ?* and *Anno Domini* are important paintings which draw on this contrast, the first being a Christian martyr, the second developing the theme of false idolatry with a new seriousness. Long echoed these concerns in later paintings dealing with idolatry and martyrdom such as *A Love Feast, Callista* and *Alethe.* Within these paintings Long turned to fictional accounts as his primary source. In particular he used two novels written by Roman Catholic cardinals written in the mid 1850s: *Fabiola, or the Church of the Catacombs* (1855) by Cardinal Patrick Stephen Wiseman and *Callista: A Sketch of the Third Century* (1856) by Cardinal John Henry Newman. Both works are fictional reconstructions of the early Christian church and shared a remarkably similar intent according to their introductions. Wiseman wished to "introduce us to some view of the morals and opinions of the pagan world, as a contrast to those of the Christians,"[74] and Newman wished to "attempt to imagine and express . . . the mutual feelings and mutual relations of Christians and Heathens . . . "[75] Long used not only the same aims of the writers in many of his pictures but also the texts of both for a pair of paintings hung at Burlington House in 1887.

72. In a film narrated by Sir Hugh Casson about the Russell-Cotes Art Gallery and Museum, Sir Hugh repeats this story although his source is unknown and was in fact told to him by someone else.
73. LG 1885, p. 32.
74. Cardinal Wiseman, introduction to *Fabiola* (London, 1855).
75. Cardinal Newman, introduction to *Callista*, dated 13 September 1855 (London: Burn and Dates, 1856).

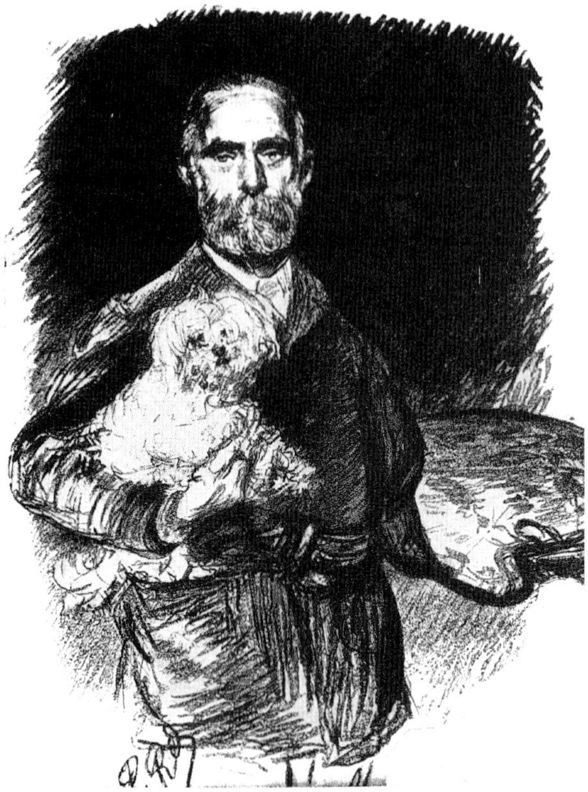

LEFT *Fig. 5.* Edwin Long with his palette and pet companion. Drawing by Paul Renouard, from *The Graphic*, 9 June 1888.

OPPOSITE *Fig. 6.* Edwin Long working on *The Crown of Justification*, in a drawing by Paul Renouard, from *The Graphic*, 9 June 1888.

A Love Feast depicts a scene from *Fabiola* where Syra, the slave, shares a meal with Caecilia, the blind girl, on the marble steps of Fabiola's house. *Callista, the Image Maker* depicts a scene where Callista, a Christian martyr, is seen in her early life as a maker of pagan religious imagery. Long had explored a similar subject in *The Gods and Their Makers* although *Callista* differed by including the subject of martyrdom as an integral part of the work. The tone of the painting, however, is predominantly light in treatment and the forthcoming martyrdom is nowhere evident in this particular scene. The same is true of *Alethe* which is derived from a poem and novel by Thomas Moore telling of a priestess of Isis and her Christian martyrdom. In both paintings we see an exotic scene of ancient Egypt. Long's insistence on using religious themes as the subject for these ancient genre scenes reveals a great deal about an artist who increasingly needed to present these exotic subjects with a Christian rationale.

In 1887 Long commissioned Richard Norman Shaw to design for him a second house. He chose a site next door to the *Labyrinth* at Netherhall Gardens. It is interesting that Long did not need to move for any practical reason. The motivation for the commission stems from Long's perception of his home and studio as a profound reflection of where his status in the world, which had changed significantly enough since Fitzjohn's Avenue to merit a change in home. The proximity of the new Shaw house to the first, and the retention of the house's name, indicated a change that was not so radical. He moved around the corner to Netherhall Gardens and, if the first *Kelston* had pretensions of being a family seat, the new home expressed the same in even grander terms. The doors that Long designed himself for the house were a sign of gravitas and invented provenance. These doors would greet the visitor on arrival at the house, and no

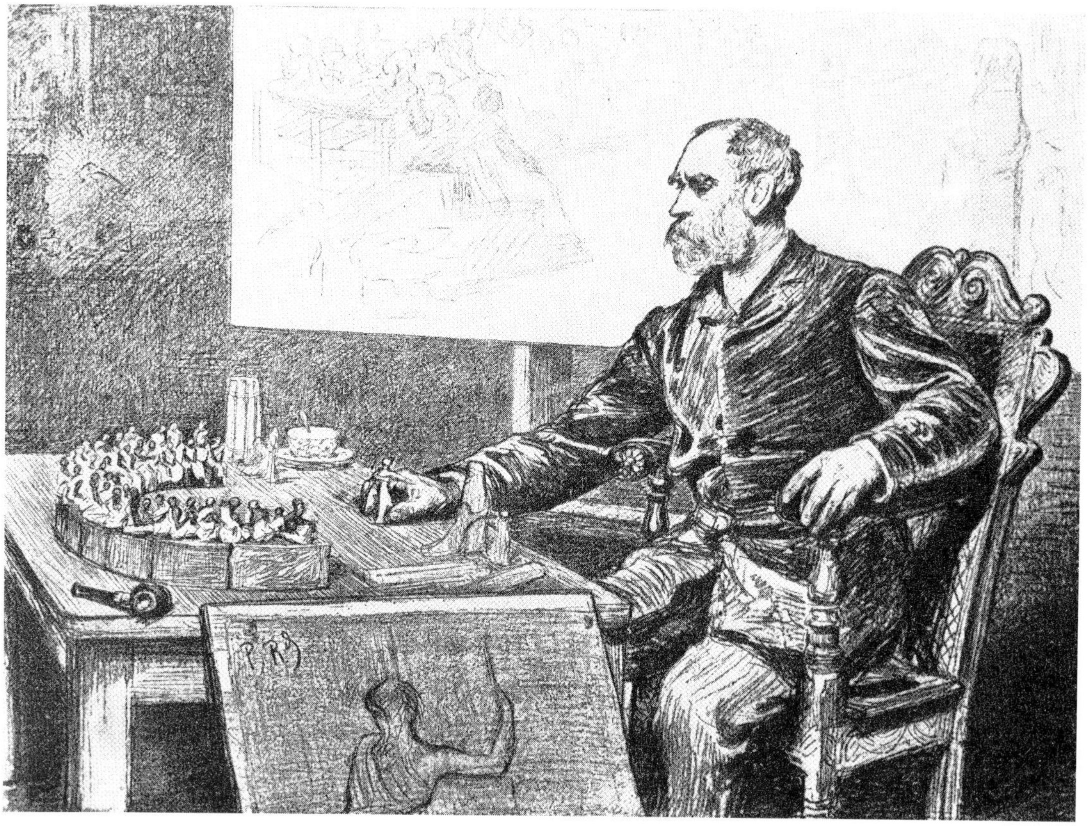

doubt made a monumental and imposing impression. As Spielmann described them on his visit there: "The front door, as it glistens under the ample porch, is a marvel to look at, consisting as it does of brass plates beaten into the representation of a mediaeval knight at the wars- his departure, his victories, and his glorious return."[76]

The interior similarly reflected Long's desire to give the impression of a family seat by including a corridor which ran the whole length of the house. This striking feature was recalled by Sir Merton Russell-Cotes on visiting in 1891[77] and by Spielmann after his visit in 1888: "the splendid corridor that has been designed it would seem, to allow of the inmates taking extensive walking exercise on a rainy day, or for hanging up long rows of Elizabethan ancestors."[78] This impressive feature marked the route to the studio on the first floor so that visitors would be struck by the grand staircase and myriad examples of the painter. His enormous studio was decorated with hundreds of oil sketches of heads that he had painted from his models and from the local people he encountered on his visits to Europe and the Middle East.

Its large size allowed him to paint the scale of paintings that people had come to expect of Long. When M. H. Spielmann and M. Renouard of *The Graphic* visited Netherhall Gardens in 1888 to research their 'Painters in their Studios' series, Long was engaged in painting his huge work *The Crown of Justification* based on a text by Diodorus Siculus which described the ancient

76. Spielmann, 'Painters in Their Studios', p. 612.
77. Russell-Cotes, *Home and Abroad*, p. 709.
78. Spielmann, 'Painters in Their Studios', p. 612.

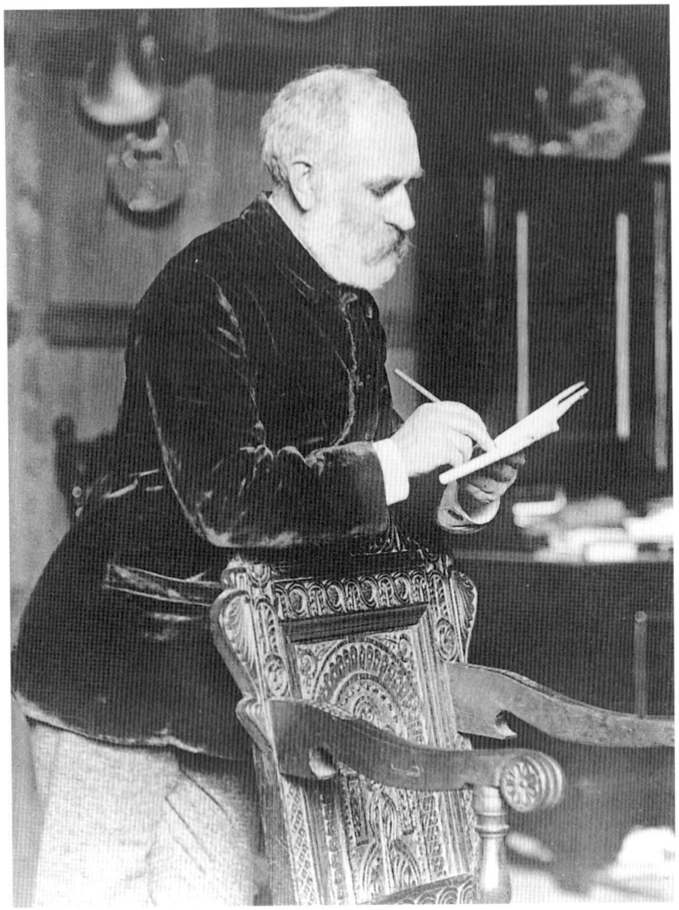

Fig. 7. Edwin Long in his Netherhall Gardens studio. Photograph by Ralph W. Robinson, published in 'Members and Associates of the Royal Academy of Arts, 1891, Photographed in Their Studios' (1892).
COURTESY OF THE NATIONAL PORTRAIT GALLERY, LONDON.

custom of judging the dead. Renouard's sketches of Long show him working on this painting. In one, Long is portrayed in painter's smock with palette and brushes in one hand and his pet terrier in the other which, Spielmann notes, "he loves to have with him while he paints."[79] The other sketch depicts Long actually painting the work from a model arena that he had built peopled by dressed wax figures. As Spielmann wrote, "To facilitate matters in this work – which has given him twelve months hard labour – Mr Long modelled the whole 'mis-en-scene' as well as the 'dramatis personae' in clay or wax, clothing the latter with rags round them, or with little robes from the diligent hand of his wife."[80]

This interesting insight into Long's working method reveals the grand theatricality of his compositions which foretells the influence that he and other neo-classical painters of this period were to have on early cinema. These ambitious reconstructions of the ancient world presented in tableaux became an important source for the early film directors, who saw their art form as an extension of painting.[81] In 1891, Long painted his largest work, *The Parable of the Sower,*

79. Spielmann, 'Painters in Their Studios', p. 612.
80. Ibid.
81. See Bernard Henson, 'D. W. Griffith: Some Sources', *Art Bulletin* no. 54, December 1972, pp. 493–515, for a discussion of the influence of the *Babylonian Marriage Market* on D. W. Griffith's film *Intolerance* (1916).

which Sir Merton Russell-Cotes saw when he visited the studio:

It was one of the finest studios I have ever entered, both for size and light. He explained to me that it extended over the whole house. He was at that time working on a huge canvas depicting our Saviour preaching from a boat on the Sea of Galilee. He also had in hand at the time several other fine works. I expressed my admiration for his works, which seemed to please him very much.[82]

The painting, measuring about seventeen by nine feet, was a tribute to Long's growing religious conviction. Its importance to him is reflected in the fact that he refused 5,000 guineas for it.[83] In 1891 Long was at the height of his reputation. Ironically when the *Parable of the Sower* finally went under the hammer in 1908 it sold for the relatively meagre sum of £131 5s.

The role of Long's wife Margaret in his career was not limited to dressing wax dolls for the great artist's model sets but involved the fundamental social role that society ascribed, in the presentation of the Long household to the world and, more especially, potential clients. In many ways, to be the wife of an artist was not an easy one, supporting her husband through initial difficulties, showing potential clients around the house, raising the family whilst remaining in the shadow of her husband's reputation. A studio house was after all a home. The new 'Kelston' was a show house and home, grander and more dignified, perhaps, than his previous houses, but a household nevertheless.[84] Margaret's importance in Long's career becomes particularly evident after his death when she continued to promote and exhibit his work.

In the May of 1891 an influenza epidemic reached the Long household. Edwin, Margaret and his daughter Ethel were all struck down. Edwin's condition became increasingly grave as it turned to sequela pneumonia. On 15 May his illness became so critical that at eleven o'clock in the morning he instructed his eldest son Maurice to call for his financial advisor, James Edward Milles to make out a will.[85] On his arrival between twelve noon and one he was shown into Long's bedroom. Long told Milles that "There is a possibility of my not getting over this illness, but I think I shall" and asked him to write the will.[86]

Long's estate at this time amounted to around £120,000, a tribute to his commercial success as an artist. The will stated that Milles was to be sole trustee and executor of the will and that Long's estate should continue to be managed at "his discretion". From this Milles would give £1,000 a year to Ethel for the rest of her life; Maurice, who had other means, £500 a year for life; and £250 a year for life to Ernest, where some provision had already been made. "The rest of the income from my estate to be paid to my dear wife my house known as Kelston, Netherhall Gardens, Hampstead, and also my furniture, pictures, and fine art, as well as stabling, carriages, and horses."[87] The will was signed by Long and witnessed by his coachman, W. Loader and Flora Joiner, a nurse attending him.

82. Russell-Cotes, *Home and Abroad*, p. 709.

83. *Daily Telegraph*, 1908, undated review in Bath Reference Library.

84. He had a stables and coach house built and employed a coachman who lived with his wife above these outbuildings.

85. James Edward Milles, of 30 Moorgate Street, Secretary to the North British Australian Company, had looked after Long's estate and financial interests for some time.

86. Reported in *The Times*, 12 December 1892, p. 14.

87. Ibid.

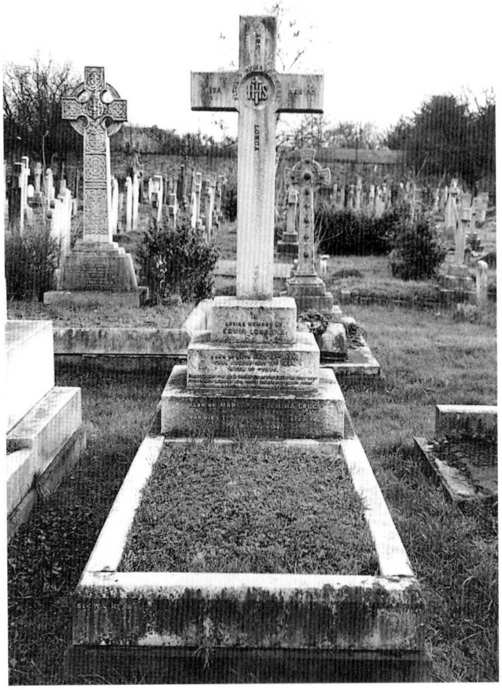

Fig. 8. Edwin Long's grave at West Hampstead cemetery. The stone bears the words '*Ars longa, vita brevis*'. PHOTOGRAPH BY FRANCIS MARSHALL.

The actual events of the afternoon that followed are unclear. As Maurice, Long's eldest son, had died on 23 September 1892, his testament did not appear in the case. However, Milles's account of the events were that Maurice asked what would become of the estate on the death of his mother. It was agreed between them that a separate codicil should be made. It is certain that a lawyer, a Mr Harris, was summoned to Netherhall Gardens at around 3.30pm on 15 May to write the codicil. At around six o'clock this was executed in the presence of W. Loader, Flora Joiner and Maurice Long. At this stage Edwin was critically ill and only able to sign his name with a cross. Loader, who could not see this action properly asked for it to be signed again. Edwin was only able to nod his head in assent. After it was signed, Maurice read prayers to his father and asked him if he would like to see a clergyman to which he agreed. Long's religious convictions had always been strong and his move towards orthodoxy and a higher church faith during his life was, to some extent, typical of the time. This change was also a reflection of his new status in society. The last rites, a ritual only practised within the highest Anglican and Catholic communities, were carried out at nine o'clock in the evening of 15 May as he lay dying. Maurice stated that "after nine in the evening he was assisting a clergyman to administer the Holy Communion to Mr. Long, and that the dying man had just partaken of the bread, but that, as he was putting the wine to his father's lips, Mr. Long sank back and expired."[88]

The codicil stated that on the death of Mrs Long the entire estate would be divided equally between the living children. This was to be managed by a sole trustee and executor, Mr Milles, who would be paid well, from the date of Long's death, for his services. Margaret contested this

88. *The Times*, 13 December 1892, p. 3.

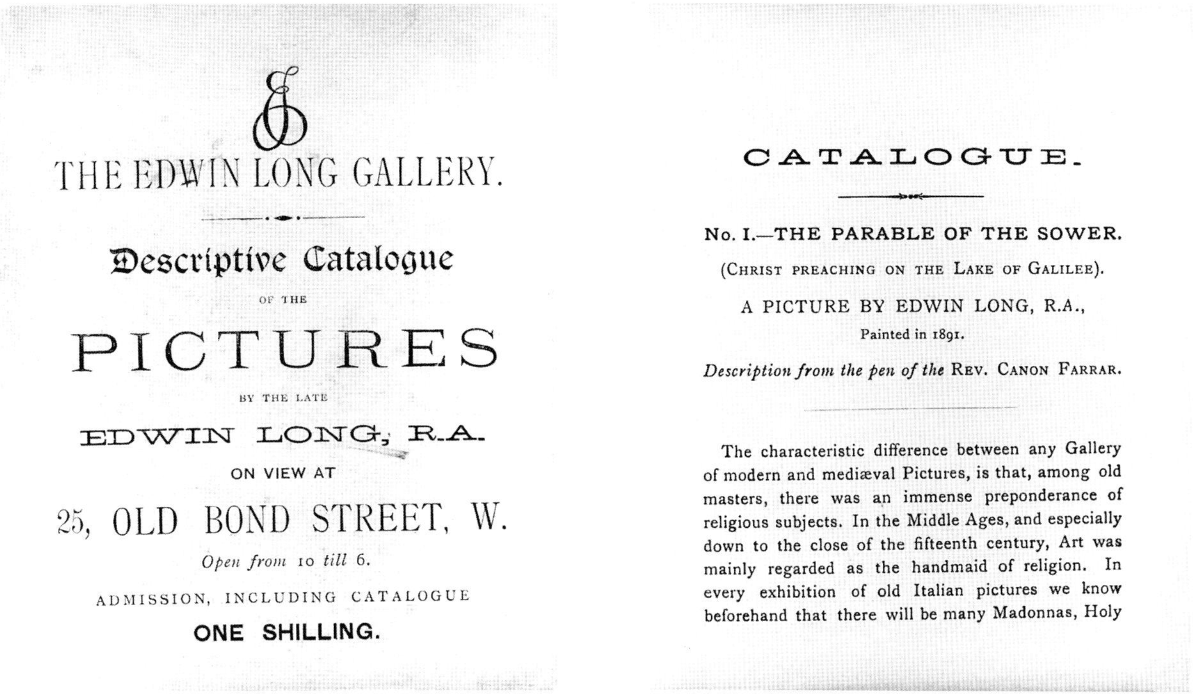

THE EDWIN LONG GALLERY.

Descriptive Catalogue

OF THE

PICTURES

BY THE LATE

EDWIN LONG, R.A.

ON VIEW AT

25, OLD BOND STREET, W.

Open from 10 *till* 6.

ADMISSION, INCLUDING CATALOGUE

ONE SHILLING.

CATALOGUE.

No. I.—THE PARABLE OF THE SOWER.

(CHRIST PREACHING ON THE LAKE OF GALILEE).

A PICTURE BY EDWIN LONG, R.A.,

Painted in 1891.

Description from the pen of the REV. CANON FARRAR.

The characteristic difference between any Gallery of modern and mediæval Pictures, is that, among old masters, there was an immense preponderance of religious subjects. In the Middle Ages, and especially down to the close of the fifteenth century, Art was mainly regarded as the handmaid of religion. In every exhibition of old Italian pictures we know beforehand that there will be many Madonnas, Holy

Fig. 9. The front cover and first page of the Edwin Long Gallery catalogue, 1894. Note Long's distinctive monogram on the cover.

codicil on the grounds that her husband "was not of sound or disposing mind, that he did not know and approve of its contents, that it was not read to him, and at the time of its execution he was in '*articulus mortis*' and incapable of understanding the nature of the act."[89] The case went to court in December 1892 and it arose that Mr Milles had already gained a 5½ per cent commission on the gross of the estate, and paid out of the estate the cost of a separate accountant as well as paying himself a further £132. Further, the section of the codicil referring to Milles's employment was added to by Milles himself after Mr Harris had made it up. The court case was stopped when agreement was made in favour of Mrs Long. Mr Milles retired from trusteeship of the estate with no stain or accusation against his character. Miss Ethel Long who had supported Milles was never reconciled with her mother after the court case.

Long's funeral was held at St Augustine's, on Park Road in Kilburn, and was led by the senior representative of the Anglo-Catholic faith based there, the Reverend Richard C. Kirkpatrick. This church, which was at the centre of the Anglo-Catholic movement, was some distance from Netherhall Gardens which lay in the parish of St John, Hampstead. The service was assisted by the Reverend A. Wright and the Reverend F. W. Smailes and was 'fully choral'[90] The organist, Mr Alfred Redhead played Chopin's funeral march and the dead march from Handel's *Saul*.[91] The church service was crowded and included many artists from the Hampstead and other commu-

89. Ibid.
90. *The Times*, 23 May 1891, p. 11.
91. Handel's oratorio *Saul* was one of Long's favourite pieces of music. He had based two companion paintings on it, *Merab* and *Michal*, in 1883.

nities. Notably present were Lord Leighton, P. H. Calderon and John Burgess, as well as dealers and patrons such as William Agnew. Wreaths were sent by the Baroness Burdett-Coutts, Henry Irving and the Duchess of Teck.[92] His son Maurice St Clair was the principal mourner as Margaret and Ethel Long were still convalescing from illness and Ernest was in South Africa. Long was buried at West Hampstead Cemetery with a simple cross which bears the inscription, '*Ars longa, vita brevis*'.

After Long's death, his reputation began to decline. As an artist who made much of his impact through the creation of large works which thrilled a contemporary audience the lack of new sensations resulted in a dearth of interest. The Doré Gallery changed its name to the Gallery of Sacred Art in order to present their existing works afresh with the inclusion of other large sacred works by Frederick Goodall. Its owners, Fairless and Beeforth, even changed the name title of *Anno Domini* to *The Unknown God.* Although the gallery continued to exhibit religious works it never found a successor to Long and eventually closed in 1896.

Long's presence on Bond Street was not limited to the Gallery of Sacred Art however. Margaret Long, in an attempt to revive the interest in Long and sell some of the works she had in her possession, set up the Edwin Long Gallery at 25 Old Bond Street in 1893. The gallery exhibited a large number of large-scale works including *The Parable of the Sower* as well as the large collection of paintings of heads that Long had displayed in his studio. It was open from ten until six and charged one shilling which included a catalogue with text by the Reverend Canon Dean Farrar. The works continued to prove popular amongst many of the clergy including Lewis Carroll who visited the new Gallery.[93] The success of the venture was short-lived however and the gallery closed in the following year. Most of the large works remained unsold.

Margaret Jemima Long died on 27 January 1907 and was buried next to her husband at West Hampstead Cemetery. She died intestate and her estate, including Long's paintings, was divided equally amongst her two remaining children, Ethel and Ernest. The studio effects that Margaret had kept were sold at a sale at 'Kelston' in the following October. The largest and most important works were sold at Christie's on 1 February 1908. The sale, the largest and most important of works by Long, was also an indicator of the decline of interest by the public and art world in the artist. In the sixteen years after Long's death, the art world was completely transformed and Long's reputation had plummeted. *The Crown of Justification* sold for only £157 10s and *The Parable of the Sower* sold for a meagre £131 5s. With the exception of Richard Quick who purchased *The Pharaoh's Daughter* for Bristol City Art Gallery, the rest were dispersed amongst private collections. The dealer W. W. Sampson who purchased several works, including *The Parable of the Sower* and *The Crown of Justification,* offered them to the nation: "I would be willing, if the nation would take them, to take cost price for either or both of them."[94] The offer, however, was not taken up by the trustees of the Tate Gallery.

92. "Amongst the mourners being Sir F. Leighton PRA, Mr P. H. Calderon RA, Mr John Burgess RA, Mr E. J. Poynter RA, Mr J. L. Pearson RA, Mr T. Brock RA, Mr Lumb Stocks RA, Mr J. E. Hodgson RA, Mr Andrew Gow TA, Sir A. W. Blomfield ARA, Mr G. Aitchison ARA, Mr G. A. Storey ARA, Mr Seymour Lucas ARA, Mr John Brett ARA, Mr Henry Moore ARA, Mr Val Princep ARA, Mr Trenta Costa, Mr William Agnew, Mr Arthur Lucas, Mr Robert Manuel, and Mr Zeno Diemar. Amongst many other artists present were Edward Goodall, T. H. Maguire, H. Weigall and J. Cother Webb. Wreaths were sent by the Duchess of Teck, the Baroness Burdett-Coutts, Mr Henry Irving, the Council of the Royal Academy and many others." *The Times,* 23 May 1891, p. 11.

93. Lewis Carroll visited the new gallery on three occasions in 1893. See note 62.

94. W. W. Sampson quoted in the *Daily Telegraph,* 1908, undated review in Bath Reference Library.

THE LIFE AND WORKS OF EDWIN LONG

Edwin Long's reputation declined in the face of the general reaction against Victorian art which occurred at the beginning of this century. Unlike many of his contemporaries however, Long's status has never recovered. His whole-hearted embracing of the popular taste of his own age has ensured that he has in many respects remained much less known than his peers such as Leighton, Alma Tadema and Poynter. Long's individuality is to be found, however, in his rare depiction of archaeological detail and in the extensive historical research linked with his deep interest in religion. His unique juxtaposition of religious subjects and female beauty expressed through historical, biblical and fictional texts reveals an artist who tied his own interests with a keen sense of the popular. That he was supremely popular within his own age is indisputable, but this is not to overshadow his own high ambitions and important achievements.

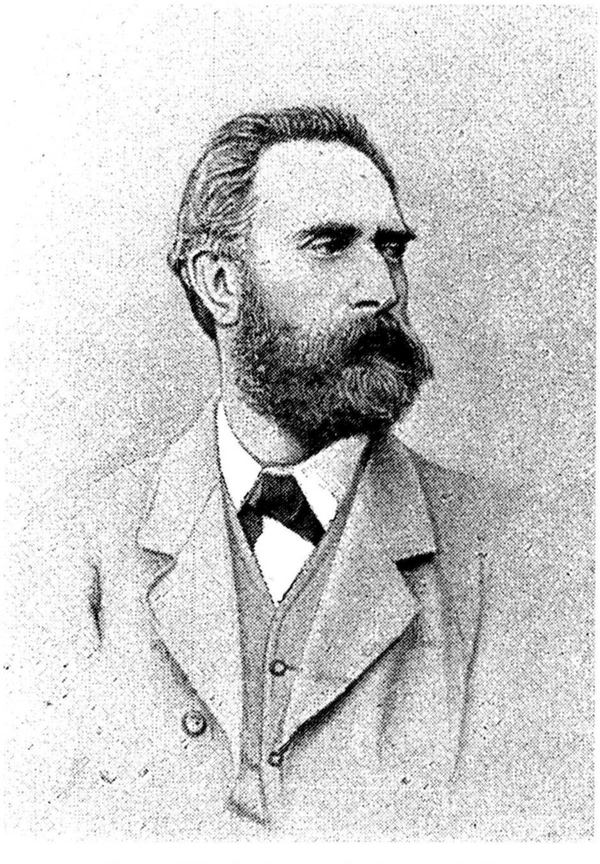

Fig. 10. Edwin Long. *Art Journal*, 1891.

APPENDIX I
LONG'S RESIDENCES AND STUDIOS

c. 1849–53	Portrait studio in 15 Old Bond Street, Bath.
1853–58	Portrait studio at 28 River Street, Bath.
1858–60	53 Upper Berkley Street West, off Portman Square, London.
1860–75	22 Ovington Square, London sw3, on the outskirts of the Chelsea artists community.
1875–80	19 Marlborough Hill with extensive renovations including a pavilion studio 'Long's Den' in his garden at 1a Carlton Hill, St John's Wood, London.
1880–88	Long's first 'Kelston', a studio house designed by Norman Shaw at 61 Fitzjohn's Avenue, Hampstead, London.
1888–91	Second 'Kelston', a studio house designed by Shaw and Lethaby at 42 Netherhall Gardens, next door to 61 Fitzjohn's Avenue.

APPENDIX II
COMMERCIAL BOND STREET GALLERIES THAT EXCLUSIVELY EXHIBITED WORKS BY LONG

Owner: Fairless & Beeforth, Fine Art Publishers

1868–92	The Doré Gallery,* 35 New Bond Street
1892–96	The Gallery of Sacred Art, 35 New Bond Street
1884–89	The Galleries (The Lawrence Gallery), 168 New Bond Street
1893–94	Lawrence & Beeforth, Publishers, 128 New Bond Street

Owner: Mrs Margaret Jemima Long

1893–94	The Edwin Long Gallery, 25 Old Bond Street

*The Doré Gallery after becoming the Gallery of Sacred Art became Lemercier & Co Ltd, French Art Prints and Lemercier Gallery and Tissot Exhibition in 1897. It returned to its title as the Doré Gallery by the early years of the twentieth century.

"MR. LONG HAS THE FINEST STUDIO IN LONDON . . . "*

Juliet Kinchin

ALONGSIDE HIS SUCCESS as a history painter, Edwin Long showed considerable flair for progressive tendencies in design. Within a twelve-year period he had commissioned not one, but two custom-built studio houses from the most fashionable architect of the day, Richard Norman Shaw. Their construction bracketed the most critically and financially successful phase of Long's career, visibly demonstrating that he had 'arrived' as the epitome of a wealthy and socially esteemed Victorian artist. There was more to these houses, however, than the expression of status and the combined provision of comfortable studio and domestic accommodation. The 'artist's house' had become viewed as a work of art in its own right, a monument to its owner's taste and creativity. On a professional level it was therefore an important vehicle for the projection of a public persona. Moreover, as part of Long's business concern these houses provided a vital location for socialising geared around the display and sale of his paintings. The custom-built studio home was an altogether new phenomenon which operated as a sophisticated model of the business town house – in other words, a living, working and salesroom environment all rolled into one.

To channel so much money and creative energy into house-building was not unusual in Long's day.[1] In this preoccupation, as in so many others, he was shadowing the example set by more established Academicians. The paradigm was Leighton who had embarked on the building of his own glamorous studio house in Holland Park Road on the strength of being elected as an Associate of the Royal Academy in 1864. This developing interest among top artists and architects was a distinctive phenomenon which contributed to Britain's world-wide reputation for 'artistic homes' in the 1870s and 1880s. In a folio volume devoted to artists' houses published in 1883, Long's name appeared in the company of the social superstars of his day – painters like Leighton, Stone, and the architects Burges and Norman Shaw. As the preface noted:

Not to Architects alone, but to Painters, and to Sculptors, remained the task of embodying in practical form the teachings and influences of those who had charmed by their writings; and the Public looked, with reason, to Artists to show them how best to profit by the lessons learned from the first workers in our modern Art-Revival. Those Artists who have been enabled to build houses for their own occupation have had the opportunity of practically embodying special ideas of what 'Art at Home' really means, as they have introduced, with more or less success, their own individualities into their dwellings.[2]

* *The Architect*, November 1879.

1. For an excellent discussion of the whole phenomenon, see G. Walkley, *Artists' Houses in London 1764–1914* (London: Scolar Press, 1994).
2. Preface to M. Stone, *Artists' Homes* (London: Batsford, 1883).

The Aesthetic Movement had helped to focus attention on the home to express both individual tastes and artistic discrimination, to become a kind of 'outer garment of the soul'. Being more aesthetically aware than the majority, artists were also seen as having a role to play in the development of public taste. Although it now rings with a patrician arrogance, Leighton was in fact expressing a commonly held view when he suggested that great artists like himself, through their "manners and method of existence . . . might furnish models to mankind in general, and elevate the tone and taste of nations."[3] Without the pressure of the commercial imperative driving speculative builders, architects and the now affluent artists could work together to create houses combining modern convenience and comfort with beauty and 'exquisite' poetic feeling.

High profile coverage was accorded to artists' houses in fashionable magazines and the professional press. Both of Long's were reviewed in glowing terms in publications such as *The Architect*, the *Art Journal*, the *Building News* and *The Graphic*. Given the competitive nature of the art world, this type of positive publicity and its implicit confirmation of professional status was arguably as important in constructing Long's critical reputation as any reviews of his actual paintings. Building a studio house had become a major public relations exercise, and public expectations of a successful artist's lifestyle were changing: "Studios like this are suggestive of the altered condition of art and artists in England. Gone are the days when studios could be improvised out of the rooms of common dwelling-houses, or those over shops and warehouses."[4] Clients like Lady Burdett-Coutts or Sir Russell-Cotes were not going to be lured to a dingy little studio in Soho. For them, part of the attraction of an artist like Long was that they could relate to him as a social and intellectual equal, and through him become involved in the lively, stylish scene of areas like St John's Wood or Holland Park where many such houses were clustered.

Victorians were fascinated by the notion of the 'creative genius' and what made each one tick. In this respect the cult of the artist as a personality converged with the growing interest in the domestic house as an artwork. There had already been a comparable focus on literary figures and their homes in Britain, most notably Sir Walter Scott at Abbotsford which had become a tourist-trap in the novelist's own lifetime. In a similar vein, an artist's house could be viewed as a key to the understanding of his (and, very occasionally, her) paintings: "In many of the leading studios one finds the mind of the master curiously apparent, for as surely as a painter's work is but the reflex of himself, with equal certainty his artistic tastes and sympathies are to be discovered in the abode he has chosen".[5] Visiting, or reading about such houses gave a new dimension to the art compared to viewing it in the context of a gallery. There was a desire to connect already familiar images with the source of their inspiration, to almost relive their conception in the studio, while also previewing their creator's latest offering. Domestic spaces impressed all the senses and worked on the imagination, giving the experience a voyeuristic intensity. Such was their emotional draw that even before Long's first house was fully completed, one magazine was recommending a visit.[6]

To be an artist was to enter a risky, unstable profession, often at the mercy of a fickle public,

3. Leighton's autobiography, quoted in Louise Campbell, 'The design of Leighton House: The Artist's 'Palace of Art', in *Lord Leighton 1830–1896 and Leighton House* (London: *Apollo Magazine* publication, 1996).
4. *The Architect*, vol. 22 (15 November 1879), p. 286.
5. *Art Journal*, 1883, p. 72.
6. *The Architect*, vol. 22 (15 November 1879), p. 286.

although the rewards for those at the top were evidently colossal, and their lifestyle tantalisingly glamorous. Compared to Leighton's meteoric rise to fame, Long's career path had followed a lower, more wobbly trajectory. It took an artist of stamina to survive the setbacks and critical panning which his work had received early on. Yet, from being turned down for enrolment as a student in the Academy on two separate occasions in the late 1840s, he had progressed to the lofty status of a full Academician by 1881. To achieve this transformation Long had patiently consolidated his career and social standing on a number of different fronts. Investment in house-building and decoration was an important strategy in this whole process, and his series of house moves in London paralleled the dogged development of his painterly skills, and his shrewd exploitation of the market.

At the age of twenty-nine, Long had finally felt ready to cast off the provincialism and faded gentility of Bath, and moved to London with his wife and young daughter. After a couple of years in Upper Berkley Street (off Portman Square), they settled in 33 Ovington Square which was to be home for the next fifteen years. This address was convenient for the growing complex of museums and the School of Art and Design at South Kensington. From here it was a tricky business judging when and where to move, as an artist's house sent out such complex and significant signals, both to the art world and to prospective patrons. The example of contemporaries like Leighton and Marcus Stone had taught Long that the right move could enhance a reputation and improve an artist's client base. On the other hand, there were plenty of casualties – artists who perhaps had inadvertently moved into, or stayed too long in areas classified as a social desert; others crippled themselves financially, gambling with mortgages on grandiose homes and an associated lifestyle which ultimately failed to improve their earning potential, or were perceived as inconsistent with their reputation at the time.

In 1875, flush with the financial and critical success of *The Babylonian Marriage Market* and his election as an Associate of the Royal Academy, Long was poised to begin dabbling in property development. While the bachelor Leighton had only had himself to think about, Long now needed to accommodate a wife and three children, plus a growing number of servants. As the producer of more big pictures than any other living member of the Royal Academy, the scale of his canvases also justified building a gigantic studio.[7] As one critic noted dryly of the studio he eventually built, "it seems no longer possible for a good picture to be produced unless the painter can regard every stroke of his brush from a long distance."[8] What he lacked in painterly finesse, Long certainly made up for in size and grandeur of theme. Within Academy circles a hierarchy of subject matter still prevailed in the late nineteenth century, with history painting viewed as the most elevated and prestigious of the art forms. Having started out as a portraitist, Long was now self-consciously styling himself as an 'historical painter'.[9]

His initial foray into building was a studio extension at the back of 19 Marlborough Hill, his new home in St John's Wood. (In a rare flash of punning humour he labelled this property 'Long's Den' after his middle name, Longsden.) But with an eye to becoming a full Academician, he clearly had a bigger project in mind – a whole new house, and was on the look out for a suitable architect and a site. Both were close at hand.

Sensibly, he did not try to muscle in on the Holland Park enclave of artists' houses where

7. M. H. Spielmann, 'Painters in Their Studios, II. – Mr. Edwin Long R.A', *The Graphic* (9 June 1888), p. 612.
8. *The Architect*, vol. 22, 15 November 1879, p. 286.
9. 1881 Census.

he would have been outclassed by the likes of Leighton, and also steered clear of the somewhat too bohemian Chelsea of Whistler and his circle. Instead Long opted for nearby South Hampstead. (A couple of years before him, Henry and Kate Holiday had already beaten a path in exactly the same direction from Marlborough Road, to a new house designed for them by Basil Champneys.)[10] The area had all the right credentials, offering the aura of rural gentrification without being too stuffily respectable. One could combine the best of city and country – controlled development, good water, air quality and extensive views, with easy access by cab or local train to the theatres and restaurants of the city centre. Nearby Hampstead was also rich with literary and artistic associations. The famous Heath had continued to draw artists since the days when Constable and Linnel had painted there (particularly after the introduction of the suburban railway in the 1860s). Shelley and Keats had rambled over the bosky meadows to the south of Hampstead, and Leigh Hunt had composed sonnets on the slopes there.

Fortunately for Long, an extensive area of rising meadowland in the vicinity was sold for development in 1875 by the Maryon Wilson family (Lords of the Manor of Hampstead).[11] A new broad avenue (named Fitzjohn's, after one of the family's estates in Essex) was to be created following the line of an old footpath which linked St John's Wood to Hampstead Village. Long immediately got hold of one of the best plots, a commanding corner site with a large garden and extensive views to the rear over open fields. The site adjoined Fitzjohn's Avenue and a smaller road named Netherhall Terrace in 1877, after the Maryon Wilsons' Sussex estate.[12] Such titles enhanced the 'lineage' of the area. Long subsequently added a further layer of association by calling both his houses 'Kelston', the area his family came from in Somerset. In effect he was creating in London a family seat that never was. The name conveyed suitable gravitas, and superimposed Long's family heritage over that of the Lord of the Manor. The status and quality of the development was also ensured by the breadth and planting of the avenue, the size of the individual plots, and the stipulation in every contract that no house worth less than £3,000 could be erected.[13]

Long's choice of site was probably advised by his architect, Richard Norman Shaw, who at the time was in the process of building a house for himself around the corner in Ellerdale Road. Stylistically, he was able to strike just the right note of inconspicuous refinement, 'homeliness' and genuine distinction that Long required. Like Long, Shaw was an Associate Academician, and very much the coming man in architectural circles. In 1875 he had already designed houses to a budget of over £5,000 for both Marcus Stone and Luke Fildes in Melbury Road.[14] Where possible he would indulge clients, but always with a keen eye for practicalities and the fundamentals of modern living like good lighting and up-to-date plumbing. On one of the drawings for Long, for example, Shaw brought the discussion down to earth with the firm note: "You must have a larder, wine and beer cellars and place for heating apparatus". Plumbing was a particular hobby-horse; his drawing for a drain from the house to the sewer not only specified the size and type of piping but also the form of the ventilating shaft to allow for repairs.[15]

10. The Holidays stayed at 5 Marlborough Road from 1868 till 1873, when their ceiling fell in.
11. Fifty acres were sold to developers for £50,000.
12. Netherhall Terrace was subsequently renamed Netherhall Gardens.
13. C.Wade, ed., *The Streets of Belsize* (London: Camden History Society, 1991), p.54.
14. For a fuller account of these commissions, see A. Saint, *Richard Norman Shaw* (New Haven: Yale University Press, 1976), pp. 153.
15. Drawings in Royal Academy Collection (Norman Shaw, 61 Fitzjohn's Avenue).

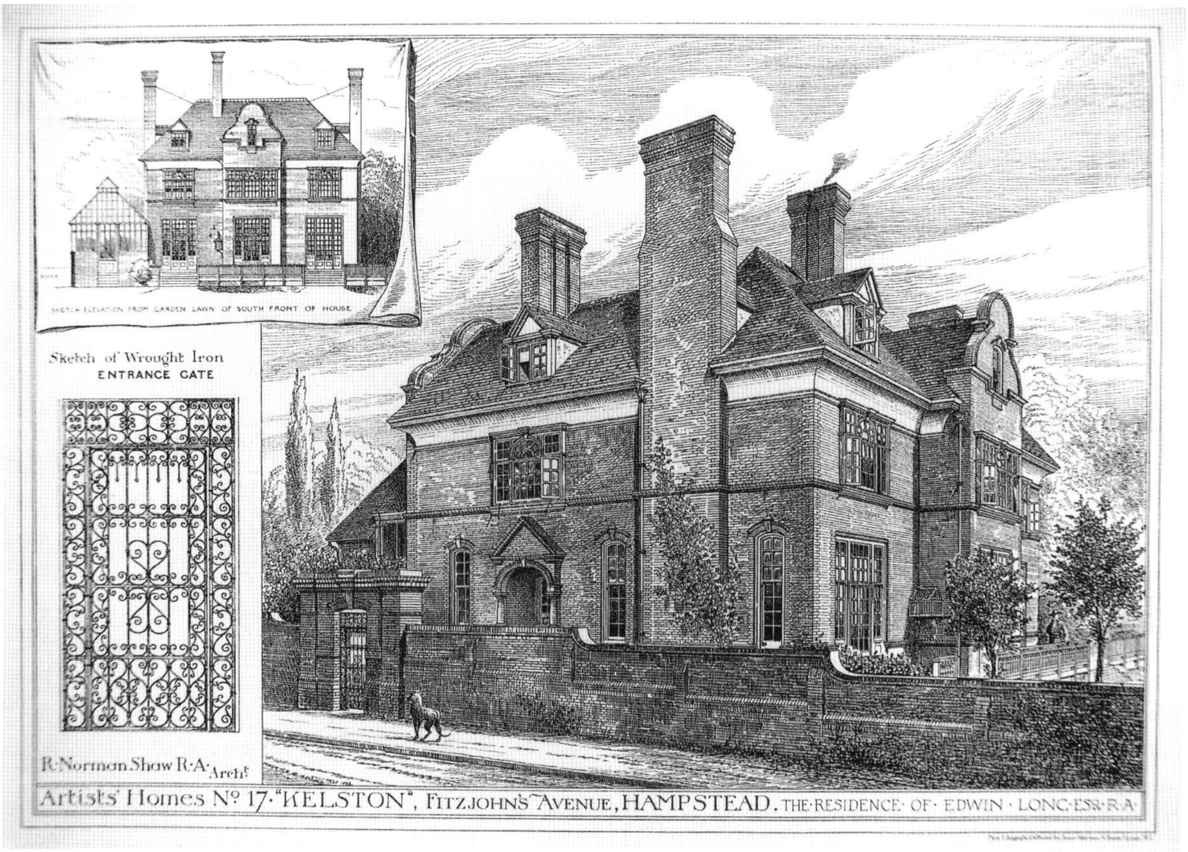

Fig. 11. Designs for Long's first house by Norman Shaw, published in the *Building News*, 1883. Although the elevation viewed from Netherhall Gardens gives an accurate impression of the house as built, the inserted elevation reflects one of the several layouts rejected by Long in what turned out to be a protracted planning process. From M. Stone, *Artists' Homes* (London: Batsford, 1883). COURTESY OF EDINBURGH PUBLIC LIBRARIES.

Like Shaw's other 'Queen Anne' houses in London, 61 Fitzjohn's Avenue was built in sober, exposed red brick with stone dressings and very little ornamental work. In contrast to the expensive speculative building nearby, Long's house was pointedly restrained in its external detailing. The plain stretches of walling were not offset by bands, panels and string courses of pressed brick; similarly the roof tiles were plain with no elaborate cresting tiles and finials to distract the eye. Visual interest was however created through the irregularity of the overall massing and fenestration. With an extensive site to play with, Shaw was able to let the house sprawl over a good deal of ground, creating various effects of grouping from different angles, with curved gables, chimney stacks and projections on different levels. The creepers working their way up the wall in the *Building News* perspective suggested the way in which nature and time would further mellow the picturesque effect.

Shaw seems to have deliberately underplayed the commanding site. Approached from Fitzjohn's Avenue, the house settled comfortably behind a wall, set well back from the pavement. Nevertheless distinctive features of the house – the apsidal protrusion of the studio and its great chimney stack marking the inglenook within – were immediately obvious from the road.

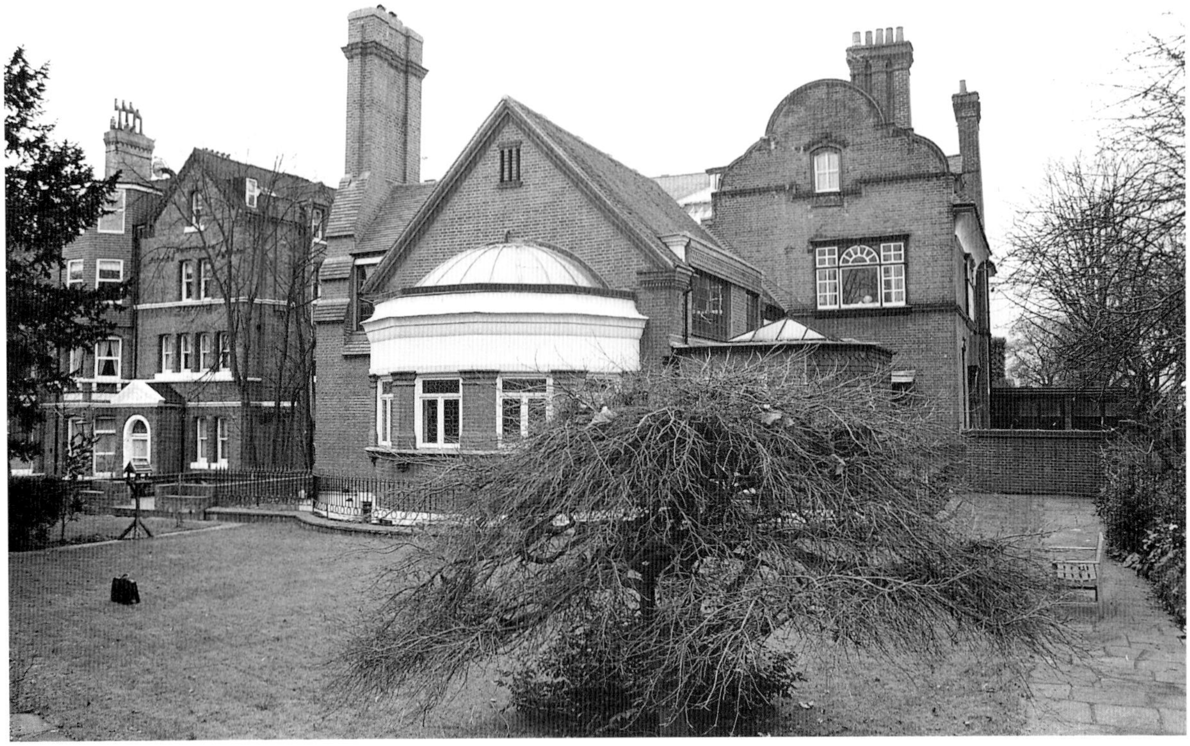

Fig. 12. Exterior of the 'Labyrinth', the first house designed for Long by Norman Shaw, viewed from Fitzjohn's Avenue. Although now subdivided within, the picturesque massing of Norman Shaw's design has remained intact from this viewpoint. The apsidal projection of the substantial studio would have made this house instantly recognisable as an artist's home. PHOTOGRAPH SHAUN GARNER.

In contrast to neighbouring properties under construction which thrust ostentatious, lofty façades upon the Avenue, Long's house self-consciously stuck its rump towards the thoroughfare. Although the address was Fitzjohn's Avenue, the main entrance to the house had been switched round to the side road in the last reorientation of the plan. Ironically it was therefore the servants, tradesmen and models who ended up entering from the Avenue. Shaw seems to have had an ability to express the personality of his clients indirectly. From the outside the unassuming yet dignified character of 'Kelston', as it was named, matched the description of Long's temperament as "reticent and retiring".[16] This outer reticence was complemented by the more ostentatious flavour of the interior which seemed to express another facet of Long's character, his inner confidence, traditionalism, and determination to succeed as a painter on a grand scale. The building certainly exuded a feeling very different from Shaw houses in the vicinity for other artists. A glittering frontage of oriel bays was designed a few years later at the other end of the Avenue for the more extrovert painter Frank Holl, while Kate Greenaway's house round the corner at Frognal (1879) was spoken of as 'pretty' and 'quaint'.

16. Spielmann, 'Painters in Their Studios', p. 612.

Shaw was renowned for his planning. Rather than tinkering with a programmatic formula he would approach a commission from scratch, developing a solution in collaboration with each client. He was already experienced in dealing with artists and their specific practical requirements like good north light for the studio, and facilities for painting equipment, models and props. Designing an artist's home also made complex demands in terms of circulation and interrelating public and private space. Family, clients, visitors, models and servants had to coexist, but could only converge at points acceptable in terms of propriety and convenience. At Kelston, Shaw provided comfortable family accommodation on the garden side and first floor, and a spacious ground-floor studio where practical work and business with clients could be conducted. The models had their own entrance so that their comings and goings were kept at a discrete distance from Mrs Long's domain. An establishment of this size operated with a considerable number of servants who in this case were squeezed into the basement at the back, and the attic. In 1881, a cook, housemaid and page were recorded as living in. The family who later rented the house needed a ladies' maid, cook, parlour-maid and two housemaids at hand twenty-four hours a day.[17]

An additional factor with which Shaw had to contend in juggling all these requirements was a meddling client with strong views on matters of art and taste. Over the years Long certainly tested his architect's ingenuity and patience to the full. They needed three attempts at the first house, and through the sequence of drawings one can reconstruct the creative play of Shaw's imagination in response to his client's tiresome, shifting intentions. In all the shuffling, two distinctive elements remained constant – a twenty-five-foot square inner hall round which the whole house was ranged, and an enormous ground-floor studio (about thirty-three feet long) with an inglenook. Even after beautiful contract drawings had been signed and sealed in June 1878, the guts of the house were swivelled round to face Netherhall Gardens before construction began. A subsequent sheet of elevations (in pencil, with more rubbing out) is marked 'as built'. It comes as no surprise that the perspective and plan published in the *Building News* did not match up, and that Long took to calling his project 'The Labyrinth'.[18]

Entering through an attractive wrought iron gate on Netherhall Gardens visitors faced the front door, marked with a simple triangular pediment. Immediately inside to the left was a waiting room with cloakroom facilities for clients; beyond, a magnificent inner hall, off which lay a sequence of different sized rooms – domestic accommodation to one side and the studio suite to the other. On his travels Long was evidently much taken by the central 'patio' of many Spanish and Arabic houses, and in all his vacillation over the plans the idea of having a spacious glass-roofed courtyard at the core of his house remained a constant. The floor was paved with stylised floral mosaics which added to the decorative, enclosed exoticism of the space. Visual isolation from the outside world, the light flooding in from above, and underfloor heating all added to the fantastical, hothouse atmosphere.

Crossing the corner of the patio, clients and visitors were conducted into the huge studio, regarded by the *Art Journal* as Shaw's best to date.[19] As in many of the artists' houses in Melbury Road, there was an adjoining glasshouse for outdoor effects and finishing work. The painting area was larger than most to allow Long the necessary space for manoeuvre, and the windows,

17. 1891 Census.
18. This name appears on the local Drainage Register, 14 November 1878.
19. *Art Journal*, 1881, p. 109.

cleverly managed so as to secure high, slanting and even light from the north. As was typical at this time, Long's approach to historical subjects entailed peopling acres of canvas with authentically researched detail. Before bringing in any models, he would often plot a canvas by placing chairs around the studio to mark the place of the various characters in the design. He would then "contemplate the view from different points of the compass, arranging, altering, re-arranging, until the resemblance to the original becomes more or less remote."[20] Opposite the window giving north light was a massive fireplace with inglenook, and over it a good-sized gallery from which Long's canvases could be viewed, while also giving access to the side compartments. The studio's barn-like dimensions were given an air of sanctity by the addition at one end of a gilt-lined 'apse' with a raised marble mosaic floor, reminiscent of Leighton's studio, and a pipe organ with an elaborate screen to one side; "at first sight this looked like a church" wrote the reporter of the *Architect*.[21] The studio, felt to be drenched in the spiritual culture and poetic feeling of the artist, was the highpoint of any visit and such theatrical, semi-religious overtones helped instil a reverential attitude in the viewer come to worship at the altar of art. The messy and racy side of painting – the models' changing room, easel store and sink for oily brushes – was kept carefully out of sight. On the garden side of the house the public rooms also functioned as a showcase for Long's art and collections. The circulation was carefully planned to allow an enticing glimpse of key works from one room to the next, as between the dining and morning rooms.

Having been ensconced in his new house for little over a year, in 1881 Long finally broke into the ranks of the fully fledged Academicians. Significantly the Diploma painting which he chose to present to the Academy was entitled *Nouzhatoul-âouadat*, ('The Delight of the Home'). The theme highlighted the two preoccupations around which his life centred at the time, the arts of the home combined with the colourful exoticism of travels which had liberated his imagination.

Long had chosen well, and in the context of Fitzjohn's Avenue he and Shaw were trail blazers. The rapidity with which Shaw conceived new architectural types and set new fashions was evident in the way many of his ideas were rather crassly recycled in other houses along the Avenue. When 'Kelston' was being built it offered extensive views over the receding fields, but these were soon being covered in bricks and mortar. Development was rapid with houses being sold almost as soon as built. Nevertheless the "disastrous torrent of extravagant vulgarity" being poured down both sides of this road provided an excellent foil to Kelston; the houses were not cheap or shoddily built, but were formulaic in their design and encrusted with 'expensive and meaningless features and ornament.'[22] After a bout of intensive building in the mid 1880s the street still had the rather raw look of a recently vacated builder's yard. It had not yet matured into the "commanding, tree-beautified avenue of stately dwellings" described in the 1912 *Annals of Hampstead*. Nevertheless the area had mopped up a creditable number of fashionable artists, justifying Long's choice of location. Some critics remained rather snooty:

It is not altogether obvious to an outsider why artists of late have shown such a predilection for Fitzjohn's Avenue, South Hampstead. It is not a countrified spot, but rather a wilderness of brick fast being converted into houses more or less aping the Queen Anne style. It is, after all, just a long,

20. Spielmann, 'Painters in Their Studios', p. 612.
21. *The Architect*, vol. 22 (15 November 1879), p. 286.
22. *Art Journal*, 1881, p.181.

uninteresting London street, with only this difference, that many of the houses are detached, and most make pretensions to artistic beauty–pretensions which in very few cases are justified . . . Yet this street is now the high artistic fashion, and the artists who of late have followed the modern tendency among their brethren of building houses for themselves after their own plans or ideas have pitched them here.[23]

This sneering tone was taken up in Bernard Shaw's play *Mrs Warren's Profession* in which one of the characters claims to have learned about art from "some artistic people in Fitzjohn's Avenue". The 'arty types' were however mixed in with other respectable professions such as civil engineers, manufacturers, insurance brokers. Next door to the Longs in 1881 was Arthur Newton, of Windsor and Newton fame, and at number 69, Charles Weld, an artists' colourman employing fifty-six men and twenty-two boys.[24] Initially Kelston had been, quite literally, the most highly rated property on the Avenue.[25] Although it remained one of the most substantial and expensive, however, it was soon upstaged by the arrival of fellow artists' houses. John Pettie set up at no. 2, while Frank Holl had gone to Norman Shaw for the flashy 'Three Gables' (no.6). Evaluated in a crudely monetary league according to rateable values, Pettie came out on top at £392, followed by Holl at £350, and Long at £317.[26] Alma Tadema lived away down the Grove End Road and MacWhirter just opposite. Sir Max Pemberton recalled how this group of artists gave a distinctive character to St John's Wood. As a boy he was mesmerised by the influx of fashionable figures on 'Show Sunday' when these studio homes were opened to the public in advance of the Royal Academy opening; 'The Sunday parade should have been a source of inspiration and delight to the makers of fashion plates.'[27] Additional colour was provided by bohemian types like Carl Haag, who had turned the top floor of his house, Ida Villa, into a kasbah. At Oak Tree House, the Holidays held famed musical soirées. Nearby on Fitzjohn's Avenue intellectuals such as Professor Huxley and the numerous musicians added to the rich cultural mix.

As already noted this house-building was a competitive business among artists and soon Long was itching to reassert his artistic lead with another strong architectural statement, one which would reflect his status as a more established Academician. Not content with a few tinkering modifications to the existing house, the planning of which had become something of an intractable problem, he wanted a second shot at starting from scratch. Within only seven years of taking up residence in 'Kelston', he took the unprecedented step of building another grand house, this time at the bottom of his garden. He had the requisite capital to sink into the project without having to realise his assets from the first Kelston (which was subsequently leased), and enough land in his back garden to develop without impinging on his neighbours. He obviously liked the area, and liked his architect, as he went straight back to Shaw a second time. The move could not be justified on the practical grounds of a growing family and household, nor of the need for more studio space. Far from having been put off by the protracted planning process of his 'Labyrinth', it seems that Long had become addicted to house building.

This time Shaw kept greater control over his client, and held him at a distance, devolving much of the project to his chief assistant, William Lethaby. There were certainly fewer tussles

23. Helen Zimmern, *Magazine of Art*, 1885, pp. 144–45.
24. 1881 Census.
25. 'Kelston' had a rateable value of £292 in 1881.
26. Poor Rates, St John Hampstead Vestry, 1890.
27. M. Pemberton, *Sixty Years Ago and After* (London: Hutchinson, 1936), p. 81.

over the plan, and Long seems to have been kept happy searching for interesting mosaics to incorporate into the plan, and designing a resplendent front door. The beaten bronze panels depicted a narrative of knights (possibly Crusaders) assembling, sailing off to war, fighting and returning triumphant. This theme was tinged with the religiosity and exoticism to be found in Long's art. In *The Moorish Proselytes of Archbishop Ximenes, Granada, 1500*, for example, Long homed in on the point of contact between Europe and the Orient, between Christian and Islamic culture. Moreover the spirit of antiquarian medievalism was widespread in both fine and decorative arts of the period, and was felt to be particularly appropriate in the entrance to a grand house, where antique weapons and armour were traditionally displayed. Entering the hall the visitor was immediately carried yet further back to antiquity by the richness of the colours and finishes, in particular the Roman mosaics allegedly excavated from the site of Carthage. Such details drawn from classical archaeology were echoed in many of Long's paintings.

Working with a smaller site this time Shaw decided to go for a first floor studio. For visitors this meant trailing the length of the house from the front door along a spacious passage. En route they could admire examples of Long's paintings and his typically eclectic collection of decorative arts including booty from his travels. In a photograph of 1891 one can make out specific items such as the Pompeian-style metal table featured in *The Chosen Five*, a Spanish-looking *vagueno*, or travelling cabinet on an eighteenth-century stand, various unupholstered

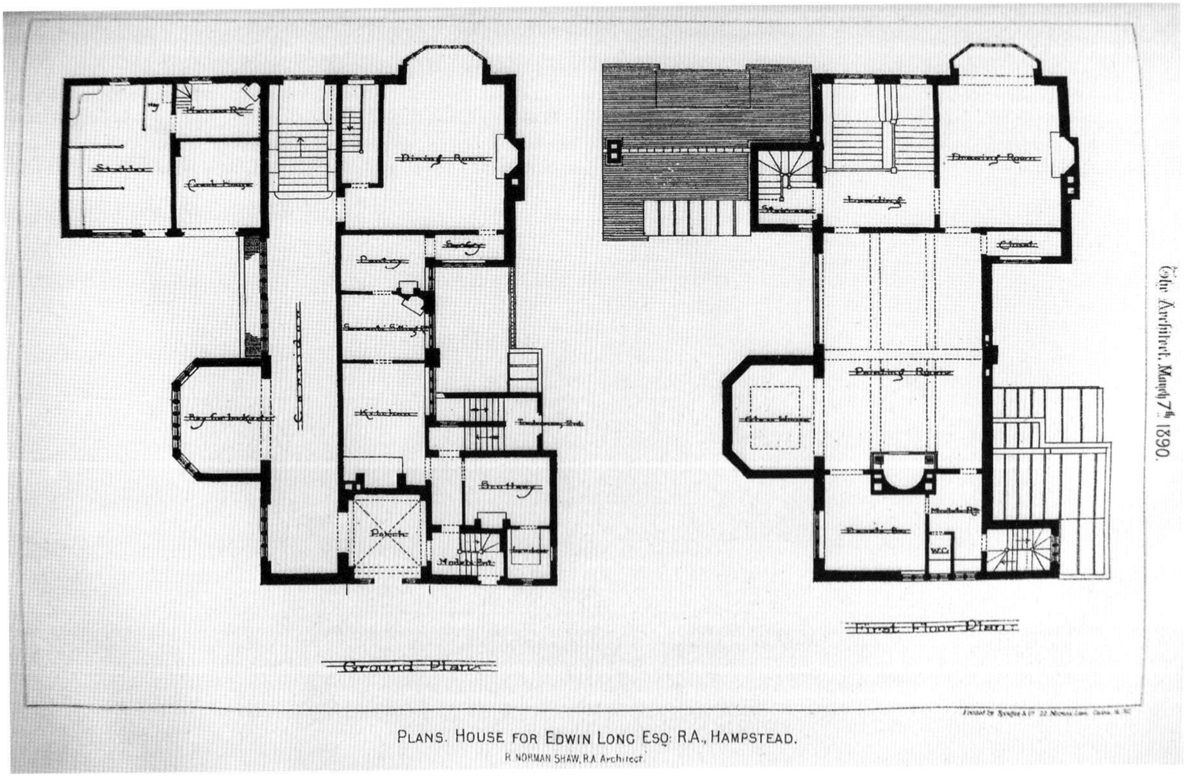

Fig. 13. Plans of the second 'Kelston', 42 Netherhall Gardens, 1900. This time round Shaw and his pupil Lethaby were working with a more compact site and offered Long a spectacular first floor studio running the full length of the house. Models entered at the opposite end to visitors and clients. From *The Architect*, 7 March 1890. COURTESY OF EDINBURGH PUBLIC LIBRARIES.

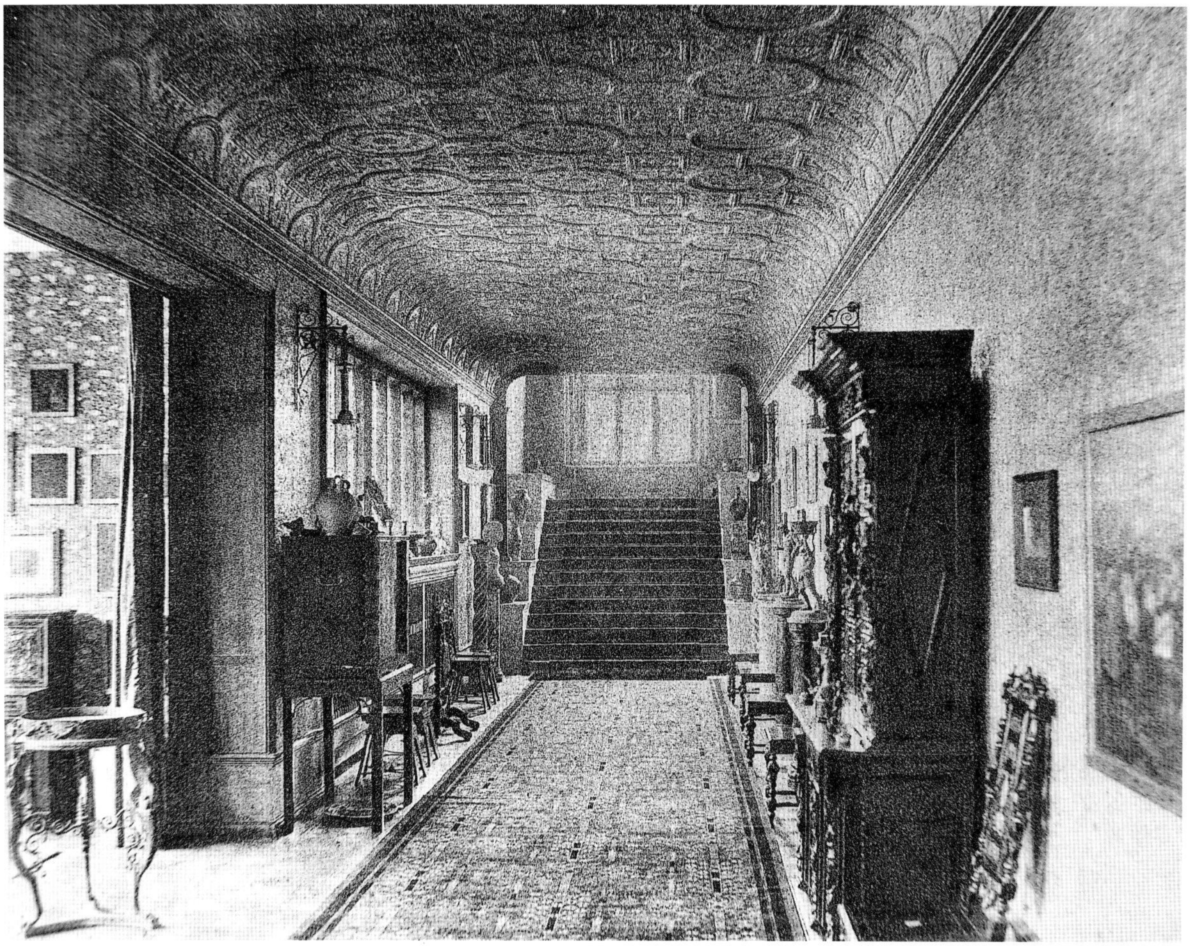

Fig. 14. 42 Netherhall Gardens, view along the ground floor corridor, 1890. Proceding along this corridor on their way to the first floor studio, clients and visitors were able to preview examples of Long's art on the walls, and admire his broadranging taste as a collector of artistic furnishings. Some of the furniture was used as props in his paintings. From *The Architect*, 7 March 1890. COURTESY OF EDINBURGH PUBLIC LIBRARIES.

hall chairs and seventeenth-century high backed chairs, an elaborately carved Flemish-style cabinet, and oriental ceramics on the stairs at the far end. This was the "beautiful mansion" which Sir Russell-Cotes recalled visiting with a painting for Long's opinion:

He afterwards invited me to go up with him into his studio, which was reached by a wide corridor running the whole length of one side of the house, and a grand staircase at the other end. It was one of the finest studios that I have ever entered, both for size and light. He explained to me that it extended over the whole of the house. He was at work at that time on a huge canvas depicting our Saviour preaching from a boat on the Sea of Galilee. He also had in hand at the time several other fine works.[28]

Models entered at the opposite end of the house from the visitors, where the main stairs

28. Sir Merton Russell-Cotes, *Home and Abroad* (Bournemouth: privately printed, 1921), vol. 2, p. 708.

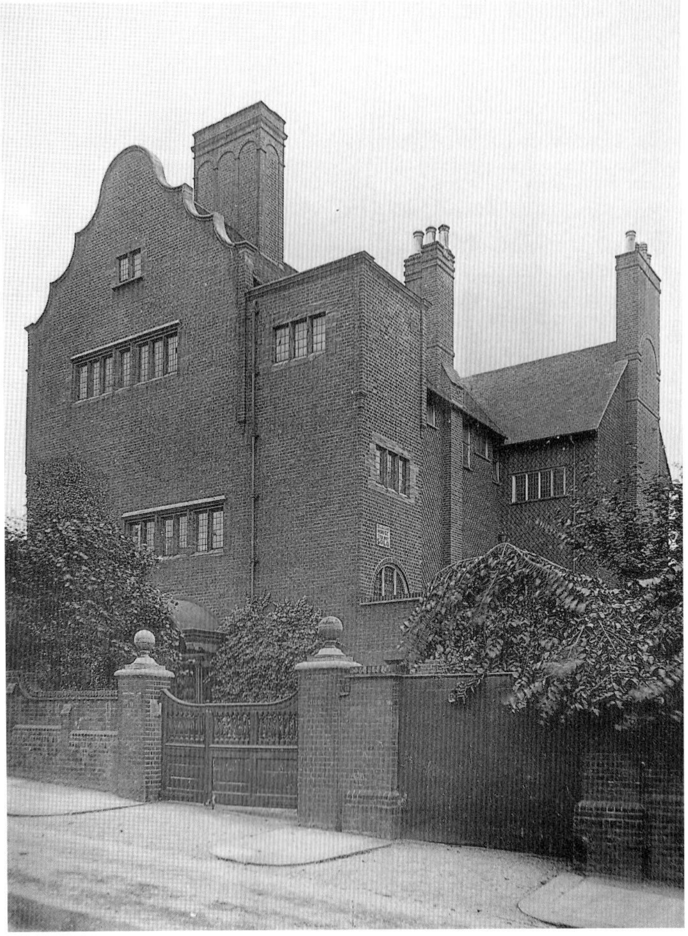

Fig. 15. Exterior of the second Kelston viewed from Netherhall Gardens in a photograph taken c. 1900. This dramatic elevation contrasts with the more retiring, picturesque feel of the previous house. Its gaunt aspect is heightened by the sign 'TO BE SOLD' and a broken window. Always expensive to maintain, the property was acquired by the Elgars before being put back on the market in 1921 and subsequently demolished in 1937. From H. Muthesius, *Englische Baukunst* (Berlin: 1900). COURTESY OF EDINBURGH PUBLIC LIBRARIES.

also led down to a Billiard Room in the basement. Servants had a better deal this time, with roomy ground-floor accommodation. A cook was accommodated in the main house, while a coachman with his wife and three children all lived above the stables.[29] The acquisition of a personal carriage was a new and important indicator of status for the Longs.

Having taken up residence in 1888, Long was only to enjoy his new house for three years before dying suddenly in May 1891. Although he had left his wife and children in a healthy financial position, without him the business and the family rapidly fell apart.[30] At the same time his critical reputation began to plummet. The great studio houses had had their day and were no longer the epicentre of fashionable life. At least he was spared the family bickering

29. 1891 Census (RG12 107).
30. At his death his personal estate was valued at £74,411. According to a report on the case surrounding his will in *The Times*, Long's personal and real estate amounted to around £120,000.

over the will hastily drawn up on the day he died, the estrangement of his daughter, and the premature death of his eldest son the following year. His widow rattled around in the second Kelston on her own for a further sixteen years after which the house lingered on the market for several more. It was given a brief reprieve as 'Severn House', however, by Lord and Lady Elgar who moved in on New Year's Day, 1912. Lady Alice appears to have been the driving force behind the purchase. She was instantly drawn to the imposing, dignified character of the house which she felt would do justice to her husband's status while providing him with a comfortable environment in which to work. The spacious studio was readily adapted to composing and chamber music. But such an elephantine property was an incredible drain on resources. Even Britain's best known composer admitted having to accept commissions for trifling theatrical works to keep up with the running costs. Repairs were a constant worry and, unlike in Long's day, the whole place was run with only one ageing servant who lived out.[31] As one local later recalled, "Severn House asked to be burgled. We children passing on sunny days thought it was uninhabited".[32] It was clearly Lady Alice, a general's daughter, who kept the show going, and after her illness and eventual death in 1920 the house was back on the market. By this time Long's posthumous reputation was at such a low ebb that his involvement in the house passed without remark in the sale catalogue. Instead Sir Edward Elgar's property was advertised as "A 'Norman Shaw' House of an Altogether Unusual Character".[33]

Today it is difficult to recreate a sense of the smart and elegant buzz of what *Harper's* described in 1883 as "one of the noblest streets in the world".[34] Many of the most spectacular houses which once graced the avenue are now gone; others have been brutally converted into flats or turned over to institutional use. The earlier Kelston has survived, but only by virtue of being chopped up internally into six flats and the rear gardens sold off for development. The second Kelston outlived its usefulness and in 1937 was demolished. (To date the magnificent bronze doors have not been traced but surely such features must have been salvaged?) A plaque now marks the site, but is a further damning indication of the collapse of Long's critical fortunes in that it celebrates the occupancy not of the artist who inspired and helped create the house, but the subsequent owner, Sir Edward Elgar.

31. *The Times*, 30 July 1919.
32. Dr Louie Eickhoff, *The Elgar Society Journal*, January 1988, p. 11.
33. Sale Catalogue of 'Severn House', November 1921 (Camden Historical Archives).
34. Wade, *The Streets of Belsize*, p. 54.

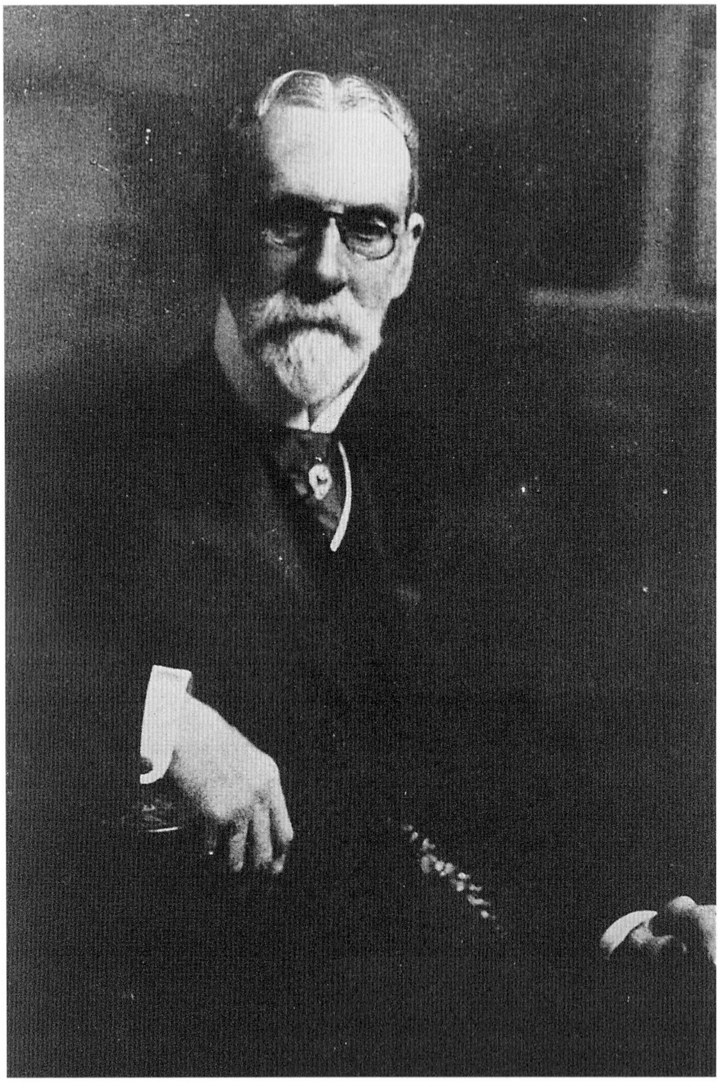

Fig. 16. Merton Russell-Cotes

EDWIN LONG AND MERTON RUSSELL-COTES

Simon Olding

THE RUSSELL-COTES ART GALLERY AND MUSEUM, Bournemouth, holds the largest single public collection of works by Edwin Long, currently numbering sixteen oil paintings and a group of engravings. The founder of the museum, Sir Merton Russell-Cotes, is known to have bought ten works by Long, of which seven paintings remain in the permanent art collections of the museum. Merton and his wife Annie (the museum's co-founder) moved to Bournemouth in the 1870s as illness dictated that he find a suitably healthy location to mitigate the long term effects of bronchitis and other disorders. The couple took over the management of the Bath Hotel (later the Royal Bath Hotel) in 1876, quickly turning it into a luxurious, fashionable and highly artistic hotel for the developing and aspirational resort town. Both Merton and Annie threw themselves enthusiastically into a wide range of philanthropic works and local improvement schemes, Merton becoming Mayor in 1894–95.

They quickly saw the potential of the hotel as a venue from which to advertise these public and social interests, and Merton's own promotional abilities ensured that the name, reputation and high style of the Royal Bath Hotel, as well as the good name of the Russell-Coteses, was never far from the public eye. In addition Merton was very keen to establish a reputation for himself as a philanthropist, gentleman-scholar and cultivated man of the world. By today's standards he did this in a rather ingratiating manner. His long, pedantic autobiography *Home and Abroad* contains frequent, and, it has to be said, tiresome references to regular contact with the minor aristocracy, minor royalty, and other local dignitaries.[1]

Once the Russell-Coteses had achieved financial and social stability in Bournemouth, they quickly set about the rapid upgrading and rebuilding of the Royal Bath Hotel. They travelled enthusiastically and at length to Japan, New Zealand, the South Pacific, America and Russia – these travels inevitably turning into collecting trips. The core of the Russell-Coteses substantial ethnographic and decorative art collections from Japan were added to displays which covered public and private rooms in the Royal Bath Hotel at the end of the nineteenth century. The hotel gained something of a reputation as an artistic haven too, since Merton Russell-Cotes, who took full charge of collecting in the area of fine art, added prodigious amounts of sculpture and paintings for display in the hotel at this time.[2]

The founders of the museum soon found that space was severely limited, even within their

1. Sir Merton Russell-Cotes, *Home and Abroad: An Autobiography of an Octogenarian*, 2 vols. (Bournemouth: privately printed, 1921). See also, Shaun Garner, 'The motives for the foundation of a museum in Bournemouth by Merton and Annie Russell-Cotes at the turn of the century' (unpublished MA thesis, University of Leicester, 1992).
2. Oscar Wilde is quoted as saying: "you have built and fitted up with the greatest beauty and elegance, a palace, and fitted it with gems of art, for the use and benefit of the public at hotel prices". Russell-Cotes, *Home and Abroad*, vol. 1, p. 36.

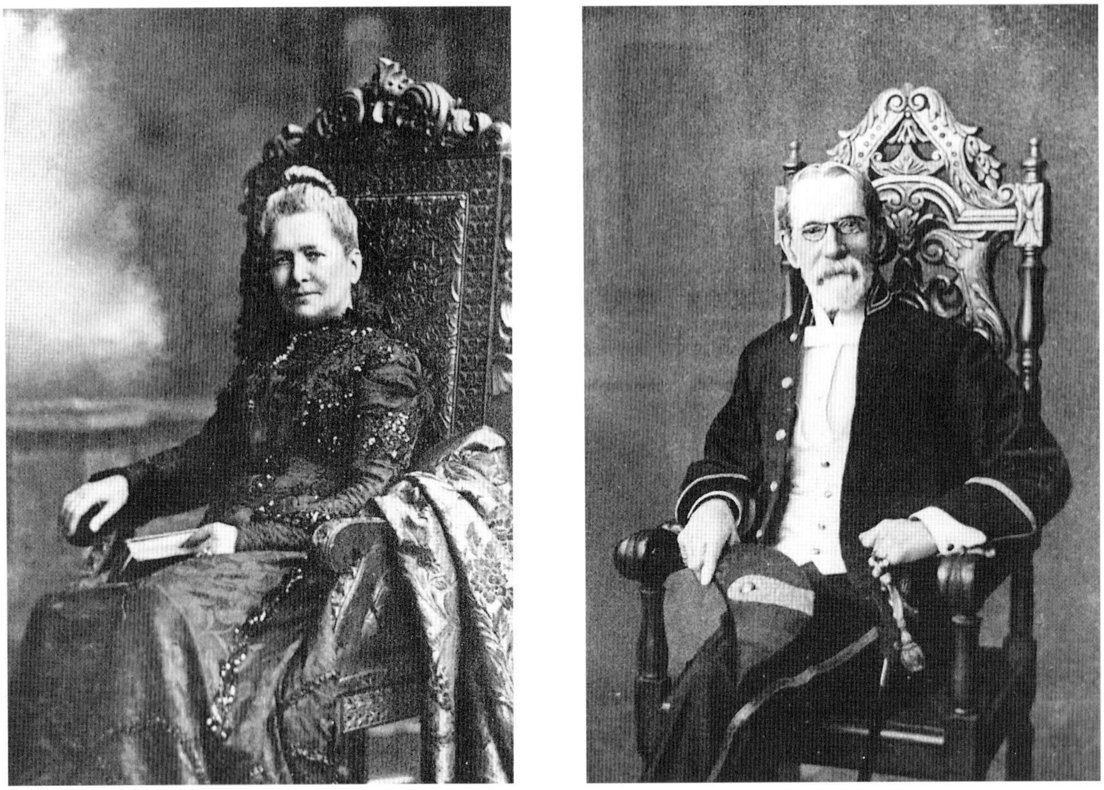

Fig. 17. Annie and Merton Russell-Cotes in 1909.

expanding hotel empire. The couple developed a scheme to build a new property in the grounds adjacent to the hotel on Bournemouth's East Cliff. The initial plans and building works to create their new home were made in 1897. The result, East Cliff Hall, is the Victorian heart of today's Russell-Cotes Art Gallery and Museum. Conceived in a dramatic and extravagant style with echoes of an Italian villa, Scottish baronial castle, Moorish temple and French chateau, the house is a colourful and exotic tribute to their artistic tastes. East Cliff Hall was designed by the Bournemouth-based architect John Frederick Fogerty. Merton's interest in artist's studio houses (he had visited Leighton House and two of Long's London houses prior to 1897) influenced the planning of his own grand home. East Cliff Hall reflects, to some degree, the baronial atmosphere and artificial provenance (creating a new 'family seat' for the Russell-Coteses), and the exotic elements characteristic of Long's Netherhall Gardens residence. The mosaic pool and a Moorish alcove in East Cliff Hall are more directly influenced by the great Arab Hall in Leighton's studio house.

The building also afforded new opportunities for the display of fine art, sculpture, ceramics, ethnographic works, Japanese material, and Annie's own natural history collections. Contemporary photographs show the interior of East Cliff Hall full to overcrowding with these works. Merton's preference for fine art began during his boyhood, when he remarks that he was "always enamoured with pictures".[3] Predictably, little evidence is given of serious purchases to

3. Russell-Cotes, *Home and Abroad*, vol. 1, p. 36.

the fine art collection until Merton had sufficient wealth to indulge his favourite habit. The 1880s were an important decade in the establishment of the collection, with its emphasis on established British artists. His taste was for the conventional, the decorative and the narrative, with a particular interest in the female nude, a subject which occurs frequently in the works of art he purchased. Merton, in one uncharacteristically frank admission, describes his zeal for fine art in the same terms as his zeal for property development. Whilst he clearly wanted to be regarded as a connoisseur and collector, it becomes clear on reading his autobiography that paintings are, at worst, marketable commodities, at best, agreeable symbols of wealth and prestige, rather than evidence of sophisticated visual taste. He writes that

one of the most important inducements that seems to present itself to me was that by purchasing the Royal Bath Hotel Estate I should be enabled to gratify my special genius for the love of art and my weakness for building and developing property, and also afford me an opportunity to form an art gallery eventually for the art treasures, of which I had a large collection.[4]

One of Merton's more endearing features was the genuine regard he held for the artists with whom he sought regular personal and professional contact, and whose works formed the core of his personal collection. He continued to buy and sell works energetically throughout the late nineteenth and early twentieth centuries.

The original Russell-Cotes collection was purchased for public and semi-public display, as well as for the Russell-Cotes's private rooms within the Royal Bath Hotel. In these circumstances they could not choose works which would offend or outrage respectable hotel clients. Rather, paintings were conceived as a very superior form of intensive wall-covering. Local press reports indicate that every wall, door and every available window were covered with designs by the hotel's resident artists, John and Oliver Thomas, who as staff members introduced elaborate historicist decorative schemes throughout the hotel. They continued this work in East Cliff Hall. The *Black and White* magazine of October 1891 describes the lengthy corridors of the Royal Bath Hotel "hung with specimens of the choicest work of such artists as Turner, Corot, Tadema, Sidney Cooper, Edwin Long, Jno. Linnell, Landseer, David Murray, W. L. Wyllie, Herkomer, Fildes, Etty, Webster, Dendy Sadler, Waterlow and hosts of others".[5] The display of this collection, intended by Merton to demonstrate both his artistic sympathies and his liberal patronage of art, also showed his tastes to be predictable and conservative.

Merton had another mission besides the decoration of his grand hotel. He put together around 250 paintings from his private collection, distinct from the collection specifically brought together for the hotel, to create a travelling loan collection, which toured to municipal galleries, principally in the north of England, throughout the last two decades of the nineteenth century. Galleries in Leeds, Liverpool, Glasgow, Sheffield, Oldham, Burnley, Bradford, and Derby, with one showing in the south of England at the Victoria Art Gallery in Bath, held short or long term exhibitions from the Russell-Cotes collection. Merton states that the prime source for the purchase of these works was the annual autumn exhibition at the Walker Art Gallery, Liverpool, though he notes that he particularly enjoyed purchasing works that had been in that year's Royal Academy exhibition. He says that his loan collection included "all admirable works

4. Russell-Cotes, *Home and Abroad*, vol. 1, p. 33.
5. Quoted in ibid., p. 38.

by famous British artists (I was always in favour of the modern British School of Art, and never appreciated the work of the Old Masters)".[6]

Merton's intention was to "confer a benefit upon the public and educate them in the art of their own country".[7] The loan collection was an important feature of his life between 1884 and 1902 when the laborious arrangements of travel and exhibition, together with the pressures of having little spare space in the hotel or at East Cliff Hall to display the works, made him sell them, although he retained one third of the collection for his continued personal pleasure. The loan paintings were sold at Christie's on 11 March 1905 (including Long's *Jairus' Daughter*), and Merton describes it as "the most complete representative collection of British Art they had had through their hands".[8] The portion which remained in his private collection was then subsequently included in the gift of East Cliff Hall, together with its fine art and other collections to the town of Bournemouth.

Merton seems to have added to his collection using the advice of a very small number of dealers and auction houses, including Agnew's where he is known to have bought five works in the 1880s, including Frost's *Sea Cave*. Russell-Cotes says that Thomas H. Woods, a senior partner in Christie, Manson and Woods at the end of the nineteenth century on his retirement to Bournemouth, also helped to purchase works of art for him as did the noted dealer W. W. Sampson of Air Street, London. Undoubtedly he bought works because of the high artistic and social standing of artists, in particular adding what are now regarded as copies of works by Albert Moore, and a large number of nude studies by William Etty. However much Merton sought out the acquaintance of the artists from whom he purchased work, he was not beyond sending paintings back to be 'improved' (he asked Solomon J. Solomon to add "a few little things" to *Bather's Alarmed*).[9] The addition of a substantial number of works by Edwin Long seems to have taken place between 1900–11, and certainly paintings such as *Anno Domini* are known to have been displayed in East Cliff Hall. However, with the addition of four purpose built art galleries to the east wing of the house during the 1920s, the paintings by Long were given special prominence, having their own dedicated room (Gallery III). The transition of a hotel and domestic art collection integrated into the fabric of the two buildings, to a fully fledged public museum display took Russell-Cotes over thirty years to achieve. The scale of his chosen works became more substantial to match the grand size of the galleries, although contemporary photographs show the typical dense late Victorian hang of paintings remained until well after the full-time opening of the Russell-Cotes Art Gallery and Museum to the public in 1922, after Merton and Annie's deaths.

Russell-Cotes mentions that the purchase of his first Long painting took place in the mid-1870s with the work called *Dialogus Diversus*. He had sought Long's personal opinion on this painting believing it to be by John Phillip. He took the painting to the artist's house at 19 Marlborough Hill in St John's Wood and was given the personal assurance by Edwin Long that it was from his own hand.

Merton acquired the seven paintings now in the permanent collections of the Russell-Cotes over a period of time. He implies that the purchase of five works (*Anno Domini*, *The Chosen*

6. Russell-Cotes, *Home and Abroad*, vol. 2, pp. 686–87.
7. Ibid., vol. 2, p. 688.
8. Ibid.
9. Ibid., vol. 2, p. 721.

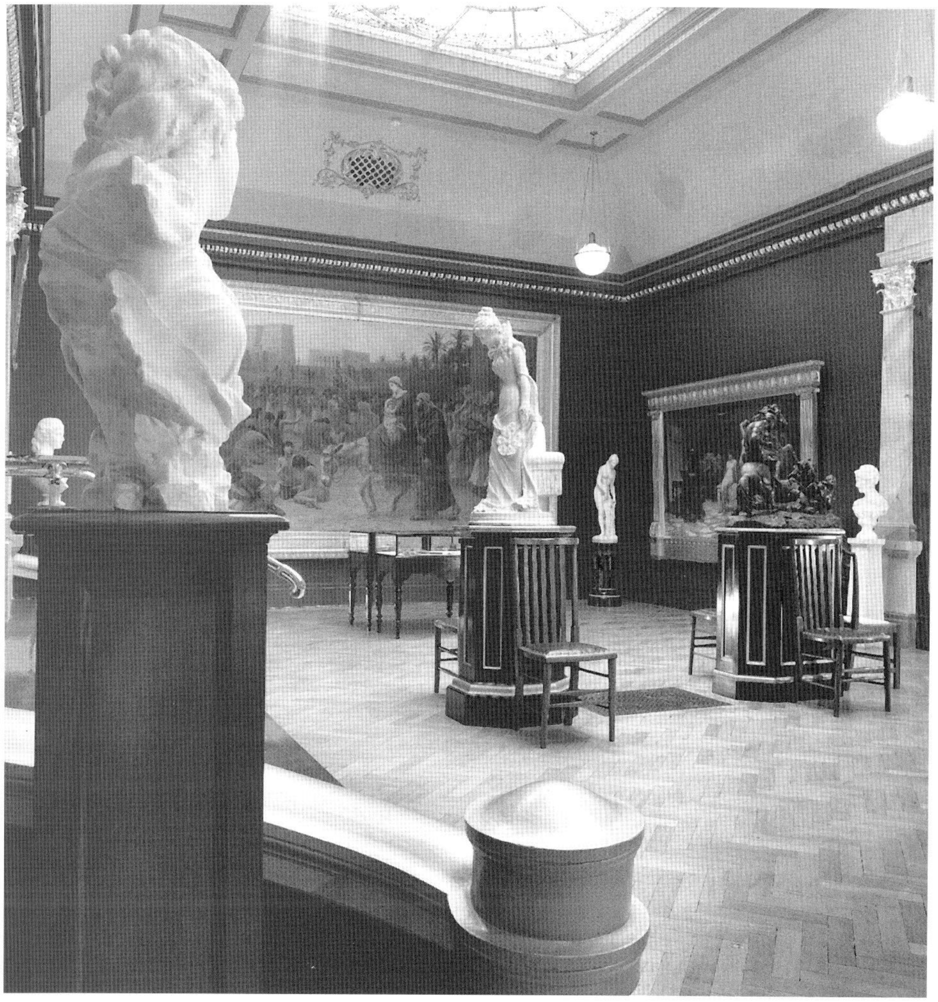

Fig. 18. Gallery 1, Russell-Cotes Art Gallery & Museum, Bournemouth.
PHOTOGRAPH BY JAMES HOWE.

Five, and the suite of three works under the heading *Jephthah's Vow*) took place at one time. It is highly likely that he would have viewed them when on extended public display in Bond Street. All of these works were purchased by Russell-Cotes at a time when their value was near its lowest level. He implies in *Home and Abroad*, recounting Long's heyday as an artist, that he was the possessor of works of significant financial value, since it is known that the group of works (with one other companion painting) were originally commissioned for £50,000.

A number of factors predisposed Merton to the purchase of his paintings. He enjoyed the personal acquaintance of the artist; he particularly appreciated the prestige and status of his chosen artist, most probably because the purchase of works would reflect glory on his personal taste and sophistication. He stuck carefully to the purchase of modern British and European works for his collection, and a number of contemporary records indicate that his loan collection as well as his personal and then museum collections, contained paintings by many modern artists of note. The paintings by Long stood alongside such well-known works as Landseer's *Highland Flood*, an oil now attributed to Turner of *St Michael's Mount*, a full-length portrait,

Edward VII by Tennyson Cole, James Archer's *Henry Irving as Charles I* and Frederick Goodall's *Subsiding of the Nile*. One of the few local artists patronised by Russell-Cotes was Lucy Kemp-Welch whose dynamic and romantic horse paintings strike an emotional note amongst the more subdued and less challenging genre scenes, historical studies and allegorical works which typified the collection. Merton and Annie donated the house and its contents to the Borough of Bournemouth in 1908 on condition that the couple were able to live in their house peaceably and quietly until their deaths in respectively 1921 and 1920. Public attendance at the 'house-museum' in this period was permissible on Wednesday afternoons, on the purchase of a ticket from the Town Clerk, and Merton would surely have been a strong personality at these viewings. He was enamoured of show and spectacle and took every opportunity to invite civic and other dignitaries to see his fine art collections. At the formal opening of the Art Gallery extension by HRH the Princess Beatrice, he was at his most ingratiating, and it has to be said, his most pompous. Merton makes his interest in his royal visitor's opinion fully known, expressing his delight when she drew particular attention to Long's paintings, as well as to works by Albert Moore.

The *Art Journal* in 1895 carried a number of studies of works from Merton's fine art collection. The anonymous writer stated that: "he has devoted considerable time to the bringing together of probably the most notable collection of modern works of art in the extreme south of England".[10] Central to this collection was the display of paintings by Long in their own dedicated art gallery. A number of factors came together to generate Russell-Cotes's interest in the works of Edwin Long. The paintings' strong, overt religious narratives and their epic scale, clearly endeared themselves to Merton with his own strong Protestant sensibilities. *Anno Domini* enabled the world-traveller to study a panorama of Egypt on the walls of his own home. Long's professional standing and status would also have attracted him and though there is no evidence that the two men struck up a particular friendship, Russell-Cotes would have made much when reminiscing about their meetings in London. Merton's second recorded, and last, meeting with Long took place early in 1891 when he visited the impressive studio at Netherhall Gardens, Hampstead, remarking in particular on the grandeur of the painting *The Parable of the Sower*.

The status of Edwin Long's paintings in the history of the Russell-Cotes Art Gallery and Museum derives then from the founder's intentions. The paintings, not least because of their physical bulk, have always maintained a strong presence in the gallery's programme. Indeed, when the refurbishment of the Art Gallery extension was undertaken in 1992, a specific decision was made to recreate the first gallery, reproducing to very high standards a decorative and colour scheme designed by Merton. In this gallery the deep brown wall paint was re-introduced, painted marbled pillars and gilt capitals were recreated, and the original lighting system restored. The picture rails were painted black as in the original scheme and the 1920s public seating was returned. Sculpture plinths, and works of sculpture known to have been displayed at the opening of the gallery were also restored. Eight works by Edwin Long, including the six paintings from Russell-Cotes's original collection are displayed in this gallery to maximum effect. In this way, the original taste of the founders is respected, the original decorative scheme of the gallery is recreated, and imposing and commanding works by Edwin Long are given an authentic and convincing historical backdrop to be seen and studied by today's visitor.

10. 'The collection of Merton Russell-Cotes, Esq., J.P', *Art Journal*, 1895, p. 83.

A CATALOGUE OF THE OIL PAINTINGS
of
EDWIN LONGSDEN LONG RA

compiled by Mark Bills

INTRODUCTION TO THE CATALOGUE

THE CATALOGUE OF WORKS BY EDWIN LONG INCLUDES ALL KNOWN FINISHED OIL PAINTINGS. It does not include the large number of oil studies that he produced, unless one specifically relates to a completed oil, and then it appears as a sub-section of the final work's number. Many of Long's studies, particularly of heads, are in one sense complete, but are not the sustained and finished works of his finished portraits. They are more comparable with the initial studies that he produced for portraits even if they were never used in more finished works. The sheer number of domestic scale works that Long produced for a commercial market ensures that there will be works that are not listed simply through lack of records. It is partly the aim of this catalogue that such works may eventually be restored to the body of Long's known works.

ORGANISATION OF THE CATALOGUE

The catalogue is organised into a chronological order with each work having a catalogue number, title, date, dimensions (in imperial and metric), medium, inscriptions, a descriptive entry, and information on its provenance, exhibitions, references and present whereabouts (where known). In the case of the catalogue number, each finished work is given a separate number. In the case of replicas, of which Long made several, a '1' has been added to the number or '2' where Long made two. The same numbering system has been used for studies of finished works.

EXHIBITIONS

All the exhibitions in which the painting has appeared are listed chronologically with its exhibition number.

REFERENCES

All books, articles and catalogues in which the work has been specifically mentioned are listed. These are listed in alphabetical bibliographic fashion with surname first rather than chronological order.

COLLECTION

The collection is listed when it is a public or institutional collection. Private collections are not specifically listed nor works where their whereabouts remain unknown.

ABBREVIATIONS

AJ	*Art Journal*
Academy Notes	Henry Blackburn, *Academy Notes, with illustrations of the principal pictures at Burlington House.*
Agnew's 1887	'Daughters of Our Empire', an exhibition by Edwin Long R.A., at Agnew's, 39 Old Bond Street, London, 1887.
Ath.	The *Athenaeum.*
BI	British Institution.
Bulletin (R-C)	*Bulletin of the Russell-Cotes Art Gallery & Museum.*
Chapel 1982	Jeannie Chapel, *Victorian Taste* (London: Royal Holloway College, 1982)
Chester 1908	Austin, Chester, 'The Art of Edwin Long, R.A.', *Windsor Magazine*, 1908, pp. 332–50.
Clayton	Peter A. Clayton, *The Rediscovery of Ancient Egypt* (London: Thames and Hudson, 1982)
De Meulenaere 1992	Herman De Meulenaere, *Ancient Egypt in Nineteenth Century Painting* (Belgium: Berko, 1992)
ELG	Edwin Long Gallery, 25 Old Bond Street, London.
ELG 1894	Edwin Long Gallery, *Descriptive Catalogue of the Pictures of the Late Edwin Long, R.A.* (London: Doherty & Co., 1894).
Home and Abroad	Merton Russell-Cotes, *Home and Abroad* (Bournemouth: privately printed, 1921)
Humbert 1989	Jean-Marcel Humbert, *L'Égyptomanie dans l'art occidental* (Paris: ACR édition, 1989)
Kestner 1989	Joseph A. Kestner, *Mythology and Misogyny* (Madison, Wisconsin: University of Wisconsin Press, 1989).
LG	Lawrence Gallery, also named The Galleries, 168 New Bond Street, London (proprietors Fairless & Beeforth).
LG 1885	Lawrence Gallery catalogue, *Anno Domini Painted by Edwin Long R.A. also Zeuxis at Crotona., etc,* (London 1885).
Ormond 1973	Richard Ormond, *Early Victorian Portraits* (London: HMSO, 1973).
Quick 1931	Richard Quick, *The Life and Works of Edwin Long R.A.* (Bournemouth: The Russell-Cotes Art Gallery and Museum, 1931).
RA	Royal Academy of Arts.
Reitlinger 1961	G. Reitlinger, *The Economics of Taste* (London: Barrie and Rockliff, 1961).
Roberts 1897	Roberts, W. *Memorials of Christie's. A Record of Art Sales from 1766 to 1896.* London: George Bell & Sons, 1897.
RSA	Royal Society of British Artists.
Spielmann 1888	M. H. Spielmann, 'Painters in their Studios, II. – Mr. Edwin Long R.A.', *The Graphic* (9 June 1888), pp. 612–14.
Walkley 1994	Giles Walkley, *Artists' Houses in London* (Aldershot: Scolar Press, 1994).

THE EARLY YEARS
1829–1856

The paintings of this period cover Long's training and his years as a portrait painter in Bath. It effectively ends with his visit to Spain with John Phillip in 1857. The majority of paintings from this period remain untraced with the notable exceptions of his portraits of eminent figures of the time and Bath dignitaries. His initial struggles and failures in London were superseded by his ability in portraiture which led to important commissions and to his first exhibition at the Royal Academy in 1855. His first commissioned portraits were of military figures and included one of the Duke of Wellington. It was, however, his portrait of Sir Hugh Gough, that fully established Long as a successful portrait painter.

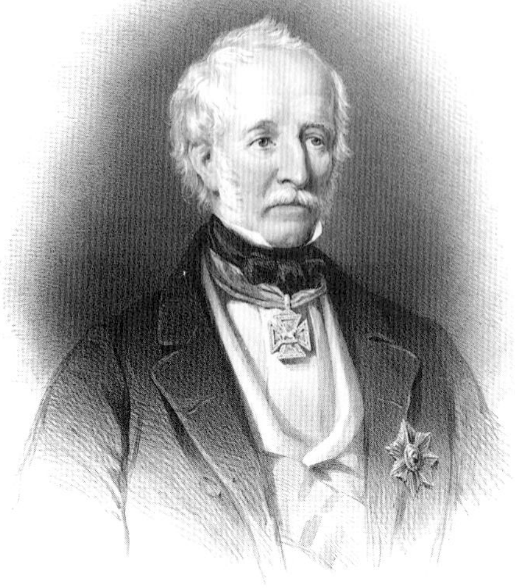

2. *Sir Hugh Gough*, c. 1850.
LITHOGRAPH BY J. H. LYNCH, COURTESY OF THE NATIONAL PORTRAIT GALLERY, LONDON

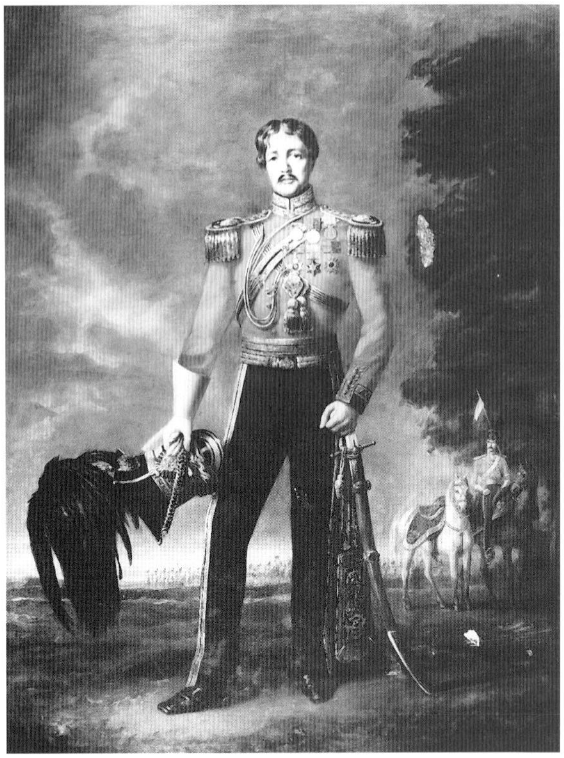

3. *Lieutenant-Colonel G. J. M. MacDowell*, c. 1850.
COURTESY OF THE DIRECTOR, NATIONAL ARMY MUSEUM, LONDON

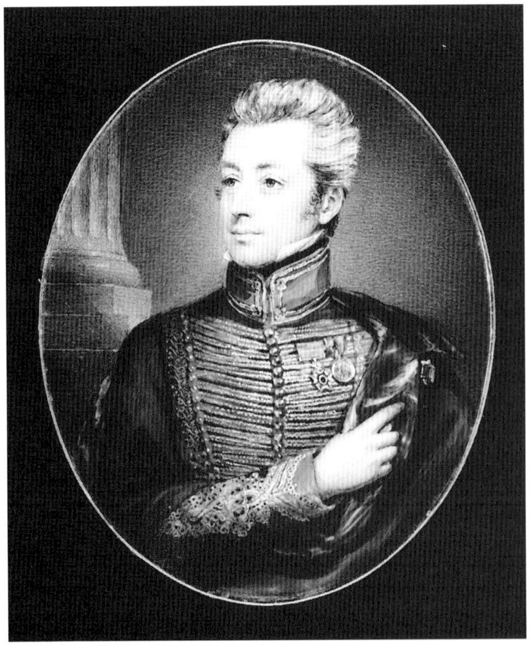

4. *General Sir Edward Charles Whinyates*, c. 1850.
CHELTENHAM ART GALLERY AND MUSEUM SERVICE

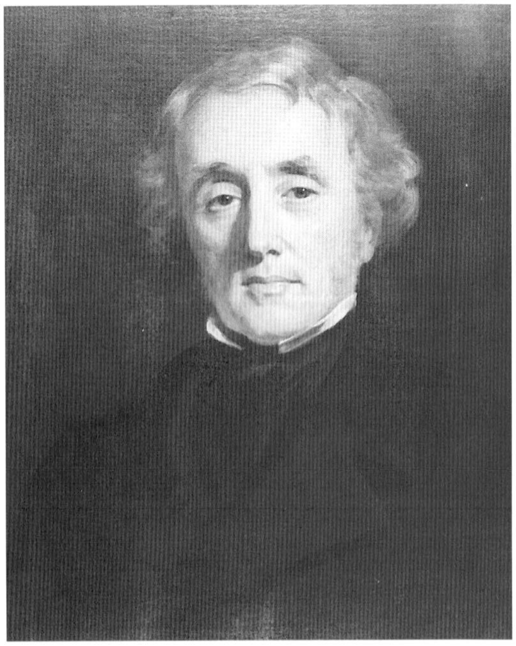

6. *James Watson, MD*, c. 1850.
HOLBURNE MUSEUM AND CRAFTS STUDY CENTRE, BATH

THE EARLY YEARS 1829–1856

1. First Portrait Painted by Edwin Long

c. 1846; size unknown; oil on canvas.

Exhibited 1893–94 at the Edwin Long Gallery as the first portrait by Long. The subject and other details of the work are unknown, but it almost certainly was in the collection of Mrs Edwin Long as most of the works in the gallery were. The work was not for sale.

PROVENANCE Edwin Long by descent to his wife.
EXHIBITIONS ELG 1893–94 (16)
LITERATURE ELG 1894, p. 23.

2. Sir Hugh Gough

c. 1850; size unknown; oil on canvas.

This is a portrait of Field Marshall Sir Hugh Gough. First Viscount Gough (1779–1867) served in the Peninsula 1808–13, became a Major-General in 1830. Between 1841–42 he served in the China War. He was made Commander-in-Chief in India in 1843 and commanded British forces during the Sikh wars, 1845–46, 1848–49. He made Field Marshall in 1862 and died in 1869. Long's portrait is mentioned in Ormond's *Early Victorian Portraits*, commenting that two copies were made from it by two other artists: the first by General A. Y. Shortt which was in the East India Sports Club, London; the other by an anonymous artist was in the collection of W. Thompson in 1897. The work was lithographed by H. Squire in 1850, and a copy of the print is in the National Portrait Gallery.

LITERATURE Ormond 1973, p. 191.

3. Lieutenant-Colonel G. J. M. MacDowell

c. 1850; 92½ × 69¾", 236 × 178 cm; oil on canvas.

A full-length portrait of Lieutenant Colonel G. J. M. MacDowell in uniform. The figure is rather stiff and ill-proportioned and untypical of Long's work. Clearly an early work, Long adopts the military style and battle setting presumably demanded by the sitter.

PROVENANCE Given to the National Army Museum in 1952 by Mr J. Eberle.
COLLECTION National Army Museum, London.

4. General Sir Edward Charles Whinyates

c. 1850; 30 × 25", 76.3 × 63.5 cm; oil on canvas.

The portrait was painted by Long while he was a young artist at Bath. It is after a miniature by Mrs Robertson (1827) from which Long made three copies. One went to the Royal Horse Artillery at Woolwich and the other two went to the sitter's family. General Sir Edward Charles Whinyates KCB, FRGS, was Colonel Commandant of 'B' Brigade, Royal Horse Artillery.

PROVENANCE Whinyates family by descent; gift to Cheltenham Borough Council in 1967.
COLLECTION Cheltenham Art Gallery.

5. The Duke of Wellington

c. 1850; 9 × 7", 23.5 × 18.5 cm; oil on board.

A half-length portrait of Arthur Wellesley, first Duke of Wellington (1769–1852). This portrait of the British Statesman and General who was Prime Minister 1828–30 was painted in his final years. The painting bears the inscription on the reverse: "The Duke of Wellington by Long". This is possibly a study for a finished painting.

PROVENANCE Ellen Titterton MD; Colonel C. V. F. Townsend; Johannesburg Art Gallery; Museum Africa, Johannesburg.

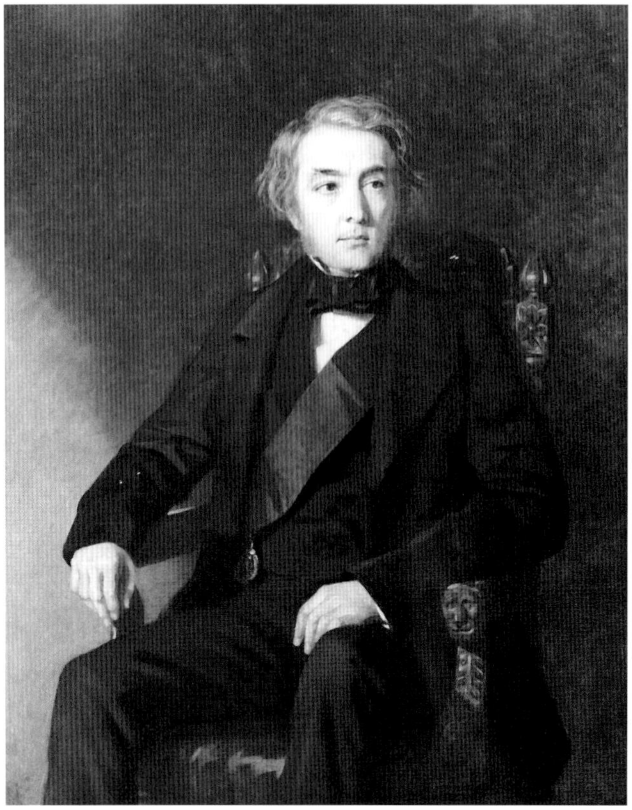

16. *Lord Ellesmere*, 1856.
COURTESY OF THE NATIONAL PORTRAIT GALLERY, LONDON

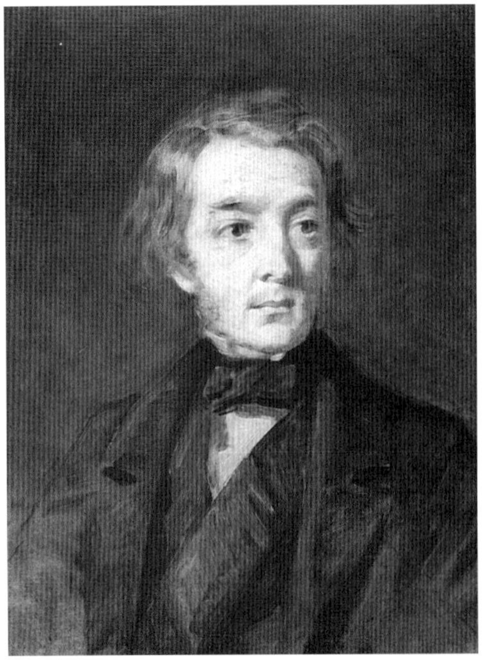

16.1. *Lord Ellesmere (study)*, 1856.
PRIVATE COLLECTION, PHOTOGRAPH BY JAMES HOWE

16. Lord Ellesmere

1856; 50 × 40⅛″, 127 × 102 cm; oil on canvas; signed.

A three-quarter-length portrait of Francis Egerton, 1st Earl of Ellesmere (1800–57), statesman and poet, wearing the ribbon and badge of a Knight of the Garter. He was an MP from 1822, a promoter of free trade and Secretary of War in 1830. In 1838 he became Rector of King's College, Aberdeen and President of the British Association in 1842. His published works include his poems, translations, historical and archaeological works. The stature of the sitter marks Long's early success as a portrait painter. The *Art Journal* commented: "A simple and unaffected portrait presenting the subject at half-length seated. In the features there is resemblance, but not, we think, personally."[1]

1. AJ, 1856, p. 168.

PROVENANCE Commissioned by sitter from the artist and then by descent; the late Miss E. I. F. Barran, R. W. Carr Esq., the trustees of the Ellesmere 1939 settlement; sold at Christie's on 15 October 1982 for £500 to the National Portrait Gallery.
EXHIBITIONS RA 1856 (326); Third National Portrait Gallery Exhibition at South Kensington 1868 (376); ELG, 1893–94 (19).
LITERATURE AJ, 1856, p. 168; ELG 1894, p. 23; Ormond 1973, p. 160; Quick 1931, p. 43.
COLLECTION National Portrait Gallery, London.

16.1 Lord Ellesmere (study)

1856; 12½ × 9¾″, 32 × 25 cm; oil on board.
A small half-length study for the portrait of Lord Ellesmere.

PROVENANCE Ms Bryony Poole.

17. Charles Greville Esq.

1856; size unknown; oil on canvas.

A portrait of Charles Cavendish Fulke Greville (1794–1865), manager of the Duke of York's stud and racing partner of Lord George Bentinck. He was Clerk to the Council between 1821 and 1859 and friends with many of the eminent statesmen of the period. His diary became famous as a primary source for political and historical research.

EXHIBITIONS RA 1856 (476).
LITERATURE Ormond 1973, p. 199.
COLLECTION Possibly the unattributed painting in the collection of the Duke of Richmond.

18. Lord Robert Grosvenor

1856; size unknown; oil on canvas.

A portrait of Lord Robert Grosvenor exhibited at the 1856 Royal Academy Exhibition.

EXHIBITIONS RA 1856 (539).
LITERATURE Quick 1931, p. 43.

THE INFLUENCE OF SPAIN
1857–1873

In 1857 Long attended classes given by John *Spanish* Phillip in his studio at 39 Gloucester Road marking an association that is key to understanding Long's work over the next sixteen years. Phillip and Long became close companions during their travels in Spain. It was there that Phillip introduced Long to the major source of his paintings and to the Spanish painters who had influenced him. Long in turn became similarly engaged with the country and from 1857 Spain was to dominate his artistic career until his visit to Egypt in 1874. Phillip exerted such an influence over Long that many of Long's paintings of this period became indistinguishable from Phillip's.[1] As well as painting similar Spanish genre scenes giving them, like Phillip, Spanish titles, Long adopted Phillip's use of dramatic lighting effects and bold use of colour. The influence of Phillip and Murillo are ever-present in this, Long's most prolific period. Indeed, Long's output in this period is incredible, as Spielmann noted "in his younger days great rapidity was amongst his remarkable gifts."[2] Consequently, many of Long's paintings remain untraced due to their sheer number, their domestic scale and their appeal to a popular market. All those mentioned in the various sources on Long have been listed and numbered despite the scarcity of information and it is certain that there are many other standard genre scenes where traces have been lost.

Within this period, however, the individual character of Long's work began to form and it is to be seen in several of his notable paintings on a larger scale, such as *The Suppliants* of 1872 and *A Question of Propriety*. These illustrate his move to grander history subjects and his burgeoning ambition. Ever-present amongst the less ambitious genre scenes too is Long's fascination with religious ritual and devotion which distinguishes him from Phillip.

1. Sir Merton Russell-Cotes recalls mistaking Long's *Dialogus Diversus* for a John Phillip. See *Home and Abroad*, pp. 708–09. Journals of the period often referred to Long's Spanish period as in the manner of Phillip.
2. Spielmann, p. 612.

19. Leaving Church (Un Ochativo por el Amor de Dios)

1857; size unknown; oil on canvas; signed and dated "Seville 1857".

According to Spielmann, this was Long's first Spanish painting derived from sketches made in Seville:

> He then determined to wait and see the religious ceremonies which were just about to begin. This decision really settled his career, for the very next day he perceived a beggar in front of a church holding aside a curtain for a lady and child to pass, and so picturesque was all the group, after the manner of Spanish beggars and ladies, that on returning to his studio he made a sketch of the scene. This was his first composition. The next year, on his return to England, he painted a picture from the sketch, but thought no more of it till his friend, Mr Hardy, suggested its contribution to the exhibition of the British Institution. The picture was then hung upon the line,[1] sold on private-view day, and was well criticised in the papers. All this success simply staggered the artist, who had built no hopes upon the matter, and evidently had been the victim of his own modesty.[2]

Mrs Margaret Long concurred with Spielmann's story and describes the picture in a letter to *The Times*: "struck by the picturesque people, he painted a small picture of a lady coming out of the Seville Cathedral with her little girl and an old beggar lifting the heavy portiere for them. This was sold at the Institute on the private view day, and so much liked that he was encouraged to paint many Spanish subjects, some of which were very fine."[3]

1. That is, hung at eye level, the most sought-after height on the gallery wall when pictures were hung above and below it.
2. Spielmann 1888, p. 612.
3. Margaret Jemima Long, letter to *The Times*, 1 November 1892, p. 7.

PROVENANCE William Herbert Esq of Cavendish House, Clapham Common; sold at Christie's on 23 April 1864 for £31 10s.
EXHIBITIONS BI 1858 (194) as *Un Ochativo por el Amor de Dios* on sale for £35.
LITERATURE Quick 1931, p. 3; Spielmann 1888, p. 612; *The Times*, 1 November 1892, p. 7.

20. Reverend William Jay of Bath

1857; 35¾ × 28¼", 91 × 72 cm; oil on canvas.

A portrait of the celebrated Reverend William Jay (1769–1853). On 30 January 1791, Jay was ordained pastor of Argyle Independent Chapel where he remained for the rest of his life. Dubbed by John Foster the 'prince of preachers', his sermons were well regarded nationally, many being published, including *Final Discourses at Argyle Chapel* in 1854. The painting has a note attached to its back: "28 River Street Bath 25 May 1857 It is my desire that the portrait / of the late Revd W Jay which I / intend shortly to present to my / Father should at his death become / the property of my sister Mrs Ostler / or of her husband Mr J M Ostler / Edwin Long." The painting is an interesting reflection of Long's religious background described by his son Maurice Long as an 'Independent' or 'Congregationalist' dissenter.[1]

1. Letter dated 12 October 1888, quoted in Chapel 1982, p. 109.

PROVENANCE Edwin Long gift to his father by descent to Long's sister; by descent to James Ostler who gifted it to the Victoria Art Gallery, Bath.
EXHIBITIONS ELG, 1893–94 (20).
LITERATURE Chapel 1982, p. 109; ELG 1894, p. 23.
COLLECTION Victoria Art Gallery, Bath.

21. Viscount Massereene and Ferrard

1858; size unknown; oil on canvas.

A portrait of Viscount Massereene and Ferrard in the uniform of the Royal Antrim Artillery. The *Art Journal* found it "An excellently painted portrait; the pose is easy and natural; very carefully finished, and in all respects a work of the best order."[1]

1. AJ, 1858, p. 166.

EXHIBITIONS RA 1858 (293).
LITERATURE AJ, 1858, p. 166; Quick 1931, p. 43.

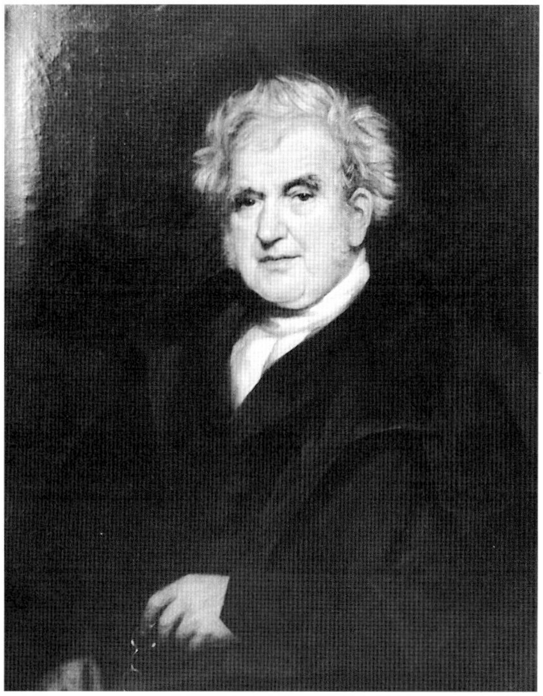

20. *Reverend William Jay of Bath*, 1857.
VICTORIA ART GALLERY, BATH & NORTH EAST SOMERSET COUNCIL

22. The First Visit of Prince Charles to Spain

1858; 39 × 49", 99 × 124.5 cm; oil on canvas.

One of Long's first history paintings depicting the visit of Prince Charles to Spain.

PROVENANCE Sold at Christie's on 19 February 1898 for £25 4s; sold at Christie's on 15 December 1900 as *Charles the First at Madrid* for 17 guineas.

EXHIBITIONS Exhibited at Liverpool before 1898.

23. Bravo el Toro!

1858; 40 × 50", 101.7 × 127 cm; oil on canvas.

Long's painting of a bullfight at Valladolid and his first Spanish subject exhibited at the Royal Academy. The catalogue describes the subject: "The usual shout when an accident occurs in the arena; another *espada* instantly takes the place of the disabled one, who is carried off to the care of the doctor or priest, as his case may require."[1]

1. RA exhibition catalogue, 1858.

PROVENANCE Sold at Christie's on 2 March 1907 as *Bravo, El Toro: Scene at a Bull Fight, Valladolid* for £31 10s to Sampson.

EXHIBITIONS RA 1859 (312)

LITERATURE Chester 1908, p. 334; Quick 1931, p. 44.

24. Lord Ebury

1859; size unknown; oil on canvas.

A portrait of Lord Ebury exhibited at the 1859 Royal Academy Exhibition.

EXHIBITIONS RA 1859 (19).

LITERATURE Quick 1931, p. 43.

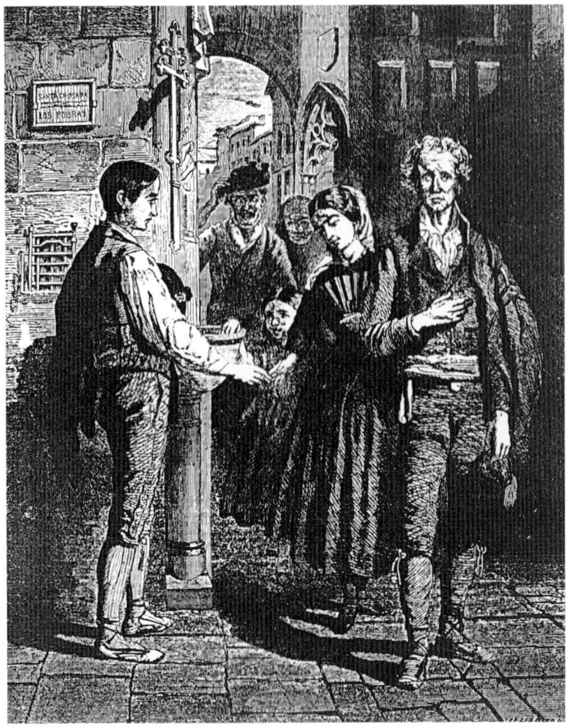

28. *Agua Santa*, 1859. Engraving.

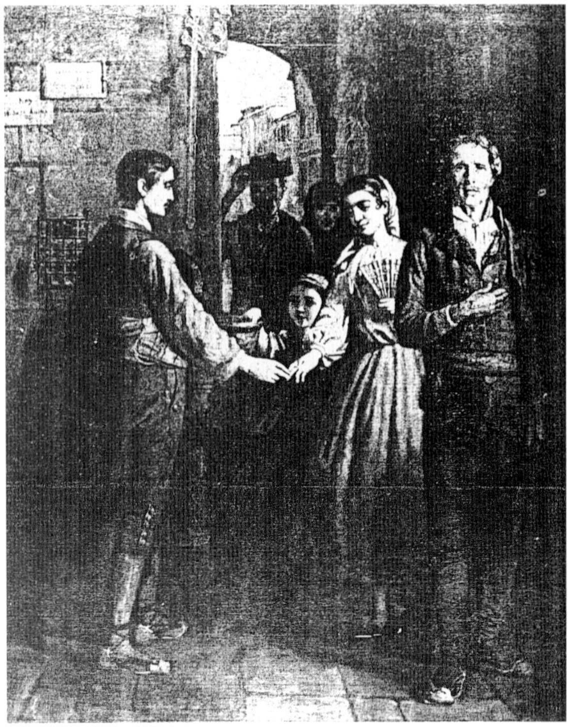

28.1. *Agua Santa*, 1860.
CHRISTIE'S IMAGESS

25. Lady Helen McDonnell

1859; size unknown; oil on canvas.

A portrait of Lady Helen McDonnell exhibited at the 1859 Royal Academy Exhibition.

EXHIBITIONS RA 1859 (578).
LITERATURE Quick 1931, p. 43.

26. The Young Student

1859; size unknown; oil on canvas.

A portrait of a young student exhibited at the 1859 Royal Academy Exhibition.

EXHIBITIONS RA 1859 (52).

27. An Old Castillian Couple at Burgos

1859; 29¾ × 25", 76 × 65 cm; oil on canvas; signed, inscribed and dated.

A painting of an old Castillian couple painted on a canvas with a rounded top.

PROVENANCE Sold at Christie's on 26 April 1974 for £273.

28. Agua Santa, (1)

1859; approx. 46 × 37", 116 × 95 cm; oil on canvas.

A painting set at Santa Crosada Los Pobras, Burgos, depicting a group passing through the entrance of the church receiving holy water. *Agua Santa* was exhibited at the British Institution of 1859 with the following description: "The custom in Spain of passing holy water by touch, often gives a lover his first opportunity of approaching the object of his affection."[1] The combination of religious ceremony and lovers was a popular theme for Long in his Spanish genre paintings. The figure of an old man crossing himself after receiving the water is followed by the figure of a young woman touching the hand of her lover. The *Art Journal* wrote: "The locale here is the entrance to the church, where a youth passes holy water by his own hand to that of a girl to whom he is attached. The costume is correct to undue severity, and the figures are somewhat stiff."[2]

1. BI exhibition catalogue, 1859.
2. AJ, 1859, p. 81.

EXHIBITIONS BI 1859 (78), on sale for £100.
LITERATURE AJ, 1859, p. 81; an engraving after the painting appears in a periodical of 1859 (unattributed source), Bath Reference Library (ill.).

28.1 Agua Santa (2)

1860; 46 × 37½", 116.8 × 95.2 cm; oil on canvas; signed with monogram and dated "Burgos 1860".

A replica of Long's British Institute painting of 1859 *Agua Santa*. Auctioned at Christie's in 1977 under the title *The Spanish Betrothal*.

PROVENANCE Sold at Christie's on 29 July 1977 as *The Spanish Betrothal* for £850.

29. The Hon. Mrs Scott Murray

1860; size unknown; oil on canvas.

EXHIBITIONS RA 1860 (228).
LITERATURE Quick 1931, p. 43.

30. Thomas Barrett, Mayor of Bath 1860

1860; 30 × 25", 76 × 64 cm; oil on canvas.

A portrait of Thomas Barrett, JP, MD, (1815–68), Mayor of Bath in 1860.

PROVENANCE Victoria Art Gallery, purchased from J. F. Meelan in 1914.
COLLECTION Victoria Art Gallery, Bath.

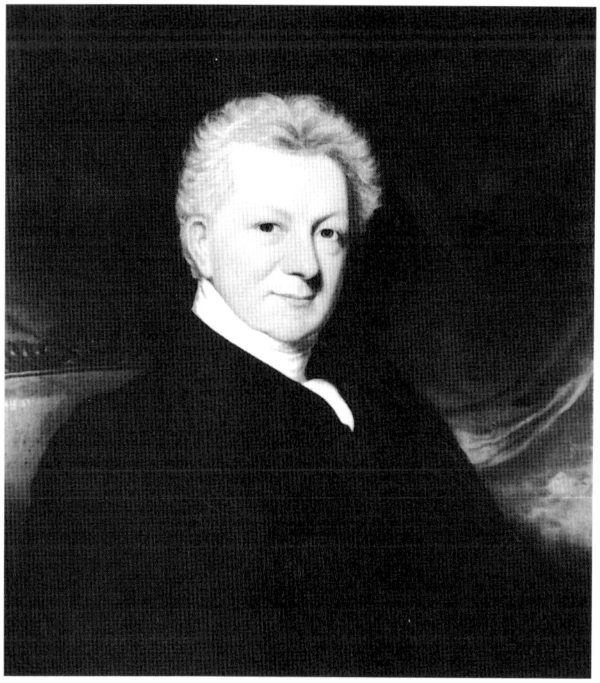

30. *Thomas Barrett, Mayor of Bath, 1860*, 1860.
VICTORIA ART GALLERY, BATH & NORTH EAST SOMERSET COUNCIL

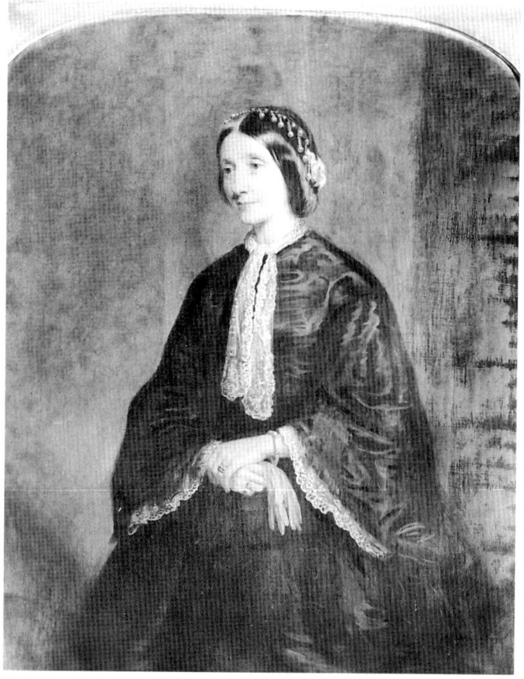

31. *Viscountess Bangor*, 1860.
THE BANGOR COLLECTION, CASTLEWARD (THE NATIONAL TRUST), PHOTOGRAPH COURTAULD INSTITUTE OF ART.

31. Viscountess Bangor

1860; 49½ × 39½", 124.5 × 100 cm; oil on canvas.

A three-quarter-length portrait of Harriet Maxwell, Viscountess of Bangor, wearing a cape and holding gloves. The daughter of the Reverend Henry Maxwell, later sixth Lord Franham, she married twice, the 3rd Lord Bangor and Major Andrew Nugent.

EXHIBITIONS RA 1860 (521).
LITERATURE Quick 1931, p. 43.
COLLECTION National Trust, Castleward.

32. Susan Irlam MacCallum

1860; 43½ × 33½", 110.5 × 85 cm; oil on canvas; signed and dated, inscribed labels on back.

A three-quarter-length portrait of Susan MacCallum wearing a brown coat, set in a landscape. Exhibited at the 1863 Royal Academy Exhibition as *Mrs. MacCallum.*

PROVENANCE Sold at Christie's on 18 October 1974.
EXHIBITIONS RA 1863 (259).
LITERATURE Quick 1931, p. 43.

33. The Hon. Mrs Legge

1860; size unknown; oil on canvas.

A portrait of Mrs Legge exhibited at the 1860 Royal Academy Exhibition.

EXHIBITIONS RA 1860 (51).
LITERATURE Quick 1931, p. 43.

34. L'Ama de Cria

1860; size unknown; oil on canvas.

From its sale price, *L'Ama de Cria* (literally 'the soul of a young creature') appears to be one of Long's small scale Spanish genre scenes exhibited at the 1860 British Institution Exhibition.

EXHIBITIONS BI 1860 (28), on sale for 20 guineas.

35. John Phillip

c. 1860; size unknown; oil on canvas.

A portrait of John Phillip (1817–67). Not only did Phillip introduce Long to Spain but was responsible for developing his interest in the Spanish painters Velasquez[1] and Murillo. For many years Long's work bore more than a passing resemblance to those by Phillip. This painting by Long is referred to by Ormond as "a painting by E. Long [of Phillip]. In the collection of Mrs. Long in 1904."[2]

1. Phillip owned a portrait of Velasquez by Long which was sold on his death at Christie's in 1867.
2. Ormond 1973, p. 377.

PROVENANCE By descent to Mrs Margaret Jemima Long in 1904.
LITERATURE Ormond 1973, p. 377.

36. The Surrender of Breda (after Velasquez)

c. 1860; 49 × 69", 124.5 × 175.2 cm; oil on canvas.

A copy of the picture by Velasquez in Madrid which remained in the artist's possession throughout his life.

PROVENANCE By descent to Mrs Margaret Jemima Long; sold at Christie's on 1 February 1908 for 10 guineas.

37. At Mass

c. 1860; 32 × 19¼", 81.3 × 48.9 cm; oil on canvas; signed.

A full-length Spanish woman with an open prayer book at a mass in a Spanish church.

PROVENANCE John Scott; sold at Christie's on 25 July 1986 for £750; sold at auction on 11 December 1984 as *In Church* for £1,200.

38. A Scene in Church, Madrid

1861; size unknown; oil on canvas

Long's painting of two men praying at the Church of the Knights of Calatrava, Madrid. In the Royal Academy catalogue he subtitles it: "Two men went up into the temple to pray, the one a Pharisee and the other a Publican."[1]

1. RA exhibition catalogue, 1861.

EXHIBITIONS RA 1861 (193).
LITERATURE Quick 1931, p. 44.

39. Miss Adela Astley

1861; size unknown; oil on canvas.

A portrait of Miss Adela Astley exhibited at the 1861 Royal Academy Exhibition.

EXHIBITIONS RA 1861 (531).

40. Charles Penruddocke Esq.

1861; size unknown; oil on canvas.

A portrait of Charles Penruddocke exhibited at the 1861 Royal Academy Exhibition.

EXHIBITIONS RA 1861 (86).

41. The Little Botanists, 1861.

1861; size unknown; oil on canvas.

A genre painting exhibited at the 1861 British Institution Exhibition.

EXHIBITIONS BI 1861 (206).

42. Seated Girl in an Interior

1862; 27½ × 35", 70cm × 89 cm; oil on canvas; signed and dated at lower right.

A genre painting of a girl seated in a kitchen.

PROVENANCE Sold at Bonham's on 2 February 1984 for £480 as *Kitchen Interior with a Girl*; sold at Phillips' on 14 December 1993.

43. Dialogus Diversus

1862; 51 × 40", 129.5 × 101.6 cm; oil on canvas.

This is an interesting example of Long's Spanish genre painting which shows two priests discussing a difficult question in a street in Seville. Their absorbing dialogue, possibly theological, makes them impervious to the other action in the picture. All the elements of popular Spanish genre painting are here: lovers, fruit-sellers and matadors. The influence of John Phillip is particularly clear in this painting which was mistakenly bought as a Phillip by Sir Merton Russell-Cotes: "It is a very beautiful picture, but, as I said, I felt certain, knowing his work so well, that it had been painted by my old friend John Phillip, R.A."[1] Merton took the work to Long to ascertain the true authorship of the work which was confirmed by Long to be by him. The *Art Journal* saw the merit in the priests while being less than flattering about its other elements: "An affected title to a picture which has in it some good points overborne by striking weaknesses. The dialogos are carried on by two monks (principal figures) and two or three other pairs, two lovers, a fruit woman and her customer, and perhaps a second pair of lovers. In the two priests there is much to praise, but all that is good is negated by the other components."[2]

1. *Home and Abroad*, p. 708.
2. AJ, 1862, p. 70.

PROVENANCE Bought by Sir Merton Russell-Cotes, c. 1860s; by descent to Mrs Lee Duncan (Sir Merton's granddaughter); sold at auction in October 1964.
EXHIBITIONS BI 1862 (600), on sale for £150; on display at the Royal Bath Hotel, Bournemouth, until 1963.
LITERATURE AJ, 1862, p. 70; *Bulletin (R-C)*, vol. II, no. 2 (June 1923), p. 16; Quick 1931, p. 4, p. 10 (ill.), p. 44; *Home and Abroad*, pp. 708–09.

44. The Muleteer's Courtship

1862; 45 × 31", 114.3 × 78.8 cm; oil on canvas; signed and dated.

This Spanish genre scene shows a muleteer seated on his mule in the foreground kissing the hand of his lover through a window grill. The rest of the scene comprises of a typical Spanish town setting.

PROVENANCE By descent to Margaret Jemima Long; sold at Christie's on 1 February 1908 for £24 3s; bought by Bristol City Art Gallery and Museum who sold it in 1947 to Messrs Frost and Reed.
LITERATURE Quick 1931, p. 14 (ill.), p. 44.

45. La Valenciana

1862; 20 × 18", 50.8 × 45.7 cm; oil on canvas; signed with monogram and dated.

A three-quarter-length portrait of a resident of Valencia painted on a canvas with a rounded top. She is depicted with her right hand holding her face while her left on her hip holds a plaited straw frail with fruit.

PROVENANCE Gift of Alderman Cedric Chivers to the Victoria Art Gallery in 1922.
EXHIBITIONS BI 1863 (412), on sale for £30.
COLLECTION Victoria Art Gallery, Bath.

46. Spanish Beggars

1862; 28½ × 23½", 72 × 59.5 cm; oil on canvas.

A small Spanish genre painting of beggars.

PROVENANCE By descent to Mrs Margaret Jemima Long; sold at Christie's on 1 February 1908 for 5 guineas; H. L. Hargreaves gift to Oldham Art Gallery.
COLLECTION Oldham Art Gallery.

47. Jairus' Daughter (1862)

1862; 33½ × 44", 84 × 112 cm; oil on canvas.

Religion was a primary concern to Long although he did not paint many subjects directly from the New Testament, with the very notable exceptions of *Anno Domini* (1883) (cat. no. 197) and *The Parable of the Sower* (1891) (cat. no. 278). He painted two versions of *Jairus' Daughter* taking St. Mark, v: 22–43 as his subject. Each deal with different stages of the story, this first version dealing with Christ's arrival at Jairus' house: "And he cometh to the house of the ruler of the synagogue, [Jairus] and seeth the tumult, and them that wept and wailed greatly." The *Art Journal* wrote that:

> This is an example in some sort of propriety in dealing with such a passage. The girl lies a corpse upon a couch, and near her stands her Mother weeping. In both forms there is an absence of grace; but the incident is properly felt by an appeal to the sympathies rather than by a parade of colour and characters. We see through the window the approach of the saviour. There is a strong tincture of French Manner in it, and so much of good that it might have been better.[1]

1. AJ, 1862, p. 131.

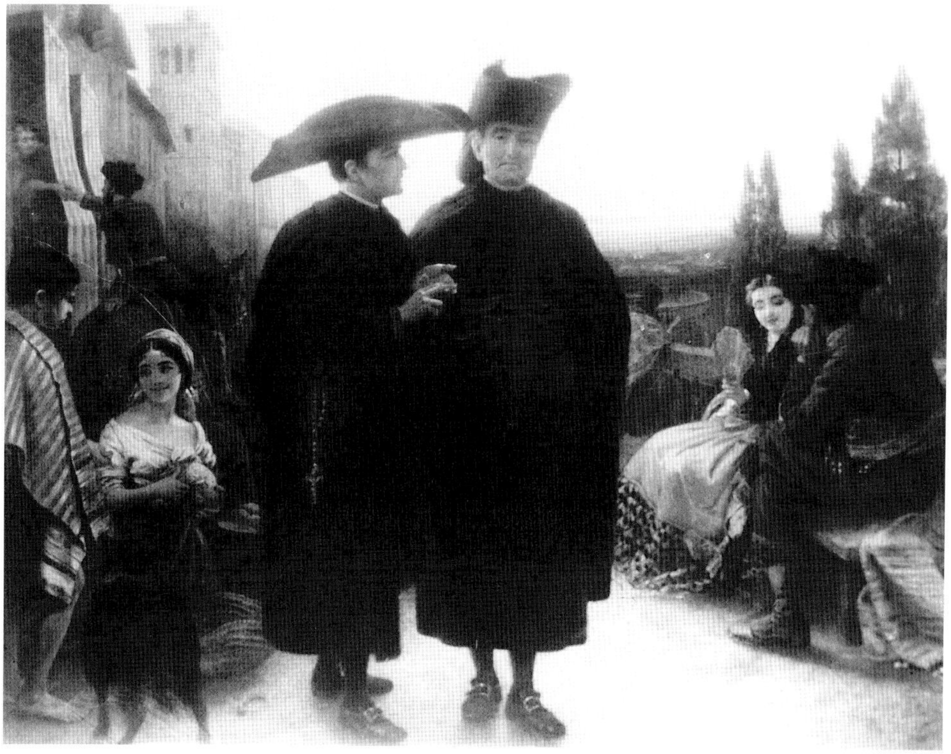

43. *Dialogus Diversus*, 1862.

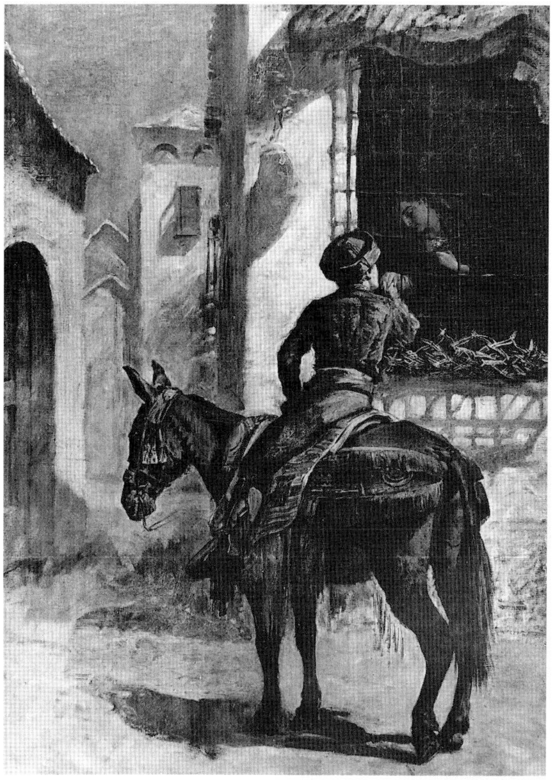

44. *The Muleteer's Courtship*, 1862.

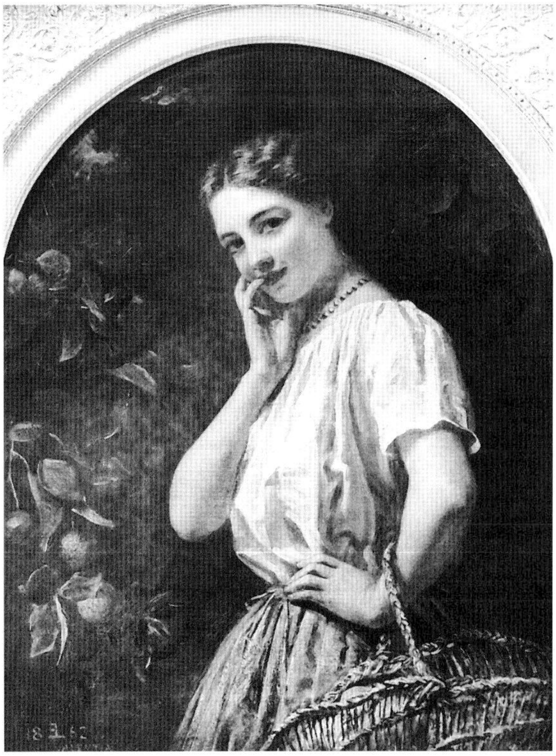

45. *La Valenciana*, 1862.
VICTORIA ART GALLERY, BATH & NORTH EAST SOMERSET COUNCIL

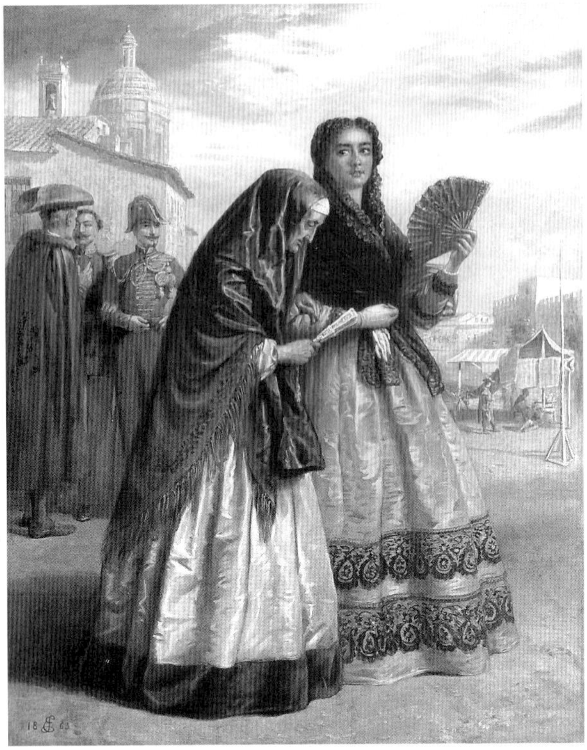

50. *Good Advice* (also called *Age and Youth*), 1863.
COURTESY OF SOTHEBY'S, LONDON

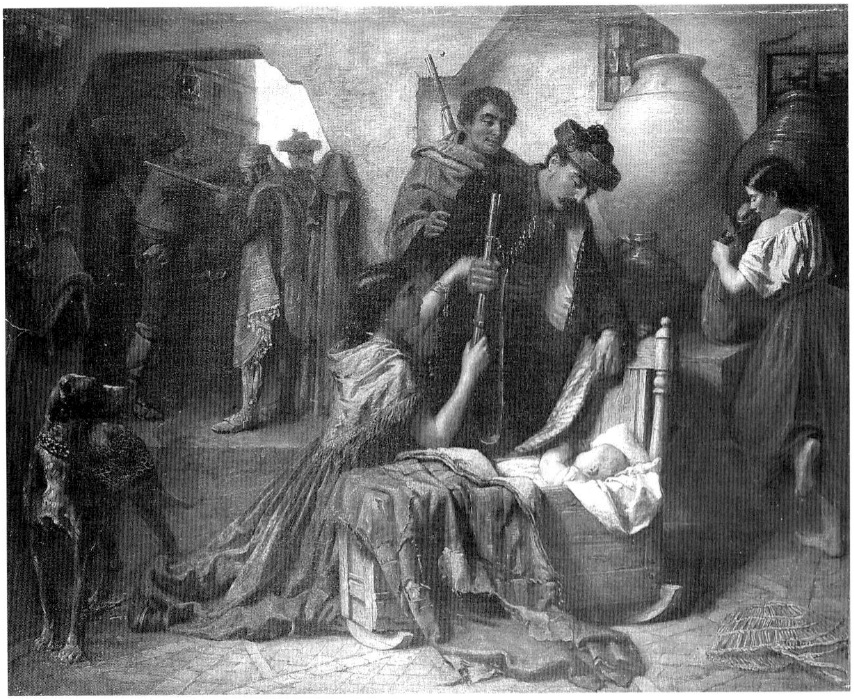

52. *Her Tender Prayers*, 1863.
CHRISTIE'S IMAGES

PROVENANCE Sold at Christie's on 23 May 1890 as *The Raising of Jairus' Daughter* for 60 guineas; Sir Merton Russell-Cotes sold at Christie's on 11 March 1905 for £52 10s to McLean.
EXHIBITIONS RA 1862 (529), on sale for £136 10s, remained unsold.
LITERATURE AJ, 1862, p. 131.

48. La Posada (Don Quixote)

1863; size unknown; oil on canvas.

One of Long's large essays in Spanish fiction, a scene from *Don Quixote.* Using Smollett's translation of Cervantes[1] it depicts a scene showing Don Quixote on his knees in front of a posada. It was exhibited at the British Institution and the Royal Academy in 1864, titled as *Don Quixote, Having Mistaken a Posada for a Castle* at the British Institution, and *La Posada* at the Royal Academy. The *Art Journal* reviewed the painting writing:

> Mr. Long's 'Don Quixote', as might be expected, is a comedy. The knight in full armour decked, has just sunk to his knees before two strolling dancers, which he mistakes for high-born damsels. The picture contains some capital painting. The execution, however, is unequal, and the component parts of the composition are a little too scattered, waiting to be brought together.[3]

1. The first edition was published in 1755, and by the 1860s there were many editions available.
2. The *Daily Telegraph* (date unknown, 1908) titles it as *Reading from Don Quixote* which refers to the accompanying quote in the 1864 RA exhibition catalogue.
3. AJ, 1864, p. 88.

PROVENANCE D. Schloss, Esq., bought the painting for 1,100 guineas; sold at Christie's on 13 February 1888 for £105.
EXHIBITIONS BI 1864 (154), on sale for £120; RA 1864 (515).
LITERATURE AJ, 1864, p. 88; *Daily Telegraph*, unknown date, 1908; *Magazine of Art*, July 1891, p. xl.

49. The Diligence

1863; size unknown; oil on canvas.

A painting depicting a religious diligence.

PROVENANCE Sold at Christie's on 17 July 1897 for £478 to Sampson.

50. Good Advice (*also called* Age and Youth)

1863; 41¾ × 33¼", 106 × 84.4 cm; oil on canvas; signed with monogram and dated.

The first of Long's 'Good Advice' paintings, the second painted eight years later in 1871. It bore its Spanish title *Buenos Consejos* (good advice) when it was exhibited at the Royal Society of British Artists in 1864. It also became known as *Age and Youth,* a popular nineteenth-century genre theme. The contrast is clearly apparent as a young Spanish woman leads her aged counterpart past two soldiers and a priest. One of the soldiers looks on as the other is engaged in conversation with the priest. The back of the picture has an old label bearing the number 1.

PROVENANCE Sold as *Buenos Consejos* at Christie's on 20 May 1882 for £105; sold at Christie's on 21 March 1903 as *Buenos Consejos* for £21 to Lister; sold at Sotheby's 6 December 1977 as *Age and Youth*; property of N. L. Eckersley Esq., the artist's great-grandson; sold at Christie's on 29 February 1980 as *Good Advice.*
EXHIBITIONS RSA (648), on sale for £100; Bristol City Art Gallery 1907 (88).

51. A Spanish Beggar Boy

1863; size unknown; oil on canvas.

A Spanish genre scene of a beggar boy.

PROVENANCE Albert Grant Esq.; sold at Christie's on 20 June 1868 for £73 10s.

52. Her Tender Prayers

1863; 41 × 52″, 104 × 132 cm; oil on canvas; signed and dated; signed on reverse.

Exhibited at the Royal Academy with the following verse:

> Her tender prayers lack skill to win his heart
> From evil comrades prompting evil deeds,
> Yet, ere the die is cast, he turns to where
> In cradled innocence lies the minister
> Of Heaven's and Nature's strongest, last appeal,
> His sleeping babe – image of life instained –
> Whose dumb, unconscious pleading doth awake
> The drugged memories of another time
> When he, too, was sinless.

The large scene illustrates the unattributed poem. The baby in the foreground is the lightest part of the picture. The mother is shown on the ground pleading with the father as he looks over the cot.

PROVENANCE Sold at Christie's on 3 November 1989 for £5,000.
EXHIBITIONS RA 1863 (623).

53. Laura, Countess of Antrim

1863; size unknown; oil on canvas.

A portrait of Laura, Countess of Antrim exhibited at the 1863 Royal Academy Exhibition.

EXHIBITIONS RA 1863 (296).
LITERATURE Quick 1931, p. 43.

54. La Zingara

1864; size unknown; oil on canvas.

A portrait of an Italian gypsy woman exhibited at the 1864 Royal Society of British Artists Exhibition.

EXHIBITIONS RSA 1864 (282), on sale for £20.

55. La Caridad

1864; 28 × 21″, 70 × 53 cm; oil on canvas; signed with monogram and dated.

A large scale Spanish scene depicting an act of charity, a popular theme in Spanish genre painting.[1]

1. For example John Phillip's *Charity, Seville, 1857.*

PROVENANCE Sold at Christie's as *Charity* on 29 November 1988 for £1,037.
EXHIBITIONS BI 1865 (489) priced at £75.

56. Gitanitas

1864; 20¼ × 15⅞″, 51.5 × 40.4 cm; oil on canvas; signed with monogram and dated.

Two young Spanish gypsy women in a Spanish street, one dances while the other claps the rhythm. Inscribed on verso: "33 Ovington Square" (Long's 1864 address).

PROVENANCE Mr N. Draper.
EXHIBITIONS BI 1866 (256), priced at 50 guineas.

57. La Gitana

1864; 28 × 20″, 71 × 51 cm; oil on canvas; signed with monogram and dated.

A three-quarter-length portrait of a Spanish gypsy woman wearing a shawl and holding an earthenware vase.

PROVENANCE W. Roberts; unsold at Christie's, 12 June 1880; sold at Christie's on 14 March 1881 for 94 guineas; Sir Arthur James Brakison; sold in 1944 to W. H. Parry; by descent to Alan Kemp.

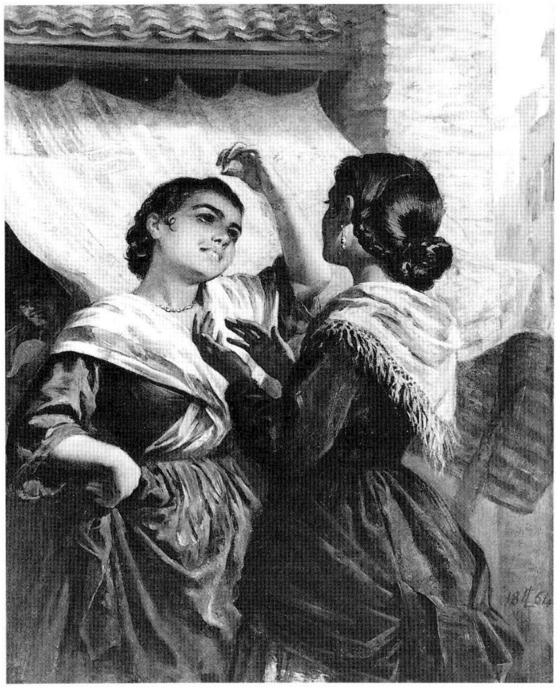

56. *Gitanitas*, 1864.
COURTESY OF NORMAN DRAPER

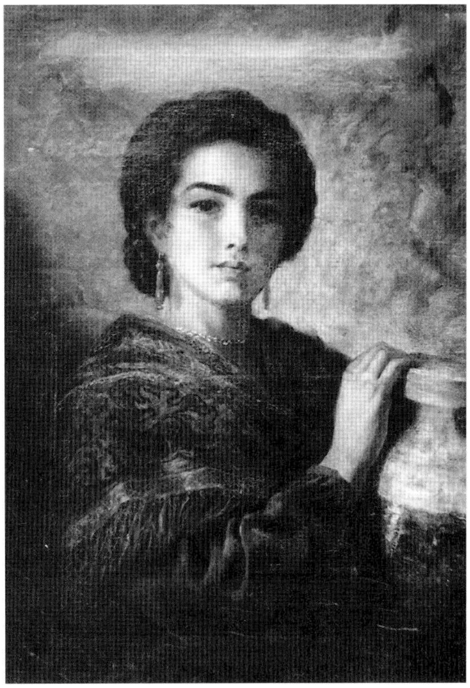

57. *La Gitana*, 1864.
COURTESY OF ALAN KEMP

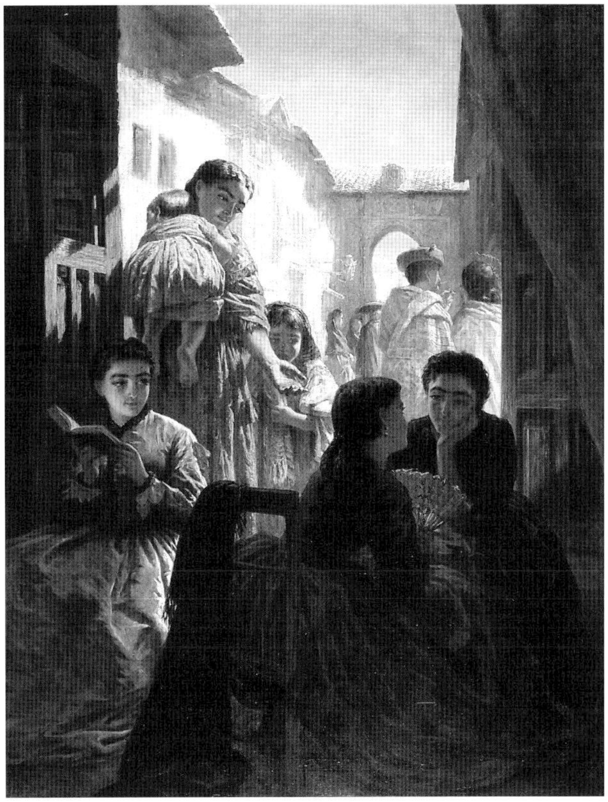

58. *The Suppliants (1864)*, 1864.
RUSSELL-COTES ART GALLERY AND MUSEUM, PHOTOGRAPH JAMES HOWE

58. The Suppliants (1864)

1864; 44 × 34″, 111.8 × 86.4 cm; oil on canvas; signed with monogram and dated on lower left.

In style, subject and colour, this scene with Spanish gypsies owes a lot to Phillip. Long dealt with the same subject in a completely different way and on a much larger scale in the 1872 painting of the same name.

PROVENANCE Purchased by the Russell-Cotes Art Gallery and Museum from Messrs Frost and Reed, February 1929.
LITERATURE *Bulletin (R-C)*, vol. VIII, no. 2 (June 1929), p. 18, p. 20 (ill.); Chapel 1982, p. 107; Quick 1931, p. 44.
COLLECTION Russell-Cotes Art Gallery and Museum, Bournemouth.

59. Giving Alms

1864; 27½ × 20½″, 70 × 52 cm; oil on canvas; dated.

PROVENANCE Sold at Christie's on 3 July 1905 for 8 guineas to Mitchell.

60. Un Gitanito

1865; size unknown; oil on canvas.

EXHIBITIONS BI 1865 (14), for sale at £30.

61. Dorniendo

1865; size unknown; oil on canvas.

A painting of Spanish figures sleeping exhibited at the 1865 Royal Society of British Artists Exhibition.

EXHIBITIONS RSA 1865 (435), on sale for £35.

62. Donna Inez

1865; size unknown; oil on canvas.

EXHIBITIONS RSA 1865 (727), on sale for £20.

63. Quien Quiere Carros

1865; size unknown; oil on canvas.

EXHIBITIONS BI 1865 (401), on sale for £45.

64. Love has its Little Cares

c. 1865; size unknown; oil on canvas.

One of Long's Spanish paintings exhibited at Wallis's after his second visit to Spain.

PROVENANCE Wallis; sold in 1865 for £168.
LITERATURE Reitlinger, 1961.

65. The Anthem

1866; size unknown; oil on canvas.

The Anthem was based on Shakespeare: "'Here will we sit, and let the sound of music creep in our ears'".[1]

1. BI 1866 catalogue.

PROVENANCE George Fox Esq. of Harefield, Winslow; sold at Christie's on 11 May 1877 for £304 10s.
EXHIBITIONS BI 1866 (62), on sale for 200 guineas.

66. Spanish Peasants going to the Market, Granada

1866; 48½ × 37½″, 123.2 × 95 cm; oil on canvas.

Long painted the same subject in 1867 (see cat. no. 76 below) which may be a smaller copy of this painting.

PROVENANCE Sold at Christie's on 2 March 1934 for 12 guineas.

67. The Entry of Columbus into Barcelona

1866; 75 × 114", 190.5 × 289.5 cm; oil on canvas.

PROVENANCE Sold at Christie's on 2 March 1934 for 15 guineas.

68. Shepherds on the Mountains of Toledo

1866; size unknown; oil on canvas.

Long painted several pictures of Spanish shepherds and gypsies. According to Spielmann he even lived amongst Spanish shepherds against the advice of the British Consul.[1] His fascination with this subject is expressed in the unattributed verse which accompanied the painting in its exhibition at the 1866 British Institution Exhibition:

And cherished still by that unchanging race
Are themes wherein their ancient glories shine,
Of strange tradition, many a mystic trace
Legend and vision, prophecy and sign.

1. Spielmann 1888, p. 612.
2. BI 1866 exhibition catalogue.

EXHIBITIONS BI 1866 (483).
LITERATURE Spielmann 1888, p. 612.

69. Uncle Tom's Cabin

1866; 30 × 44", 76 × 111.8 cm; oil on canvas; signed and dated on door, lower right.

A scene from *Uncle Tom's Cabin* (1851) by Harriet Beecher Stowe (1811–96). Throughout his career Long painted several fictional genre scenes focusing particularly on the novel's heroines. Long clearly reflects a colonial Victorian attitude in his depiction of the central figure as a enlightened and pure white girl.

PROVENANCE The Russell-Cotes Art Gallery and Museum purchased from Mrs Cottrell, 12 March 1976.
LITERATURE *Images of People*, catalogue to an exhibition at Russell-Cotes Art Gallery and Museum, Bournemouth, 1992, p. 14 (ill.), pp. 23–25 (ill.).
COLLECTION Russell-Cotes Art Gallery and Museum.

70. Begging for the Monastery

1867; 32¼ × 44½", 82 × 113 cm; oil on canvas; signed "Edwin Long / Rome" on lower right.

One of the four pictures known to have been painted as a result of Long's visit to Rome in 1867. John Phillip had visited Rome and Florence a year earlier and may have been instrumental in encouraging Long to go there. The setting for this painting is a Roman street market. The central figure of a monk, followed by his donkey, is begging for provisions for the monastery and has approached a fruit seller who is seated to the right.

PROVENANCE Sold 1886 for 205 guineas; sold at Sotheby's on 2 November 1994 for £7,500.
EXHIBITIONS RA 1867 (no. 568), on sale for 250 guineas, remained unsold.
LITERATURE *Daily Telegraph*, unknown date, 1908; Quick 1931, p. 44.

71. The Catechism or The Recitation

1867; 41 × 60", 104.2 × 152 cm; oil on canvas; signed and inscribed "Rome 1867".

Long's interest in religious ritual is explored in this Italian scene. Its treatment is very familiar to those he painted in Spain. The picture depicts a scene in a Roman church with a young girl standing on a table covered by a carpet answering questions. A large group stands in front of her, a monk behind her looking on. Another young girl is preparing for her time on the table.

PROVENANCE Sold at Christie's on 2 March 1934 for 10 guineas as *The Recitation*; sold at Christie's on 29 February 1980 (unframed) for £1,600.

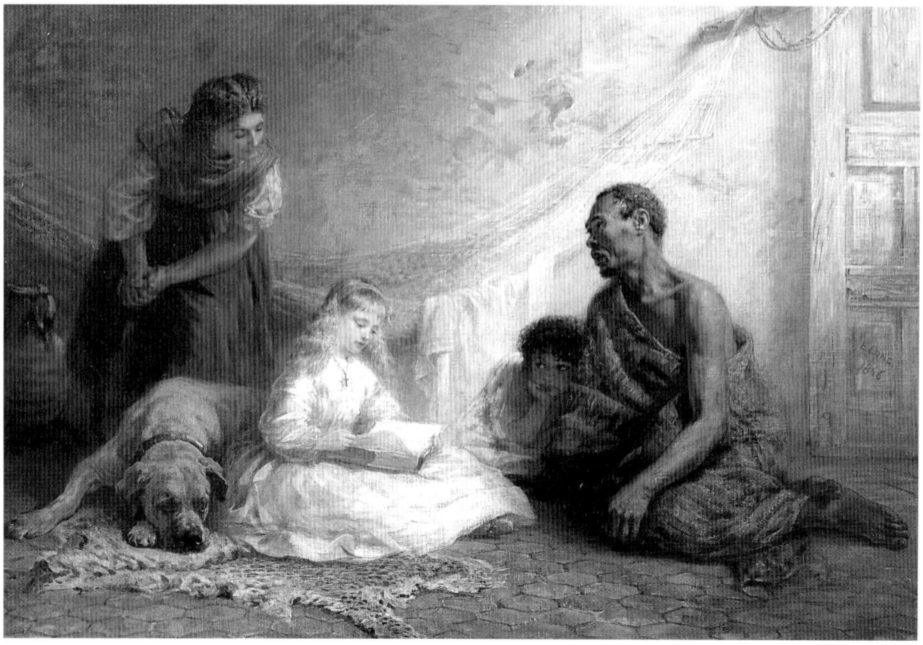

69. *Uncle Tom's Cabin*, 1866.
RUSSELL-COTES ART GALLERY AND MUSEUM, PHOTOGRAPH JAMES HOWE

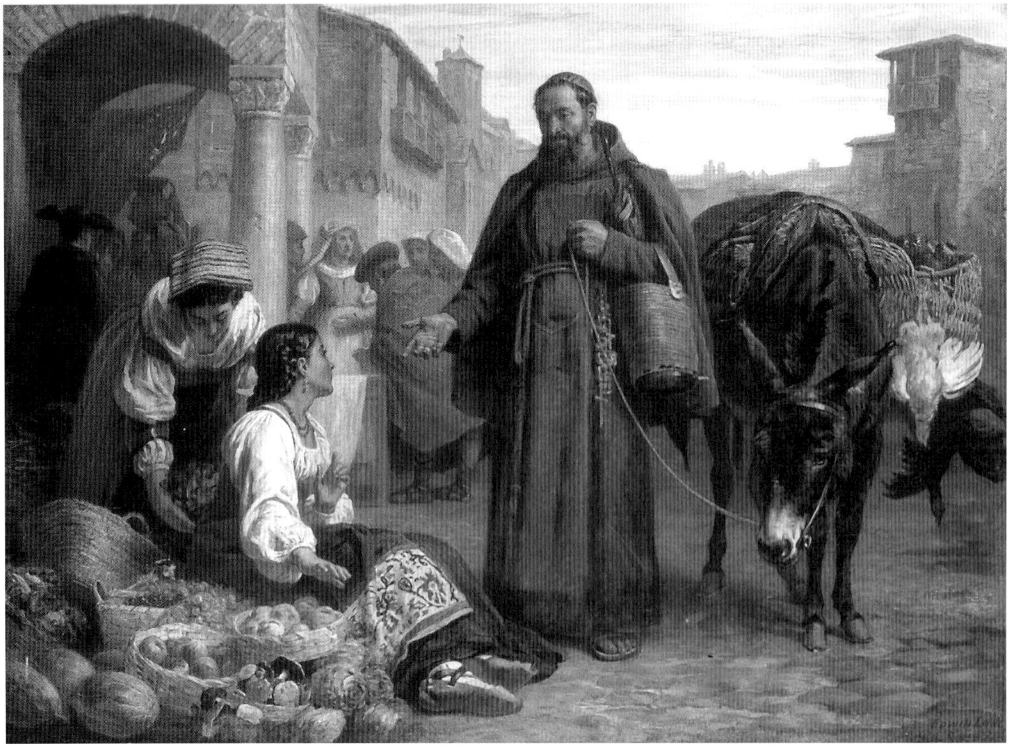

70. *Begging for the Monastery*, 1867.
COURTESY OF SOTHEBY'S, LONDON

72. St. Anthony's Day

1867; size unknown; oil on canvas.

The most ambitious of Long's two 1867 Roman paintings exhibited at the Royal Academy. It depicts a drover approaching three priests to gain his certificate of benediction for his cattle. The *Art Journal* praised it as

> a commendable work. A drover of the campagna, a handsome fellow, but rather too much of a heap and a bundle in his drapery, comes to the office of the church to get a certificate that his cattle have duly received the saint's benediction. The story is spiced with satire. Three priests sit at the table; one may be said to represent learning, another jovial good cheer, and the third, who is napping, sloth. The picture is remarkably well painted, and the colour rich and harmonious. It is with great pleasure we accord to Mr Long this praise, because it has been our painful duty to tell him, that in certain large and showy works, he was squandering his talents.[1]

The Times noted: "Mr E. Long has a clever picture (542) of a Roman herdsman paying his fee, and receiving his certificate of the due benediction of his bestie on St. Anthony's day. The business-like air of the waking priests, and the heavy-headed somnolence of the slumberer, are capitally caught. You may hear the sleeper snore."[2]

1. AJ, 1867, pp. 142–43.
2. *The Times*, 9 May 1867, p. 6.

PROVENANCE Kay Knowles; sold at Christie's on 14 May 1887 for 410 guineas; bought by Sir Prescott Newett on 9 April 1926 for £96 12s.
EXHIBITIONS RA 1867 (542), sold at the exhibition.
LITERATURE AJ, 1867, pp. 142–3; Quick 1931, p. 44; Roberts 1897, vol. II, p. 126; *The Times*, 9 May 1867, p. 6.

73. Roman Water-Carrier

1867; size unknown; oil on canvas.

A painting of a Roman water-carrier from Long's 1867 visit to Rome and the Roman Campagna.

PROVENANCE Sold at Christie's on 2 March 1934 as a pair with *Spanish Children* for 13 guineas.

74. Peter's Pence

1867; 32½ × 44½″, 83 × 110.5 cm; oil on canvas; signed and dated.

PROVENANCE W. F. Bruford Bequest to Wolverhampton Art Gallery, 1951.
COLLECTION Wolverhampton Art Gallery.

75. A Portrait of Velasquez

1867; size unknown; oil on canvas.

This portrait, owned by Long's mentor, John Phillip, was sold on Phillip's death in 1867.

PROVENANCE John Phillip RA; sold at Christie's on 31 May 1867 for £36 15s.

76. A Spanish Scene – To Market

1867; 35 × 29″, 90 × 73 cm; oil on canvas; signed with monogram and dated.

A scene of a Spanish family going to market. The mother and her young children travel on a decorated donkey covered by a parasol and loaded with chickens. The father walks alongside with a rifle over his shoulder with the dog following on. This is possibly a copy of Long's slightly larger *Spanish Peasants Going to Market, Granada* (1866) (see cat. no. 66 above).

PROVENANCE Sold at auction on 24 October 1989 for £3,025.

77. A Spanish Flower Seller

1867; 29½ × 44″, 75 × 112 cm; oil on canvas; signed and dated lower left.

A Spanish genre scene which is reminiscent of John Phillip in its subject, modelling and dramatic use of colour and shadow.

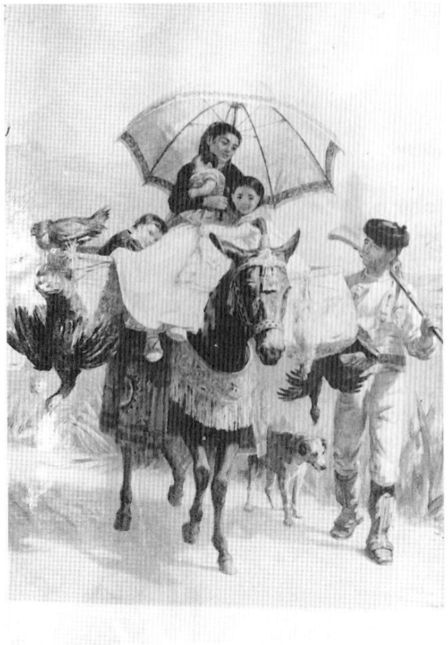

76. *A Spanish Scene – To Market*, 1867.

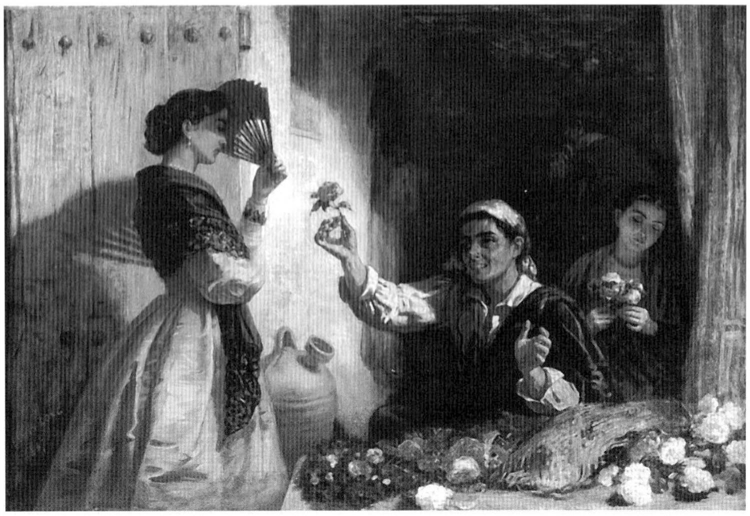

77. *A Spanish Flower Seller*, 1867
RUSSELL-COTES ART GALLERY AND MUSEUM, PHOTOGRAPH JAMES HOWE

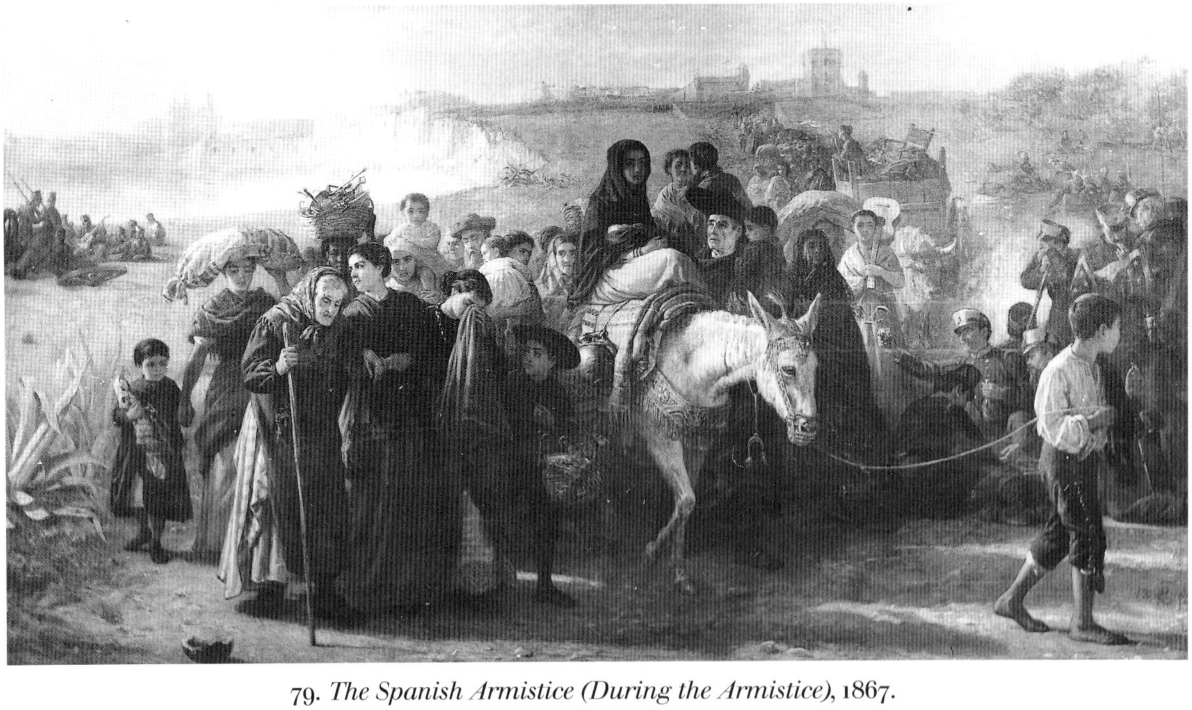

79. *The Spanish Armistice (During the Armistice)*, 1867.
SALFORD ART GALLERY

PROVENANCE Upway Manor Collection; purchased for the Russell-Cotes Art Gallery and Museum from Messrs H. Duke and Sons, 1932.
LITERATURE *Bulletin (R-C)*, vol. XI, no. 3 (September 1932), p. 30, p. 32 (ill.); Quick 1931, p. 34 (ill.), p. 44.
COLLECTION Russell-Cotes Art Gallery and Museum.

78. News From the War

c. 1867; size unknown; oil on canvas.

One of Long's paintings bought and exhibited at Wallis' on his return from a visit to Spain.

PROVENANCE Purchased from Wallis by Thomas Agnew and Sons on 15 May 1870; sold to Brassey, 20 July 1870; sold in 1906 for 90 guineas.
LITERATURE *Daily Telegraph*, unknown date, 1908.

79. The Spanish Armistice (During the Armistice)

1867; 53½ × 93", 136 × 237 cm; oil on canvas; signed and inscribed "b.i. 18 e 67".

Its full RA title, *During the Armistice – Free Passage for Women and Children*, shows the siege of Cadiz, one of Long's early depictions of a serious Spanish subject. The picture has, like much of his work, strong religious overtones. The picture depicts a large procession of women, children, and elderly people fleeing Cadiz with their possessions overlooked by encamped troops. The central figure of a young woman with a baby travelling on a donkey looks forward to *Anno Domini, or the Flight into Egypt* (1883) (cat. no. 197 below). The priest gazing at this central groups adds to the parallels made with the Holy Family. Spielmann in his interview with Long gives an interesting history of the painting:

> While painting he bribed one of the uncouth shepherds of Andalucia to sit to him, and struck by the enthusiasm raised by the man, to whom he had paid a peseta, actually allowed himself to be persuaded to join the man and his companions, and live with them for a month or more upon the mountains far away in the heart of the country, and this in spite of the urgent warnings with which he was hotly plied by the English Consul. The result laid the foundation of his later success. 'The Seige of Cadiz' was the outcome–a large picture full of small figures, and tiny but very carefully painted heads. This picture was skied at the Academy, and has since been sold at Christie's for £2,000.[1]

The Times reviewed the work: "E. Long's 'During the Armistice' shows a sad train of women, children, and other non-combatants passing from a Spanish town during a temporary suspension of hostilities between the parties engaged. With a great deal of nicely-observed character and clever grouping and painting, the picture sins, as Mr. Long's pictures very often do, by a want of concentration and a profusion of episode which fatigues and distracts. That 'half is more than whole' is truer of nothing than of his pictures."[2]

1. Spielmann 1888, p. 612.
2. *The Times*, 1 May 1869, p. 12.

PROVENANCE Sold at Christie's for £2,000 before 1888; bought by Alderman Isadore Frankenburg for £78 15s on 23 April 1910; presented in 1919 to Salford Art Gallery by Mrs. I. Frankenburg in memory of her late husband.
EXHIBITIONS RA 1869 (102), on sale for £735, remained unsold.
LITERATURE Spielmann 1888, p. 612; *The Times*, 1 May 1869, p. 12.
COLLECTION Salford Art Gallery.

80. Gipsy Schools Going to Vespers, Andalucia

1868; 51 × 98", 129.5 × 249 cm; oil on canvas.

Painted as a result of Long's extensive visit to Andalucia, this work combines Long's interest in Spanish gypsies and religious ritual.

PROVENANCE Sold in 1883 for 1,000 guineas; sold at Christie's on 2 May 1885 for 810 guineas.
EXHIBITIONS RA 1868 (409), on sale for £682 10s, remained unsold.
LITERATURE *Daily Telegraph*, unknown date, 1908; Quick 1931, p. 44.

81. The Proposal

1868; 34½ × 26¾", 82 × 68 cm; oil on canvas; signed with monogram and dated.

The Proposal is a Spanish genre scene of lovers sat in a garden with their *duenna* in the background with her back facing towards them. The metal railings that they are leaning against bears an engraved heart. Both of the central figures are in full traditional Spanish costume.

PROVENANCE Mr Thomas Jackson in 1930; sold at Sotheby's on 13 November 1973 for £380.

82. Billeting in Cadiz

1868; 62 × 44", 157.5 × 112 cm; oil on canvas; signed and dated.

A Spanish scene of soldiers billeting in Cadiz, a subject which relates to Long's *Spanish Armistice* of a year earlier.

PROVENANCE Edward Hermon Esq., MP; sold at Christie's on 13 May 1882 for £525; sold at Christie's as *Billeting Soldiers* on 13 July 1934 for £29 8s.

LITERATURE Rettlinger, 1961; Roberts 1897, vol. 1, p. 328.

83. La Duenna

1868; size unknown; oil on canvas; signed with monogram and dated.

A painting depicting a Spanish chaperone.

PROVENANCE Sold at the Hampshire Gallery, Bournemouth.

84. Wandering Thoughts

1868; 33½ × 52", 85 × 132 cm; oil on canvas.

A genre scene of a central figure lost in thought.

PROVENANCE Robert Wharton Esq.; sold at Christie's on 18 March 1899 for £59 17s.

85. Harvest Thanks and Blessing

1868; 54 × 90", 137 × 228.5 cm; oil on canvas; signed and dated.

A large painting depicting a harvest festival.

PROVENANCE Sold at Woolley and Wallis, Salisbury, on 30 September 1973 for £2,551.

86. The Dancer

1868; 33¼ × 57", 85 × 145 cm; oil on canvas; signed with monogram and dated, inscribed on verso.

An outdoor scene of a large group of Spanish gypsies. One of Long's Spanish period which shows the considerable influence of Spanish artists and that he was not solely influenced by John Phillip. The picture shows a woman with a guitar while another dances with a tambourine, the large group of men to the right of the picture are being served drink from a large earthenware jug.

PROVENANCE Sold at Sotheby's on 9 March 1976.

EXHIBITIONS Leeds 1868.

LITERATURE *Burlington Magazine*, no. 118 (February 1976), p. xix (ill.).

87. A Spanish Gypsy

1869; 39½ × 12", 100 × 30.5 cm; oil on canvas; signed and dated.

A small portrait of a Spanish Gypsy.

PROVENANCE Sold at Christie's on 10 May 1875 for £105.

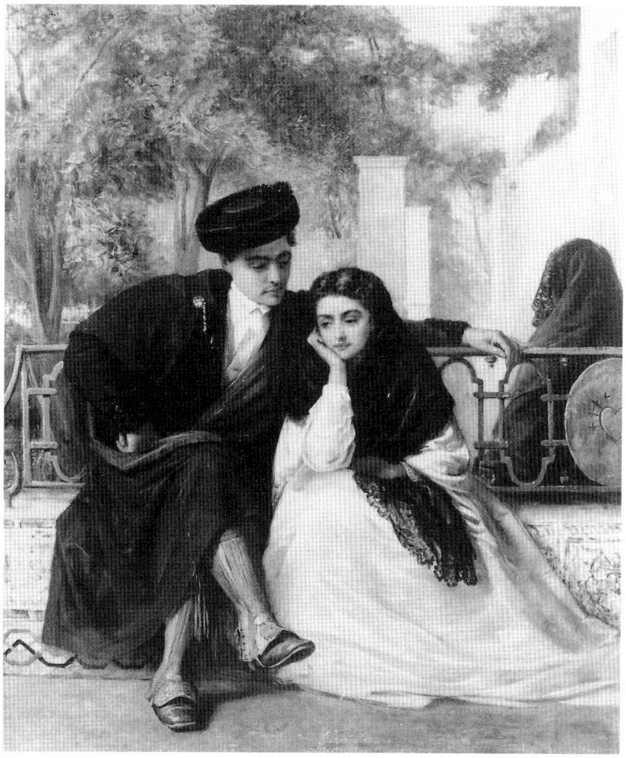

81. *The Proposal*, 1868.
COURTESY OF SOTHEBY'S, LONDON

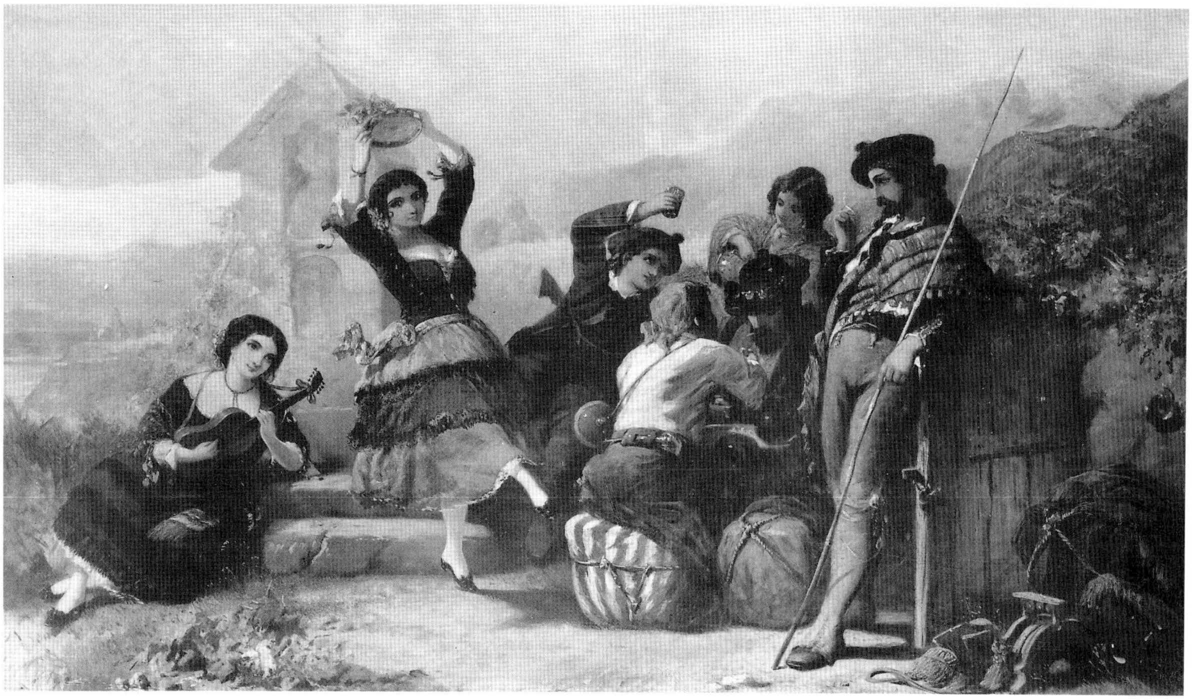

86. *The Dancer*, 1868.
COURTESY OF SOTHEBY'S, LONDON

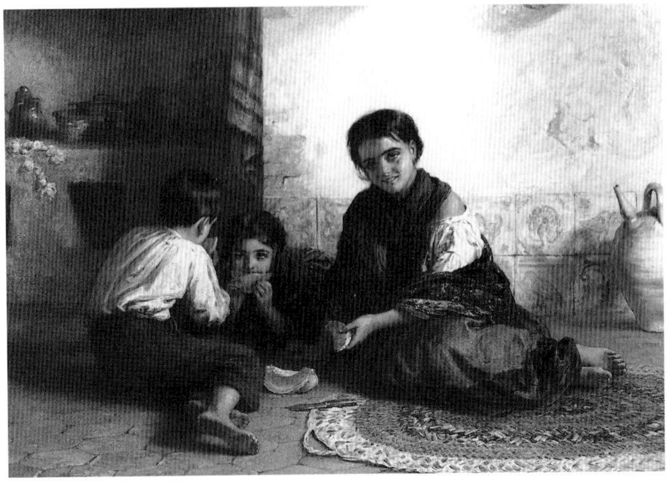

88. *Usted Gustra? (Spanish Children)*, 1869.
CHRISTIE'S IMAGES

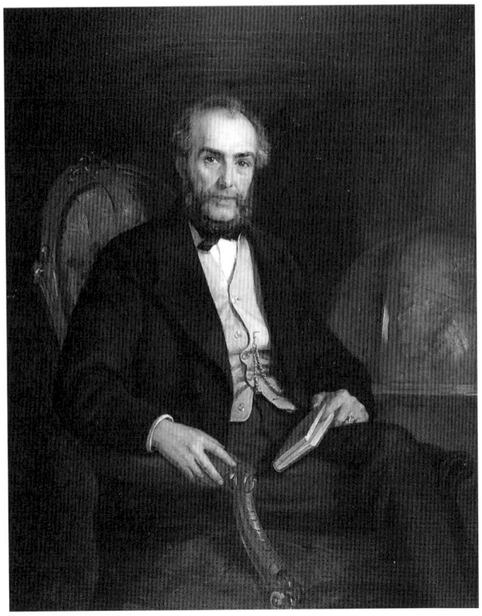

89. *Peter Douglas Esq.*, 1869.
RUSSELL-COTES ART GALLERY AND MUSEUM, PHOTOGRAPH JAMES HOWE

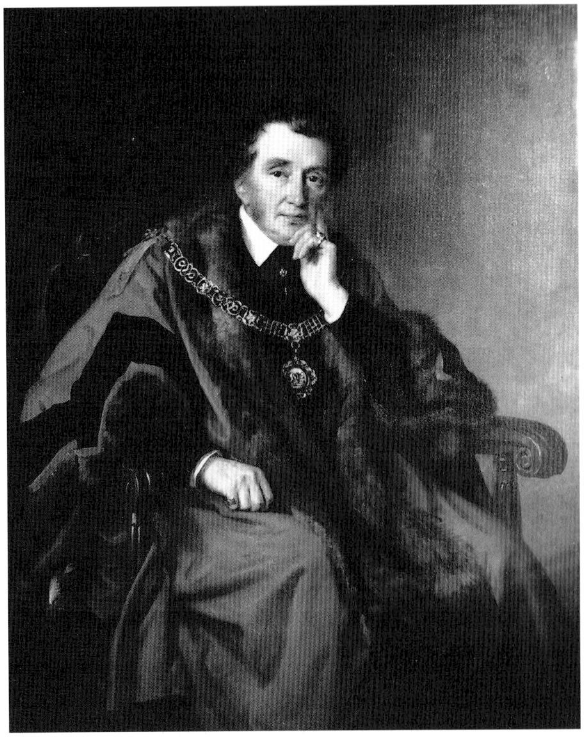

90. *William Hunt, Mayor of Bath*, 1869.
VICTORIA ART GALLERY, BATH & NORTH EAST SOMERSET COUNCIL

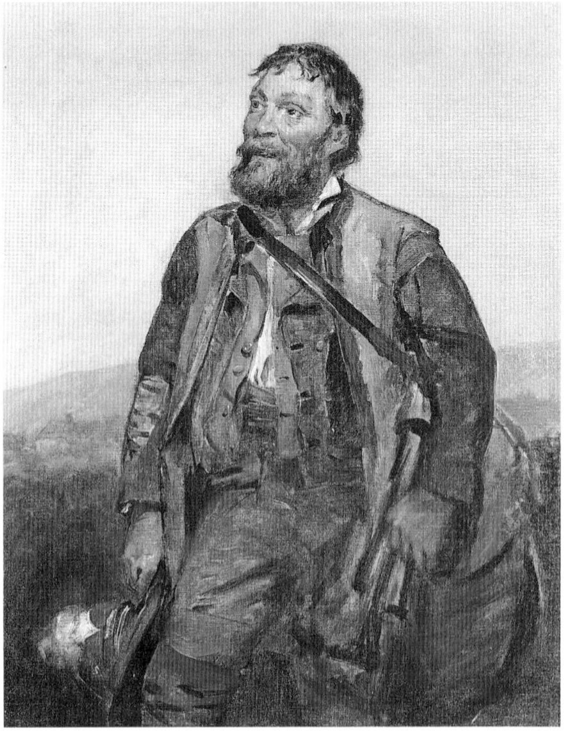

91. *The Gamekeeper*, 1869.
RUSSELL-COTES ART GALLERY AND MUSEUM, PHOTOGRAPH JAMES HOWE

88. Usted Gustra? (Spanish Children)

1869; 31 × 43″, 80 × 109 cm; oil on canvas; signed with monogram and dated.

A scene of Spanish children eating and selling a water melon. Its Spanish title *Usted Gustra?* (literally 'do you like?') is directed at the viewer as the central figure looks directly out of the painting. In this picture Long shows a particular debt to Murillo. The same scene is repeated in *Sympathy* (1875) (cat. no. 135) and in reverse (with the central figure looking at another figure in the painting) as part of a larger composition in *A Street Scene in Spain* (1871) (cat. no. 105). It was exhibited as *Usted Gustra?* at the 1869 Royal Academy Exhibition.

PROVENANCE Sold at Christie's on 2 March 1934 as *Spanish Children* with *A Roman Water-Carrier* for 13 guineas; Peter Stuart; sold at Christie's on 23 October 1987 as *Spanish Children* for £4,000.
EXHIBITIONS RA 1870 (890).

89. Peter Douglas Esq.

1869; 49 × 40″, 150 × 125 cm; oil on canvas; signed with monogram and dated, lower left.

A three-quarter-length seated portrait of Peter Douglas. To the right of the painting, by the sitter's left hand, is a globe.

PROVENANCE Commissioned by Peter Douglas from the artist; by descent to Miss Maude Douglas; Donation to the Russell-Cotes Art Gallery and Museum by Maude Douglas November 1942.
COLLECTION Russell-Cotes Art Gallery and Museum, Bournemouth.

90. William Hunt, Mayor of Bath

1869; 50 × 39¾″, 127 × 101 cm; oil on canvas.

A portrait of William Hunt (1800–85), Mayor of Bath.

PROVENANCE Bequest of Alderman William Hunt on his death in 1885.
COLLECTION Victoria Art Gallery, Bath.

91. The Gamekeeper

1869; 20 × 16″, 51 × 40.5 cm; oil on canvas.

A small study of a bearded gamekeeper.

PROVENANCE Gift of Mr Biddlecombe on 2 March 1976 to the Russell-Cotes Art Gallery and Museum.
COLLECTION Russell-Cotes Art Gallery and Museum, Bournemouth.

92. A Question of Propriety (1)

1870; 52 × 81″, 132 × 205 cm; oil on canvas; signed and dated.

The subject is taken from *Arte de la pintura* by Francesco Pacheco (1638) which Long consulted in the archives of the Simancas. It tells of a gypsy woman called before the inquisition on the charge of corrupting public morals. The painting was begun in 1870 where it was seen incomplete in Long's studio on 18 April by Alfred Thomas Taddy who commissioned a copy for the Victoria Art Gallery on the strength of it. It was sold to Wallis before it was completed in August, 1870. It was not long after this that Wallis sold it to Thomas Taylor. "Mr. Wallis has already sold Long's picture although it is no further advanced than it was when he bought it, for Long has bestowed all his time upon your replica, the two works are now at the same stage and are progressing simultaneously-I fear he will be unable to complete them before August."[1] The replica was complete by 5 August and was kept by Long for several days after so that it could be used to inform the original. The original, and smaller, of the two was exhibited at the Royal Academy of 1871 where, according to Thomas, it was hoped by Long to ensure his associateship.[2] Long sold the copyright to James L. Fairless of the Doré Gallery on 5 June 1873. The reviews were admiring although he did not achieve his desired election until four years later, *The Athenaeum* writing of the dancer: "this is a capital figure, full of spirit and elegance; and, except for a disproportionate small head, well drawn and brilliantly coloured. Mr. Long's sense of humour has been aptly employed in making the dancer forget her position, so that she proves the case for her accusers. The story is perfectly told."[3] The *Art Journal* review noted: "E. Long improves though we shall expect still better work than this. The painter strives to be within allowed limits, and in his endeavour his picture scarcely escapes heaviness. Yet the characters are delineated with rare insight, and the execution equals the conception."[4]

1. Alfred Thomas Taddy, letter to the National Gallery of Victoria, c. April 1870, National Gallery of Victoria archive.
2. "He thinks it would insure his election to the honours of associateship." Alfred Thomas Taddy, letter to the National Gallery of Victoria, c. August 1870, National Gallery of Victoria archive. Long did not achieve this status until 1875.
3. Ath., 1871.
4. AJ, 1871, p. 150.

PROVENANCE Bought by Wallis from the artist (before complete) in 1870; sold by Wallis (before complete) to Thomas Taylor (Aston Rowant Gallery, Oxfordshire); Thomas Taylor sale at Christie's on 28th April 1883; Thomas Taylor sold to Thomas Agnew & Sons on 1 March 1890; sold to S. G. Lister in March 1890; in the collection of the Earl and Countess of Swinton in 1973.

EXHIBITIONS RA 1871 (43).

LITERATURE AJ, 1871, p. 150; Ath., 1871; *Bulletin (R-C)*, vol. II, no. 2 (June 1923), p. 16; Chester, 1908, p. 336; *Daily Telegraph*, unknown date, 1908; *The Portfolio*, June 1891, obituary; Quick 1931, p. 3, p. 44; Roberts 1897, vol. II, p. 48.

92.1 A Question of Propriety (2)

1870; 69 × 84½", 175.2 × 275 cm; oil on canvas.

The largest version of this painting was commissioned for the National Gallery of Victoria, Melbourne by Alfred Taddy Thomas. He wrote to the Gallery in 1870, "I have arranged with Long to paint you an enlarged replica of it on a canvas 9 × 5ft., in which the figures will be nearly one half larger, which he considers the size he can paint most effectively; he undertakes to complete it during the month of July."[1] The painting was finished by 5 August, before the original version but was retained "in order that he may progress with the original picture which he is now painting from your replica."[2] The original painting was selected for exhibition at the Royal Academy: "Long regrets that his larger picture cannot be sent to the Academy next year, as he feels that he cannot succeed as well as the smaller one."[3] A copy by Sir John Longstaff (signed and dated 1887) is in the Shepparton Art Gallery, Victoria.

1. Alfred Thomas Taddy, letter to the National Gallery of Victoria, Melbourne, c. April 1870, National Gallery of Victoria archive.
2. Ibid.
3. Ibid.

PROVENANCE Commissioned by A. Thomas Taddy for the National Gallery of Victoria for 600 guineas.

LITERATURE *Daily Telegraph*, unknown date, 1908.

COLLECTION Purchased with the assistance of a Government Grant, 1871, National Gallery of Victoria, Melbourne, Australia.

92.2 A Question of Propriety (3)

1875; 52 × 85", 132 × 215 cm; oil on canvas; signed and dated "E. Long 1875".

The second replica of *A Question of Propriety* (1870) almost the same size as the original. The majority of it was painted by a studio assistant but was completed by Long. It was engraved by John Ballin (exhibited at the Royal Academy in 1877, no. 1230).

PROVENANCE Thomas Taylor, Aston Rowant Gallery, Oxfordshire; sold at Christie's on 28 April 1883 for 1,200 guineas; D. H. Evans in 1897; sold at Sotheby's on 14 June 1989 for £10,000; sold at Christie's on 14 June 1990 for £8,000.

EXHIBITIONS 1897 Earl's Court (318).

LITERATURE *Daily Telegraph*, unknown date, 1908.

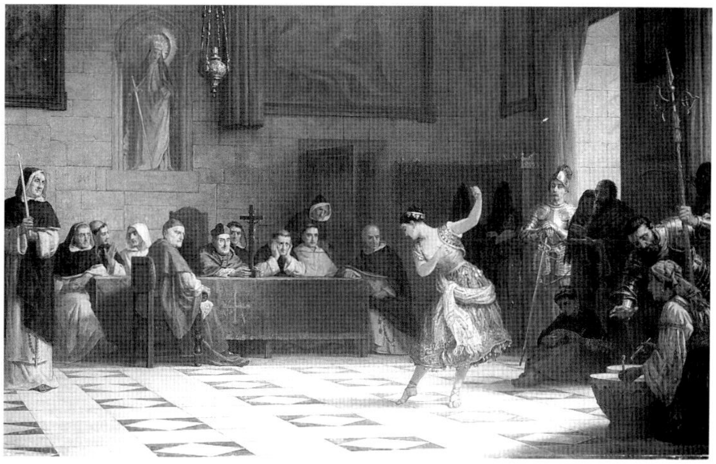

92.1. *A Question of Propriety*, 1870.
NATIONAL GALLERY OF VICTORIA, MELBOURNE

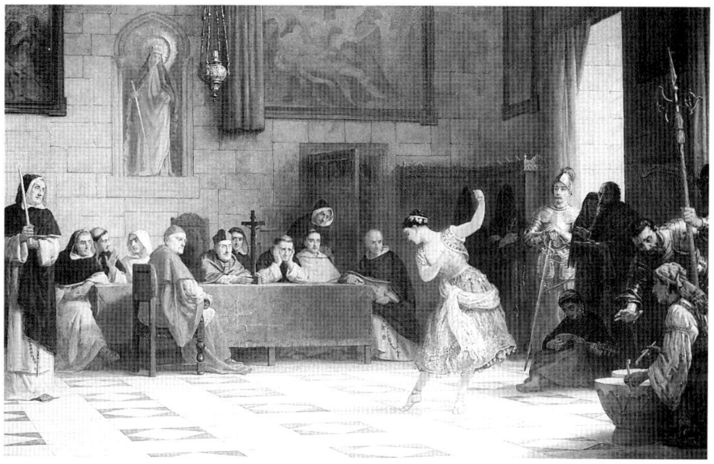

92.2. *A Question of Propriety*, 1870.
COURTESY OF SOTHEBY'S, LONDON

93. Lazarillo and the Blind Beggar

1870; 42 × 55", 106.5 × 139.5 cm; oil on canvas; signed and dated.

Long's fascination with Spain led him to produce paintings based upon fictional Spanish works. The source for this work was by Diego Hurtado de Mendoza's (1503–75) *Lazarillo de Tormes* (1554). The work was available in English as *Lazarillo, or the Excellent History of Lazarillo de Tormes, the witty Spaniard*, translated by David Rowland and published in over twenty-five editions; in 1852, it was revised by William Hazlitt. Long's painting illustrates a scene from the third chapter and shows Lazarillo and the blind beggar. The *Art Journal* found the painting "Very powerful, but lacking delicacy, is a work not unworthy of the proved ability of E. Long."[1]

1. AJ, 1870, p. 168.

PROVENANCE Adamson; sold at Christie's on 10 May 1875 for £315; Stephen J. Holland Esq.; sold at Christie's on 25 June 1908 for £241 10s to Agnew's; sold at Sotheby's on 22 February 1972 for £220; sold at Christie's on 28 July 1972 for £231.

EXHIBITIONS RA 1870 (497).

LITERATURE AJ, 1870, p. 168; *Magazine of Art*, July 1891, p. xl; Reitlinger, 1961.

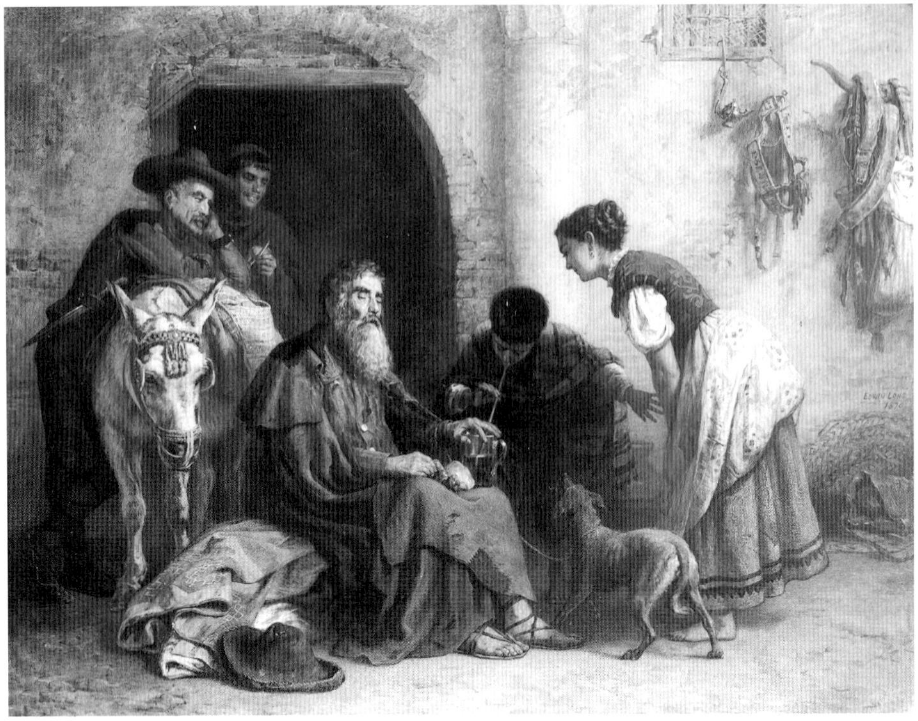

93. *Lazarillo and the Blind Beggar*, 1870.
COURTESY OF SOTHEBY'S, LONDON

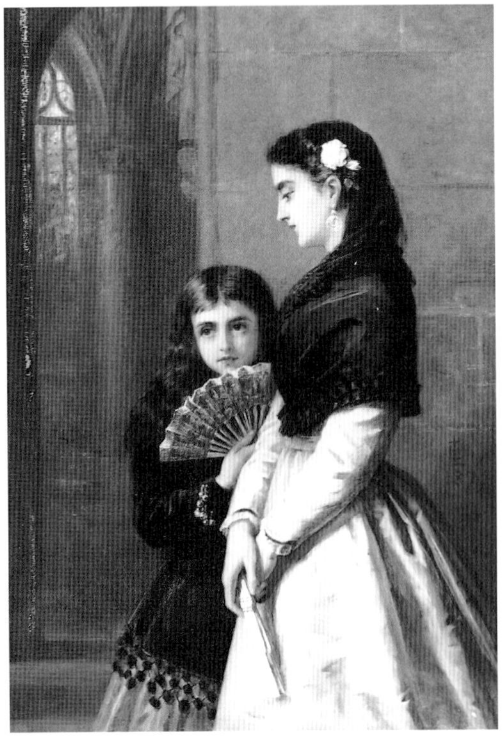

94. *At the Church Door*, 1870.
CHRISTIE'S IMAGES

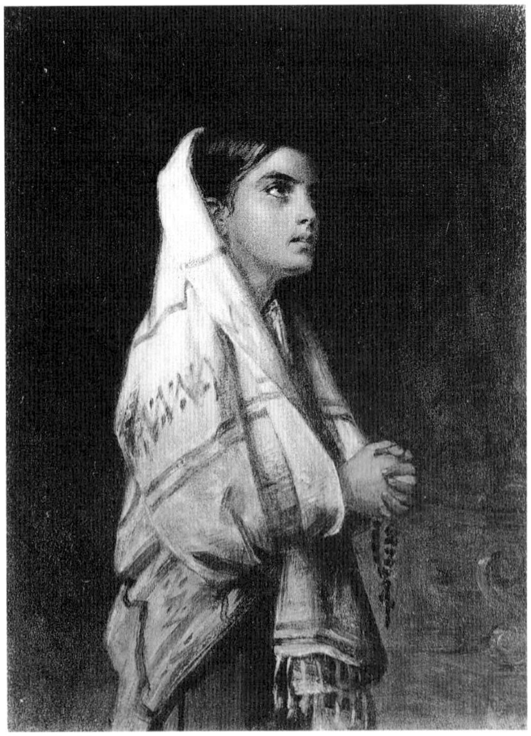

97.1. *Spanish Girl Praying*, c. 1870.
CITY OF ABERDEEN ART GALLERY & MUSEUMS COLLECTIONS

94. At the Church Door (1)

1870; 36 × 24″, 91.3 × 60.9 cm; oil on canvas; signed with monogram and dated.

This is the first version Long painted of *At the Church Door* showing a young Spanish woman and girl in church.

PROVENANCE Sold at Christie's on 27 September 1990.

94.1 At the Church Door (2), 1879.

1879; 30 × 21″, 76 × 53 cm; oil on panel; signed with monogram and dated.

A copy of *At the Church Door* (no. 94), this version being slightly smaller and painted on panel rather than canvas. In a 1990 Christie's sale it was titled *Listening to the Anthem* (cat. no. 98), the title of a very different painting by Long.

PROVENANCE A. & J. Polck, Manchester; sold at Christie's on 14 June 1991 as *Listening to the Anthem.*

95. Confession Hour

1870; size unknown; oil on canvas; signed and dated.

A Spanish religious genre painting.

PROVENANCE Sold at Christie's on 16 June 1888 for £115 10s.
EXHIBITIONS Exhibited at Birmingham before 1888.

96. Padre Francisco

1870; 42 × 57½″, 107 × 146 cm; oil on canvas.

A large scale genre painting.

PROVENANCE George Fox Esq., of Harefield Winslow; sold at Christie's on 11 May 1877 for £237; sold at Christie's on 13 December 1929 for 12 guineas.

97. A Young Peasant at Her Devotions

1870; 36 × 24″, 91.3 × 60.9 cm; oil on canvas; signed with monogram and dated.

A three-quarter-length painting of a young girl with shawl and rosary performing her devotions in church. This is a more complete version of the half-length *A Spanish Girl Praying* which appears to be its study.

PROVENANCE Sold at Christie's on 27 September 1990.

97.1 Spanish Girl Praying

c. 1870; 15 × 11″, 38.2 × 27.8 cm; oil on canvas.

A half-length painting of a young Spanish girl at her devotions wearing a shawl carrying out her devotions with rosary beads in church. It appears to be a study for *A Young Peasant Girl at Her Devotions.*

PROVENANCE Bequest of Alexander MacDonald to Aberdeen Art Gallery.
LITERATURE Quick 1931, p. 11 (ill.), p. 44.
COLLECTION Aberdeen Art Gallery.

98. Listening to the Anthem

c. 1870; 31½ × 18½″, 80 × 47 cm; oil on canvas; signed.

The same subject and model as *A Spanish Girl Praying* and *A Young Peasant Girl at Her Devotions* of the same year. This version is in a different pose than the other two and is full-length. It shows the girl leaning against a church column wearing the same shawl carrying out her devotions with her rosary beads.

PROVENANCE Sold at Sotheby's on 12 April 1985 for £1,000.

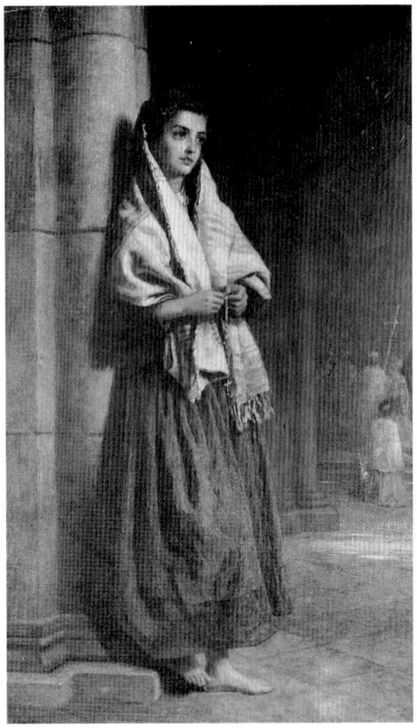

98. *Listening to the Anthem*, c. 1870.
COURTESY OF SOTHEBY'S, LONDON

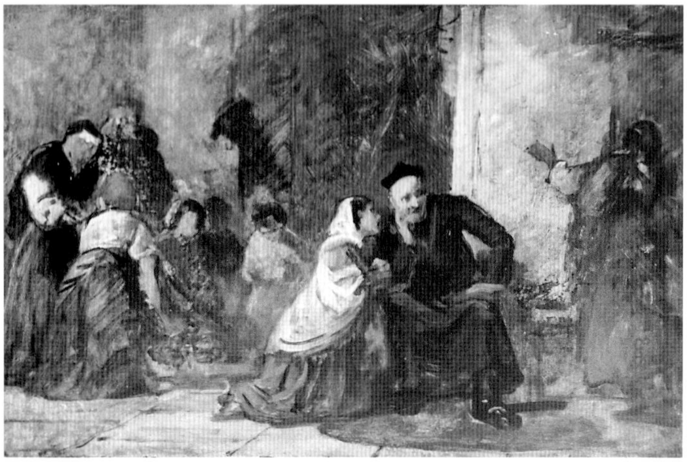

102.1. *An Easter Vigil* (study), 1871.
MR CLIVE BLOUNT

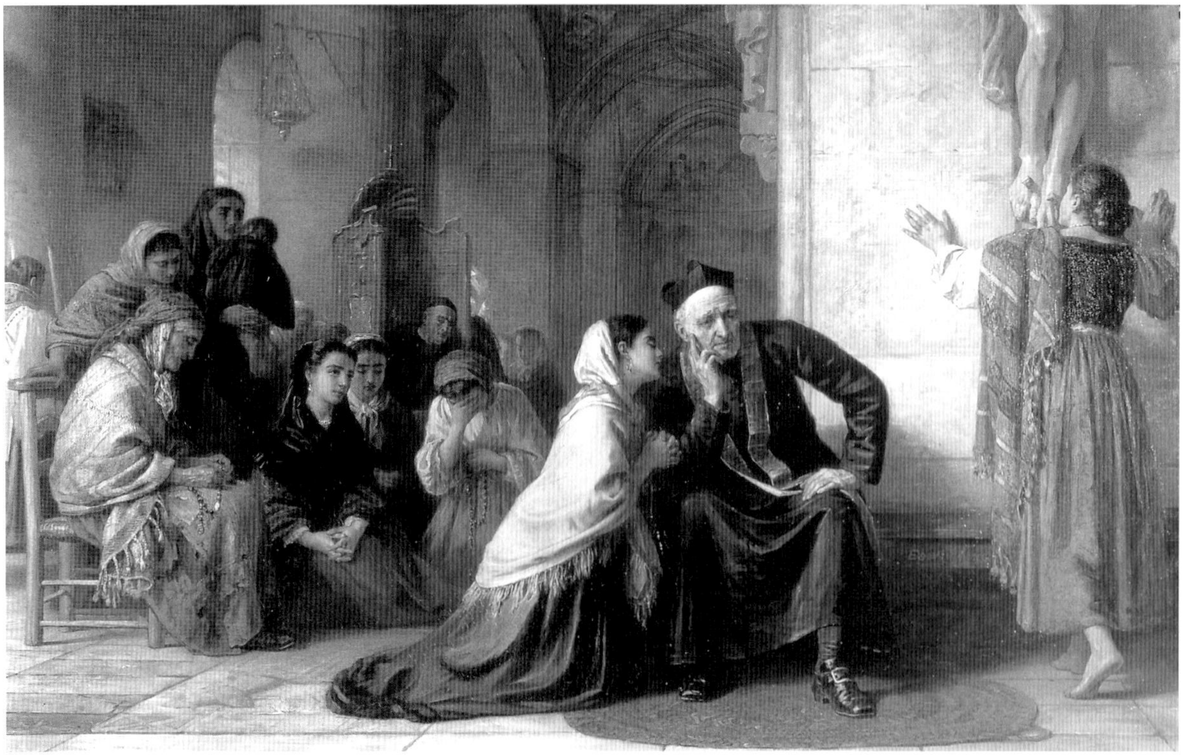

102. *An Easter Vigil in a Cathedral at Seville*, 1871.
THE FORBES MAGAZINE COLLECTION NEW YORK, ALL RIGHTS RESERVED

99. Agape

c. 1870; size unknown; oil on canvas.

PROVENANCE Purchased from Wallis by Agnew's on 4 December 1871; sold to J. K. Cross on 20 March 1872.

100. Hubert

1870; size unknown; oil on canvas.

A portrait exhibited at the 1870 Royal Academy Exhibition. The *Art Journal* noted that "Hubert is brilliant and skilful: the face is in a light key relieved from a background in half tone, expression and transparency are thrown into the eyes".[1]

1. AJ, 1870, p. 167.

EXHIBITIONS RA 1870 (321).
LITERATURE AJ, 1870, p. 167.

101. Andrew Mulholland

c. 1870; size unknown; oil on canvas.

A three-quarter-length portrait of Andrew Mulholland seated in a chair.

LITERATURE *Country Life*, 2 March 1967 (ill.).

102. An Easter Vigil in a Cathedral at Seville

1871; 52 × 80¾", 132 × 205 cm; oil on canvas, signed and inscribed on label on stretcher.

The setting is Seville Cathedral where a woman is whispering her confession to the priest. In composition and subject, the painting bears many similarities to *The Catechism* but lies closest to *Good Advice* (1871) (cat. no. 103) where Long portrays the same central characters in a similarly religious genre scene. The two pictures form two parts of the same narrative. The *Art Journal* noted: "This artist is becoming more careful, and studious, but his style is still rather showy and convential".[1]

1. AJ, 1871, p. 177.

PROVENANCE Daniel Roberts Esq.; sold at Christie's on 5 May 1883 for £1,165 10s; sold in 1887 for £1,030; Charles Neck Esq.; sold at Christie's on 3 May 1890 for 880 guineas; sold at Christie's on 18 March 1983 for £2,000; Forbes Magazine Collection.
EXHIBITIONS RA 1871 (486), on sale for 800 guineas, remained unsold.
LITERATURE AJ, 1871, p. 177; *Daily Telegraph* , date unknown, 1908; Quick 1931, p. 44; Roberts 1897, vol. II, p. 50, p. 144.
COLLECTION Forbes Magazine Collection, New York.

102.1 An Easter Vigil (study)

1871; 15¾ × 23½", 40 × 60 cm; oil on canvas.

PROVENANCE Madame Tussauds; by descent to Mr Clive Blount.

103. Good Advice

1871; 38 × 51¾", 96.5 × 131.5 cm; oil on canvas; signed and dated.

Good Advice,[1] using the same models as *An Easter Vigil*, is the second part of the narrative begun in that painting. Set in a Spanish church, a crucifixion triptych is visible to the right. The young woman looks coyly downwards as the priest points to a letter she has brought him for advice. This work bears the same title as a painting by Long of 1863, and although they both deal with the popular theme of age advising youth, it is a completely different picture in mood and characterisation.

1. This painting is not to be confused with *Age & Youth*.

PROVENANCE Sold at Christie's on 6 May 1983; sold at auction on 29 November 1983 for £1,300; sold at Sotheby's on 18 March 1980.

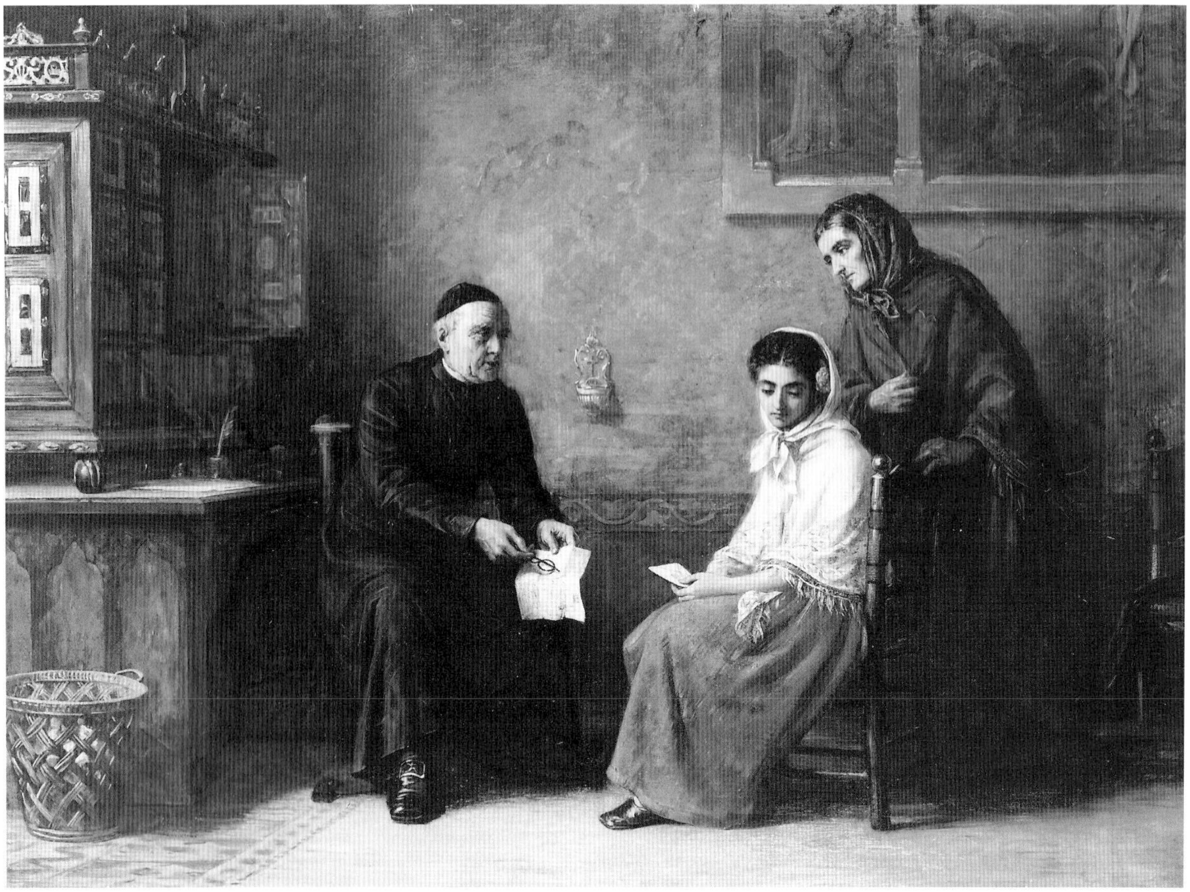

103. *Good Advice*, 1871.
COURTESY OF SOTHEBY'S, LONDON

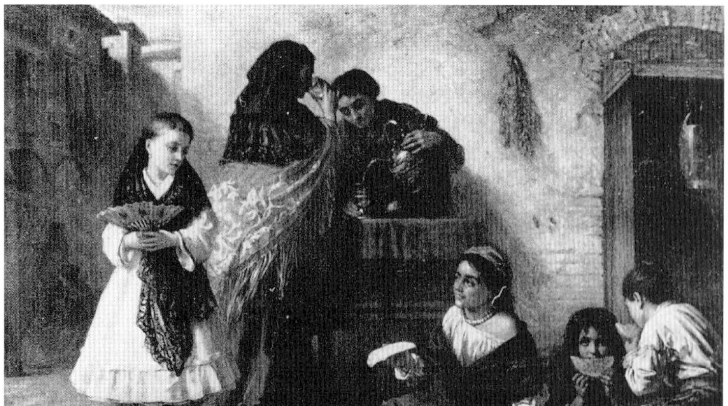

105. *A Street Scene in Spain*, 1871.
RUSSELL-COTES ART GALLERY AND MUSEUM

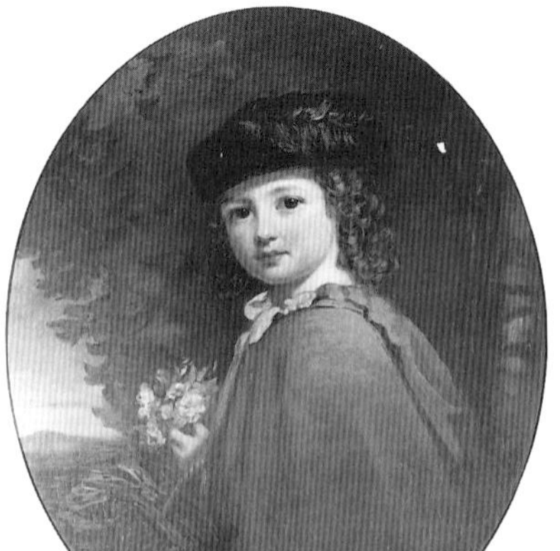

106. *Florence Amy Marler*, date unknown.
COURTESY OF SOTHEBY'S, LONDON

104. Off Duty

1871; 33 × 43½", 84 × 110.5 cm; oil on canvas.

PROVENANCE Sold at Christie's on 3 August 1933.

105. A Street Scene in Spain

1871; 45 × 66", 152 × 206 cm; oil on canvas; signed and dated on lower left.

This painting shows an affluent girl being offered water melon by a group of children, while in the background a water-seller is serving the girl's mother. The same group of children, who owe much to Murillo, appear in two other paintings by Long, *Usted Gustra?* (1869) (cat. no. 88) and *Sympathy* (1875) (cat. no. 135). This exemplifies the often formulaic treatment of the subject matter in Long's Spanish genre scenes, and perhaps indicates his tiring of such genre paintings in general.

PROVENANCE Bought from the artist by Thomasson; by descent to Mr F. Thomasson and bought from him by the Russell-Cotes Art Gallery and Museum, 20 April 1932.
LITERATURE *Bulletin (R-C)* vol. XI, no. 2 (June 1932), p. 18, p. 20 (ill.); Quick 1931, p. 33 (ill.).
COLLECTION Russell-Cotes Art Gallery and Museum, Bournemouth.

106. Florence Amy Marler

date unknown; 28¼ × 23", 71.8 × 58.5 cm; oil on canvas.

An oval portrait of Florence Amy Marler as a young girl holding a small posy.

PROVENANCE Sold at Sotheby's on 14 June 1977.

107. Alone

1871; size unknown; oil on canvas.

PROVENANCE Sold at Christie's on 23 May 1871 for 80 guineas.

108. Listening

1872; 23½ × 17½", 59.8 × 44.5 cm; oil on canvas.

PROVENANCE Sold at Christie's on 7 March 1908 for £9 19s 6d by Sampson.

109. Fanchette

1872; 49 × 31", 125 × 79 cm; oil on canvas; signed, dated and inscribed.

A three-quarter-length portrait of Miss Isabella Bateman in the role of Fanchette. Isabella Bateman was the daughter of Hezekiah Luithicum Bateman, manager of the Lyceum Theatre in 1871. The Batemans had just arrived in London from the United States in 1870 and *Fanchette; or, the Will-of-the-Wisp* was the first drama of the new management opening on 11 September 1871.[1] The central role of the heroine was aimed to launch the career of their daughter, but failed to do so. Long's painting illustrates act 2, scene 3 of the play: "I did not mean to make you quarrel with the girl you love so much". The painting received short but more favourable mentions than the play, the journals noting, "A highly meritorious life-sized study, the arm and hand, however, are somewhat heavy for the figure".[2] "We shall consider the artist's 'Fanchette' (1069) on another occasion, and, meanwhile, we may correct the mistake which a transposition of memoranda caused us to commit last week, when we styled this as a love scene".[3] "His other picture is a graceful half-length (1,069) of Miss Isabella Bateman in the character of Fanchette".[4]

1. *Fanchette* was written by Mrs Bateman and based on a German dramatic version of George Sand's *La Petite Fadette*.
2. AJ, 1872, p. 185.
3. Ath., 11 May 1872, p. 596.
4. *The Times*, 4 May 1872, p. 5.

PROVENANCE Sold at Sotheby's on 19 October 1983; and on 29 March 1984, for £600.
EXHIBITIONS RA 1872 (1069).
LITERATURE AJ, 1872, p. 185; Ath., 11 May 1872, p. 596; *The Times*, 4 May 1872, p. 5.

110. The New Dress

1872; 24 × 17", 60 × 44 cm; oil on canvas, signed and dated.

A half length portrait of a young girl wearing a new white dress, seated on a blue chair.

PROVENANCE Sold at Sotheby's, Chester, on 30 March 1984; sold at Christie's on 19 December 1991.

111. The Suppliants: Expulsion of the Gypsies from Spain (1872)

1872; 72 × 113", 182.8 × 286 cm; oil on canvas; signed and dated.

In this painting, Long proved to his critics that he was able to successfully paint a large scale historical painting that was both convincing in its composition and accomplished in its painting technique, as well as owing little to John Phillip. In this sense it is a clear turning point in Long's career and although he continued several pleasant Spanish genre scenes, his ambitions to be taken seriously as a painter of historical scenes became increasingly clear. The depth of research that Long carried out to produce the painting further indicated his seriousness of purpose, a point that was reiterated in criticism of this and later works. Its only real precedent in terms of originality, ambition and technical prowess is *A Question of Propriety* (1870) (cat. no. 92) which was preferred over *The Suppliants* by the *Athenaeum*.[1]

The subject of the painting was inspired by the writings of Pacheco, a source Long had used in his *Question of Propriety*. The documents of the Secretary of the Inquisition, preserved in the archives of Simancas, tell of Phillip III's proposal to expel the gypsies from Spain. Long wrote later of the work:

> The Gypsies in Spain have always been considered a very degraded race, they were at that time excommunicated & consequently not allowed to enter a church. It is supposed the edict of expulsion would have been carried out, as in the case of the Jews in the time of Ferdinand & Isabella, but for the timely deputation which the picture attempts to represent when the King & the Cardinal [Gonzales] were descending the steps of the Santa Annunciata in Valladolid, and for the compassionate intervention of the young queen, who may be seen in the corridor above.[2]

Long's research for the painting was not limited to consulting Pacheco's historical records, as he also visited the Prado to sketch the portraits of the King, Queen and Cardinal to achieve greater accuracy. Long also visited the Santa Annunciata in Valladolid, a place he had visited on his first trip to Spain in 1857.[3] Further, his depiction of gypsies in the painting were modelled from their descendants still living in Spain.

The painting achieved great critical acclaim on its exhibition at the Royal Academy exhibition of 1872, the 'Annual Register' comparing it to Veronese's *Family of Darius before Alexander* in the National Gallery. *Punch* praised the painting, beginning with the phrase which was later to appear on Long's grave: "'Ars longa, Vita brevis' But to Art we do no wrong, If, while LONG such work can give us Vita longa, we wish LONG".[4] *The Times* noted that "No painter of the year has made a more decided advance than Mr. Long . . . "[5] *The Graphic* too was generous in its praise, but the *Art Journal* saw its real importance not only as "a manifestation of the new that is rising in English Art" but as

> a picture of a very high class, painted by E. Long, who could not have produced a composition like this without having already shown tokens of being on the road to high achievement; and so we have predicted of this rising painter . . . It is an admirable work, and we cannot compliment Mr Long more highly than by saying there is not a person in his picture who has not something appropriate to urge.[6]

1. "E. Long's picture, 'The Suppliants' (64), will not please so many as 'The Inquisition' of last year pleased". Ath., 1872, p. 596.
2. Edwin Long, letter to Thomas Holloway, 1 June 1882, in the Royal Holloway Archives, London.
3. *Bravo El Toro* (1858) depicts a bullfight at Valladolid.
4. *Punch*, 25 May 1872, p. 213.
5. *The Times*, 4 May 1872, p. 5.
6. AJ, 1872, p. 149.

PROVENANCE Purchased by Edward Hermon MP of Wyfold Court, Henley on Thames for £1,575[?]; sold at Christie's on 13 May 1882 with copyright for £4,305 to Martin for Thomas Holloway.

EXHIBITIONS RA 1872 (64).

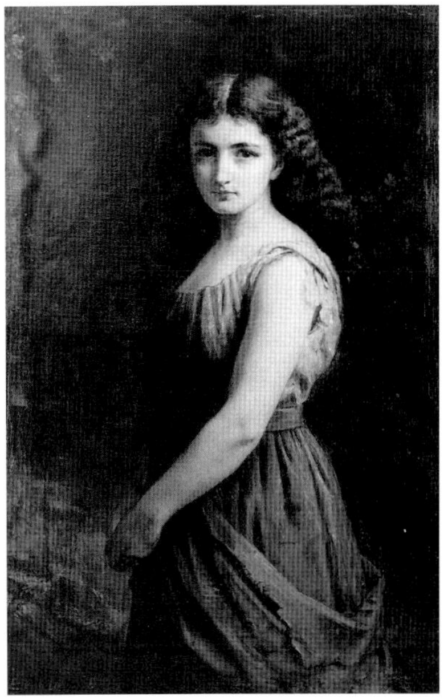

109. *Fanchette*, 1872.
COURTESY OF SOTHEBY'S, LONDON

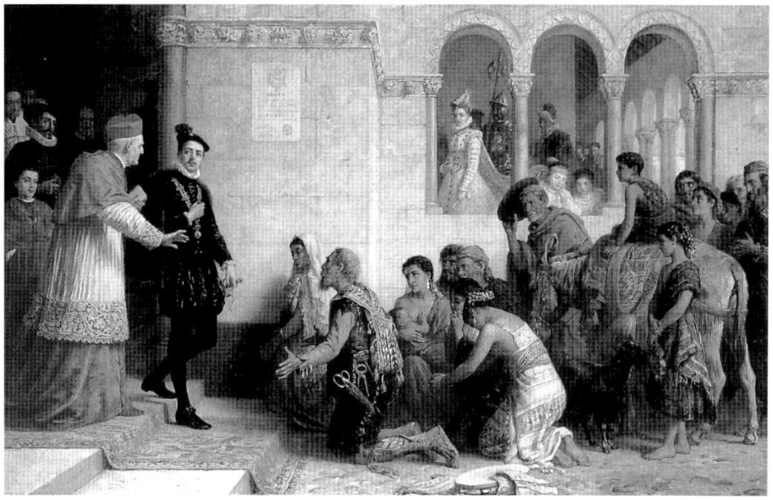

111. *The Suppliants: Expulsion of the Gypsies from Spain (1872)*, 1872.
ROYAL HOLLOWAY & BEDFORD NEW COLLEGE, SURREY.
PHOTOGRAPH BRIDGEMAN ART LIBRARY

LITERATURE *Annual Register*, 1872, p. 363; AJ, 1872, p. 149; *Art Pictorial and Industrial*, vol. III (1872), p. 89; Ath., 4 May 1872, p. 564, and 11 May 1872, pp. 595–96; Chapel 1982, pp. 107–08 (ill.); Chester 1908, p. 334; *The Examiner*, 1 June 1872, p. 549; *Fraser's Magazine*, July 1872, pp. 27–28; *The Graphic*, 1 June 1872; *Illustrated London News*, 18 May 1872, p. 486; *Punch*, 25 May 1872, p. 213; *Saturday Review*, 8 June 1872, p. 729; Spielmann 1888, p. 612; *The Times*, 4 May 1872, p. 5, and 16 May 1882, p. 4; Quick 1931, pp. 3–4, p. 12 (ill.), p. 44; Roberts 1897, vol. I, p. 328.

COLLECTION Royal Holloway College Picture Collection, London.

112. The Moorish Proselytes of Archbishop Ximenes, Granada, 1500

1873; 74 × 108", 188 × 274.3 cm; oil on canvas, signed and dated on a chair, lower left.

In this picture, Long attempted to repeat his success of the previous year. He created another pictorial scene from Spanish history, setting it in Granada around 1500 shortly after the Christians had taken the city. The historical source for the painting is William H. Prescott's *History of the Reign of Ferdinand and Isabella the Catholic* which described the plight of the remaining Moorish contingent: "The greater part made their peace by embracing Christianity; many others sold their estates and migrated to Barbary, and the remainder of the population, whether from fear of punishment or contagion of example abjured their ancient superstition, and consented to receive baptism . . . ".[1] The picture shows the Archbishop Ximenes overseeing the baptism of the Granada Moors.

The picture received widespread reviews, due, in part, to the success of his Royal Academy picture *The Suppliants* of the year before. This was to acclaim in the *Illustrated London News* which produced an engraving after the painting and which noted in its obituary of Long in 1891: "His earlier work attracted little notice; although some – such as the 'Baptism of the Moors of Granada by Cardinal Ximenes,' exhibited in 1873 – were often ambitious in design and creditable in composition".[2] *The Athenaeum* wrote:

> The scene is an interior: The Moors who chose to be converted rather than expelled from Spain are abjuring the faith of their fathers before the sharp-witted and suspicious Ximenes. This is rather an 'illustration' than a picture, with several suggestive, but not particularly pathetic, figures, and sufficiently good painting. The subject hardly seems to have interested Mr. Long. He has done much better and he has done much worse than this.[3]

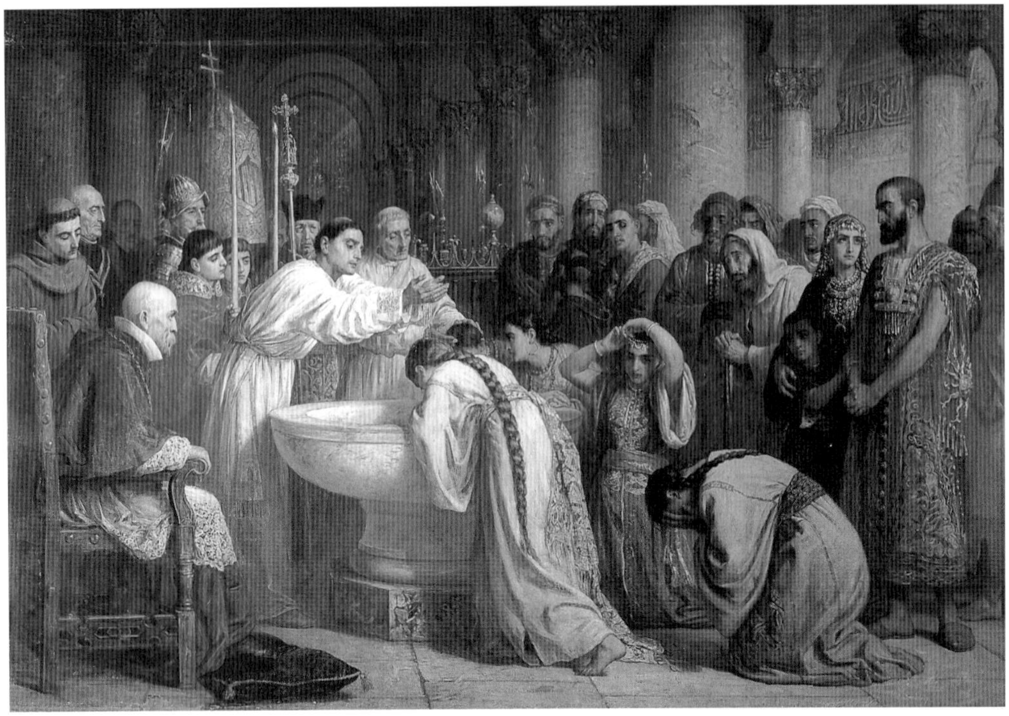

112. *The Moorish Proselytes of Archbishop Ximenes, Granada, 1500*, 1873.
RUSSELL-COTES ART GALLERY AND MUSEUM. PHOTOGRAPH JAMES HOWE.

The Times made a direct comparison with *The Suppliants* of 1872:

> Here is a palpably dramatic subject, which, however, Mr. Long has clearly turned to far less successful account than he did in his expulsion of the Gitanos last year. The reason is, probably, that Mr. Long could find in and about Granada and Seville plenty of models for his gypsy suppliants; Whereas he is thrown mainly on fancy or the chapter of accidents for models of his Moors, particularly his Moorish matrons and maidens. The Cardinal is properly grim and rigid, but the whole group of perfunctory converts seems to us theatrical and without national character.[4]

The *Art Journal* commented rather more positively in writing:

> This picture is large and ambitious in style, and suggests the need of more deliberation in the grouping of the figures. A crowd of this sort is not easy to manage; and if the result is to be harmonious, considerable thought must be expended upon the drawing and arrangement. Mr Long has, however, abundant energy and cleverness, which are exhibited without stint in the present work.[5]

1. William H. Prescott, *History of the Reign of Ferdinand and Isabella the Catholic*, 2 vols. (London: R. Bentley, 1837).
2. *Illustrated London News*, May 1891, obituary of Edwin Long.
3. Ath., 31 May 1873, p. 700.
4. *The Times*, 19 May 1873, p. 6.
5. AJ, 1873, p. 236.

PROVENANCE Sold in 1876 for £1,200; collection of Mr. Hamilton Fletcher; purchased by the Russell-Cotes Art Gallery and Museum from Messrs H. Duke and Son on 25 June 1932.

EXHIBITIONS RA 1873 (628).

LITERATURE AJ, 1873, p. 236; Ath., 31 May 1873, p. 700; *Bulletin (R-C)*, vol. XI, no. 3, (September 1932), p. 30, p. 31 (ill.); Chester 1908, p. 336, p. 340, p. 343; *Illustrated London News*, 13 December 1873 (ill.); *Illustrated London News*, May 1891 (obituary); Quick 1931, p. 32 (ill.), p. 44, and front cover (ill.); *The Times*, 19 May 1873, p. 6.

COLLECTION Russell-Cotes Art Gallery and Museum, Bournemouth.

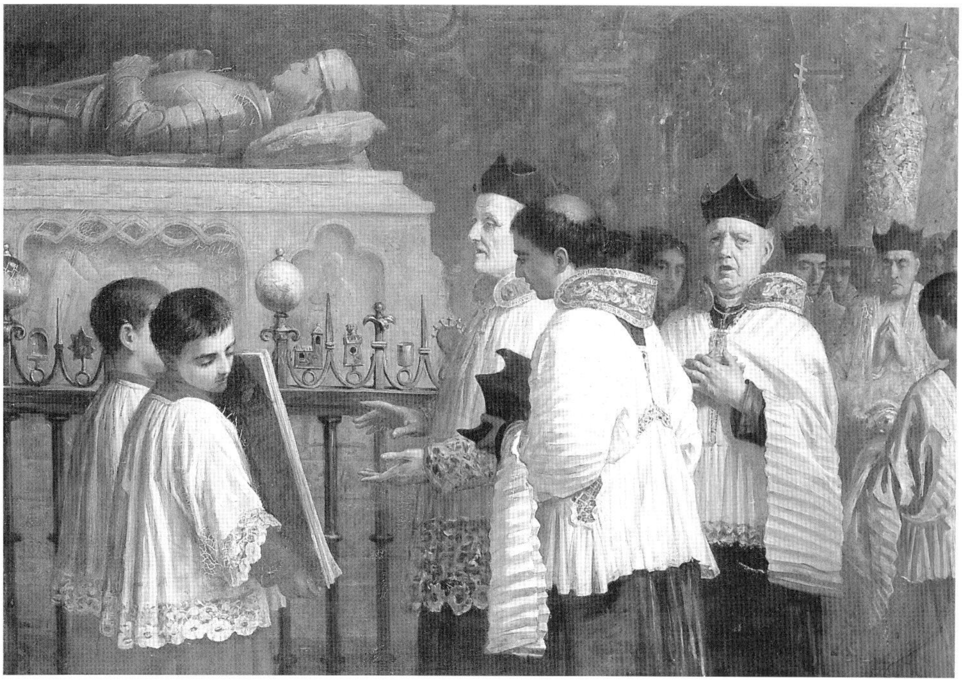

113. *Primero Segundo y Basso Profundo*, 1873.
CHRISTIE'S IMAGES

113. Primero Segundo y Basso Profundo

1873; 41½ × 58″, 105.4 × 147.3 cm; oil on canvas, signed with monogram and dated.

The title of this Spanish religious genre scene translates as 'First, second and deep bass'. In the background, to the left, is the tomb of a knight, to the right, a large congregation of priests.

PROVENANCE H. Roberts; sold at Christie's on 12 March 1881 for 255 guineas; sold at auction on 26 February 1985 for £440; sold at Christie's on 14 February 1986; sold at Christie's on 19 December 1991.

114. Velasquez, Spanish Painter

1873; 108 × 41″, 274.3 × 104.2 cm; oil on canvas.

The second, much larger, painting by Long of Velasquez is painted on a gold ground.

COLLECTION Victoria and Albert Museum, London.

115. The Pleasures of the Coupé

1873; size unknown; oil on canvas.

A Spanish genre scene of a couple sitting in a two-seated carriage from 1873.

PROVENANCE Sold at Christie's on 2 July 1874 for 70 guineas.

116. Madrid

c. 1873; 55 × 84″, 139.7 × 213.4 cm; oil on canvas.

A Madrid street scene, originally titled *Madrid* but later referred to as *A Street Scene in Madrid*. Referred to in W. Roberts' *Memorials of Christie's* as "*Madrid* or *Liberty of Creed*, priests discussing with the people in the streets" (vol. I, p. 274).

PROVENANCE Baron Albert Grant; sold at Christie's on 28 April 1877 for £675; Sir Julian Goldmid; sold at Christie's on 13 June 1896 for £546 as *A Street Scene in Madrid*.

LITERATURE Reitlinger 1961; Roberts 1897, vol. I, p. 274, vol. II, p. 289.

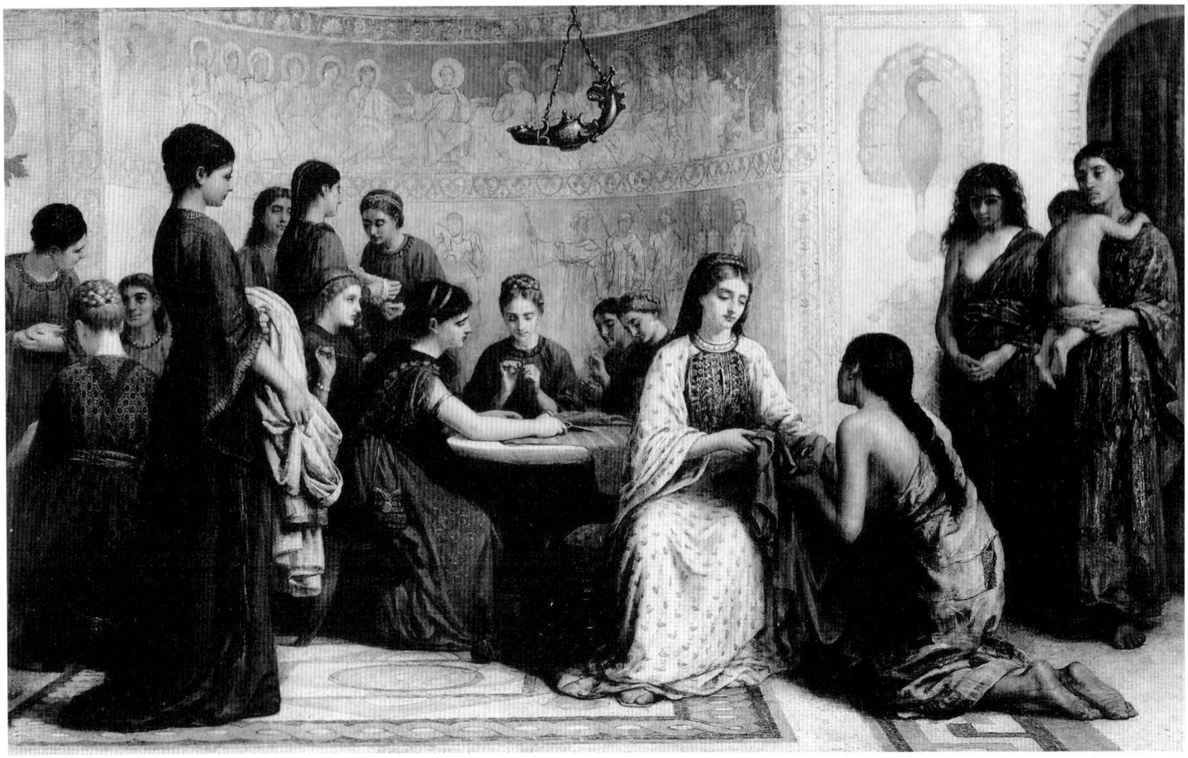

117. *A Dorcas Meeting in the 6th Century*, 1873–77
THE ART GALLERY OF NEW SOUTH WALES, SYDNEY

117. A Dorcas Meeting in the 6th Century

1873–77; 53 × 85¾", 134.6 × 217.5 cm; oil on canvas; signed and inscribed "18 EL 73 / finished 1877" on lower right.

This is an important painting which marks a transition between Long's Spanish and Classical works. Long himself refers to the work as such and the fact that he struggled with it for four years is an indication of its importance as well as the initial difficulties he had in first painting a classical subject. It was started in 1873 when Long was still primarily concerned with Spain and completed after he had established himself as a painter of Antique subjects. Within it there are elements of both periods which are not thoroughly resolved and Long remained unhappy with the final result.

The subject he chose is a Dorcas meeting in the sixth century.[1] In the foreground, the central figure, defined by her lighter costume and pallor, is handing clothes to the grateful poor. The other figures of the poor and the Dorcas Society in darker dress surround the central grouping. The decoration of the interior appears a mixture of early Christian and Spanish design, the composition a mixture of formality and informality.

In a letter to the National Gallery of New South Wales Long wrote of the work:

> It was my very first attempt at anything like a classic subject, a sort of transition picture between modern Spanish and the Antique and I am sorry to say it was considered a dead picture when shown for a few weeks at Wallis's. It then remained in my possession for some years until the sale of the 'Babylonian Marriage Market'. It was exhibited, when the dealers all wanted my works and at one of the sorties to my Studio I sold it to Mr. Vokins which I have always regretted and only lately have offered to buy it back (for the price I received for it) from Mr. Holland who has just parted with it, my object being to seriously alter or destroy it. I must confess I am very vexed for I have a very strong feeling that in a National Collection like yours it is a great honour to be represented and that only the best examples should be placed there.[2]

1. The Dorcas Society was formed in 1847. It was a ladies' society who, like their namesake, in association with the church, made and provided clothes for the poor. The sixth-century setting comes from the biblical reference of the Society's namesake mentioned in Acts, IX: 36–43: "Now there was at Joppa a certain disciple named Tabitha, which by interpretation is called Dorcas: the woman was full of good works and alms deeds which she did . . . shewing the coats and garments which Dorcas made, while she was with them".
2. Edwin Long, in a letter dated 11 July 1889, in the Art Gallery of New South Wales, Sydney.

PROVENANCE Purchased from the artist by Mr Holland; Messrs Vokins, c.1882; purchased by the London Selection Committee from Vokins in 1889 with the Edith Walker Fund for £1,400; Art Gallery of New South Wales, Sydney.
EXHIBITIONS Wallis's Gallery, London c. 1877; 'Victorian Olympians', Art Gallery of New South Wales, Sydney, 1975 (22).
LITERATURE *Magazine of Art* 1890, p. iii; *Victorian Olympians*, catalogue to an exhibition at the Art Gallery of New South Wales, Sydney, 1975, p. 20 (ill.).
COLLECTION The Art Gallery of New South Wales, Sydney.

118. At Prayer

date unknown; 50 × 34″, 127 × 86.4 cm; oil on canvas, signed with monogram.

A Spanish genre scene depicting religious devotion.

PROVENANCE Horsman Bequest in 1886 to Wolverhampton Art Gallery.
COLLECTION Wolverhampton Art Gallery.

119. Mary Clifden, Wife of 6th Viscount Clifden

date and size unknown; 50 × 40″, 127 × 101.6 cm; oil on canvas.

A three-quarter-length portrait of Mary wife of the 6th Viscount Clifden, seated and playing a Spanish guitar.

PROVENANCE Collection of Viscount Clifden, Lanhydrock House, commissioned from the artist and family by descent.

120. Peccados e Peccadillos

date and size unknown; 40 × 31″, 101.6 × 18.7 cm; oil on canvas.

A Spanish genre scene titled *Peccados e Peccadillos* ('crimes and misdemeanours').

PROVENANCE Sold at Christie's on 27 March 1897 for 16 guineas.

121. Dancers

date and size unknown; oil on canvas.

A painting of Spanish dancers.

PROVENANCE Sold to Taylor, London, in 1883.

122. Margurite

date and size unknown; oil on canvas.

A Spanish portrait of Margurite exhibited at the Edwin Long Gallery between 1893 and 1894.

EXHIBITIONS ELG 1893–94 (7).
LITERATURE ELG 1894, p. 21.

123. Christmas Day at Seville

date unknown; 52 × 84″, 132.1 × 213.4 cm; oil on canvas.

PROVENANCE Sold at Christie's on 2 May 1885 for 890 guineas.

124. Pottery Painting in Spain

date and size unknown; oil on canvas.

PROVENANCE Bought from the artist by Thomas Agnew's & Sons; sold to T. Beasley on 13 October 1873; sold at auction as *Seville Pottery* in 1903 for £190.

LITERATURE *Daily Telegraph*, unknown date, 1908.

125. Life of Guzman d'Alfarache

date and size unknown; oil on canvas.

PROVENANCE J. G. Holland in 1888.

EXHIBITIONS Exhibited in Glasgow 1888 (298).

126. A Spanish Promenade

date and size unknown; oil on canvas.

PROVENANCE Sold at Christie's on 19 July 1890 for £50 8s.

127. A Spanish Lady

date and size unknown; oil on canvas.

PROVENANCE James Dunnachie Esq.; sold at Christie's on 30 March 1895 for 15 guineas.

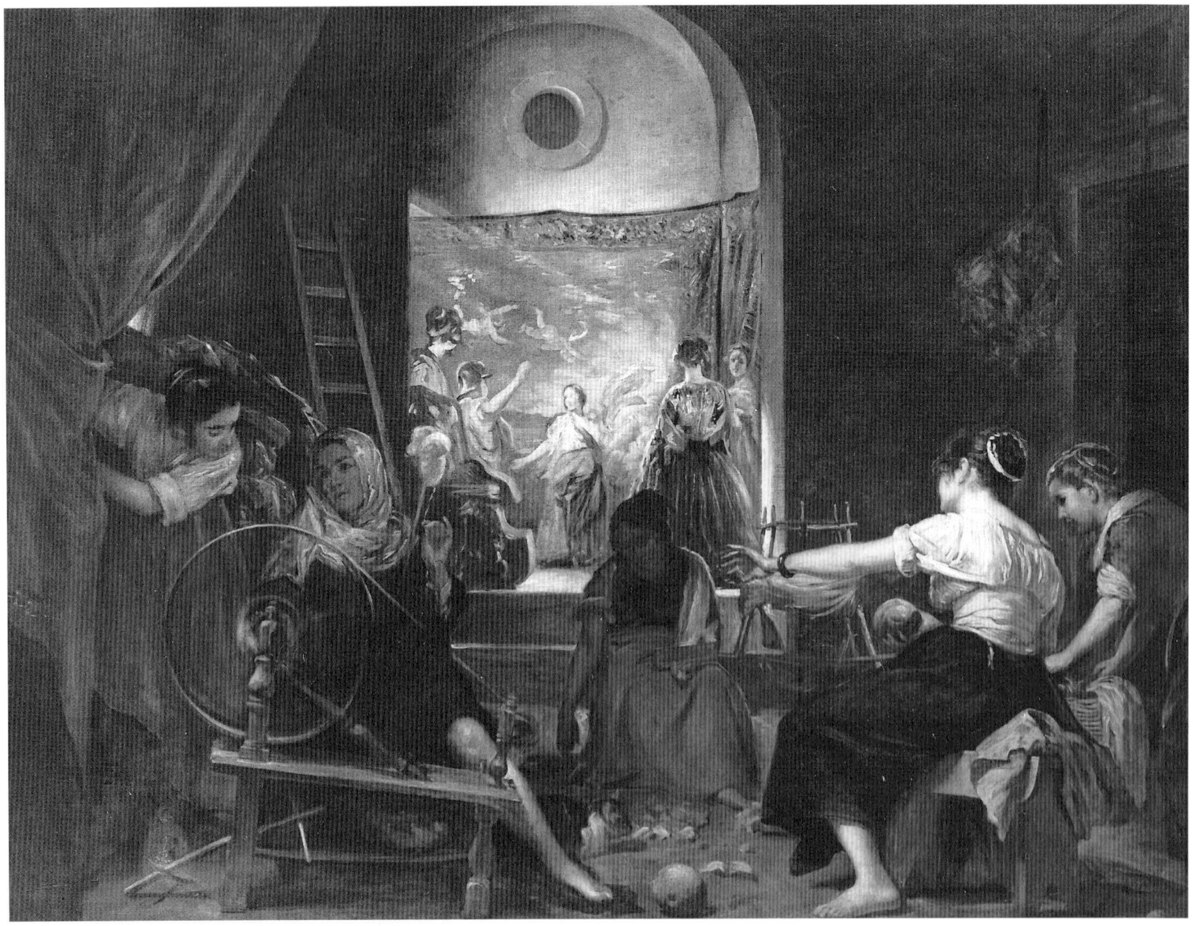

132. *Las Hilanderas (after Velasquez)*, date unknown.
THE ROYAL ACADEMY OF ARTS, LONDON

128. Vespers

date unknown; 35½ × 27½″, 90.2 × 70 cm; oil on canvas.

A Spanish genre scene around the theme of age and youth depicting an old and young woman at their devotions. The *Magazine of Art* noted in 1893: "'Vespers' by the late Edwin Long, R.A., is noteworthy for the intense feeling of devotion which the artist has thrown into a girl's face, who is seated by an old woman bending over beads. Though weak in the outline of the head, it displays much better work than Long did for many years".[1]

1. Alfred T Story, 'Mr W. Y. Baker's Collection at Streatham Hill', *Magazine of Art*, 1893, p. 232.

PROVENANCE W. Y. Baker Esq.; sold at Christie's on November 1916 for £50 8s.
LITERATURE *Magazine of Art*, 1893, p. 232.

129. Spanish Lady with a Fan

date and size unknown; oil on canvas.

PROVENANCE Sold at Willis's Rooms on 25 October 1928 for 5 guineas.

130. On the Almeda, Seville

date and size unknown; oil on canvas.

LITERATURE Quick 1931, p. 44.

131. The Secret

date unknown; 36 × 27″, 91.4 × 68.6 cm; oil on canvas.

PROVENANCE Henry Dewhurst Esq.; sold at Christie's on 19 April 1890 for 140 guineas.

132. Las Hilanderas (after Velasquez)

date unknown; 50 × 64″, 126 × 163 cm; oil on canvas.

Long's brilliant copy of Velasquez's *Las Hilanderas* (c. 1657, Prado Museum) was possibly painted in 1857 when "Long made the acquaintance of John Phillip, and the two journeyed to Spain to sit at the feet of Velasquez".[1] The work was given as a gift to the Royal Academy in 1943 by Sir George Clausen, formerly a student of Long's. It was exhibited in 1908 in an exhibition of British artists' copies. These were chiefly copies of works from private or foreign collections to allow greater access to the art-going public. The *Art Journal* wrote: "Among the copies at the recent Whitechapel Exhibition was Long's charming and brilliant transcription of 'Las Hilanderas,' which suggests capacity to walk in a very different aesthetic way from that which he actually chose. In several of his pictures of the sixties and seventies he seems, as a solemn preliminary to have invoked Velasquez as his patron saint".[2]

1. AJ, 1908, p. 175.
2. Ibid.

PROVENANCE Presented to the Royal Academy by George Clausen RA in 1943.
EXHIBITIONS Whitechapel Art Gallery, 1908 (78); 'Art into Art' exhibition, Sotheby's, 34–35 New Bond Street, London, September 1971 (216).
LITERATURE AJ, 1908, p. 175; *Art into Art*, catalogue to an exhibition held in London, 1971, p. 43.
COLLECTION Royal Academy Collection, London.

133. The Young Bride

date unknown; 36 × 23″, 91cm × 58 cm; oil on canvas, signed with monogram.

A portrait of a young bride.

PROVENANCE Sold at Pearsons, Winchester, on 25 June 1979 for £900.

EGYPT, BABYLON AND ASSOCIATESHIP TO THE ROYAL ACADEMY 1874–1880

The beginning of this period is marked with an extensive visit to Egypt and Syria. Consequently Long's output within 1874 was small as his energies were spent exploring what effectively was his new subject area. Before his visit, Spielmann tells us that Long had chosen Herodotus's description of a Babylonian marriage market as a subject for a large scale painting.[1] This work was realised in 1875 when it was exhibited at Burlington House giving unprecedented success to Long. *The Babylonian Marriage Market* is his most important painting of this period, if not his career, because it marked the real beginnings of his depictions of the ancient world and because he was considered more seriously by critics from this point on. It was also the important vehicle that raised him to the status of ARA. The majority of his works of this period, including *The Babylonian Marriage Market,* were painted at his new studio in St John's Wood at 19 Marlborough Road, the house where Sir Merton Russell-Cotes first visited Long.[2] Other key works from this period are *An Egyptian Feast* and *The Gods and Their Makers* which developed further his interest in the ancient world. Long also made more contacts and patrons at this time including the influential philanthropist Baroness Burdett-Coutts who commissioned many portraits from Long. Within this period Long finally established his own individual artistic character and style for which he subsequently became known.

1. According to Spielmann Long came across this passage in Herodotus in 1873 and was struck by its potential as a subject for a painting. Spielmann, p. 612.
2. "I drove to the artist's beautiful mansion in St. John's Wood." *Home and Abroad,* p. 708.

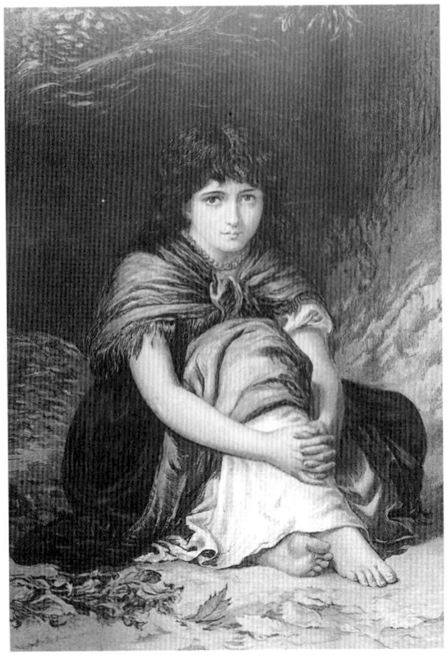

134. *M'liss*, 1874
PRINT BY LEIGHTON BROTHERS
COPYRIGHT BRITISH MUSEUM

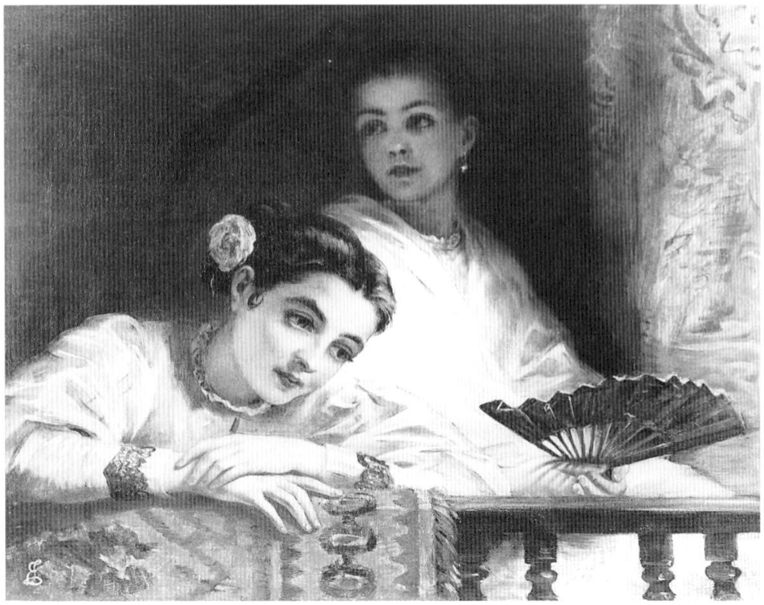

136. *The Balcony*, 1875.
CROYDON MUSEUM AND HERITAGE SERVICE

134. M'liss

1874; size unknown; oil on canvas.

Edwin Long painted very few finished paintings in 1874 as he spent most of the year travelling through Egypt and Syria. This is the only recorded painting of this year which was his only representation at the 1874 Royal Academy Exhibition, and is singularly unambitious in size and scale. The subject for the painting is taken from a novelette by the American writer, Francis Bret Harte (1836–1902). 'M'liss' is about a young girl's adventures in the gold rush community of California. The painting is a full-length portrait of her seated holding her legs with clasped hands, wearing a shawl and set in a shady grove. Harte's novels were popular and an engraving of Long's painting was made for the *Illustrated London News*.

PROVENANCE Owned by T. J. Hirst in 1887.

EXHIBITIONS RA 1874 (1354); Manchester Jubilee Exhibition 1887 (26).

LITERATURE *Illustrated London News*, Extra Supplement, 21 February 1877 (ill.); J. Edgar Pemberton, 'Harte's Life' (undated and unreferenced review in archive of the Russell-Cotes Art Gallery and Museum, Bournemouth) (ill.); Quick 1931, p. 43.

135. Sympathy

1875; 44 × 66", 122 × 168 cm; oil on canvas; signed with monogram and dated.

Although Long moved to antique subjects as the source for his paintings in 1874, he did not immediately abandon Spanish genre painting and several date from 1875. In *Sympathy* he adopts the formula that had served him successfully for many years and the painting includes the same group of children eating a water melon that he had used in *Usted Gustra?* (1869) (cat. no. 88) and *A Street Scene in Spain* (1871) (cat. no. 105). The picture depicts its title through a middle-class Spanish girl looking at three peasant children eating a melon.

PROVENANCE Sold at Parke-Bernet, New York, on 30 October 1980; in the collection of Mrs K. Lytton in 1982.

136. The Balcony

1875; 17 × 21", 43 × 53 cm; oil on canvas; signed with monogram and dated at lower left.

A Spanish genre scene depicting two young women looking out from a balcony. The first is bathed in light whilst the second is in the shadow of the room holding a fan.

PROVENANCE Given to Croydon Art Collection by William Ford Stanley, by the trustees of his estate in 1934.
EXHIBITIONS 'Croydon Art Collection', an exhibition of paintings, Croydon Art Gallery, 1988.
LITERATURE *Croydon Art Collection*, an exhibition of paintings, 1988, p. 43.
COLLECTION Croydon Art Gallery.

137. The Gypsy Mother

1875; 48 × 35", 122 × 89 cm; oil on canvas; signed and dated.

PROVENANCE Sold at auction 26 July 1988 for £900.

138. A Gypsy Encampment

1875; 48 × 34", 121 × 86 cm; oil on canvas, signed and dated "E. Long 1875".

PROVENANCE Sold at auction on 30 March 1984 for £420; sold at auction on 5 October 1984 for £420; sold at Christie's on 12 March 1992.

139. An Eastern Beggar and Child

1875; 39 × 28⅓", 99 × 72.4 cm; oil on canvas.

A painting from Long's visit to Egypt and Syria.

PROVENANCE Sold at Christie's on 22 February 1908 for £3 13s 6d.

140. Cairo

1875; 17 × 13", 43 × 33 cm; oil on canvas; signed and dated.

A small oil painted during Long's visit to Cairo in 1875.

PROVENANCE William Lee Esq.; sold at Christie's on 28 May 1883 for £157 10s.

141. Head of an Egyptian Girl, Cairo

1875; 13⅝ × 9⅝", 34.6 × 24.4 cm; oil on canvas; signed with monogram and dated.

A finished painting of an Egyptian girl painted during Long's visit to Cairo in 1875.

PROVENANCE Sold at Christie's on 11 April 1891 for £67 4s to Agnew's; sold to Frank Heallins as *Egyptian Girl, Cairo* on 2 March 1897 for £78; W. W. Sampson and Sons in 1921; sold at Christie's on 25 March 1994.

142. The Babylonian Marriage Market

1875; 68 × 120", 182.8 × 269.9 cm; oil on canvas; signed and dated.

The Babylonian Marriage Market is undoubtedly one of Long's most important works. Not only did it achieve an auction house record but elicited for Long unprecedented critical acclaim. It marked a grand change in subject and was a true turning point in Long's status and achievements. The work was commissioned by Edward Hermon MP for a reputed 1,700 guineas.[1] In 1882 the work was sold at Christie's for £6,625 (including copyright) to Thomas Holloway for his collection. This was a Victorian sale-room record for the work of any living English artist, not to be beaten until 1892.

Long took his subject from George C. Swayne's *The History of Herodotus*:

> Herodotus records one of their customs, which, whether in jest or earnest, he declares to be the wisest he ever heard of. This was their wife-auction, by which they managed to find husbands, for all their young

> women. The greatest beauty was put up first, and knocked down to the highest bidder; then the next in order of comeliness – and so on to the damsel who was equidistant between beauty and plainness, who was given away gratis. Then the least plain was put up, and knocked down to the gallant who would marry her for the smallest consideration – and so on till even the plainest was got rid of to some cynical worthy, who decidedly preferred lucre to looks. By transferring to the scale of the ill-favoured the prices paid for the fair, beauty was made to endow ugliness, and the rich man's taste was the poor man's gain.[2]

The story of its conception was described by Spielmann:

> Fired in his imagination by the types to which he had been devoting himself, and ambitious of producing a work more important than any he had yet painted, he set about the study of ancient history, so that he might combine Art and Archaeology in a more thorough manner than he or others were at the time attempting. In 1873, while reading Mr. Swayne's 'Herodotus', he was struck by the description of the ingenious process whereby the Babylonians procured husbands for their maidens . . . This subject, hitherto untouched, was difficult of realisation. It was so full of promise that the artist clung to it for a couple of years or so without being able at the time to realise the composition of the scene. Suddenly, one night, whilst playing whist, as I have heard him tell, the whole picture, much as it stands now, with the figures of the maidens all in a row, flashed across his mind, and he could hardly sleep that night for the eagerness with which he waited for the morning.[3]

Long's conscientiousness in the research he carried out for his historical paintings can be seen in earlier paintings such as *The Suppliants* (1872). With *The Babylonian Marriage Market* however this was of a different order, as Spielmann was to later stress. Long had made an extensive tour of Egypt and Syria in 1874–75 which almost certainly added to his knowledge of Ancient Babylon. Visits to the British Museum and his use of Rawlinson's extensive texts and illustrations[4] reinforced his site visits. As Spielmann and many other critics were to stress, Long had, they believed, made possible a harmonious connection between art and archaeology. Ruskin's writing on the painting in 1875 reinforced this view:

> A painting of great merit, and well deserving purchase by the Anthropological Society. For the varieties of character in the heads are rendered with extreme subtlety; while, as a mere piece of painting, the work is remarkable, in the modern school, for its absence of affectation: there is no insolently indulged indolence nor vulgarity asserted dexterity – the painting is good throughout, and unobtrusively powerful.[5]

Ruskin's voice clearly aided the painting's critical success, although most of the contemporary journals reacted favourably. On the strength of it Long made Associateship to the Royal Academy. *The Art Journal* commented, "The picture, in our eyes, is historic in the best sense, and does honour to the British school".[6] *The Athenaeum* noted, "The story is told in a dramatic way, so that within the range of the painter's intentions here is another complete sucess".[7] *The Times*, that "the painter has hit a popular subject which a less restrained – or what French critics would be apt to call prudish-taste in treatment might have easily made cynical in the worst sense of the word".[8] Despite its popularity it was not until 1889 that a mass-produced image of the painting was made available. This was a photogravure produced by the Fine Art Society that went against the wishes of Long who wrote: "what I am really anxious about is that if it be done at all it may be done well and I know it would be very costly to prepare it properly. Photogravure would I am quite sure be an injury to the picture and me".[9]

The painting's influence on the development of Long's work was immense. He had achieved a grand vision of Babylon, enriched with archaeological detail with a finely composed and understated theatricality. It even became the source for a seven-and-a-half minute silent sequence in D. W. Griffith's film *Intolerence* (1916). The marriage market scene in the film although displaying a variety of different moods, shows remarkable fidelity to the details in the painting. The auctioneer and the waiting women show the same poses and expressions in the painting and are dressed in the same costumes. The background tiles, the slave block and other set details show Griffith's use of the painting.[10]

1. *The Artist*, 1 June 1882, p. 173.
2. George C. Swayne, *The History of Herodotus* (London, 1870), pp. 36–37.
3. Spielmann 1888, p. 612.
4. George Rawlinson, *The Five Great Monarchies of the Ancient Eastern World; or the history, geography and antiquities of Chaldea, Assyria, Babylon, Media and Persia*, 4 vols. (London, 1862–67).

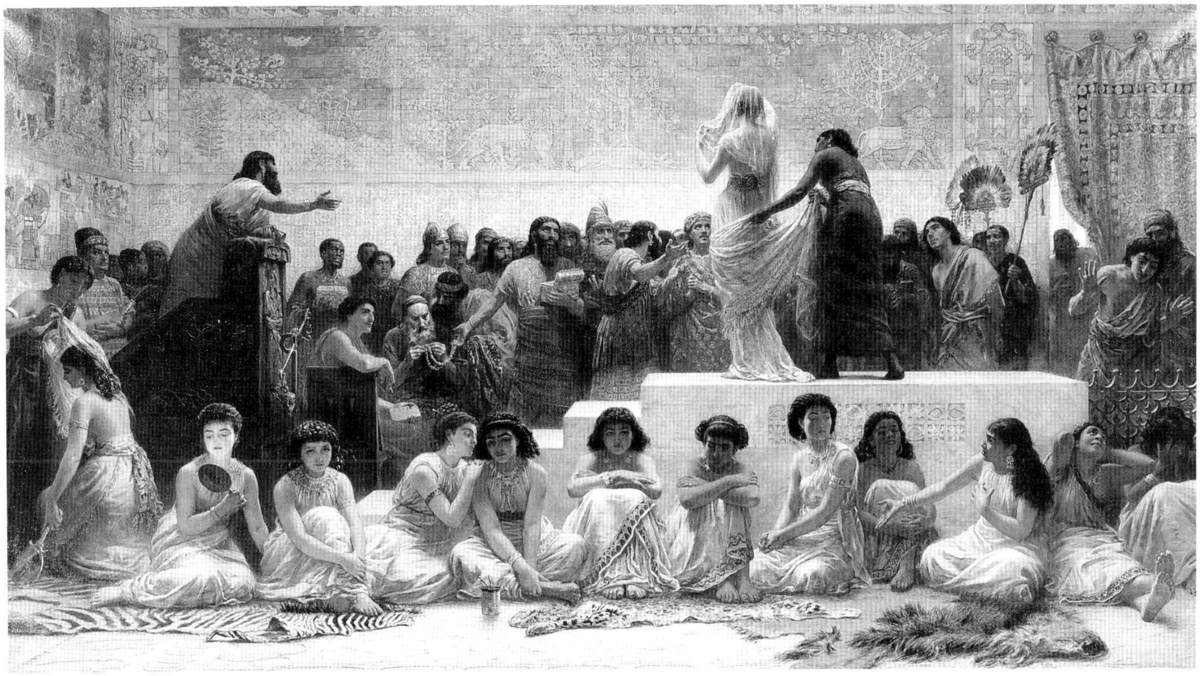

142. *The Babylonian Marriage Market*, 1875.
ROYAL HOLLOWAY & BEDFORD NEW COLLEGE, SURREY. PHOTOGRAPH BRIDGEMAN ART LIBRARY.

5. John Ruskin, *Academy Notes*, 1875, 1902 complete ed, pp. 233–35.
6. AJ, 1875, p. 250.
7. Ath., 1 May 1875), p. 591.
8. *The Times*, 24 May 1875, p. 5.
9. Letter by Edwin Long, dated 14 May 1889, in the Royal Holloway archive, London.
10. See Bernard Hanson, 'D. W. Griffith: Some Sources', *Art Bulletin*, no. 54 (December 1972), pp. 493–515.

PROVENANCE Commissioned by Edward Hermon MP of Wyfold Court, Henley-on-Thames for a reputed £1,700; sold at Christie's on 13 May 1882 (with copyright) for £6,615 to Martin for Thomas Holloway.

EXHIBITIONS R.A. 1875 (482); Manchester Royal Jubilee Exhibition (540); Guildhall Exhibition 1897 (40); 'This Brillant Year – Queen Victoria's Jubilee 1887', RA 1977 (150); Agnew's 1981 (25).

LITERATURE *Academy*, 8 May 1875, p. 486; *Academy Notes* 1875, p. 34, p. 35 (ill.); *Annual Register*, 1875, p. 374; *Apollo*, no. 111 (June 1980), p. 452 (ill.); Walter Armstrong, *Celebrated Pictures exhibited at the Manchester Royal Jubilee Exhibition*, Manchester 1888, p. 45; *Art and Artists*, no. 12 (May 1977), pp. 14–15 (ill.); *Art Bulletin*, no. 54 (December 1972), p. 510 (ill.); AJ, 1875, p. 250; AJ, 1882, p. 317; AJ, 1908, p. 175; *The Artist*, 1 June 1882, p. 173; Arts Council of Great Britain, *Great Victorian Pictures*, 1978, p. 12, p. 45; Ath., 1 May 1875, pp. 590–91; *Blackwood's Magazine*, June 1875, p. 763; *Bulletin (R-C)*, vol. 11, no. 2 (June 1923), p. 16; A. C. R. Carter, *Let Me Tell You* (London: Hutchinson, 1940), pp. 37–40; Chapel 1982, pp. 109–9 (ill.); Ernest Chesneau, *The English School of Painting* (London: Cassell, 1885), p. 268; Chester 1908, p. 339 (ill.), and p. 349; *The Examiner*, 1 May 1875, p. 501; *The Examiner*, 22 May 1875, p. 585; John Forbes-Robertson, 'Art at the Manchester Jubilee Exhibition', *Magazine of Art*, 1887, p. 283; *The Graphic*, 1 May 1875, p. 415; *The Graphic*, 29 May 1875, p. 518; John Evans Hodgson, *Fifty Years of British Art* (London and Manchester: John Heywood, 1887), pp. 82–83; *Illustrated*

London News, 1 May 1875, p. 415; Kestner, 1989, p. 229, p. 231; Jeremy Maas, *Victorian Painters* (London: Barrie and Jenkins, 1969), p. 184 (ill.); Jeremy Maas, *The Victorian Art World in Photographs* (London: Barrie and Jenkins, 1984), p. 42; Quick 1931, p. 5, p. 13 (ill.), p. 44; Harry Quilter, *Preferences in Art, Life and Literature* (London, 1892), pp. 317–19; Reitlinger 1961, pp. 159–60 (ill.); Roberts 1897, vol. 1, p. 328; John Ruskin, *Academy Notes*, 1875 (London: George & Allen, 1902 edition of complete works), pp. 233–35; *Saturday Review*, 1 May 1875, p. 567; *Saturday Review*, 15 May 1875, p. 625; *The Spectator*, 22 May 1875, pp. 661–62; Spielmann 1888, p. 612; *The Studio*, no. 162 (November 1961), p. 193 (ill.); A. G. Temple, *The Art of Painting in the Queen's Reign* (London, 1897), pp. 291–92; *The Times*, 1 May 1875, p. 12, p. 24; *The Times*, 24 May 1875, p. 5; *The Times*, 16 May 1882, p. 4; Walkley 1994, p. 109; Gleeson White, *The Master Painters of Britain* (Birmingham: Combridge, 1910), p. 218; Christopher Wood, *Dictionary of Victorian Painters* (Woodbridge: Antique Collectors Club, 1971), p. 91, p. 319 (ill.); Christopher Wood, *Olympian Dreamers* (London: Constable, 1983), p. 146, p. 205, p. 253.

COLLECTION Royal Holloway College Picture Collection, London.

143. Thisbe (1)

1875; 55½ × 36″, 141 × 91.4 cm; oil on canvas; signed and dated.

Long's first painting of Thisbe uses his knowledge of ancient Babylon to depict her seated on a wall of Babylonian wall painting. Thisbe is depicted full-length dressed in robes and an amulet, leaning to hear the whispers of Pyramus through the chink in the wall. Long took his subject from Ensden's translation of Ovid quoted in the Christie's sale catalogue that accompanied the work in 1908:

> In Babylon where first her queen, for state,
> Rais'd walls of brick maginificently great.
> Liv'd Pyramus and Thisbe . . .
> A closer Neighbourhood was never known,
> Tho' two the houses, yet the roof was one.
> When the division wall was built,
> A chink was left, the cement unobserv'd to shrink;
> So slight the cranny that it still had been
> For centuries unclosed, became unseen.
> But oh, what thing so small, so secret lies,
> Which 'scapes, if formed for love, a lover's eyes".[1]

Long produced a copy of this *Thisbe* and painted a later version in 1884.

1. Ovid, *Metamorphoses*, book IV, translated by Ensden. This translation was first published in 1717 and went through many editions.

PROVENANCE Bought by Thomas Agnew & Sons on 23 July 1889; sold to Stephen G. Holland on 24 July 1889 for £1,350; sold at Christie's in June 1908 for £346 10s to Agnew's.

143.1 Thisbe (2)

1875; 37¼ × 22″, 94.6 × 55.8 cm; oil on canvas; signed and dated.

A smaller copy of Long's Babylonian *Thisbe* sold at Christie's in 1983.

PROVENANCE Sold at Christie's on 23 November 1983 for £6,000.

144. Ernie

1875; size unknown; oil on canvas.

Ernie was the only picture by Long to accompany *The Babylonian Marriage Market* at Burlington House in 1875.

EXHIBITIONS RA 1875 (117).

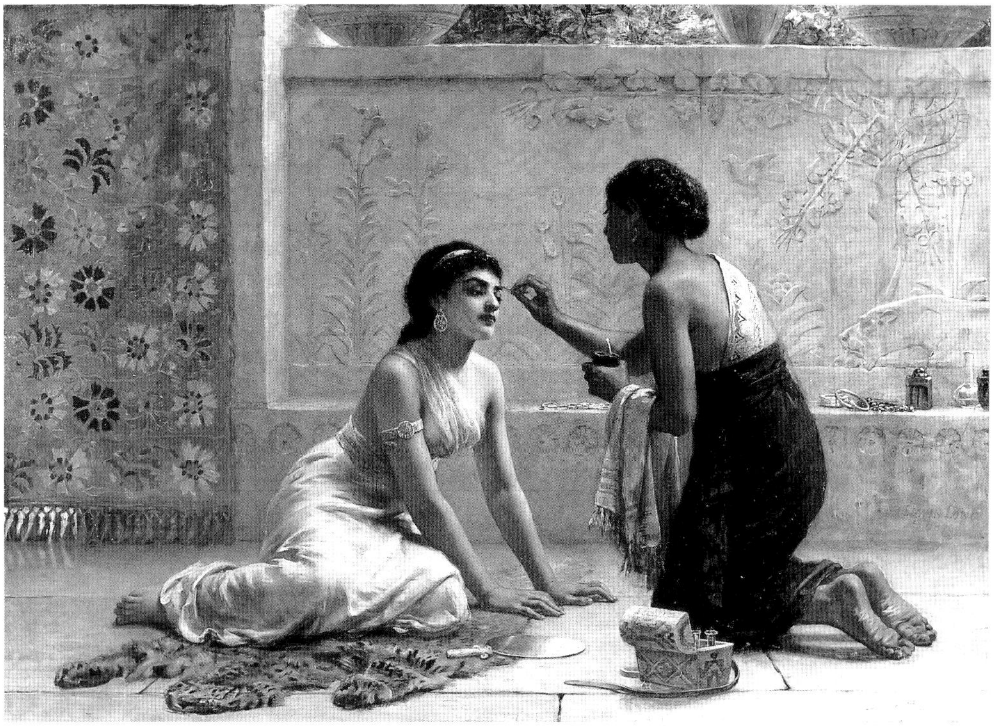

145. *An Ancient Custom*, 1876.
COURTESY OF PHILLIPS FINE ART AUCTIONEERS, LONDON

145. An Ancient Custom (1)

1876; 39½ × 54", 100cm × 138 cm; oil on canvas; signed and dated.

A scene depicting two central figures, a mistress and servant. The mistress is more lavishly dressed, seated on a leopard skin rug while the black servant applies perfume and make-up. The background shows a Babylonian relief and textiles. The *Academy Notes* described it as "Two figures nearly life-size; A Nubian girl on her knees painting the eyebrows of her young Egyptian mistress.!"[1] According to Long the painting was "the original study" for *Esther* "on a smaller scale, and afterwards completed for the purpose of engraving".[2]

1. *Academy Notes* 1877, p. 21.
2. Edwin Long, letter to *The Times*, 7 June 1879, p. 8.

PROVENANCE Sold in 1897 for £400; bought by Thomas Agnew & Sons on 25 June 1907; sold to L. R. Erskine on 15 June 1908; sold at Phillips on 31 October 1989 for £29,000.

EXHIBITIONS RA 1877 (163).

LITERATURE *Academy Notes* 1877, p. 21; AJ, 1877, p. 197; Chester 1908, p. 333 (ill.); *Daily Telegraph*, date unknown, 1908; Kestner, p. 229; Quick 1931, p. 19 (ill.), p. 45; *The Times*, 7 June 1879, p. 8.

145.1 An Ancient Custom (2)

1877; 28 × 37½", 71.1 × 95.2 cm; oil on canvas.

A copy of the 1877 Royal Academy painting of the same name. Long notes in a letter to *The Times* that "with the exception of one other picture entitled 'An Ancient Custom' . . . I have not made any duplicates of my pictures, or any portions of them, for some years past".[1]

1. *The Times*, 7 June 1879, p. 8.

PROVENANCE R. A. Cosier Esq; sold in 1887 for £680; Stephen G. Holland Esq.; bought by Thomas Agnew & Sons at Christie's in June 1908 for £178 10s.

LITERATURE Roberts 1897, vol. II, p. 119–200; *The Times*, 7 June 1879, p. 8.

146. Bethesda

1876; 105 × 69", 266.7 × 175.2 cm; oil on canvas.

Exhibited at the Royal Academy exhibition of 1876 as *Bethesda*, but ever since the painting has been referred to as *The Pool of Bethesda*. Its subject is taken from the Gospel of St. John:

> Now there is at Jerusalem by the sheep market a pool, which is called in the Hebrew tongue Bethesda, having five porches. In these lay a great multitude of impotent folk, of blind, halt, withered, waiting for the moving of the water. For an angel went down at a certain season into the pool, and troubled the water: whosoever then first after the troubling of the water stepped in it was made whole of whatsoever disease he had.[1]

The picture depicts the still pool with the prominent figure of a mother with her child in the centre, lighter than the other figures staring heavenward. In the background a sick child is being carried to the pool, and to the left the figure of an old man is crawling to reach it. The *Art Journal* bestowed praise on the work writing:

> With 'Bethesda' we are much pleased. The face of the mother in the centre of the work beams with faith and holiest devotion. To some, the picture may seem scarcely equal of the "Babylonian Marriage Market" of last year; but to others, and these we suppose to be the more thoughtful, it will appear as a scriptural subject of beauty and significance.[2]

The Times wrote at length of the painting. The *Babylonian Marriage Market* had caused a sensation at the previous year's Academy and critics were anxious to assess Long's development. The subject of Bethesda was a popular one although they felt that it "will hardly disturb the recollection of his 'Babylonian Marriage Market'. It has the merit of unhackneyed treatment of an often painted subject . . . ".[3] It cast doubt upon Long's effectiveness in expressing the spirit of the story and characterisation of its main protagonists. It found within it, however, cleverness of composition and masterful handling of the still pool and its reflections. The *Magazine of Art* in its 1891 obituary on Long recalled the painting as one of Long's key paintings: "'Bethesda' appeared in 1876, and greatly moved many who did not affect high standards of invention, poetry, or art. Mr Ruskin, to the immense surprise of his followers, testified more or less equivocally in its favour".[4] Blackburn's *Academy Notes* found that the painting was a

> serious and, in some respects, important contribution to the religious art of our time . . . The costumes and votive offerings that hang round the pillar have all been studied in the East. The picture is most successful in the face of the principal figure . . . We hear it is to be engraved.[5]

According to Long's notes the work was painted between 14 January and 3 April 1876. He wrote of the painting: "Painted on a rough French canvas, covered with three solid coats of Flake White more than two years ago. The last coat yellowish. Copal, oil, turpentine with also a little Robinson's medium in parts. Indian, the principal red in flesh a good deal of Wharmrins ash, other colours. Flesh laid in without much detail with solid grey rather lighter than tone required finished over this as much as possible at once".[6]

1. John, v: 2–4.
2. AJ, 1876, p. 263.
3. *The Times*, 8 May 1876, p. 9.
4. *Magazine of Art*, July 1891, p. xl.
5. *Academy Notes* 1876, p. 557.
6. Long's notes for the 1876 Royal Academy exhibition, in the Royal Academy Library.

EXHIBITIONS RA 1876 (891).

LITERATURE *Academy Notes* 1876, p. 57 (ill.); AJ, 1876, p. 263; Chester 1908, p. 337 (ill.), p. 343; *Magazine of Art*, July 1891, p. xl; *The Times*, 8 May 1876, p. 9; Quick 1931, p. 19 (ill.), p. 44.

147. Interested

1877; size unknown; oil on canvas.

PROVENANCE Henry Dewhurst Esq.; sold at Christie's on 19 April 1890 for 19 guineas.

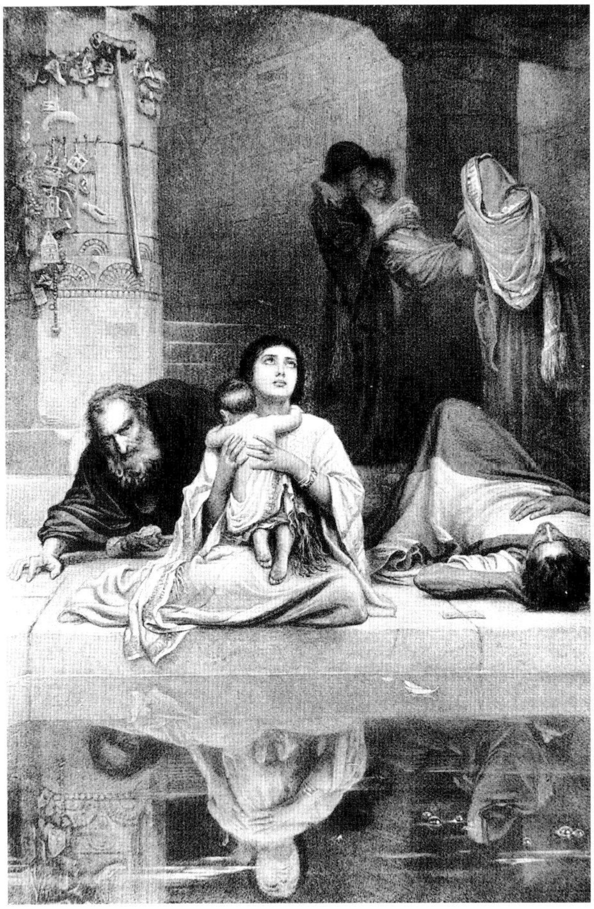

146. *Bethesda*, 1876.

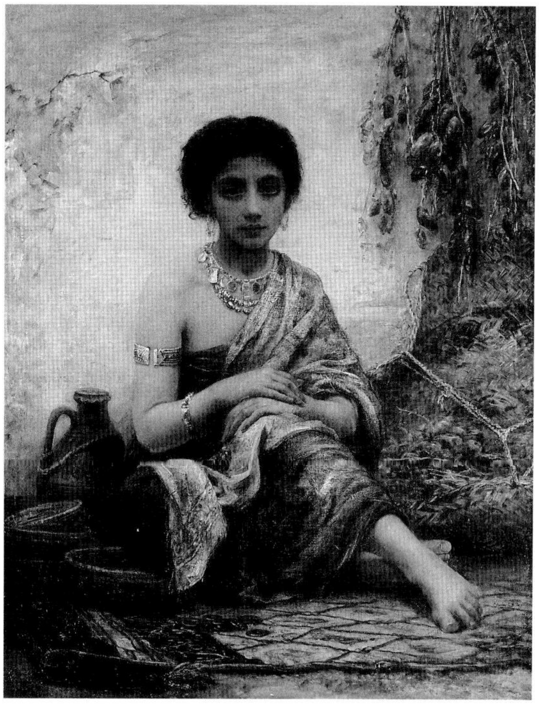

148. *The Date Seller*, 1877.
COURTESY OF SOTHEBY'S, LONDON

148. The Date Seller (1)

1877; 41½ × 23½", 105.4 × 59.7 cm; oil on canvas.

A young Eastern girl seated and selling dates.

PROVENANCE Sold at Christie's on 18 July 1919 for £75 12s to Sampson; sold at Christie's on 28 November 1990.

148.1 The Date Seller (2)

1877; 29 × 22", 74 × 56.3 cm; oil on canvas; signed and dated.

A slightly smaller version of a young Eastern girl seated and selling dates.

PROVENANCE Sold at Woolley and Wallis, Salisbury, on 23 April 1986 as *The Date Girl* for £2,000; sold at Christie's on 25 July 1986 for £3,000.

149. A.M.F.R.

1877; size unknown; oil on canvas.

A small sketch portrait of a young woman in a grey dress.

EXHIBITIONS RA 1877 (30).

LITERATURE AJ, 1877, p. 197.

150. An Egyptian Feast

1877; 74½ × 150", 189.2 × 381 cm; oil on canvas; signed with monogram and dated bottom right.

An Egyptian Feast marked Long's return to Herodotus for his major picture of 1877. It is of a similar size to the *Babylonian Marriage Market* and seems to display Long's desire to repeat the success of his 1875 painting. In this case he uses Herodotus to produce a scene from ancient Egypt: "In social meetings among the rich, when the banquet is ended, slaves bring round to the several guests a bier on which there is a wooden image of the corpse, carved and painted to resemble nature as nearly as possible. As it is shown to each guest in turn, the attendant says, 'Gaze here, and drink and be merry; for when you die, such will you be . . . "[1]

In its composition, size and subject the painting is a sequel to the *Babylonian Marriage Market.* Both are rituals using Herodutus, overtly theatrical in their composition and showing Long's desire to present a well-researched reconstruction of ancient history. It is his first major tackling of ancient Egypt as his subject; up until now his depictions of the ancient world had focused on Babylon.[2] Long in this picture is also rather freer in his use of Herodotus than he had been in his earlier work. Its critical reception similarly reflected that of the *Babylonian Marriage Market. The Times* wrote at length:

> In this room is what will no doubt be the picture of the year – E. Long's Egyptian Feast, worthy for dimensions and pictorial merits to rank with his Babylonian slave market, the 'sensation' of two years ago. We have all read of the death's head at the Egyptian feast. This momento of the transitoriness of earthly delights was no death's head, but the wooden image of a mummy, here shown as a large mummified corpse, drawn round by slaves, preceded by one who proclaims to each group of feasters, 'Look here; drink and be merry; for when you die, such will you too be.' Herodotus indicates a smaller image than Mr. Long has painted, describing it as of a cubit, or two cubits long, at most, and carried round by one man, who preached the sermon; not a full-sized mummy dragged round on a painted and carved boat of Osiris by a team of slaves, preceded by a preacher, as we see here. No doubt the alteration supplied the painter with valuable pictorial material and motive; and seeing that he has seated his feasters in a gigantic hall, decorated with whole ranges of hieroglyphs, such as are found in the temples and tombs on the banks of the Nile, a hall of dimensions such as we have not reason to think would have been possible in any ordinary, or even palatial Egyptian house, he may have felt there was room for such a slave team and full-sized mummy as he had used to point the moral of the ghastly emblem. Allowing for this exaggeration, Mr. Long's work is worthy of the highest praise for the cleverness in the arrangement of the guests, not seated tamely at long boards, but gracefully and variously seated in little groups of both sexes and all ages, with youth and beauty predominating, round those light carved tables of palm wood, of which so many have been brought to light from the tombs; the judicious treatment of the hieroglyph painted walls in the background, so as to get all the effect of their bright, pleasant, and characteristic colour without interference with the figures; the ingenious variety of grouping, combined with the symmetry essential to the subject, and the interest of the expressions, which it is a pleasant occupation to decipher, from that of the white-headed 'jeune femme', a Lady Kew of the 'beau monde' of Thebes or Memphis, who takes the lesson of the mummy even ostentatiously to heart – as one who is very far indeed, as yet, from that sort of thing – to that of the lovely girl on her left hand who sits with serene, wide-open eyes and an innocent smile as if the lesson of mortality, instead of finding an echo in her heart, left only wonder whether there can be a world of sadness and shadows and oblivion beyond this brightness and joy and love. But we might go the round of the picture in this way, reading the expressions of the various guests. The group of musicians on the left makes an admirable pendant to the feasters, and gracefully completes the composition.[3]

The picture displays a wealth of archaeological detail in the Egyptian murals, architecture and mass of objects, from the musical instruments to the statuary around the hall. Long's sources for these were various, and include objects observed in the British Museum, articles on Ancient Egyptian excavations and books on the subject, in particular J. G. Wilkinson's *Manners and Customs of the Ancient Eygptians* (6 vols., London: 1837). The *Art Journal* praised this aspect of Long's work: "There is the great outcome of a teeming imagination, constrained and guided by a rigid scholarship . . . The merits of Mr. Long's work lie in his archaeological knowledge as already hinted."[4] Spielmann noted later that "In this work, rising higher than he had hitherto touched, he carried his antiquarian research to its furthermost point. Indeed, the artist went so far as to introduce a pineapple into the feast on the authority of a certain recent traveller, who had discovered modelled representations of the fruit in recently-unearthed tombs, which proved

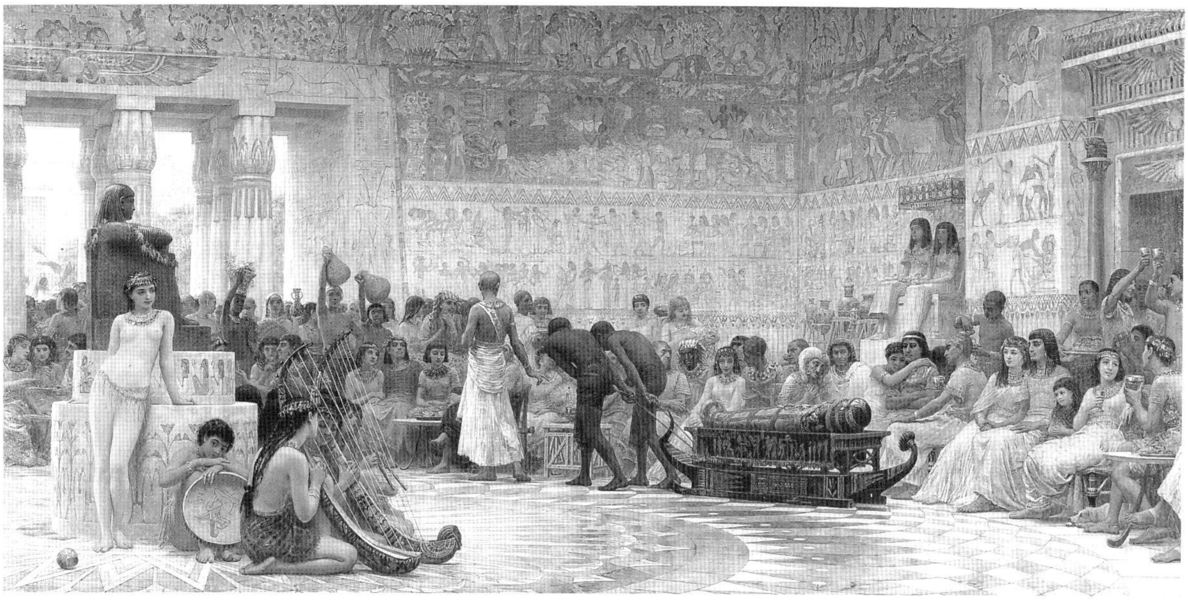

150. *An Egyptian Feast*, 1877.
CARTWRIGHT HALL ART GALLERY, BRADFORD. PHOTOGRAPH BRIDGEMAN ART LIBRARY

them to have been not unknown at the period of the picture".[5] The painting received widespread admiration across the board of criticism; *The Athenaeum* called it "a most important and attractive picture . . . ",[6] whilst *Punch* wrote: "An Egyptian Feast by E. Long, A. The mummy at the feast reminds the revellers of their fate. The motto should have been, 'Ars longa, vita brevis.' And a very fine specimen of the ars longa, too".[7] A print of the work was produced by the Fine Art Society.

1. George C. Swayne, *The History of Herodotus* (London, 1870).
2. Such as *Babylonian Marriage Market* (1875), *Thisbe* (1875) and *An Ancient Custom* (1876).
3. *The Times*, 5 May 1877, p. 12.
4. AJ, 1877, p. 197.
5. Spielmann 1888, p. 612.
6. Ath., 5 May 1977, p. 582.
7. *Punch*, 19 May 1877, p. 217.

PROVENANCE In the possession of J. Lord, Maloise Hall; Cartwright Hall Art Gallery, Bradford.

EXHIBITIONS RA 1877 (83); Rodman's Art Gallery, 41 Donegall Place, Belfast, 29 March–13 April 1878 (probably part of a solo tour of the British Isles); Royal Yorkshire Jubilee Exhibition, Saltaire, 1887 (421).

LITERATURE *Academy Notes* 1877, pp. 15–16 (ill.); AJ, 1877, p. 197; Ath., 5 May 1877, p. 582; Chester 1908, p. 338 (ill.), pp. 349–50; *Daily Telegraph*, date unknown, 1908; Kestner 1989, p. 229; LG 1885, p. 15, p. 19; *Magazine of Art*, July 1891, p. xl; *Punch*, 12 May 1877, p. 209; *Punch*, 19 May, p. 217; Quick 1931, p. 4, p. 8, p. 18 (ill.), p. 45; Spielmann 1888, p. 612; *The Times*, 5 May 1877, p. 12; Gleeson White, *The Master Painters of Britain* (Birmingham: Combridge, 1910), p. 218.

COLLECTION Cartwright Hall Art Gallery, Bradford.

151. Rich and Poor

c. 1877; size unknown; oil on canvas.

A genre painting from around 1877 .

PROVENANCE Bought by Thomas Agnew & Sons from H. Edwards in 1877; sold to Hauldsworth on 30 June 1877 for £126; sold to R. Humphrey on 6 December 1888.

152. Queen Esther (1) (*also called* The Favourite)

1877–78; 84 × 65", 214.5 × 166 cm; oil on canvas; signed and dated.

Two of Long's paintings exhibited in the 1879 Royal Academy exhibition were illustrations of the queens from the book of Esther. Although painted in different years and not exhibited side by side at Burlington House, *Vashti* (October 1878–April 1879) was painted as a companion piece to *Queen Esther* (December 1877–June 1878). The reviews of 1879 were keen to note that: "These important pictures, in which there is much dignity and beauty of design should be examined together. It is to be regretted they are not in the same gallery".[1] The backgrounds for both paintings are taken from Esther: "Where were white, green, and blue, hangings, fastened with cords of fine linen and purple to silver rings and pillars of marble; the beds were of gold and silver, upon a pavement of red, and blue, and white, and black, marble".[2]

The other sources of historical details are various but primarily volume III of George Rawlinson's *The Five Great Monarchies of the Ancient Eastern World* (1862–67). The walls are the Persepolis reliefs from Layard's work at Nineveh. Many of the objects, like the stool and jewel box are nineteenth century. The dresses were taken from the Talmud and Apocrypha "in both of which 'Esther' is said to have been accompanied by two of her maidens, on one she leaned and the other bore up her train".[3] In scale and composition the paintings are almost identical and it seems unusual that they were hung in separate galleries at the Royal Academy exhibition. They depict two queens of the Persian king Ahasuerus, one about to be divorced, the other to become Queen. The *Magazine of Art* compared the two principal figures: "Both pictures are eminently attractive studies of feminine beauty, with which is combined much emotional expression. Esther is the more solemnly heroic, Vashti the more majestic".[4] *Esther* takes the point in the story where she enters the King's palace unbidden and faces death for the chance to plead for her people. She stares right out from the canvas with grim determination, clasping her hands tightly together. The *Art Journal* of 1879 wrote:

> We may say at once that we have nothing but praise for the 'Esther'. She is dark-eyed, fair-skinned, and exceedingly comely. As one of her maids is about to veil her, she sits passively on her ebony and ivory stool, and, with her fingers interlaced at her side, she looks at you from out of her melancholy yet resolute eyes, and says in low, measured tones "and so will I go in unto the king, which is not according to the law: and if I perish, I perish" (Esther, iv: 16).[5]

The popularity of the paintings was made clear in a review in *The Graphic* which wrote: "The grace of Mr. Long's central figures, particularly the Esther, who is charming, the cleverness of grouping and comeliness of the attendants, the beautiful painting of backgrounds and accessories . . . carry the day over the elaborate drawings of Elijah's torso [Leighton], and the classic graces of Mr. Poynters's nymphs . . . "[6]

Long saw his *An Ancient Custom* as a preliminary to *Esther*. In costume and in subject it has its precedents but differs in its scale and ambition. Long noted the technique he used in painting the skin, familiar to many of his paintings: "Solid impasto on the flesh, prepared light warm grey afterwards finished with all colours laid on thinly so as to let the first painting through". Painted between December 1877 and June 1878.[7]

1. *Academy Notes* 1879, p. 62.
2. Esther, I: 6.
3. Taddy Thomson, records of his meeting with Long about *Esther*, National Gallery of Victoria, Melbourne. He also notes that Esther's face was painted from a Jewish model and her body completed from a second model.
4. *Magazine of Art*, 1879, p. 127.
5. AJ, 1879, p. 127.
6. *The Graphic*, 17 May 1879, p. 490.
7. Long's notes for the 1879 RA exhibition, in the Royal Academy Library.

PROVENANCE Sold at Christie's in February 1887 to Thomas Agnew & Sons; sold to A. Henderson on 28 February 1887; Gregoire Galleries Inc; sold at Parke-Bernet, New York on 25 November 1969 for £510 as *The Favorite: A Young Oriental Woman with Two Servants in a Harem.*

EXHIBITIONS RA 1879 (102).

LITERATURE *Academy Notes* 1879, p. 17 (ill.), p. 62; *Art International*, no. 15 (February 1971), p. 77 (ill.); AJ, 1879, p. 127; *Art Quarterly*, vol. 35, no. 3 (Autumn 1972), p. xv (ill.); Ath., 3 May 1879, p. 572;

Ath., 17 May 1879, p. 637; Chester 1908, p. 343, pp. 346–47; *The Graphic*, 17 May 1879, p. 490; *The Graphic*, 9 June 1888, p. 612; *Magazine of Art*, 1878, p. f; *Magazine of Art*, 1879, p. 127; Quick 1931, p. 5, p. 44; Spielmann 1888, p. 612; *The Times*, 3 May 1879, p. 5; *The Times*, 6 June 1879, p. 10; *The Times*, 7 June 1879, p. 8.

152.1 Queen Esther (2)

1878; 84 × 67", 312.5 × 170.3 cm; oil on canvas; signed "Edwin Long 1878 1–1".

A replica of *Queen Esther* commissioned on 13 April 1878 by Alfred Taddy Thomson for the Art Gallery of Victoria, Melbourne, Australia, and completed in September of that year. Long wrote of the two versions in a letter to *The Times*: "The two paintings are not nearly so identical as your correspondent supposes. The replica is of a different proportion and the attendant figures are painted from different models. Esther herself is also painted from life, and as a necessary sequence, varied in expression".[1]

1. Edwin Long, letter to *The Times*, 7 June 1879, p. 8.

PROVENANCE Commissioned in 1878 by A. T. Thomson from Long for the Art Gallery of Victoria, Melbourne, Australia; purchased by him in 1879 for £1,600.

EXHIBITIONS 'Victorian Olympians', Art Gallery of New South Wales, June–July 1975 (23).

LITERATURE E. La Touche Armstrong, quoted in National Gallery of Victoria collection catalogue, 1894, p. 39; *Book of the Public Library* (Melbourne, 1906), vol. 1; *Victorian Olympians*, catalogue to an exhibition at the Art Gallery of New South Wales, Sydney, 1975 (ill.); *The Times*, 6 June 1879, p. 10; *The Times*, 7 June 1879, p. 8.

COLLECTION National Gallery of Victoria, Melbourne.

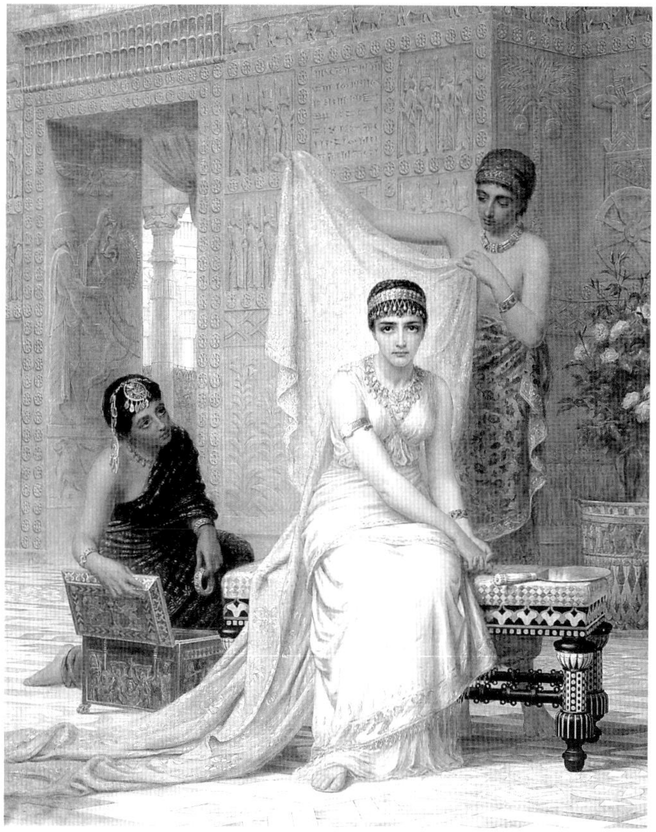

152.1 *Queen Esther*, 1878.
PURCHASED WITH THE ASSISTANCE OF A GOVERNMENT GRANT, 1879, NATIONAL GALLERY OF VICTORIA, MELBOURNE.

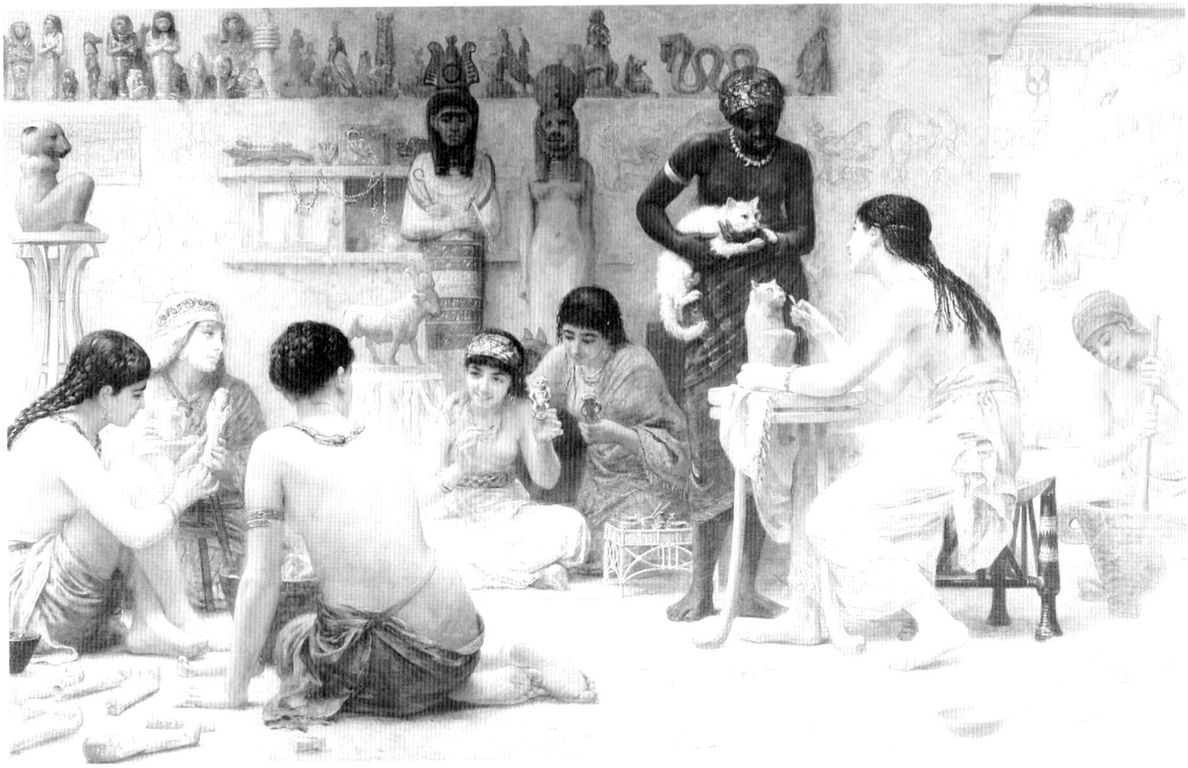

153. *The Gods and Their Makers*, 1878.
TOWNELEY HALL ART GALLERY & MUSEUMS, BURNLEY BOROUGH COUNCIL
PHOTOGRAPH BRIDGEMAN ART LIBRARY

153. The Gods and Their Makers

1878; 56 × 88", 142.2 × 233.4 cm; oil on canvas; signed and dated, upper right.

The painting was exhibited at Burlington House with the following lines from Juvenal:

> All know what monsters Egypt venerates.
> It worships crocodiles, or it adores
> The snake gorged ibis; and the sacred ape
> Graven in gold is seen . . . whole cities pray
> To cats and fishes, or the dog invoke.[1]

The picture shows the craftswomen who are producing the idols that 'whole cities' pray to. The workshop contains effigies, canoptic jars, *ushabtis* and amulets. The famous Egyptian stool from the British Museum is present in the picture which Long was to use again in *Love's Labour Lost.* This display of false idolatry that so fascinated Long is most in evidence in the central figure modelling from a cat held by a Nubian. The title itself and the light-heartedness of the scene suggests amusement in the worship of gods in the form of beasts, particularly that of the cat. As *The Times* wrote:

> . . . girls in the employment of the sacred image maker in their 'atelier', on the walls of which are 'graffiti' poking fun at the mythology whose Olympus is peopled by these snake, ape, cat, hawk, and ram-headed gods . . . Others laugh over the comical faces and attitudes of the amulets they are modelling . . . This is, as all Mr. Long's Egyptian scenes have been, a very animated, amusing and pleasing picture . . . [2]

As in many of Long's paintings, there is a wealth of archaeological detail. The presence of the beautiful craftswomen at the same time allows Long to show them exotically half-dressed and to show his own morality by highlighting the triviality of the construction of idols. According to Spielmann,

It had its origins in the sight of one of the many little shops that swarm in the neighbourhood of St. Sulpice in Paris, displaying for sale the plaster figures of the Saints. Catching sight of the manufactory beyond, his mind, now imbued with Egyptian lore, transferred the scene in imagination to the banks of the Nile, and applying and illustrating Juvenal's lines . . . produced this interesting picture.[3]

Reviews were favourable for a work which showed a lyricism lacking in some of Long's more moralising scenes. The *Art Journal* commented:

A picture illustrative of that passage in Sir Frederick Pollock's "Juvenal". The principal incident in this picture, the finest we think Mr Long has yet painted, is that of the Ethiopian woman holding a white cat, while an Egyptian girl models it. No part of the canvas, however, is left uncovered, or without stirring interest. The figures, to our mind, hold their places better, and, where required, are emphasized with a firmer and surer touch, than Mr Long has given to any of his previous creations . . . taking it all in all . . . one of the finest figure subjects in the exhibition.[4]

The *Magazine of Art* wrote of the work:

Of Mr. Long's work, whether in composition or portrait, only one opinion will be held this year, probably, and this will pronounce that the artist, after the slight weakness of last year's work, has put out all his power of drawing and modelling, and has gained greatly in sureness. The extreme refinement in colour in *The Gods and Their Makers* is very pleasing; different tones of flesh are relieved only by darker or lighter blue-greens, except in the case of the negress, who wears a red necklace, the only bit of primary colour in the picture. This group of Egyptian girls is full of fun and charm; the background tones are delicately varied.[5]

1. Sir Frederick Pollock's translation of the works of Juvenal (AD 60–c.130).
2. *The Times*, 4 May 1878, p. 12.
3. Spielmann 1888, p. 612.
4. AJ, 1878, p. 147.
5. *Magazine of Art*, 1878, p. 43.

PROVENANCE Taylor; sold in 1883 for £2,625; belonged to Jesse Howarth in 1887; sold at Christie's on 21 May for 16 guineas; purchased by Towneley Hall Art Gallery and Museum, Burnley from M. Cocker in 1952 for £130.

EXHIBITIONS RA 1878 (129); Manchester (Jubilee) 1887 (535); 'Egyptomania, Egypt in Western Art, 1730–1930', Paris, Ottawa, Vienna, (335).

LITERATURE *Academy Notes* 1878, p. 20 (ill.); AJ, 1878, p. 147; Chester 1908, p. 350; Clayton, p. 32, p. 33 (ill.); James Stevens Curl, *The Egyptian Revival* (London: Allen and Unwin, 1982), p. 152, p. 192; *Daily Telegraph* 1908; *Eyptomania*, Paris 1994–95, pp. 491–92 (ill.); John Forbes-Robertson, 'Art at the Manchester Jubilee Exhibition', *Magazine of Art*, 1887, p. 283; Humbert 1989, p. 255; LG 1885, p. 17, p. 21; *Magazine of Art*, 1878, p. 43, p. 70 (ill.); *Magazine of Art*, 1891, p. xl; de Meulenaere 1992, p. 108 (ill.), p. 138 (ill.); Quick 1931, pp. 5, 8, and 44; Reitlinger 1961; Roberts 1897, vol. II, p. 48; Spielmann 1888, p. 612; *The Times*, 4 May 1878, p. 12.

COLLECTION Towneley Hall Art Gallery and Museum, Burnley.

154. The Tambourine Player

1878; 27 × 19", 68.6 × 48.3 cm; oil on canvas; signed and dated.

PROVENANCE Robert Wharton Esq.; sold at Christie's on 18 March 1899 for 15 guineas; sold at Christie's on 15 December 1900 for 90 guineas.

155. The Right Rev Christopher Wordsworth, D.D., Bishop of Lincoln

1878; size unknown; oil on canvas.

A portrait of the Right Reverend Christopher Wordsworth, D.D., Bishop of Lincoln, painted for the Diocese. *The Athenaeum* found it an "excellent portrait",[1] whilst *Punch* wrote:

No. 1423 The Right Rev. Christopher Wordsworth D.D., D.C.L., Lord Bishop of Lincoln. EDWIN LONG, A. Property crozier against the wall- evidently for ornament not use, and a metal cross fastened by an evident elastic band round his Lordship's neck. He wears also his Scarlet Doctor's University hood. Bravo, Mr. LONG! 'Keep up the Christopher'.[2]

Long's notes refer to it as "Painted up at once, the head was unfinished on the third day after it was begun. Painted between July 1878–October 1878".[3]

1. Ath., 3 May 1879, p. 572.
2. *Punch*, 24 May 1879, p. 229.
3. Long's notes for the 1879 RA exhibition, in the Royal Academy Library.

EXHIBITIONS RA 1879 (1423).
LITERATURE *Academy Notes* 1879, p. 76; Ath., 3 May 1879, p. 572; *Punch*, 24 May 1879, p. 229.

156. Henry Irving as the Duke of Gloucester

1878; 57 × 40 , 144.8 × 101.6 cm; oil on canvas.

A three-quarter-length portrait of Sir Henry Irving as the Duke of Gloucester. Irving is portrayed in costume with a brooding expression against a mediaeval-style hanging. This is one of three portraits commissioned by Baroness Burdett-Coutts of Irving in character.

The work was well reviewed on its exhibition in 1878: "His . . . portrait of Irving as Richard III, is the best portrait yet painted of the popular tragedian and shows the skill with which he made up for Richard after the best authorities for look and action".[1] The *Magazine of Art* found that "'Mr. Irving as the Duke of Gloucester' is altogether a noble portrait".[2]

1. *The Times*, 4 May 1878, p. 12.
2. *Magazine of Art*, 1878, p. 43.

PROVENANCE Commissioned by Baroness Burdett Coutts; sold in 1912 as a set of three Irving portraits by Long for £2,100.
EXHIBITIONS RA 1878 (472); Manchester Jubilee Exhibition 1887 (392).
LITERATURE *Academy Notes* 1878, p. 47 (ill.); *Magazine of Art*, 1878, p. 43, p. f; Quick 1931, p. 6, p. 43; Reitlinger 1961; *The Times*, 4 May 1878, p. 12.

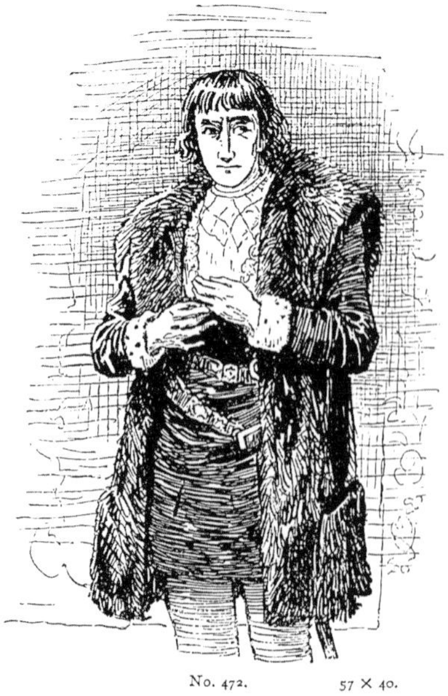

156. *Henry Irving as the Duke of Gloucester*, 1878.
Engraving from *Academy Notes*, 1878, p. 47.

156.1 Henry Irving as Richard III

1880; 56 × 38", 142.2 × 96.6 cm; oil on canvas.

A slightly smaller copy of Long's 1878 Academy portrait of Sir Henry Irving as the Duke of Gloucester.

PROVENANCE The American Shakespeare Festival Theatre and Academy, Stratford, Connecticut in 1964.
EXHIBITIONS 'Shakespeare in Art', M. Knoedler and Co., Inc., New York, 3–28 March 1964.
LITERATURE *Apollo*, no. 79 (April 1964), p. 343 (ill.).

157. Henry Irving as Vanderdecken

1879; size unknown; oil on canvas.

A portrait of Sir Henry Irving as Vanderdecken. On 8 June 1878, a new poetic drama titled *Vanderdecken* opened in London with Irving in the leading role. The play, written by Percy Fitzgerald and W. G. Wills was created for Irving and based on Wagner's *The Flying Dutchman.* Fitzgerald wrote: "Irving has never looked more impressive, more weirdly picturesque, than as Vanderdecken".[1]

Long's portrait, commissioned by the Baroness Burdett-Coutts, shows Irving in a fur hat and coat reminiscent of the costume of a seventeenth-century Dutch painting. The *Magazine of Art* noted: "Mr. Long has painted excellent portraits of . . . and of Mr. Irving in the character of 'Vanderdecken' ".[2]

1. Quoted in Charles Hiatt, *Henry Irving, A Record and Review* (London: G. Bell and Sons, 1899), p. 165.
2. *Magazine of Art*, 1879, p. 127.

PROVENANCE Commissioned by Baroness Burdett-Coutts; sold in 1912 as a set of three Irving portraits by Long for £2,100.
LITERATURE *Magazine of Art*, 1879, p. 127; Reitlinger 1961.

158. Vashti

1878–79; 84⅜ × 67¼", 214 × 171 cm; oil on canvas; signed "E Long 1879" on the servant's bracelet.

> On the seventh day, when the heart of the king was merry with wine, he commanded Mehuman, Biztha, Harbona, Bigtha and Abagtha, Zethar, and Carcas, the seven chamberlains that served in the presence of Ahasuerus the king, to bring Vashti the queen before the king with the crown royal, to shew the people and the princes her beauty: for she was fair to look on. But the queen Vashti refused to come at the king's commandment by his chamberlains: therefore was the king very wroth and his anger burned in him.[1]

The book of Esther is the subject of Long's *Vashti* along with its companion painting *Esther.* Both were exhibited at the 1879 Royal Academy exhibition although, surprisingly, not together. The similarities in the composition only help to highlight the contrast between the depiction of the central figures. The *Magazine of Art* called *Esther* the more solemnly heroic and *Vashti* the more majestic.[2] The voluptuous Persian palace (for the sources, see *Esther*, catalogue no. 152) acts as a perfect backdrop to the resolute Vashti. Her expression is a marvellous capturing of two feelings acting concurrently. As the *Magazine of Art* noted: "Her dignity as an Eastern woman, who has never been seen unveiled, is outraged; but a knowledge of the full consequences of her act is seen in her eyes".[3] *The Times* found her "swelling with a suppressed sense of courage".[4] The servants' pleading is ignored and her resolution is echoed in the retiring chamberlains, one with his arms raised despairingly. The crown that Vashti has refused to wear sits at her right. The *Art Journal* wrote of *Vashti*: "Our admiration embraces also heartily Mr Long's other grand canvas, representing the resolute and lovely "Vashti", and if the artist could only introduce a touch more of strength into his work, we should be inclined to think him almost faultless".[5] According to Long's notes, *Vashti* was painted between October 1878 and April 1879.[6] The painting was begun just after he had completed his copy of *Esther* and four months after he had completed the original.

1. Esther, 1: 10–12.
2. *Magazine of Art*, 1879, p. 127.
3. Ibid.
4. *The Times*, 3 May 1879, p. 5.
5. AJ, 1879, p. 127.
6. Long's notes for the 1879 RA exhibition, in the Royal Academy Library.

PROVENANCE Central Picture Galleries; Bob Jones University, South Carolina, USA.
EXHIBITIONS RA 1879 (955).
LITERATURE *Academy Notes* 1879, p. 62 (ill.); AJ, 1879, p. 127; AJ, vol. 29, no. 2 (winter 1969–70), p. 218, p. 220 (ill.); Ath., 3 May 1879, p. 572; Ath., 17 May 1879, p. 637; Chester 1908, pp. 346–47; *The Graphic*, 17 May 1879, p. 490; *Magazine of Art*, 1879, p. 127; Quick 1931, p. 44; Spielmann 1888, p. 612; *The Times*, 3 May 1879, p. 5.
COLLECTION Bob Jones University, Greenville, South Carolina, USA.

159. A Nubian Girl

1879; size unknown; oil on canvas.

PROVENANCE Thomas Agnew and Sons purchased from the artist on 13 October 1879; sold to G. T. Lees on 12 July 1880 for £400; in the collection of Mr Tate in 1893.
LITERATURE *Magazine of Art*, 1893, p. 247.

160. Raising the Veil

1879; 23 × 18″, 59 × 46 cm; oil on canvas; signed and dated.

PROVENANCE Sold at Sotheby's on 15 February 1983 for £420.

161. The Chieftain's Daughter

1879; 36 × 23″, 91.5 × 58.5 cm; oil on canvas; signed with monogram and dated, lower left.

A half-length portrait of a single female figure. Half-naked and bedecked in jewellery, she is depicted arranging her hair. In the background is a stone wall with two columns containing ancient relief carvings.

PROVENANCE Thomas Agnew and Sons; sold at Sotheby's on 27 November 1984 for £11,000.

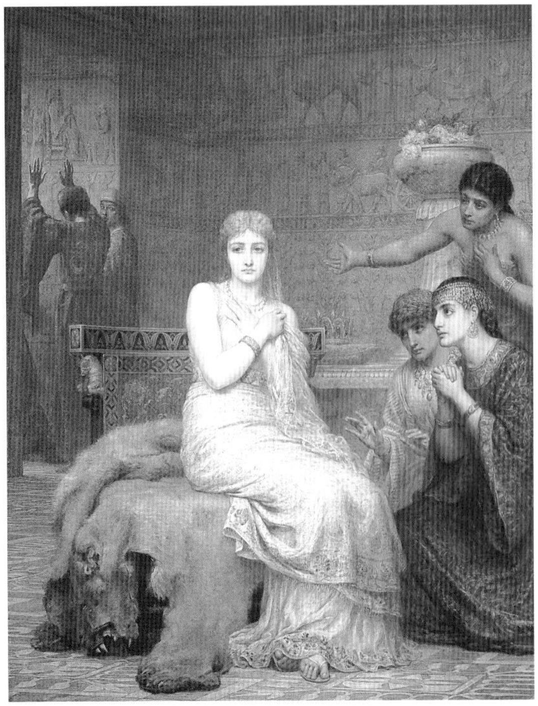

158. *Vashti*, 1878–79.
BOB JONES UNIVERSITY MUSEUM & GALLERY, GREENVILLE, USA.

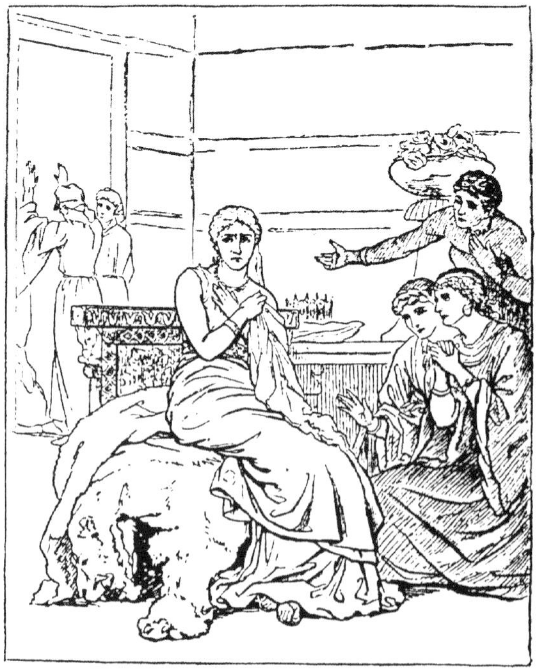

No. 955. 84 × 67.

158. *Vashti*, 1878–79.
Engraving from *Academy Notes*, 1879, p. 62.

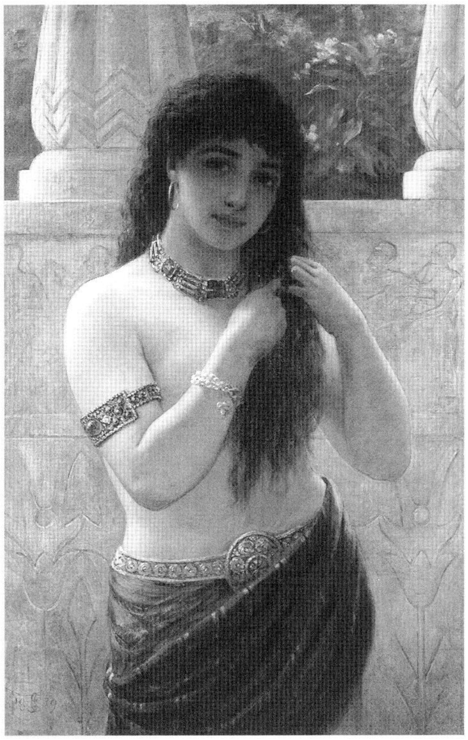

161. *The Chieftain's Daughter*, 1879.
COURTESY OF SOTHEBY'S, LONDON

162. Winter

c. 1879; 36 × 33", 91.5 × 83.8 cm; oil on canvas.

PROVENANCE Purchased from the artist by Thomas Agnew & Sons on 11 July 1879.

163. The Late Hannah Brown

1879; size unknown; oil on canvas.

A portrait of Hannah Brown commissioned by her "lifelong friend"[1] the Baroness Burdett-Coutts. Hannah Brown (née Meredith) was a close associate of the Baroness in her charitable and philanthropic work. She is portrayed as an old woman seated dressed in black, and wearing a veil. Her blindness is referred to in the painting's subtitle from St. John, "Whereas I was blind, now I see".[2] The *Academy Notes* wrote that on entering Gallery VII it was "one of the first pictures to attract attention . . . " An engraving of the work was later made by Samuel Cousins RA. According to Long's notes the work was painted between August and December 1878. He noted of the painting: "Painted for the Baroness Burdett-Coutts. Light Amber varnish mixed with oil and turpentine. Flesh modelled up in pure white then finished with all colours".[3]

1. RA 1879 exhibition catalogue.
2. John, X: 25.
3. Long's notes for the 1879 RA exhibition, in the Royal Academy Library.

EXHIBITIONS RA 1879 (562).

164. Vere, Daughter of Ellis Gosling, Wife of 7th Viscount Galway

1879; 50 × 36", 127 × 91.5 cm; oil on canvas; signed and dated.

A seated wedding portrait of Vere Gosling (married 1879, died 1920) in a silk dress.

PROVENANCE By descent to Dowager Viscountess Gosling, Selby Hall.

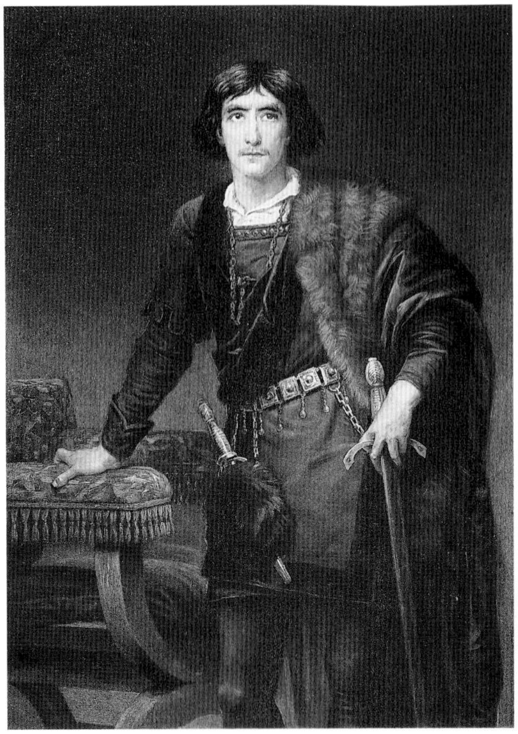

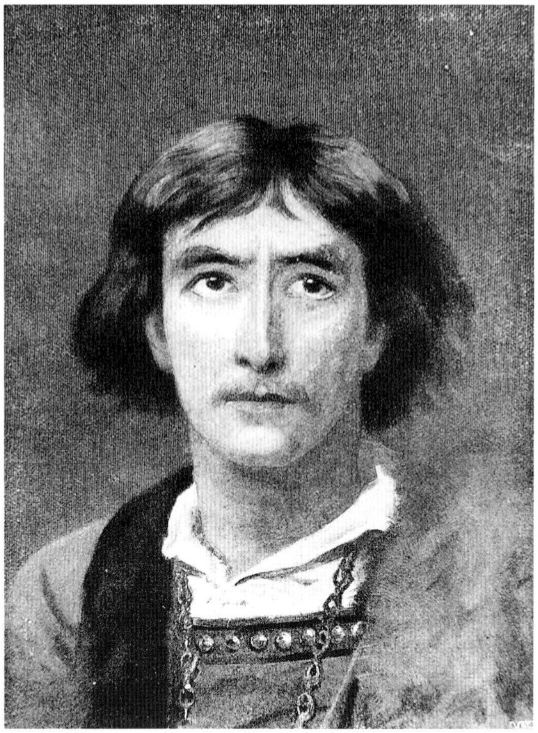

165. LEFT *Henry Irving as Hamlet*, 1880. Engraving. RIGHT Detail.
RUSSELL-COTES ART GALLERY AND MUSEUM, PHOTOGRAPH JAMES HOWE

165. Henry Irving as Hamlet

1880; size unknown; oil on canvas.

A three-quarter-length portrait of Sir Henry Irving as Hamlet. The painting of Irving in costume looking directly out of the canvas was lengthened by Long from a half-length to a three-quarter-length portrait. The clear addition was noted by the *Magazine of Art*: "There are two by Edwin Long R.A., one as Hamlet being clumsily lengthened by five or six inches,"[1] and more satirically by *Punch*:

> No. 416. Henry Irving as Hamlet; or Knee Plus Extra. E. Long, A. A three-quarter-length, and quite long enough. The Artist felt the subject would scarcely bear E-long-a-tion, and perhaps he'll give us the remainder next year. 'To be continued in our next year.' As Hamlet observes 'Very like, very like. Stay'd it Long?' &c. (Act I, s.2). Of course the answer would be – Just sufficient time to have his portrait taken.[2]

1. *Magazine of Art*, 1897, p. 171.
2. *Punch*, 8 May 1880, p. 10.

PROVENANCE Commissioned by Baroness Burdett-Coutts; sold in 1912 as a set of three Irving portraits by Long for £2,100.

EXHIBITIONS RA 1880 (416); 'Exhibition of Musical and Dramatic Art', Grafton Galleries, 1897.

LITERATURE Chester 1908, p. 336 (detail ill.); *Magazine of Art*, 1897, p. 171; *Punch*, 8 May 1880, p. 209; Quick 1931, p. 6, p. 15 (ill.), p. 43; Reitlinger 1961; *The Times*, 6 May 1880, p. 10.

166. Charles I (after Vandyck)

c. 1880; size unknown; oil on canvas.

A copy of Vandyck's head studies of Charles I, referred to in Ellen Terry's autobiography:

> Edwin Long painted him [Henry Irving] a triptych of Vandyck heads, which he always had in his dressing room, and which is now in my possession. He used to come on stage looking precisely like the Vandyck portraits, but not because he had been busy building up his face with wig-paste and similar atrocities. His

make-up in this, as in other parts, was the process of 'assisting subtly and surely the expression from within.'[1]

1. Ellen Terry, *The Story of My Life* (London, 1908), p. 180.

PROVENANCE Commissioned by Sir Henry Irving from Edwin Long; collection of Ellen Terry in 1908.
LITERATURE Ellen Terry, *The Story of My Life* (London, 1908), p. 180.

167. Mrs Angerstein

1880; size unknown; oil on canvas.

The Times described this work as "a very graceful portrait".[1]

1. *The Times*, 6 May 1880, p. 10.

PROVENANCE Thomas Agnew & Sons; sold at Christie's on 23 December 1953 to W. N. Bernard.
EXHIBITIONS RA 1880 (276).
LITERATURE Quick 1931, p. 43; *The Times*, 6 May 1880, p. 10.

168. Ernest Renan

1880; size unknown; oil on canvas.

A portrait of the philosopher and critic (1823–92).

PROVENANCE Ernest Renan, commissioned from the artist.

168.1 Study for the Portrait of Ernest Renan

1880; 14¼ × 12¼", 36 × 31 cm; oil on canvas.

A study for his portrait of Ernest Renan. An old mount is inscribed:

> The first study of Ernest Renan, author of 'Vie de Jesus' / It was painted in the year of Renan's delivery of the Hibbert Lectures in London, 1880 / I introduced the men to one another and was present in the studio when his study was begun / I bought it at a sale of Edwin Long's studio effects 24th 10th 1907 / A.L.

PROVENANCE Bought by A. Lucas from the studio sale of Edwin Long following the death of his wife on 20 October 1907; by descent to Mrs Seymour Lucas; K. E. G. Boniglioli; gift to the Ashmolean Museum in 1966.
COLLECTION Ashmolean Museum, Oxford.

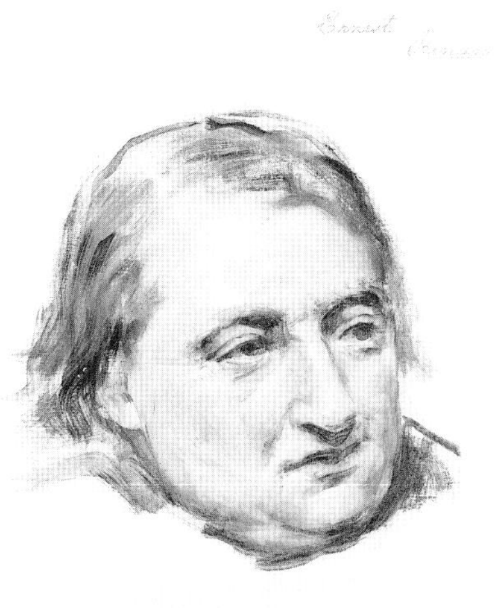

168.1. *Study for the Portrait of Ernest Renan*, 1880.
ASHMOLEAN MUSEUM, OXFORD

169. William Reed Esq.

1880; size unknown; oil on canvas.

A portrait of William Reed that *The Times* described as an "unconspicuous portrait".[1]

1. *The Times*, 6 May 1880, p. 10.

EXHIBITIONS RA 1880 (1060).
LITERATURE Quick 1931, p. 43; *The Times*, 6 May 1880, p. 10.

170. Mrs Patrick Campbell in Balkan Dress

1880; 25½ × 18½", 65 × 47 cm; oil on canvas; signed with monogram and dated.

A head and shoulders portrait of Mrs Patrick Campbell in Balkan dress comprising of a head scarf, earring, twisted pearl necklace and holding a casket. It was exhibited in 1880 at the Graphic Gallery as part of the 'Types of Beauty' exhibition which included work by Alma-Tadema, Leighton, Calderon and Tissot. They were engraved for illustration in *The Graphic*, including 'Mrs Patrick Campbell', being number IV in the series. *The Graphic* singled out the work in its advertisement for the series:

> Anyone having a heart to bestow on a muscular, strong-minded lady, with a casket in her hand, possibly suggestive of her fortune, and who looks as if she liked her own way and meant to have it, may be recommended to make acquaintance of the young lady who blooms defiant on Mr. Long's canvas.[1]

1. *The Graphic*, 21 February 1880, p. 191.

PROVENANCE *The Graphic*, commissioned from the artist; sold at Sotheby's on 27 June 1978; sold at Sotheby's on 20 March 1979 for £1,200; sold at Sotheby's on 13 December 1984 for £3,800.
EXHIBITIONS The Graphic Gallery, 190 Strand, 1881, 'Types of Female Beauty' Exhibition (15).
LITERATURE *The Graphic*, 23 July 1881 (supplement), p. 90 (ill.); *The Graphic*, 21 February 1880, p. 191; *The Thrifty Farmer and Fireside Magazine*, April 1889 (ill. as an 'art plate picture').

171. The Rest by an Oasis

1880; 16 × 25⅞", 40.5 × 65.5 cm; oil on canvas.

A painting of Arabs resting at an oasis.

PROVENANCE Mon. O. Guichard, Hotel des Ventes, Saint-Brieve; sold at auction on 9 December 1984.

172. Letter Writer of Cairo

c. 1880; size unknown; oil on canvas.

PROVENANCE Bought from the artist by Thomas Agnew and Sons on 28 June 1881; sold to H. Edwards M.P. on 28 June 1881 for £300; bought on 30 July 1881 by Thomas Agnew and Sons; sold to James Mason on 29 September 1882 for £735.

173. An Assyrian Captive

1880; 55 × 36", 139.7 × 91.5 cm; oil on canvas.

The source of the painting is a custom described in George Rawlinson's *The Five Great Monarchies of the Ancient World*. George Rawlinson's (1812–1902) work on the ancient world was an important source for Long. He utilised it in many of his paintings, not only directly as he did with *An Assyrian Captive*, but also to inform him of the architecture and decoration which he used in such pictures as *Esther* and *Vashti*. Rawlinson's work contains numerous engravings of examples of antiquities, reliefs and architecture which provided a rich visual record for Long. *An Assyrian Captive* is based on the following section from *The Five Great Monarchies*:

> The employment of captives as musicians is interesting, though we cannot say that the captives are Jews. It shows us that the Assyrians, like the later Babylonians, were in the habit of 'requiring' music from their prisoners, who, when transported into a 'strange land,' had to entertain their masters with their native melodies.[1]

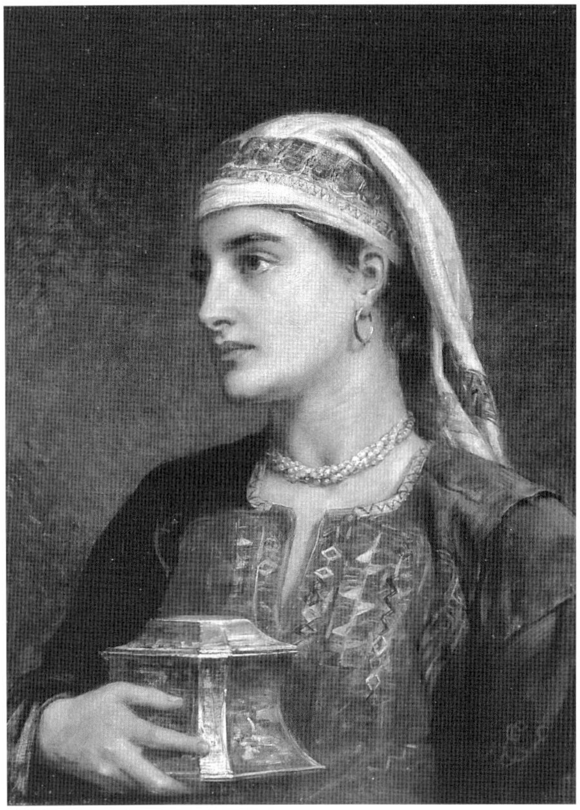

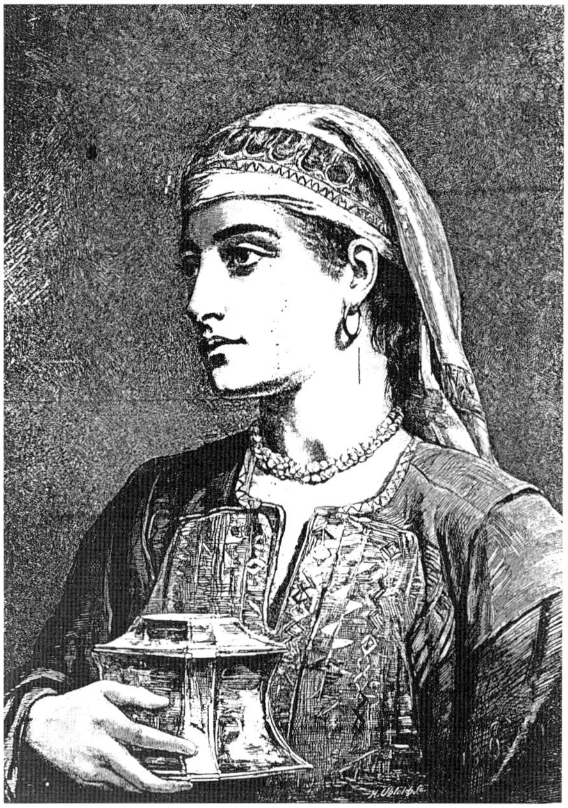

170. LEFT Mrs Patrick Campbell in Balkan Dress, 1880. COURTESY OF SOTHEBY'S, LONDON
RIGHT Engraving from *The Graphic*, 23 July 1881, p. 90.

The Times reviewed the work's appearance at the 1880 Royal Academy:

> E. Long's 'Assyrian Captive' (210), which hangs hard by, a graceful girl, crouching with her harp by her side – one of the painter's many studies for his pictures of ancient Oriental life, and nothing more. The winter fogs have interfered with Mr. Long's more important designs, and left him represented here only by this figure. . . .[2]

1. Rawlinson, *The Five Great Monarchies of the Ancient World; or the history, geography and antiquities of Chaldea, Assyria, Babylon, Media and Persia*, 4 vols. (London, 1862–67), vol. I (1862), chapter 7, p. cxxxvii.
2. *The Times*, 6 May 1880, p. 10.

PROVENANCE Sold to Arthur Anderson of Wimpole Street in 1880 for a reputed 1,500 guineas; sold at Christie's on 19 May 1894 for 440 guineas; sold at Christie's on 30–31 July 1936 for 11 guineas.

EXHIBITIONS RA 1880 (210).

LITERATURE *Academy Notes* 1880; Chester 1908, p. 349; *Daily Telegraph*, date unknown, 1908; Quick 1931, p. 44; Roberts 1897, vol. II, p. 228; *The Times*, 6 May 1880, p. 10.

174. Miriam

c. 1880; size unknown; oil on canvas.

Exhibited at the Edwin Long Gallery from 1893–94 as *Miriam, 'A Type of Beauty'* – it is unclear to what this subtitle refers. Long painted only one work for the 'Types of Female Beauty' exhibition at the Graphic Gallery exhibition of 1881.

EXHIBITIONS ELG 1893–94 (10).

LITERATURE ELG 1894, p. 22.

175. Choosing a Deity

c. 1880; size unknown; oil on canvas.

The setting is ancient Rome and what appears to be a shop selling a variety of statuettes of gods. The building is filled with toga-clad customers. One has a statuette in each hand and is attempting to make a choice between the two, whilst a group are attempting to choose between other model deities. Most of the Roman pantheon of gods are visible include Zeus, Diana and Eros. The viewing position is from behind a large marble desk full of statuettes with a woman serving. In the background, visible through the shop, are grand examples of Roman architecture.

PROVENANCE In the collection of the Worshipful Company of Painters by 1908.
LITERATURE AJ, 1908, p. 175 (ill.).
COLLECTION Collection of Painters' and Stainers' Hall, London, destroyed by bomb in 1940.

176. Ione

c. 1870s; 39 × 29", 99 × 73.7 cm; oil on canvas.

PROVENANCE Sold at Christie's on 21 July 1900 for £1 15s.

177. The Rivals

date unknown; 49 × 33", 124.5 × 84 cm; oil on canvas; signed with monogram, date indistinct.

A genre scene set in Roman dress of two lovers walking hand in hand through a garden. The man is wearing a toga, cloak and sandals whilst his lover is dressed in a full length dress and headress of the same period. In the backround her jealous rival peers out of the bushes.

PROVENANCE Sold at Sotheby's on 14 December 1988 for £900.

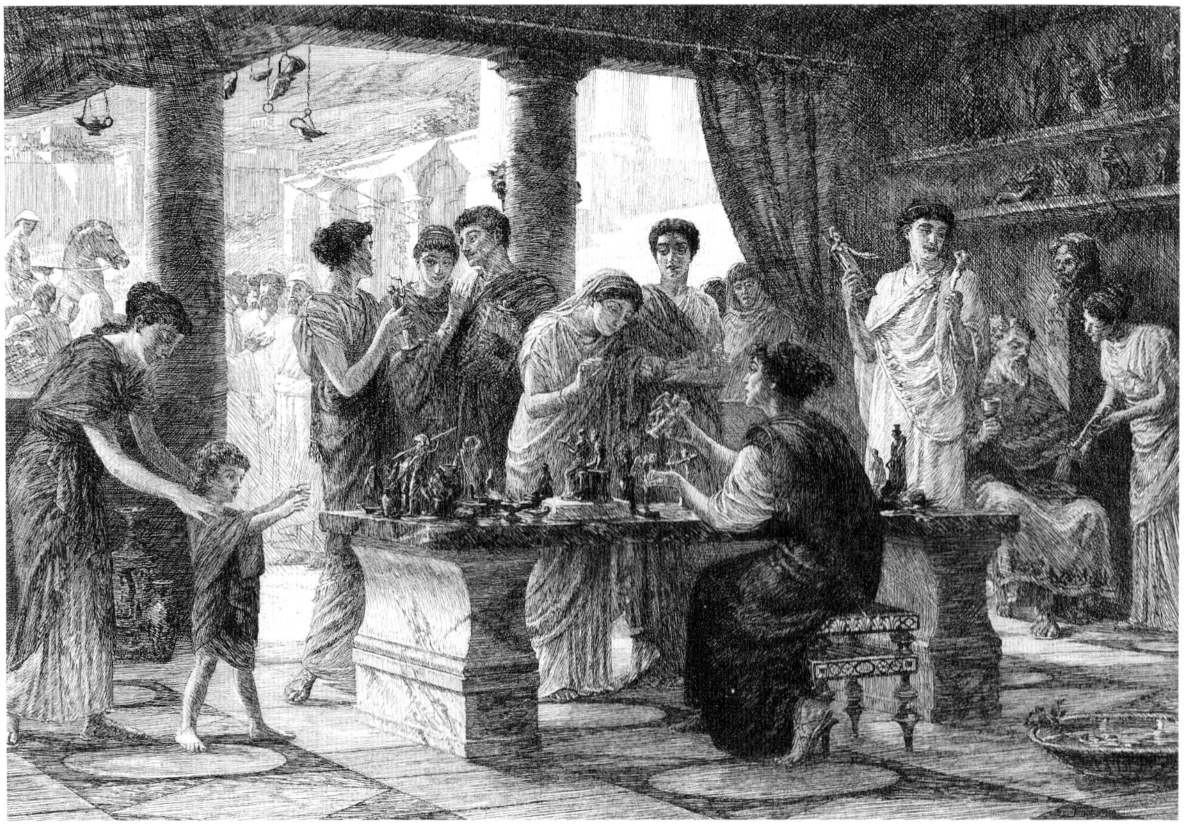

175. *Choosing a Deity*, c. 1880.

178. The Circassian Slave

date unknown; 73 × 40″, 185.5 × 101.6 cm; oil on canvas.

A large scale painting of a Circassian slave. In the nineteenth century, the Circassian women, from a group of tribes from the Caucasus, were thought to be of exceptional beauty.

PROVENANCE Sold at Christie's on 16 July 1904 for 5 guineas.

179. Moroccan Coffee.

52 × 36″, 132.1 × 91.5 cm; oil on canvas; signed, date indistinct.

A large scale painting of a group of figures taking Moroccan coffee.

PROVENANCE Sold at Charles Boardman and Sons on 6 March 1974 for £400.

180. A Greek Girl

date and size unknown; oil on canvas.

A portrait of a Greek girl.

PROVENANCE Sold at Christie's on 4 February 1888 for £94 10s.

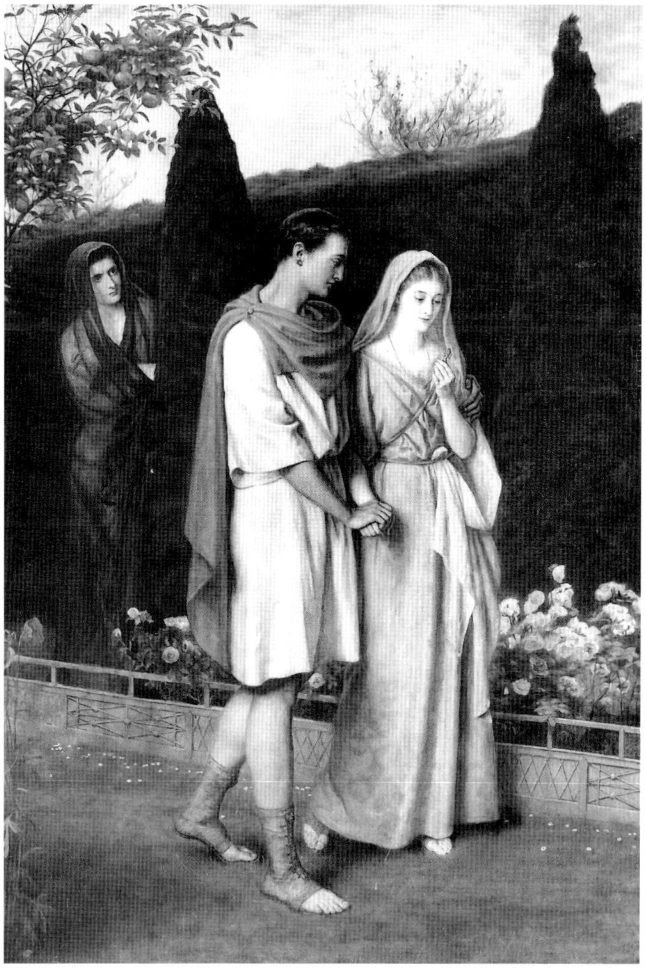

177. *The Rivals*, date unknown.
COURTESY OF SOTHEBY'S, LONDON

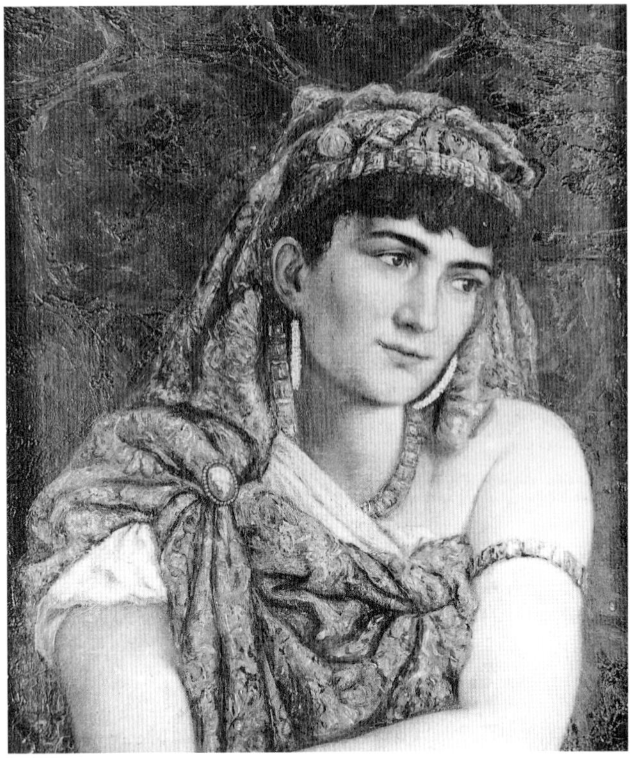

181. *A Syrian Maid*, date unknown.
COURTESY OF SOTHEBY'S, LONDON

181. A Syrian Maid

date unknown; 21 × 18″, 53.3 × 45.7 cm; oil on canvas.

A half-length painting of a young Syrian woman wearing a cape with a cameo brooch.

PROVENANCE Sold at Sotheby's on 10 March 1981.

182. Eastern Lady

date and size unknown; oil on canvas.

A portrait of an Eastern lady, sold at Christie's in 1881.

PROVENANCE Thomas Agnew and Sons; sold to Maclean on 23 June 1881.

183. The Bishop of Jerusalem

date and size unknown; oil on canvas.

A portrait of the Bishop of Jerusalem exhibited at the Edwin Long Gallery from 1893–94.

EXHIBITIONS ELG, 1893–94 (8).
LITERATURE ELG 1894, p. 21.

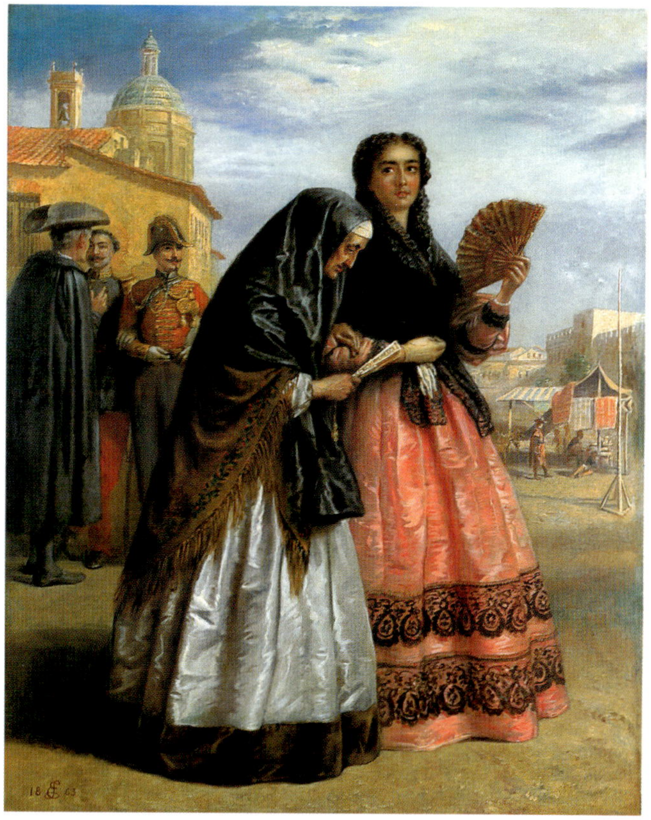

50. *Good Advice* (also called *Age and Youth*), 1863.
COURTESY OF SOTHEBY'S, LONDON

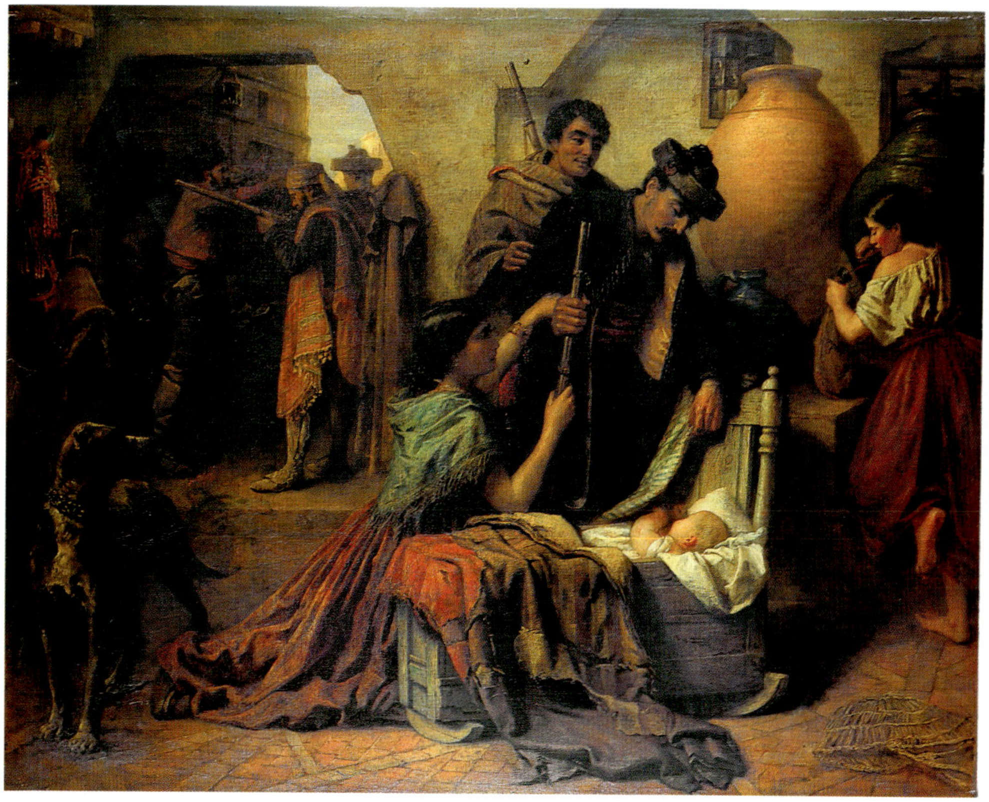

52. *Her Tender Prayers*, 1863.
CHRISTIE'S IMAGES

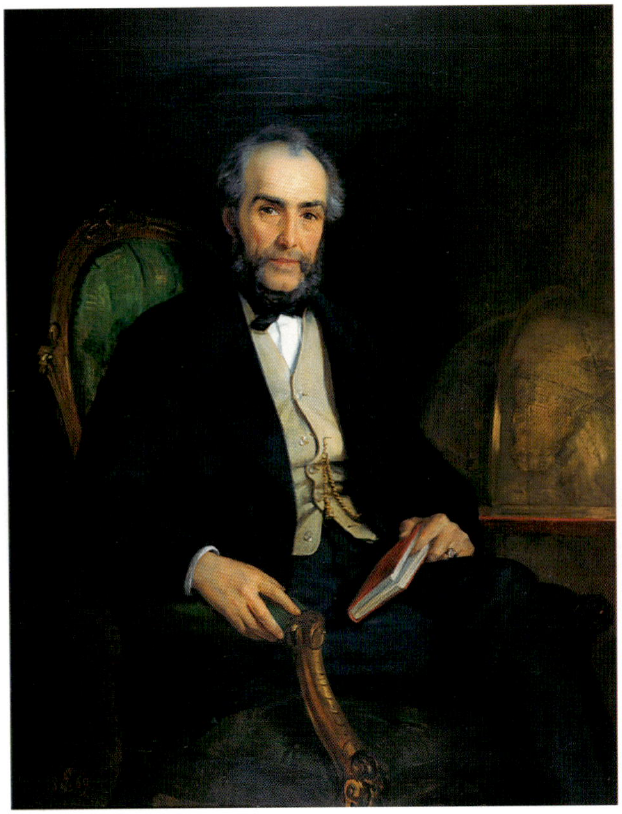

89. *Peter Douglas Esq.*, 1869.
RUSSELL-COTES ART GALLERY AND MUSEUM, PHOTOGRAPH JAMES HOWE

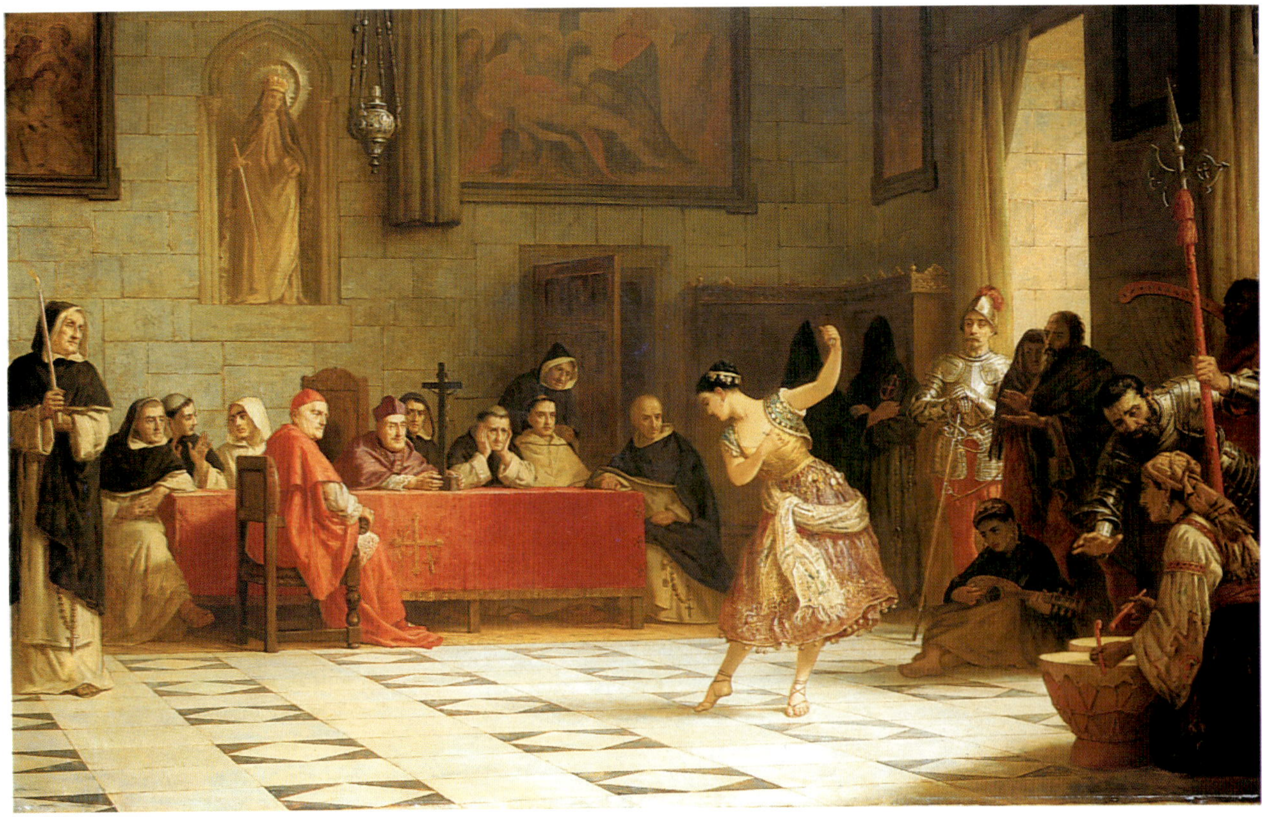

92.2. *A Question of Propriety*, 1870.
COURTESY OF SOTHEBY'S

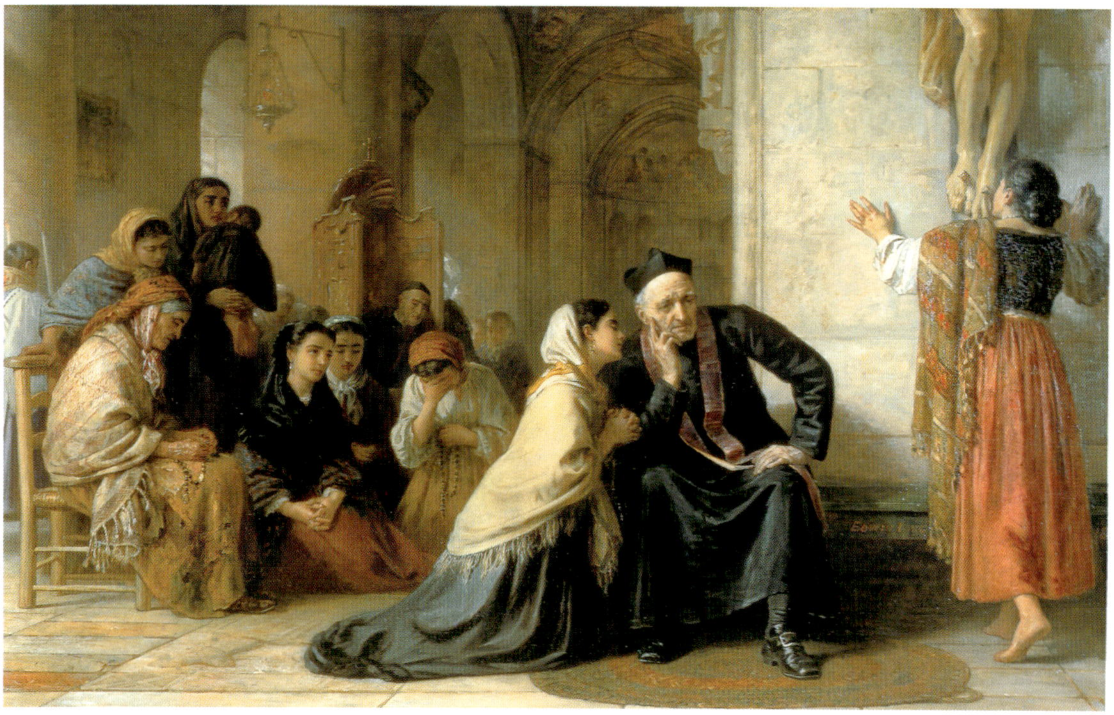

102. *An Easter Vigil in a Cathedral at Seville*, 1871.
THE FORBES MAGAZINE COLLECTION NEW YORK, ALL RIGHTS RESERVED

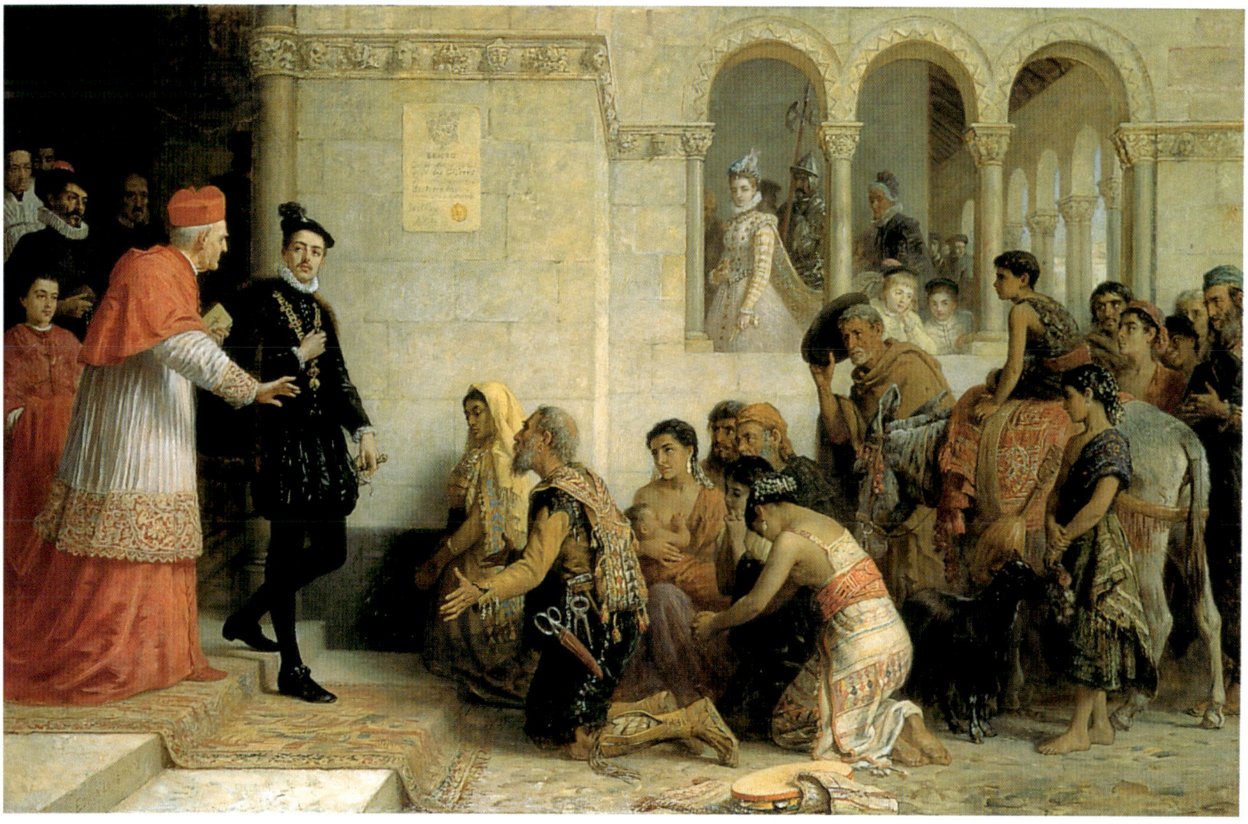

111. *The Suppliants: Expulsion of the Gypsies from Spain (1872)*, 1872.
ROYAL HOLLOWAY & BEDFORD NEW COLLEGE, SURREY. PHOTOGRAPH BRIDGEMAN ART LIBRARY

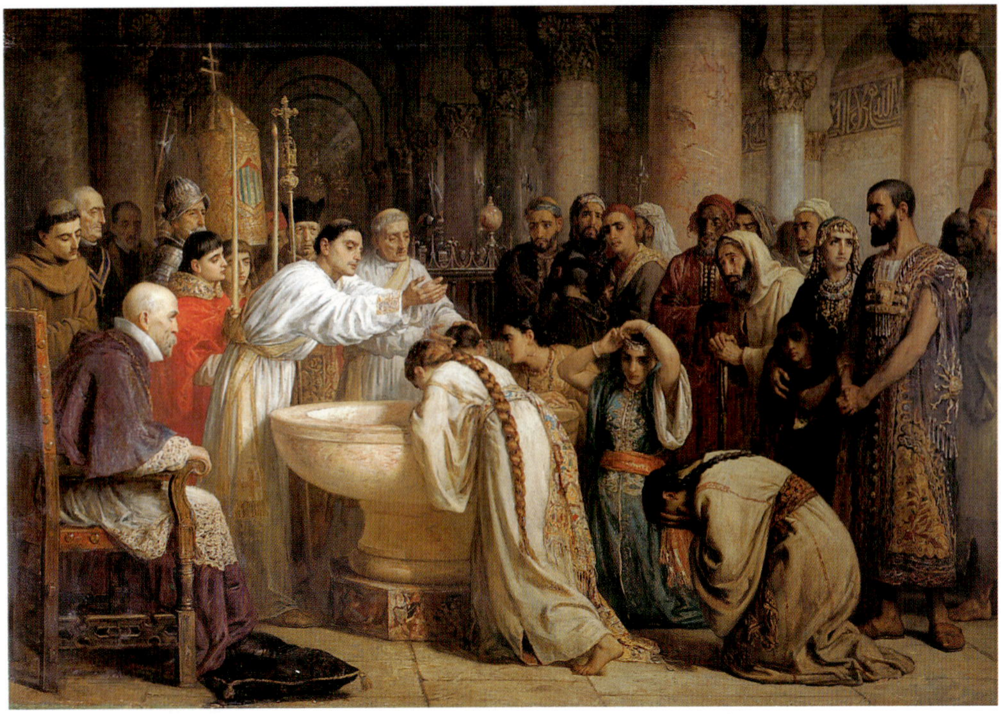

112. *The Moorish Proselytes of Archbishop Ximenes, Granada, 1500*, 1873.
RUSSELL-COTES ART GALLERY AND MUSEUM. PHOTOGRAPH JAMES HOWE.

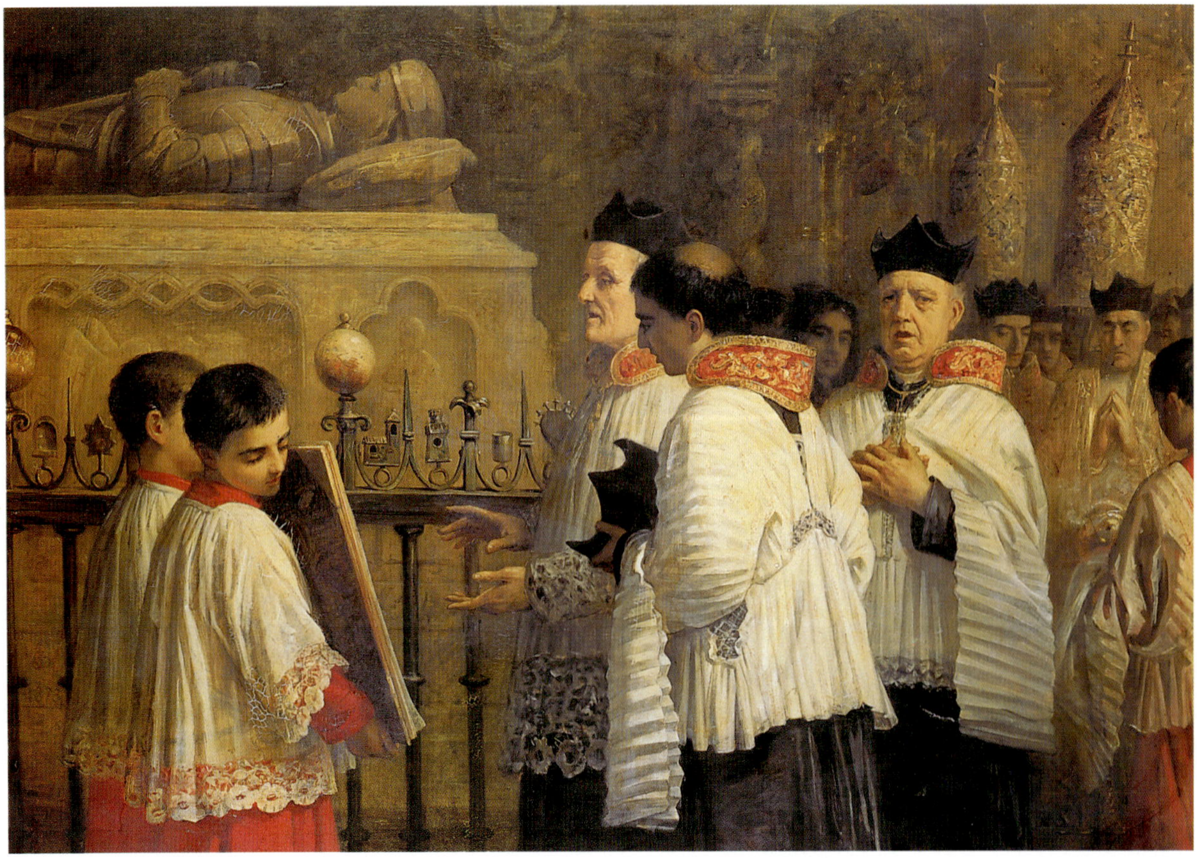

113. *Primero Segundo y Basso Profundo*, 1873.
CHRISTIE'S IMAGES

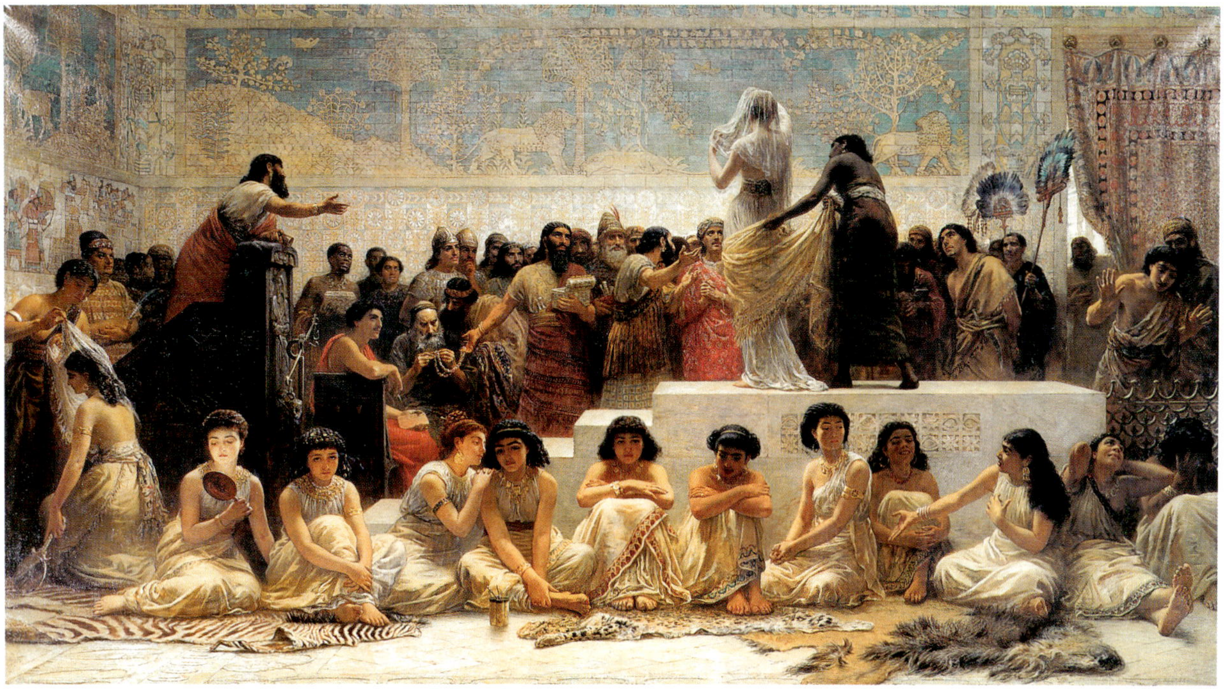

142. *The Babylonian Marriage Market*, 1875.
ROYAL HOLLOWAY & BEDFORD NEW COLLEGE, SURREY. PHOTOGRAPH BRIDGEMAN ART LIBRARY.

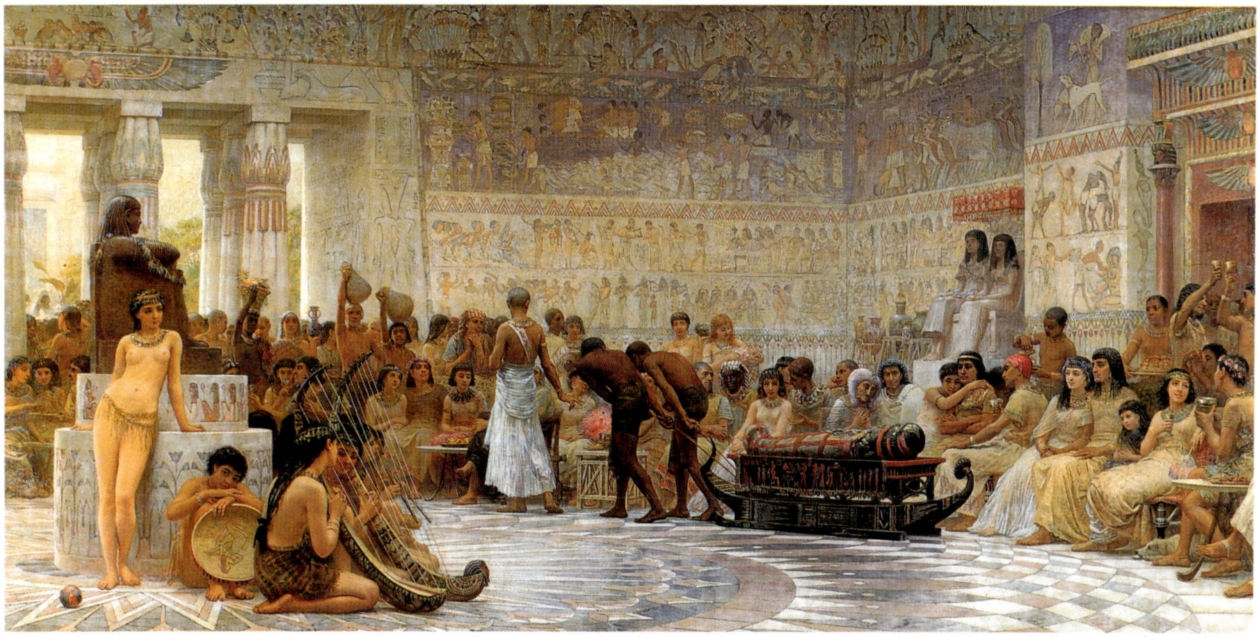

150. *An Egyptian Feast*, 1877.
CARTWRIGHT HALL ART GALLERY, BRADFORD. PHOTOGRAPH BRIDGEMAN ART LIBRARY

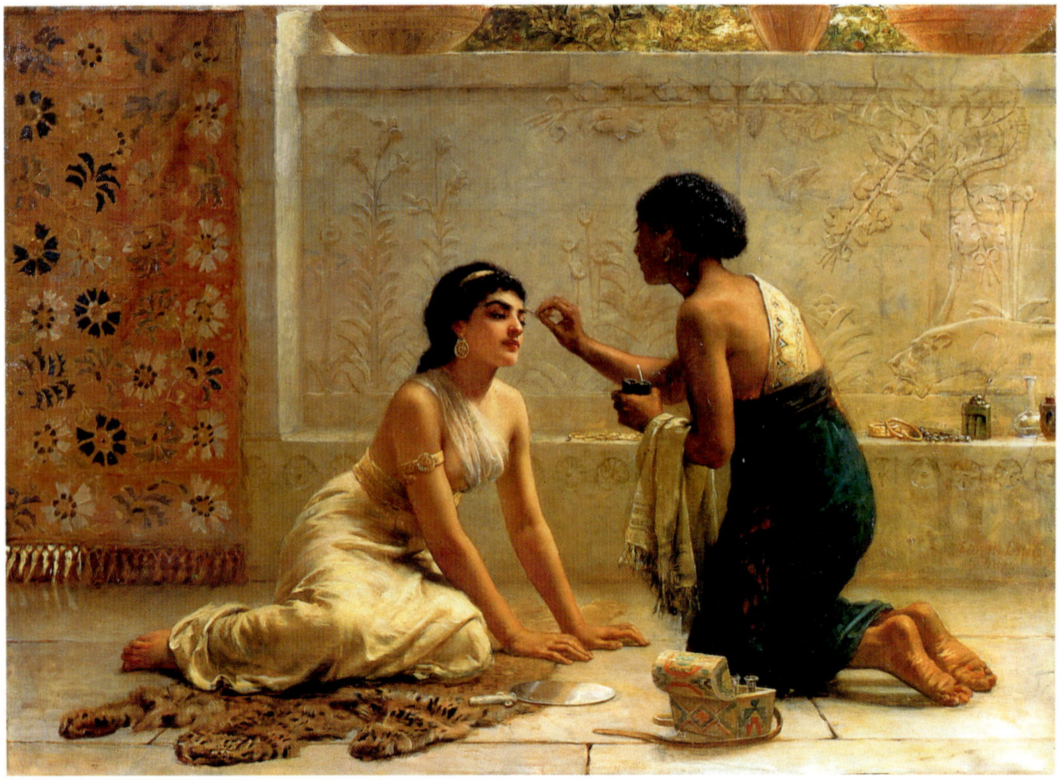

145. *An Ancient Custom*, 1876.
COURTESY OF PHILLIPS FINE ART AUCTIONEERS, LONDON

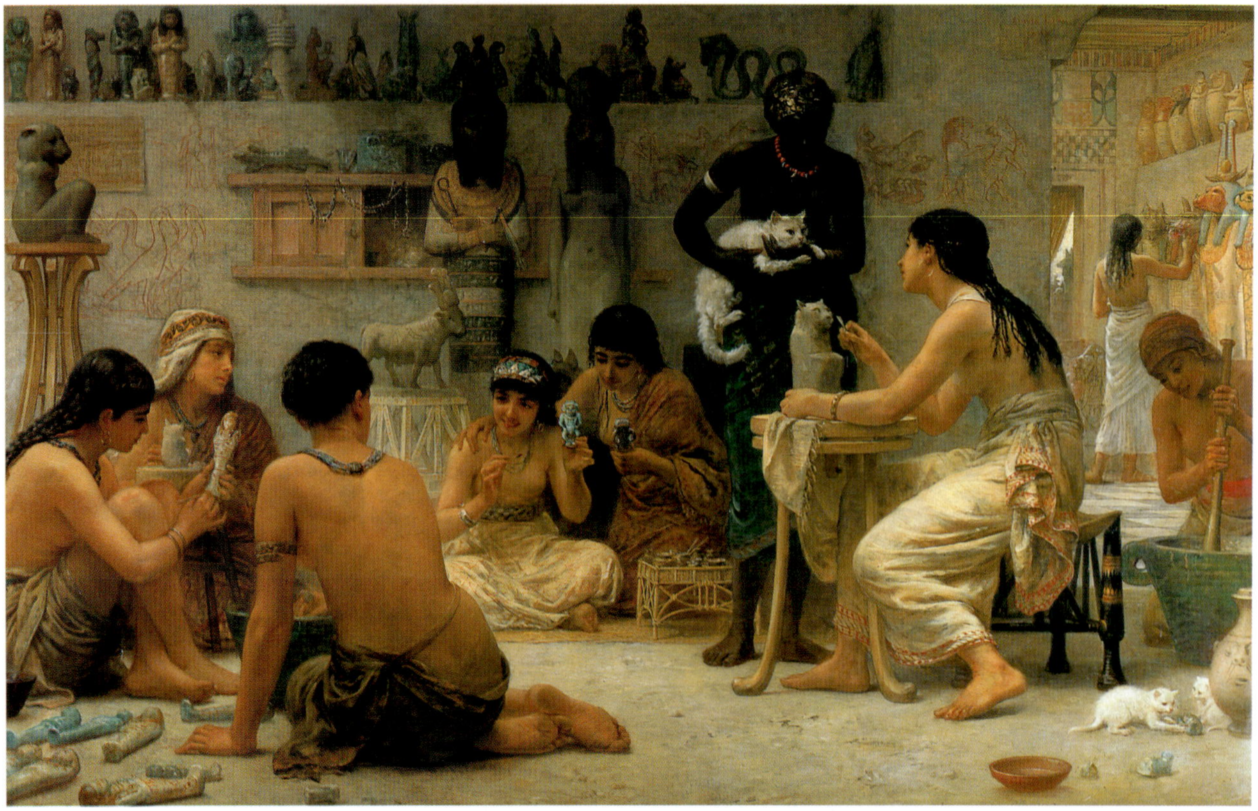

153. *The Gods and Their Makers*, 1878.
TOWNELEY HALL ART GALLERY & MUSEUMS, BURNLEY BOROUGH COUNCIL. PHOTOGRAPH BRIDGEMAN ART LIBRARY

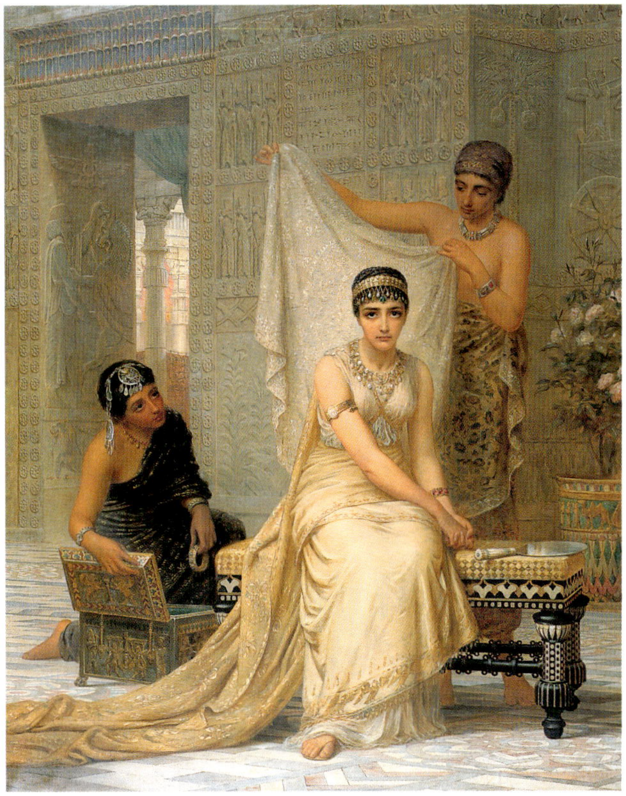

152.1 *Queen Esther*, 1878.
PURCHASED WITH THE ASSISTANCE OF A GOVERNMENT GRANT, 1879,
NATIONAL GALLERY OF VICTORIA, MELBOURNE.

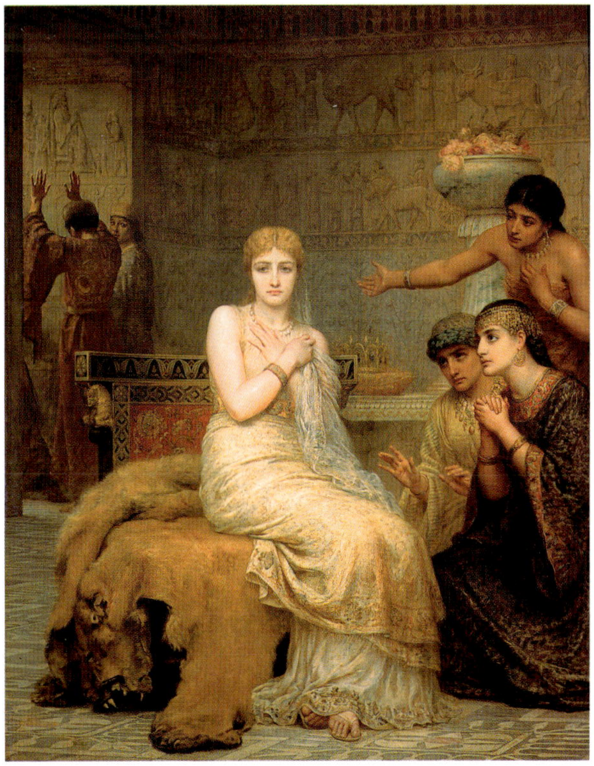

158. *Vashti*, 1878–79.
BOB JONES UNIVERSITY MUSEUM & GALLERY, GREENVILLE, USA.

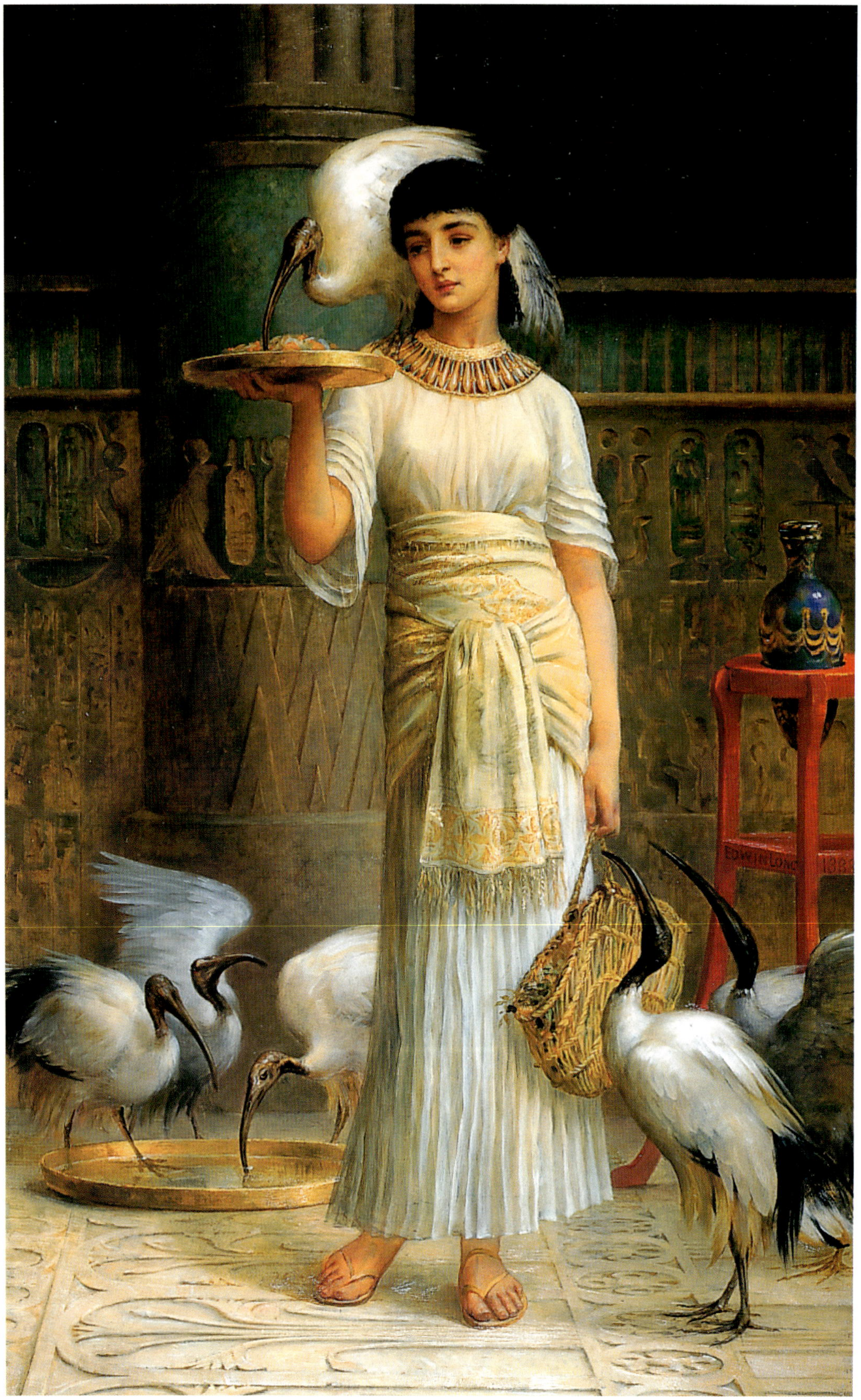

254. *Alethe, Attendant of the Sacred Ibis*, 1888.
RUSSELL-COTES ART GALLERY AND MUSEUM, PHOTOGRAPH JAMES HOWE

ROYAL ACADEMICIAN AND THE COMMERCIAL SUCCESSES OF BOND STREET 1881–1887

Long's move into Fitzjohn's Avenue in 1880 had marked Long's growing status over and above that reflected in his move to St John's Wood. In Hampstead he was closer to other artists of his own standing, indeed he was only a year there when he was made a full Academician. During this period at Fitzjohn's Avenue, Long consolidated his commercial success through his growing relationship with Bond Street. Before 1881 he had been commercially successful, his home being a clear testament to this, but by the mid-to late 1880s he achieved an even greater success, becoming an almost permanent presence on Bond Street. Fairless and Beeforth, the fine art publishers, commissioned him to paint many large scale works for their galleries on Bond Street, most notably *Anno Domini* which remained on exhibition for over ten years. The production of prints after works by Long was extremely lucrative for those who had purchased the copyright. Agnew's commissioned many paintings from Long in this period, in particular a series of twenty paintings titled *Daughters of Our Empire* which were exhibited in Bond Street in 1887 for the Royal Jubilee.

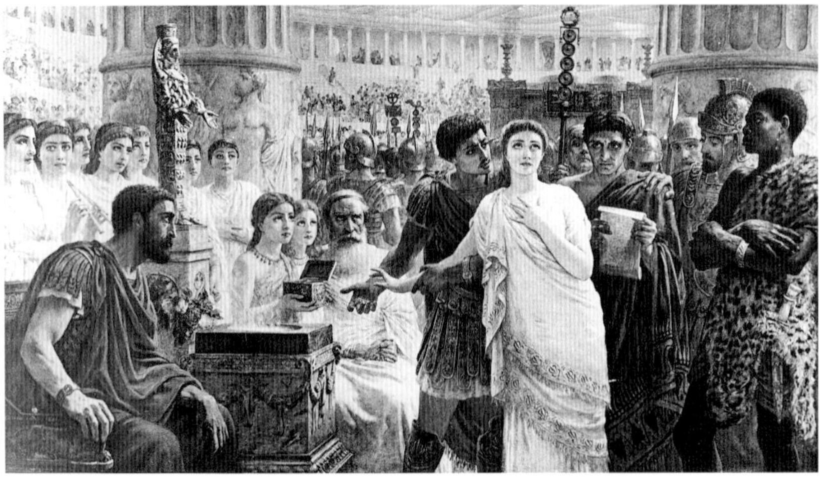

184. *Diana or Christ?*, 1880–81.

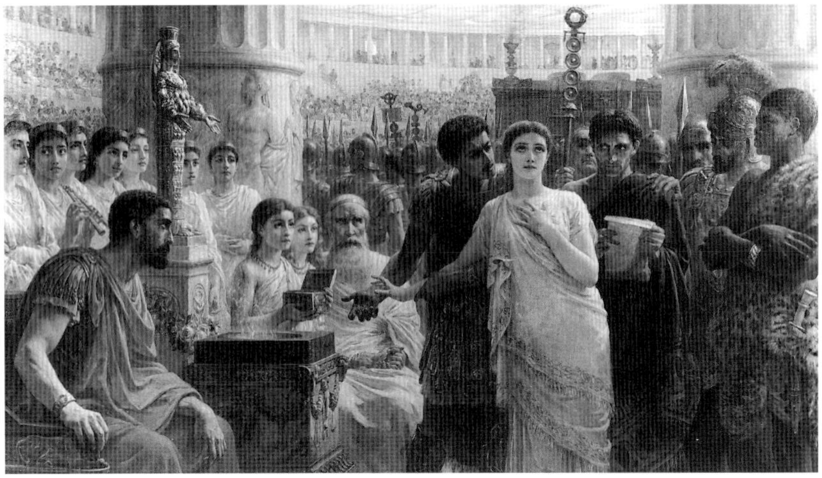

184.1. *Diana or Christ?*, 1881.
COPYRIGHT BLACKBURN MUSEUM & ART GALLERY

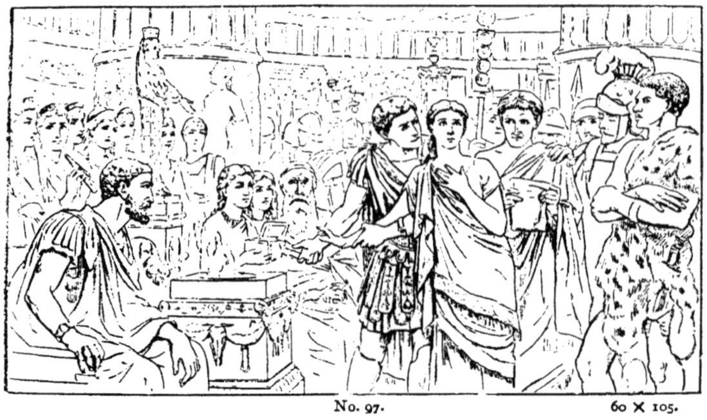

184. *Diana or Christ?*, engraving. *Academy Notes*, 1884.

184. Diana or Christ? (1)

1880–81; 60½ × 106½", 154 × 270 cm; oil on canvas; signed and dated 1881.

This painting of 1881, originally titled *Christiani ad Leones,*[1] is set in a Roman stadium at Ephesus. It depicts a Christian, offered her freedom if she will reject her God by worshipping the goddess Diana: "Let her cast the incense – but one grain, – and she is free". The stories of Christian martyrs in the ancient world was a frequent subject in Long's work. This work was exhibited in 1881 at the Royal Academy. A verse, inspired by the picture, by J. B. Greenwood was published which ends: "One pitying moment stood the crowd at bay, / Gazing incredulous, on the fearless maid; / Then the fierce tide of passion toward her swayed, / And her sweet martyr-spirit passed away."

The events are set c. 250 AD during the reign of Emperor Decius (249–51 AD) at Ephesus. Christian persecution had hitherto been sporadic and localised but an edict of 250 AD was issued for all citizens to perform a religious sacrifice in the presence of commissioners. Citizens who passed the test were issued with certificates, many of which have survived today. A large number of Christians lost their lives by refusing to carry out the ceremony, including the bishops of Rome, Antioch and Jerusalem.

Diana or Christ? shows the Christian martyr looking heavenward and refusing the grain of incense. Faces looking on, anxiously awaiting her decision, include the bureaucrat on the right with the certificate in his hands and the commissioner on the far left. The sacrifice is for the goddess Diana, Ephesus being one of the principle centres of the Diana cult (the statue to the left of the martyr is Diana-Artemis). The setting is the Odeum, a partially covered semi-circular theatre. The picture was widely reviewed on its exhibition at the Royal Academy. The majority of these were favourable with the exception of *The Times*; even the *Athenaeum*, often so critical of Long, was liberal in its praise:

> Mr. E. Long's 'Diana or Christ?'(97) is his best work, and in not a few respects the improvement is of a kind as well as of degree . . . On the whole, the design of this work is much better than we have yet seen by Mr. Long; it has been much more carefully and consistently carried out, a more solid style has been employed, the draughtsmanship is more searching and the painting better.[2]

Punch echoed the comments through its puns and surprise that the work was painted by Long: " . . . informs us that 'This is Long's'. Impossible . . . Our informant being gone, we consult the catalogue. Oh! picture 'by Mr. Long, A.' The martyr who won't incense the statue. Quite right. But that person who said simply it was 'Long's' has incensed us very much . . . "[3] The *Art Journal* responded not by surprise at the accomplishment of the work, but to what had come to be expected: "Needless to say that the silver statue of Diana, the columns of the stadium and all the antiquarian and architectural features of the scene are rendered with Mr Long's usual learning and accuracy".[4]

Long painted two versions of the painting. There was some confusion as to the identity of the original which was settled by a letter to *The Times* in 1908:

> Mr. Long's 'Diana or Christ?' – Mrs. Daniel Thwaites writes:– 'Will you allow me, through the medium of your journal to state that the original picture 'Diana or Christ?' was bought (with it all rights attached therewith) by my late husband from the studio of Edwin Long, and now is in my possession. It was exhibited at the Royal Academy in 1881, and at the Royal Jubilee Exhibition, Manchester in 1887. It has not recently been sold, nor is it now on exhibition'.[5]

1. *Magazine of Art*, 1880, p. 276.
2. Ath., 14 May 1881, p. 661.
3. *Punch*, 7 May 1881, p. 208.
4. AJ, 1881, p. 187.
5. *The Times*, 4 February 1908, p. 3.

PROVENANCE Bought from the artist by Daniel Thwaites, a Blackburn brewer; by descent to Mrs Daniel Thwaites, then to her daughter Elma Yerburgh; sold at Agnew's in 1979 to Mirra Fantenburg.

EXHIBITIONS RA 1881 (97); Manchester Jubilee Exhibition, 1887 (545); Russell-Cotes Art Gallery and Museum, Bournemouth, 1979.

LITERATURE *Academy Notes* 1884 (ill.); AJ, 1881, p. 187; AJ, November 1891; Ath., 14 May 1881, p. 661; Chester 1908, p. 335 (ill.), p. 350; John Forbes-Robertson, 'Art at the Manchester Jubilee Exhibition',

Magazine of Art, 1887, p. 283; John Evan Hodgson RA, *Fifty Years of British Art* (London and Manchester: John Heyward, 1887), p. 83; Kestner, p. 258 (ill.); *Magazine of Art*, 1880, p. 276; *Punch*, 7 May 1881, p. 208; Quick 1931, p. 5, p. 27 (ill.), p. 44; Reitlinger 1961; Spielmann 1888, p. 612; *The Times*, 6 June 1881, p. 4, 13 and 14 December 1892; *The Times*, 4 February 1908, p. 3.

184.1. Diana or Christ? (2)

1881; 48 × 84″, 122 × 213.4 cm; oil on canvas; signed and dated.

A replica of Long's *Diana or Christ?* of the 1881 Royal Academy. There are slight, differences in the two versions notably the plume on the centurion's helmet has not been included, and an additional circle on the soldier's staff. The painting is referred to in Benezit and Quick as the *Martyr of Ephesus*.

PROVENANCE Purchased from the artist by David Price of 4 Queen Anne Street; sold at Christie's on 2 April 1892 for 2,500 guineas to Fairless and Beeforth; in the collection of D. H. Evans in 1897; presented to Blackburn as a war memorial in 1919 by John Edmondson.

EXHIBITIONS Gallery of Sacred Art (Fairless and Beeforth), 38 New Bond Street, London, 1892; Earl's Court, 1897 (no. 321).

LITERATURE *Daily Telegraph*, date unknown, 1908; Roberts 1897, vol. II, p. 179.

COLLECTION Blackburn Museum and Art Gallery.

185. Nouzhatoul-âouadat, 'The Delight of the Home'

1881; 28½ × 23″, 72.4 × 58.4 cm; oil on canvas; signed and dated on vase "Edwin Long 1881".

This half-length portrait of an Eastern young woman was Long's diploma piece. Its title is the French spelling of the Arabic translated as *The Delight of the Home*. Although not widely reviewed, the *Athenaeum* found it superior to Long's other Academy pieces: "A much better picture is 'Nouzhatoul-aouadat' (1483), which Mr. Long has wisely preferred to 'The New Fugue' for his diploma work. The imaginative and technical motives are devoid of fibre and purpose, but the handling of this painting and the choice of its colours show considerable good fortune and exterity".[1]

1. Ath., 27 May 1882, p. 673.

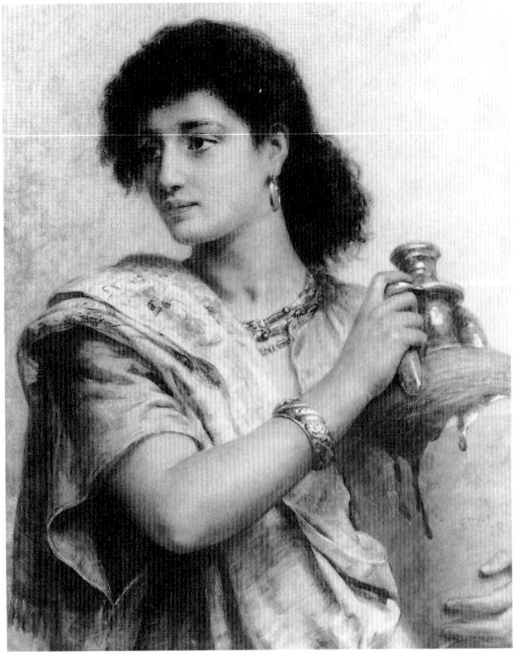

185. *Nouzhatoul-âouadat*, 1881.
THE ROYAL ACADEMY OF ARTS, LONDON

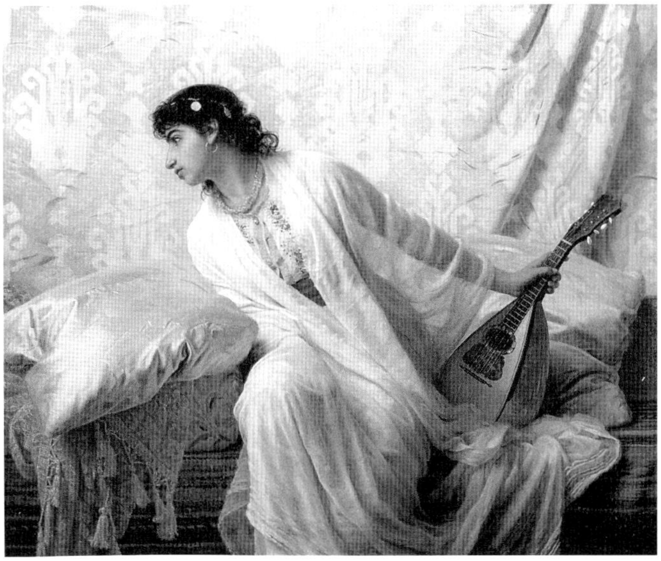

186. *Then to Her Listening Ear . . .*, 1881.
RUSSELL-COTES ART GALLERY AND MUSEUM
PHOTOGRAPH BRIDGEMAN ART LIBRARY

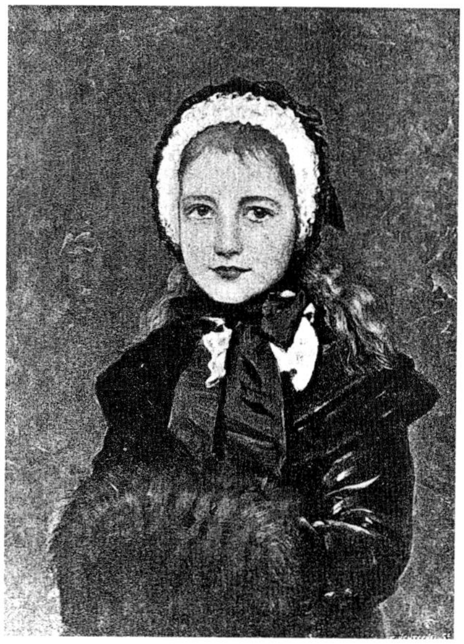

188. *Little Maud*, 1881.

EXHIBITIONS RA 1882 (1483).
LITERATURE Ath., 27 May 1882, p. 673; Sir Walter Lamb, *The Royal Academy* (London: George Bell and Sons, 1951, 1st. ed. 1935), p. 140; Quick 1931, p. 20 (ill.),p. 45; *Royal Academy Diploma Catalogue*, 141, (ill.).
COLLECTION Royal Academy Collection.

186. Then to Her Listening Ear . . .

1881; 38 × 40", 96.5 × 101.6 cm; oil on canvas; signed and dated on lower right.

One of Long's more lyrical paintings, emulating the work of Leighton. His technique in rendering the surface is more laborious and sensuous in this work. Its full title underlies its poetic rather than narrative aim: "Then to her listening ear responsive chords came familiar, sweet and low".

PROVENANCE Sir Merton Russell-Cotes before 1907; Russell-Cotes Art Gallery and Museum, Bournemouth.
EXHIBITIONS 'Fine Material for a Dream', Harris Art Gallery, Preston (1992), touring exhibition.
LITERATURE *Bulletin (R-C)*, vol. II, no. 2 (June 1923), p. 19, p. 23 (ill.); Quick 1931, p. 34 (ill.), p. 45.
COLLECTION Russell-Cotes Art Gallery and Museum, Bournemouth.

187. Ionian Pottery Seller

1881; 45 × 33½", 114.2 × 85 cm; oil on canvas.

PROVENANCE Sold at Christie's on 14 February 1936 for £5 15s 6d.

188. Little Maud

1881; size unknown; oil on canvas.

An extremely accomplished portrait by Long exhibited at the Royal Academy in 1881. The sitter depicts Miss Maud Crawley Vokins (later Mrs Arthur W. Blyth) as a young girl. The painting is a half-length portrait of Maud Vokins wearing a bonnet and muff. The quality of the painting was recognised by the contemporary periodicals who found it deserved mention: "'Little Maud' (509) by the same painter, is a vivacious portrait of a girl in black, with a crisp white lining to her bonnet, setting off a bright and clear, expressive, and intelligent face. Her hands are in a muff".[1] "'Little Maud' . . . showing Mr. Long quite at his best".[2]

1. Ath., 14 May 1881, p. 661.
2. *The Times*, 27 June 1881, p. 12.

PROVENANCE Mrs Vokins by descent to William Vokins, Esq.
EXHIBITIONS RA 1881 (509); Grafton Gallery, 1895 (311).
LITERATURE Ath., 14 May 1881, p. 661; *The Times*, 27 June 1881, p. 12.

189. Unconvinced

c. 1881; size unknown; oil on canvas.

PROVENANCE Purchased by Thomas Agnew & Sons on 2 April 1881; Christie's; sold at Christie's on 2 April 1887 to J. Mason for £385 10s.

190. Why Tarry the Wheels of his Chariot?

1882; size unknown; oil on canvas.

A large scale painting depicting a scene from the Song of Deborah: "The mother of Sisera looked out at a window, and cried through the lattice, Why is his chariot so long in coming? Why tarry the wheels of his chariot?"[1] Blackburn described the picture being of "Eastern colour and costume; the mother Sisera seated sorrowfully at the lattice with her handmaidens . . . The large picture, of which, by desire of the purchaser [Agnew's], we give no sketch, is to be engraved".[2] The *Art Journal* wrote: "The Mother of Sisera waiting among her Maidens for the return of her son. A large picture by Mr Long, remarkable for its absence of dramatic feeling, but also for fine painting".[3] *The Times* found that

> There is both expectation and dignity in the chief figure, and the contrast between the mother's anxiety and the unconcern of the attendants is carefully and not too strongly marked. The latter are just uneasily indifferent at the delay. The composition is smaller and less pretentious than Mr. Long's usual work, and there is less of the large-eyed Eastern beauty than usual. On the whole it is an advance upon former years showing more of the artist, and less of the archaeologist.[4]

1. Judges, v: 28.
2. *Academy Notes* 1882, p. 32.
3. AJ, 1882, p. 210.
4. *The Times*, 13 May 1882, p. 5.

PROVENANCE Bought from the artist by Thomas Agnew & Sons on 7 March 1882; sold to D. Thwaites on 31 March 1882 for £2,750.
EXHIBITIONS RA 1882 (302).
LITERATURE *Academy Notes* 1882, p. 32; AJ, 1882, p. 210; Chester 1908, p. 348; Quick 1931, p. 5, p. 44; *The Times*, 13 May 1882, p. 5.

191. The New Fugue

1882; size unknown; oil on canvas.

A portrait of a lady playing a new fugue on an organ. It is likely that the portrait was painted in Long's Fitzjohn Avenue studio where he had an organ installed over his large inglenook fireplace. According to the criticism of the time this was one of his least interesting Academy pictures for several years:

> A rather commonplace portrait of a young lady at the key-board of an organ, by Mr Edwin Long. Mr Long is at present deficient in the trenchant power of characterization which produces good portraits without the help of picturesque accessories, whilst he adds nothing in the way of colour or chiaroscuro to make up for their absence.[1]

The Athenaeum found it a contrast to his larger scale Biblical work at Burlington House:

> 'The New Fugue' (678) is a less ambitious, less exacting subject than the mother of Sisera waiting for the wheels of his chariot; in fact it is a tame portrait of a lady at an organ. The motive of the design is exceedingly commonplace, and nothing could be more trivial than the technical principle illustrated by the contrasts of the swans-down tippet, the black satin gown, and the fully lighted face. All other parts of the picture have

been sacrificed to these, and even they have been carried out with empty forms and perfunctory modelling, if modelling it can be called which admits of nothing like analyses of the garments, their folds and contours.[2]

Punch wrote: "No. 678 'Mind your Stops! or, Tempus Fugue it.' Female organism. EDWIN LONG RA."[3]

1. AJ, 1882, p. 236.
2. Ath., 27 May 1882, p. 673.
3. *Punch*, May 1882, p. 229.

EXHIBITIONS RA 1882 (678).
LITERATURE AJ, 1882, p. 236; Ath., 27 May 1882, p. 673; *Punch*, May 1882, p. 229.

192. Lord Iddesleigh (1)

1882; 51 × 34", 129.5 × 86.3 cm; oil on canvas; signed with monogram and dated.

A half-length portrait of Sir Stafford Henry Northcote (1818–87), first Earl of Iddesleigh. Long painted two versions of Lord Iddesleigh in 1882, both of almost identical size, one clearly being a copy of the other. This version now at Exeter appears to be the original version, as it was a gift to Lady Northcote and was the one exhibited at the 1882 Royal Academy exhibition and the 1887 Manchester Jubilee exhibition, the year of his death. The pentimenti on the hands of the 1882 National Portrait Gallery version may indicate that the painting was initially copied from this version, and that the hiding of the hand and the addition of a case were afterthoughts. The reasons for this may have been to vary the portrait, but more importantly to add

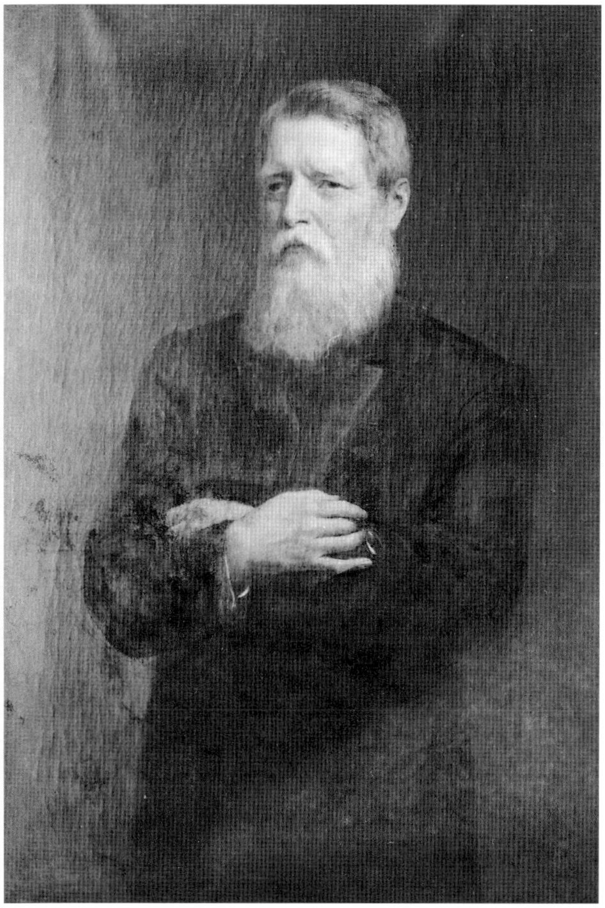

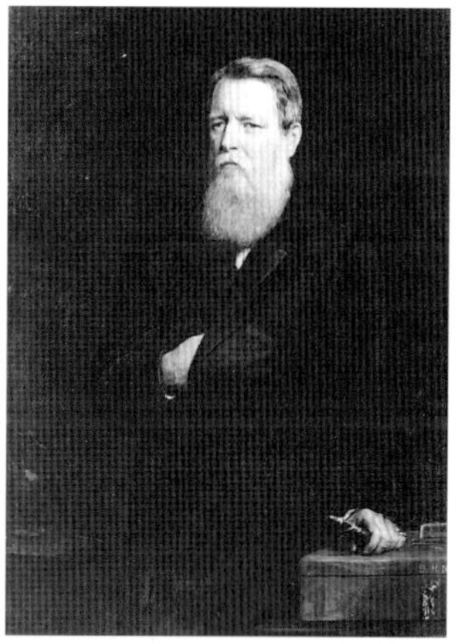

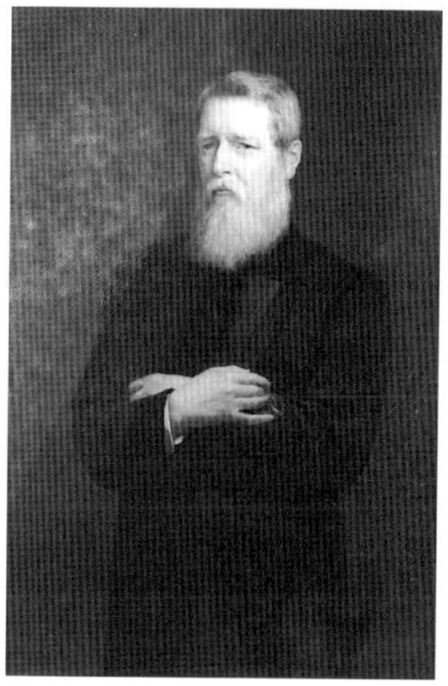

ABOVE 192. *Lord Iddesleigh*, 1882. UNIVERSITY OF EXETER
TOP RIGHT 192.1. *Lord Iddesleigh*, 1882. BOTTOM RIGHT 192.2. *Lord Iddesleigh*, 1889.
BOTH COURTESY OF THE NATIONAL PORTRAIT GALLERY, LONDON

some indication of his office. The portrait was commissioned by W. H. Smith, MP, who commissioned or bought portraits of his poitical colleagues, and the case with his initials S. H. N. may have been added to refer to his time as Chancellor of the Exchequer under Disraeli. The later modification of a copy seems quite plausible as does the original being owned by Lady Northcote. Furthermore, this was the version that Long chose to make a copy from in 1889.

PROVENANCE Presented to Lady Northcote (Countess Iddesleigh) by Devonshire Friends on 7 December 1883; in the collection of the Countess of Iddesleigh in 1887; Exeter University collection.
EXHIBITIONS RA 1882 (780); Manchester Jubilee Exhibition 1887 (522).
COLLECTION University of Exeter.

192.1 Lord Iddesleigh (2)

1882; 49½ × 36", 125.7 × 91.4 cm; oil on canvas; signed with monogram and dated.

The second 1882 portrait of Lord Iddesleigh and probably a modified copy of the Exeter version. Its notable differences are the cloaking of his right hand in his jacket and the addition of a case with his initials S. H. N. A photogravure of this version appears in Mr. Andrew Lang's *Life, Letters, and Diaries of Sir Stafford Northcote, First Earl of Iddesleigh.*

PROVENANCE Commissioned or bought by W. H. Smith, MP; given by Viscount Hambelden to the National Portrait Gallery, London, in 1938.
LITERATURE Chester 1908, p. 350; Andrew Lang, *Life, Letters and Diaries of Sir Stafford Northcote*, 2 vols. (Edinburgh and London: William Blackwood and Sons, 1890), (ill.).
COLLECTION National Portrait Gallery, London.

192.2 Lord Iddesleigh (3)

1889; 47½ × 31½", 120 × 80 cm; oil on canvas; signed with monogram and dated.

Replica of Exeter's 1882 portrait of Iddesleigh. A letter from Sir George Scharf, the National Portrait Gallery's first director, noted the main addition to the painting of one of Long's studio chairs: "Your excellent portrait of Lord Iddesleigh has arrived here this day in perfect safety, and the richly carved chair which you have introduced is a valuable addition".[1]

1. Scharf to Long, 18 July 1889, National Portrait Gallery Collection, London.

PROVENANCE Given by a Memorial Committee to the National Portrait Gallery in 1889.
LITERATURE Quick 1931, p. 6, p. 11 (ill.), p. 43.
COLLECTION National Portrait Gallery, London.

193. Samuel Cousins, RA

1882; 48 × 34", 121.8 × 86.3 cm; oil on canvas; signed with monogram and dated '1882'.

Samuel Cousins RA (1801–87) was a renowned mezzotint engraver. He was made an associate of the Royal Academy in 1835, and in 1855 was the first printmaker to achieve the full status of RA. He instituted a fund for indigent artists. As an important artistic personality, Long's portrait is one of many by several artists, including Frank Holl. J. H. Cousins (Samuel's cousin) compared the two in a letter calling Holl's painting "quite unrecognisable as a portrait of him, and in this opinion his family agreed. Subsequently however Edwin Long R.A. painted an excellent portrait of Samuel Cousins, which was appreciated by us all, and in his 84th year he made an excellent engraving from this portrait (without spectacles) and distributed proof prints amongst his relatives".[1]

1. Letter by J. H. Cousins, National Portrait Gallery Archive, London.

PROVENANCE Bequeathed by John Lane Esq. in 1925 to the Royal Albert Memorial Museum and Art Gallery, Exeter.
EXHIBITIONS RA 1883 (470).
LITERATURE Chester 1908, p. 348 (ill.); Ormond 1973, p. 118; Quick 1931, p. 6, p. 16 (ill.), p. 43.
COLLECTION Royal Albert Memorial Museum and Art Gallery, Exeter.

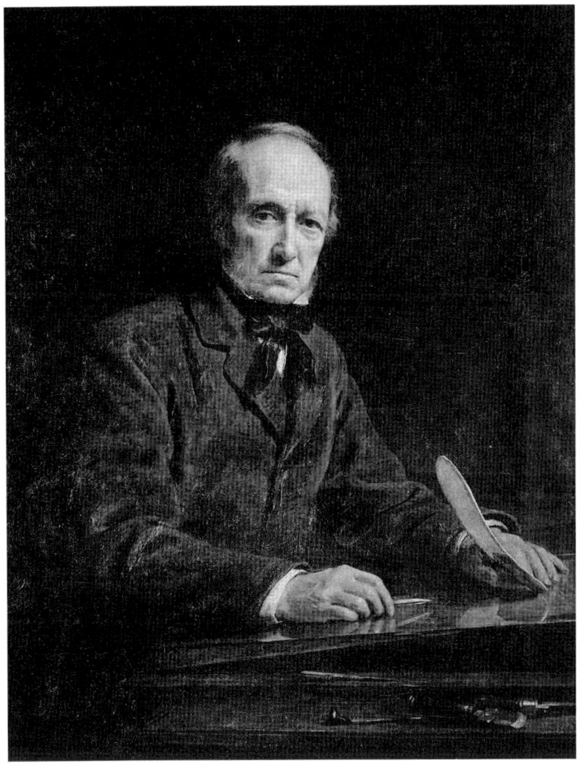

193. *Samuel Cousins, RA*, 1882.
ROYAL ALBERT MEMORIAL MUSEUM AND ART GALLERY, EXETER

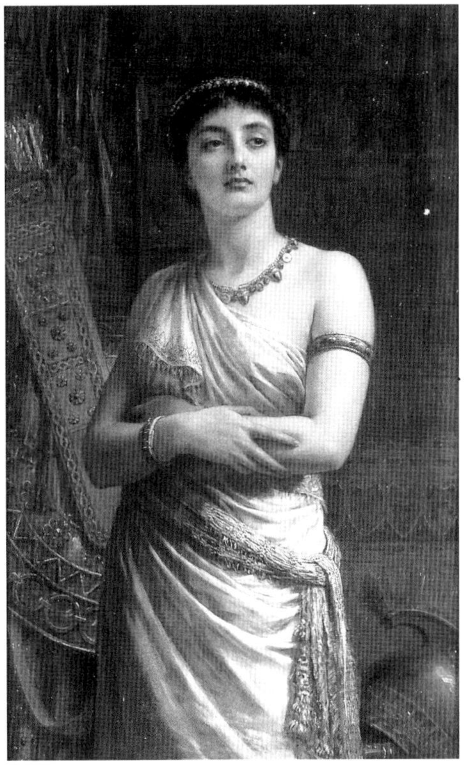

194. *Merab*, 1883.
COURTESY OF SOTHEBY'S, LONDON

194. Merab

1883; 48 × 30", 122 × 76 cm; oil on canvas; signed with monogram and dated.

In 1883, Long painted two companion paintings from the Book of Samuel. Like *Esther* and *Vashti* of 1879 they were two female portraits that illustrated contrasting expressions, in this case Long contrasts arrogance with love and devotion. Unlike his earlier pair, *Merab* and *Michal*, were smaller in scale and were this time appropriately hung close together at Burlington House. In 1885 they were exhibited together at the Lawrence Gallery beside *Anno Domini* and the companion paintings *Zeuxis at Crotona. Merab and Michal, Daughters of Saul* are both three-quarter-length portraits taken from 1 Samuel XVIII: 17–21, although Long used the words from Handel's oratorio *Saul* in the Royal Academy catalogue to emphasise the characters. Saul's eldest daughter Merab was promised to David but was instead given to Adriel the Meholathite for his wife. "And Michal Saul's daughter loved David: and they told Saul, and the thing pleased him". Merab is the arrogant elder daughter who, particularly in Handel's oratorio, scorns the thought of marriage to David: "My soul rejects the thought with scorn, That such a boy, 'till now unknown, Of poor plebeian parents born, Should mix with royal blood his own! Though Saul's commands I can't decline, I must prevent his low design, And save the honour of his line".[1] She is portrayed by Long looking insolently out of the canvas, her head held back and her arms folded. In the background armour is clearly apparent including a rich quiver and shield.

The Times, wrote at length:

> As we pass to the opposite wall of this first room the pictures that first take the eye are Mr. Long's pair of single figures which flank a rather dull conventional Faed. In default of a 'Babylonian Marriage Market' or a scene from the life ancient Egypt, Mr. Long bids visitors to the Academy content themselves with two modern portraits . . . and the highly ornamental sisters whom he has labelled with Bible names. They are Saul's two daughters – Merab and Michal – painted as they might have supposed to look in reference to the question of

marriage with David. The painter in default of much scriptural authority has sought his inspiration rather in Handel's oratorio, where the elder daughter is represented as highly indignant at David's presumption, and as by no means disposed to wed a son of the people even though he be the slayer of Goliath. What the Book of Samuel says, as the well-brought-up among Academy visitors will remember, is that a marriage between Merab and David was arranged, but that Saul broke his promise, and gave her to Adriel, Son of Barzillai the Metholathite. As the haughty damsel looks in scorn upon her suitor, what would she have given, one asks, if she could have forseen the time when King David should hand over his four sons to be hanged by the Gideonites? But Michal, as everyone knows, loved David: and her picture shows it. The painter indeed has set himself to paint two companion pictures alike in costume and surrounding and only altering in the character and attitudes of his heroines; he has set himself to paint the two strongest of feminine emotions – scorn and love – and he has embodied his types in two very picturesque but candour compels us to add uninteresting and conventional figures.[2]

1. George Frederic Handel, *Saul*, 1738. The first two lines of this verse were quoted in the Royal Academy catalogue, 1883.
2. *The Times*, 5 May, p. 12.

PROVENANCE Lawrence and Beeforth; sold at Sotheby's on 21 March 1990 for £16,000.
EXHIBITIONS RA 1883 (91); LG 1885 (89).
LITERATURE *Academy Notes* 1883; Chester 1908, p. 348; LG 1885; *Punch*, 12 May 1883, p. 220; Quick 1931, p. 44; *The Times*, 5 May 1883, p. 12.

195. Michal

1883; 48 × 30", 122 × 76 cm; oil on canvas; signed with monogram and dated.

"A father's will has authorized my love: No longer, Michal, then attempt to hide The secret of my soul. I love thee, David, And long have lov'd. Thy virtue was the cause; And that be my defence".[1] In contrast to Merab, Michal is shown hands clasped under her chin with a look of love and implied innocence. In the background are wall hangings and furs. Unlike *The Times* had suggested, that the contrast was made clear solely in expression, the backgrounds echo and reflect the different expressions. How much softer are the materials in Michal to the hard, metallic, cold and rich armour of Merab. *Punch* found space to make puns on the paintings: "Nos. 91 and 97. EDWIN LONG RA. Twin Sisters. 'Linked sweetness – Long drawn out.' Go on – can't stop Long".[2]

1. George Frederik Handel, *Saul*, 1738. The second and third lines of this verse are quoted in the Royal Academy catalogue, 1883.
2. *Punch*, 12 May 1883, p. 220.

PROVENANCE Fairless and Beeforth; sold at Sotheby's on 21 March 1990 for £20,000.
EXHIBITIONS RA 1883 (97); LG 1885-9.
LITERATURE *Academy Notes* 1883; Chester 1908, p. 348; LG 1885; *Punch*, 12 May 1883, p. 220; Quick 1931, p. 44; *The Times*, 5 May 1883, p. 12.

196. Glauké: Pensive

1883; 35½ × 27½", 90.2 × 69.8 cm; oil on canvas; signed with monogram and dated lower left.

The subject for Long's study of a pensive classical beauty is Glauke. Glauke or Glauce, also called Creusa, was the daughter of Creon, king of Corinth, who was betrothed to Jason, and slain out of jelousy by Medea by means of a poisoned robe. Long displays a young woman brooding on her fate, a subject he was to use in many of his Christian martyrs such as *Diana or Christ?* and *Alethe*.

PROVENANCE Sir Merton Russell-Cotes; sold at Christie's on 16 February 1917 for £63 to Wolf; purchased by the Russell-Cotes Art Gallery and Museum from Messrs L. Wolf on 18 June 1930 for 50 guineas.
LITERATURE *Bulletin (R-C)* vol. IX, no. 3 (September 1930), p. 25 (ill.), p. 29; Kestner, p. 230; Quick 1931, p. 35 (ill.), p. 45.
COLLECTION Russell-Cotes Art Gallery and Museum, Bournemouth.

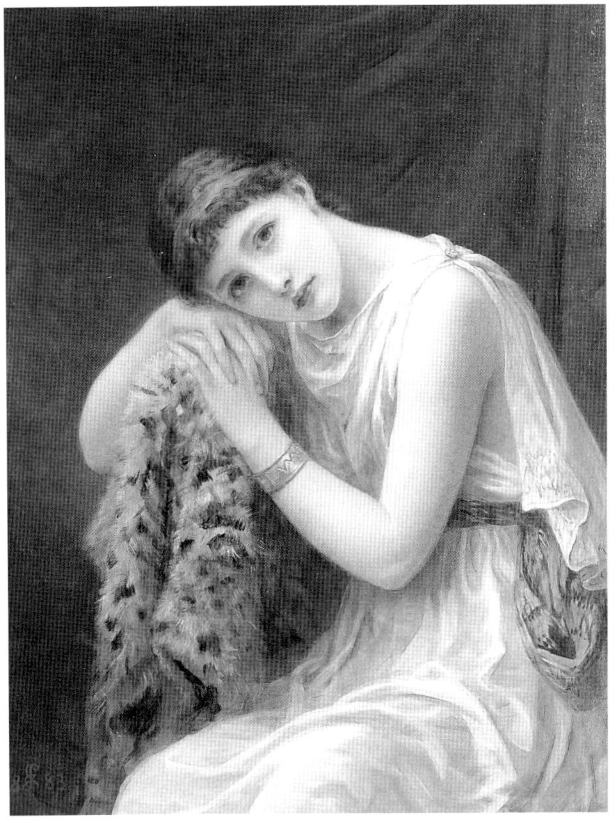

196. *Glauké: Pensive*, 1883.
RUSSELL-COTES ART GALLERY AND MUSEUM
PHOTOGRAPH BRIDGEMAN ART LIBRARY

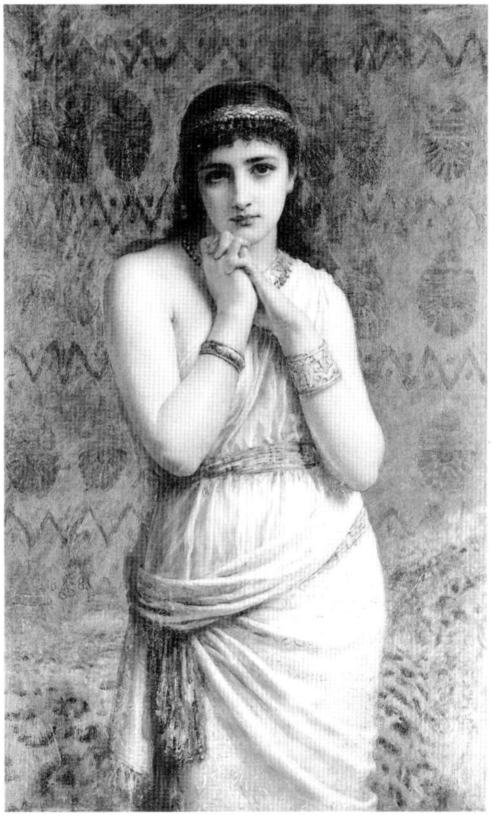

195. *Michal*, 1883.
COURTESY OF SOTHEBY'S, LONDON

197. Anno Domini, or the Flight into Egypt (1)

1883; 96 × 192", 243 × 487 cm; oil on canvas; signed and dated lower right hand corner.

> Behold, the Angel of the Lord appeared to Joseph in a dream, saying, Arise, and take the young child and his mother, and flee into Egypt, and be thou there, until I bring thee word: for Herod will seek the young child to destroy him. When he arose, he took the young child and his mother by night and departed in to Egypt.[1]

This passage of the New Testament is the main subject of this key work by Long. But as G. A. Sala describes in his catalogue essay on the work,

> The predominant and all-pervading idea of the 'Flight into Egypt' is to indicate by direct pictorial contrast, by the arrival of the Holy child and His parents a country reeking with idolatry, the coming into contact of the old and the new faiths, and to imply the conflict which, ere long, must inevitably arise between Paganism and Christianity.[2]

Long clearly explores this contrast in many of his works such as *Callista*, but *Anno Domini* is marked for its use of the New Testament to indicate such a contrast and to explore the theme on such a grand scale with such a wealth of imagery. The contrast between the Holy family and the other figures from Ancient Egypt is clear not only in the marked difference in their clothing, but in the style of each which Long has adopted in his painting in both technique and colour. The Egyptians are rich, bright and clearly delineated, the Holy family are portrayed with subtler hues with a softer focus.

Their poverty and humility is a clear contrast with the brazen imagery of Ancient Egypt. Groups of images reflect further this contrast and the image of the mother and child can be seen in various guises. The image of Isis and her son Horus can be seen as gilded statues carried by the procession of priests,

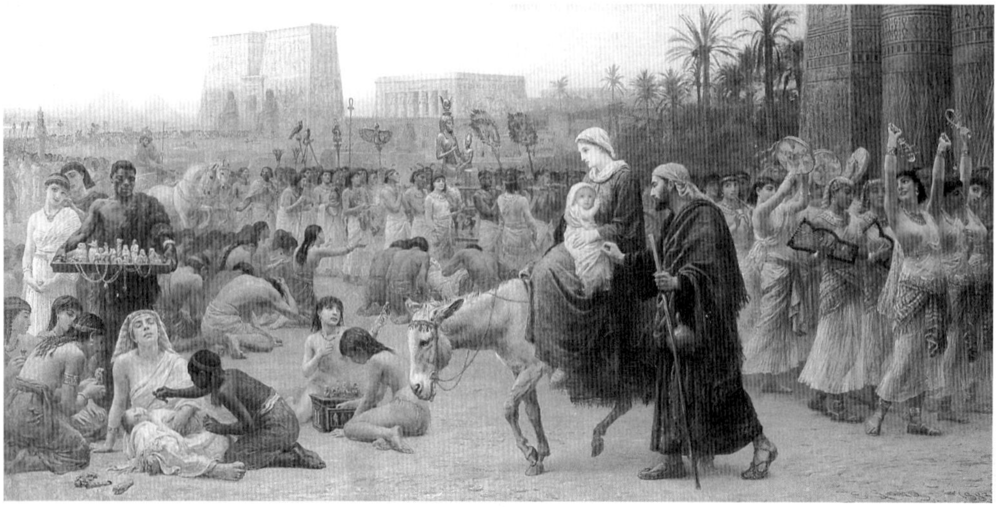

197. *Anno Domini, or the Flight into Egypt*, 1883.
RUSSELL-COTES ART GALLERY AND MUSEUM, PHOTOGRAPH JAMES HOWE

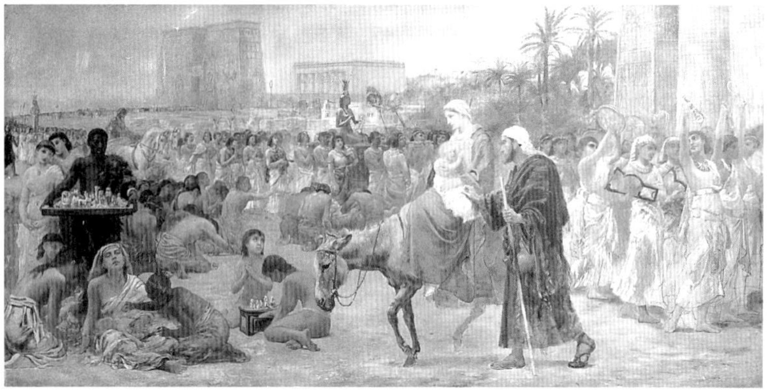

197.1. *Anno Domini, or the Flight into Egypt*, c. 1883.
CHRISTIE'S IMAGES

depicted by Long as a barren myth. From myth, the image is transformed into the lower left hand corner where a distressed mother can be seen trying to revive her dying or dead child. She is buying the icons (that Long had studied in the British Museum), to vainly reverse fate. Long has used this mother and child image to emphasise the land "reeking with idolatry". In contrast, the Holy family reflects Long's 'true' faith, the 'true' healer and spiritual family. Long also refers to myths and Sala recalls "an incident evidently suggested by the ancient tradition that, while journeying to Egypt the Madonna took a dead child, the offspring of a robber in her arms, and restored it to life".[3]

The setting shows Long's fascination with the costume and voluptuous images of the ancient world despite the picture's overt morality. It is set at dusk, a cooler time in Egypt that gives the light in the picture a beautiful evening glow. In the background is a temple with its main building and outer pylons and in the distance the pyramids are visible. Long uses temple design in general to construct the painting rather than any true view of Egypt. The temple paintings were copied from ancient remains, the pylons representing the wars of Rameses II. The procession begins at the temple and winds its way to the front of the picture, overseen by the Roman soldiers indicating the Roman rule in Egypt at this time. The female musicians at the front of the group are the 'holy women' of the temple playing, according to their status, cistrums (a kind of rattle), lyres, tabors and dual flutes. The parade is celebrating the gods Isis, Horus and

Osiris. Isis represented by the symbol of the lotus represents maternity and creativity, shown by Long as a negative contrast. Osiris is the earth-god who was put to death only to rise again, contrasted again by Long in his depiction of Christ. The bull Apis can be seen as the body of the transmigrated soul of Osiris.

Long's interest in archaeology and other religions is explored in detail in 'Anno Domini' which is so full of detail, religious symbolism and archaeology that elicited the *Art Journal* to write: "It is not possible at first view to do more than indicate the more striking features in so extensive a canvas; it is certainly in many respects a remarkable achievement, and merits further investigation and study".[4] The painting was commissioned by Fairless and Beeforth, fine art publishers who "paid half in cash and half out of receipts".[5] Fairless and Beeforth owned the Doré Gallery, a gallery set up in 1869 to exclusively show works by that artist, and made a small fortune showing his works and selling prints after them. When Doré died unexpectedly in January 1883 they needed a replacement. As the *Magazine of Art* noted

> When Gustave Doré died, the caterers for that devout and sentimental portion of the public who took unctuous delight in the wonders of the Doré Gallery could find in England no worthier heir to his mantle than Mr. Long, who exerted himself considerably on their behalf, and produced a number of gently inspired scriptural paintings.[6]

Anno Domini was exhibited firstly at their gallery at 168 New Bond Street until 1889, then it was moved, after the gallery closed, to the Doré Gallery, later their Gallery of Sacred Art until 1896 under a new title, *The Unknown God*. The picture proved to be popular and over a period of nine years Lewis Carroll visited it on four occasions. The critical reception of the work on first showing at the Lawrence Gallery was unanimous in regarding it as a major work of great importance. Reviews are to be found in many journals of the day, *The Morning Post* writing:

> The picture is in a bright, harmonious scheme of colour. The excellent type and variety of feature, and the mass of archaeological detail introduced, attest to the research and care which have been resorted to, in as great a measure as the numerous incidents depicted show the thought and diligent effort which have been expended on the work, which is one of the most important, if not the most important, which Mr. Long has ever painted.[7]

The work was engraved by Herbert Bourne in 1889 for Fairless and Beeforth.

1. Matthew, II: 13–14.
2. LG 1885.
3. Ibid.
4. AJ, 1884, p. 59.
5. *Home and Abroad*, p. 710.
6. *Magazine of Art*, July 1891, p. xl.
7. *The Morning Post*, 1884, quoted in LG 1885.

PROVENANCE Commissioned by Fairless and Beeforth in 1883; in the collection of D. H. Evans in 1897 and 1910; bought by Sir Merton Russell-Cotes before 1920; Russell-Cotes Art Gallery and Museum, Bournemouth.

EXHIBITIONS LG 1884–89; Doré Gallery, 35 New Bond Street, London, 1890–92; Gallery of Sacred Art, 35 New Bond Street, London, 1892–96 as *The Unknown God*; Earl's Court 1897 (320).

LITERATURE AJ, 1884, p. 59; *Belfast News Letter*, 1884; *Bulletin (R-C)*, vol. v, no. 3, (September 1926), p. 30 (ill.); *Bulletin (R-C)*, vol. II, no. 2, (June 1923) p. 17, p. 18 (ill.); Lewis Carroll, diary entries for 27 May 1884; 18 March, 3 April, and 28 June 1893; Clayton 1982, p. 32, pp. 33–34 (ill.); *Daily Chronicle*, 1884, quoted in LG 1885; *Daily News*, 1884, quoted in LG 1885; *Daily Telegraph*, 1884, quoted in LG 1885; *Edinburgh Daily Review*, 1884, quoted in LG 1885; *Era*, 1884, quoted in LG 1885; LG 1885; *Magazine of Art*, 1884, p. xiv, and 1885, p. xxii; De Meulenaere 1992, p. 125 (ill.), p. 138 (ill.); Quick 1931, pp. 4–5, pp. 40 (ill.), p. 41 (ill., detail), p. 44; *Home and Abroad*, p. 709; *Saturday Review*, 1884, quoted in LG 1885; Spielmann 1888, p. 612; *The Standard*, 1884, quoted in LG 1885; *The Times*, 13 and 14 December 1892; Walkley 1994, p. 109; Gleeson White, *The Master Painters of Britain* (Birmingham: Combridge, 1910), pp. 218–19 (ill.).

COLLECTION Russell-Cotes Art Gallery and Museum, Bournemouth.

197.1 Anno Domini, or the Flight into Egypt (2)

c. 1883; 60 × 120″, 152.3 × 305 cm; oil on canvas; signed with monogram.

This picture, which is unfinished appears to be a large preliminary oil sketch rather than an uncompleted replica. It even includes a faint nimbus around Christ's head which contradicts the whole meaning of the finished work.

PROVENANCE Sold by Burstow and Hewett on 21 December 1987 (122); sold at Christie's on 3 June 1988, bought by Todd for £3,000.

LITERATURE De Meulenaere 1992, pp. 124–25 (ill.), p. 138 (ill.).

198. Baroness Burdett-Coutts

1883; size unknown; oil on canvas.

Angela Georgina Burdett-Coutts (1814–1906), was a remarkable Victorian philanthropist. She was the heir of Thomas Coutts the banker and used her wealth to set up many schemes and charities for social and economic improvements and reform. She was friends with many of the important figures of her age. She was an important patron to Long commissioning several portraits from him, particularly those of the actor Sir Henry Irving who was a great friend of hers. In 1879 Long and his family joined Irving and Burdett-Coutts at Weymouth to board the yacht 'Walrus'. This was the beginning of a long Mediterranean cruise organised by the Baroness taking them to Corfu, Spain, Greece, France and Italy.[1] The *Art Journal* noted that the painting was "Very stately and composed; an excellent likeness without any pretence to flatter. Mr. Long's best work of the year".[2]

1. Lawrence Irving, *Henry Irving, The Actor and his World* (London: Faber and Faber, 1951), p. 330.
2. AJ, 1883, p. 220.

PROVENANCE Commissioned by Baroness Burdett-Coutts from the artist; by descent to S. Burdett-Coutts, in his possession in 1934.

EXHIBITIONS RA 1883 (667); Manchester Jubilee Exhibition 1887 (226).

LITERATURE AJ, 1883, p. 220; Ormond 1973, p. 81; Quick 1931, p. 6, p. 43.

199. Thisbe (3)

1884; 56 × 33″, 142.2 × 83.8 cm; oil on canvas.

Long's second version and third painting of Thisbe. The following translation of Ovid appeared in the 1886 Christie's catalogue which accompanied the sale of the painting: "An envious wall the Babylonian maid From Pyramus, her gentle lover, stayed. Yet here a tiny clink none else had seen Sufficed to bear love's messages between. They kissed its tiny mouth like lovers true, But neither side would let the kisses through".

The painting is a full length portrait of Thisbe, standing and listening, her head against the wall. In subject it is far less evocative of Babylon than his earlier paintings of the subject. The reliefs appear less well observed, the composition simpler and less effective and more like a dressed Victorian model smiling at the viewer. The *Athenaeum* was critical of the figure:

> We cannot say much for the elaborate and somewhat more vigorous 'Thisbe' (358), a figure placed near a stone wall that is wrought with emblems. She is supposed to be listening earnestly; but she does nothing and seems to do nothing. At any rate she does no harm, which Judith, did she move at all, might do –.[1]

1. Ath., 24 May 1884, p. 668.

PROVENANCE Edward Harrison Esq.; sold at Christie's 8 May 1886 for 840 guineas.

EXHIBITIONS RA 1884 (358).

LITERATURE *Academy Notes* 1884, p. 35 (ill.); Ath., 24 May 1884, p. 668; Chester 1908, p. 334 (ill.); Kestner 1989, p. 230, p. 352; Quick 1931, p. 21 (ill.), p. 44; Roberts 1897, vol. II, p. 93.

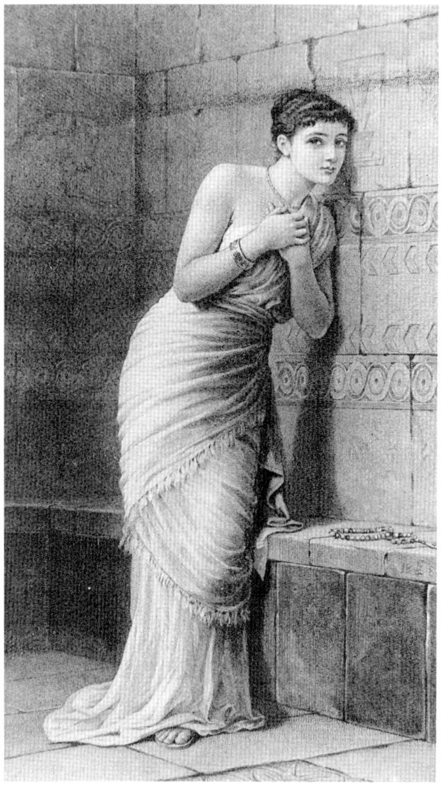

199. *Thisbe*, 1884.

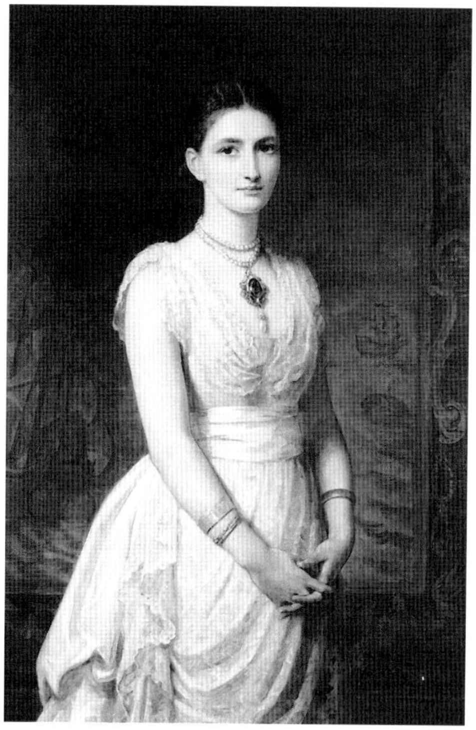

201. *Beatrice, Daughter of Sir Francis E. Drake, Bart.*, 1884.
PLYMOUTH MUSEUMS AND ART GALLERY

200. Judith

1884; size unknown; oil on canvas.

The subject of this painting is Judith, XIII: 7, the moment before she beheads Holophernes: "And approached the bed, and took hold of the hair of his head, and said, Strengthen me, O Lord God of Israel, this day". The *Athenaeum* offered a description of the work which it found weak: "The 'Judith' (28) of Mr. E. Long is one of his weakest performances. The famous Jewess was of other stuff than this. The sword hangs by a tent pole, and Judith, in the manner of a 'pose plastique,' makes believe to be impressed, turning upon her fine eyes and letting her draperies fall in order".[1] *The Times* found the painting too academical: " . . . and a 'Judith' by Mr. Long the latter likely to be popular among Mr. Long's admirers, but, to our mind, only another example of the ultra-academical manner into which this painter has fallen of late".[2] *Punch* joked: "No. 28 'Girl with an old Pump' As Claudian would say 'How Long! How Long! How – EDWIN LONG RA'."[3]

1. Ath., 24 May 1884, p. 668.
2. *The Times*, 3 May 1884.
3. *Punch*, 17 May 1884, p. 232.

PROVENANCE Bought by Thomas Agnew and Sons from the artist on 8 March 1884 (before its Royal Academy exhibition); sold to H. H. Blackwell on 2 May 1884 for £1,260 (during exhibition at the Royal Academy).

EXHIBITIONS RA 1884 (28).

LITERATURE *Academy Notes* 1884; Ath., 24 May 1884, p. 668; Chester 1908, p. 348; *Punch*, 17 May 1884, p. 232; Quick 1931, p. 44; *The Times*, 3 May 1884.

201. Beatrice, Daughter of Sir Francis E. Drake, Bart.

1884; 50¼ × 34¼", 127.6 × 87 cm; oil on canvas; signed and dated.

A three-quarter portrait of Elizabeth Beatrice Drake (Lady Seaton), the daughter of Sir Francis Elliot Drake, Bart. She is stood wearing a white dress and large necklace. The painting is briefly described in Chester: "He painted also the daughter of Sir Francis Elliot Drake, and, as the most suitable of all backgrounds, used a study of the tapestries of the Armada which are in the Houses of Parliament."[1]

1. Chester 1908, p. 350.

EXHIBITIONS RA 1885 (670).
LITERATURE Chester 1908, p. 350.
COLLECTION City of Plymouth Museums and Art Gallery.

202. The Mosque

1885; 16⅛ × 25½", 41 × 65 cm; oil on canvas; signed and dated.

A painting of a mosque with a group of Arabs and camels in the foreground.

PROVENANCE Sold at Christie's on 5 November 1993.

203. A Votary of Isis

c. 1885; 27 ×20", 68.6 × 50.8 cm; oil on canvas.

A painting depicting a worshipper of Isis painted during Long's residence at Fitzjohn's Avenue. The copyright of the painting was purchased by Arthur Tooth and Sons.

204. The Neophyte

c. 1885; 27 × 20", 68.6 × 50.8 cm; oil on canvas.

A painting depicting an early Christian convert painted during Long's residence at Fitzjohn's Avenue. The copyright of the painting was purchased by Arthur Tooth and Sons.

205. Iras

1885; unknown size; oil on canvas.

The subject is taken from Shakespeare's *Antony and Cleopatra*, Iras being one of Cleopatra's attendants who brings the Queen's cloak and crown before her suicide:

CLEO: . . . Iras, long farewell. [*kisses them. IRAS falls and dies*]
Have I the aspic in my lips? Dost fall?
If thou and nature can so gently part,
The stroke of death is as a lover's pinch,
Which hurts and is desir'd. Dost thou lie still?
If thus thou vanishest, thou tell'st the world
It is not worth leave-taking.[1]

There is a reference to this painting in Chester: "The literary is the most notable of all the elements that go into the making of Mr. Long's pictures, and when he turned to Shakespeare for inspiration, and added to it his powers of grouping and colour, his pictures from 'Anthony and Cleopatra' showed excellent qualities".

1. *Antony and Cleopatra*, v:2.
2. Chester 1908, p. 350.

EXHIBITIONS RA 1885 (149).
LITERATURE Chester 1908, p. 350.

206. Love's Labour Lost

1885; 50 × 75¼", 127 × 191.2 cm; oil on canvas; signed and dated.

This painting was exhibited at the Royal Academy with verse written by Long's eldest son Maurice St. Clair.[1]

> When like an opening bud the flower of Youth
> Unfolds its petals to the light of Truth,
> Then mimic toys and tales of wondorous lore,
> By puppets acted, charm not as before.
> Amusement wearies out her skill in vain,
> And calls the aid of music's magic strain;
> But happy childhood's limit passed for e'er
> Youth rashly craves reality and care.

Clayton in his *Rediscovery of Ancient Egypt* saw *Love's Labour Lost* as a version of the death of Cleopatra with the "young, tragic figure accepting her fate".[2] This is unconvincing in the light of the verse, the lack of tragedy in the poses and expressions of the central figures, and the fact that *Iras* explored this theme at the 1885 Royal Academy exhibition. The painting is clearly reflective of the verse. The central figure, presumably the daughter of an important Egyptian has moved into adulthood and is bored by the childish entertainments of her servants. The musicians that have been called for can be seen approaching from the right-hand entrance of the room.

The main archaeological sources for the painting come from *Manners and Customs of the Ancient Egyptians* by J. G. Wilkinson (1837), including the vase, the stand, stool and the entire mural on the back wall. The stool is a more accurate version of the British Museum one Long used in *The Gods and Their Makers* (1878). The unusually critical review in the *Athenaeum* noted:

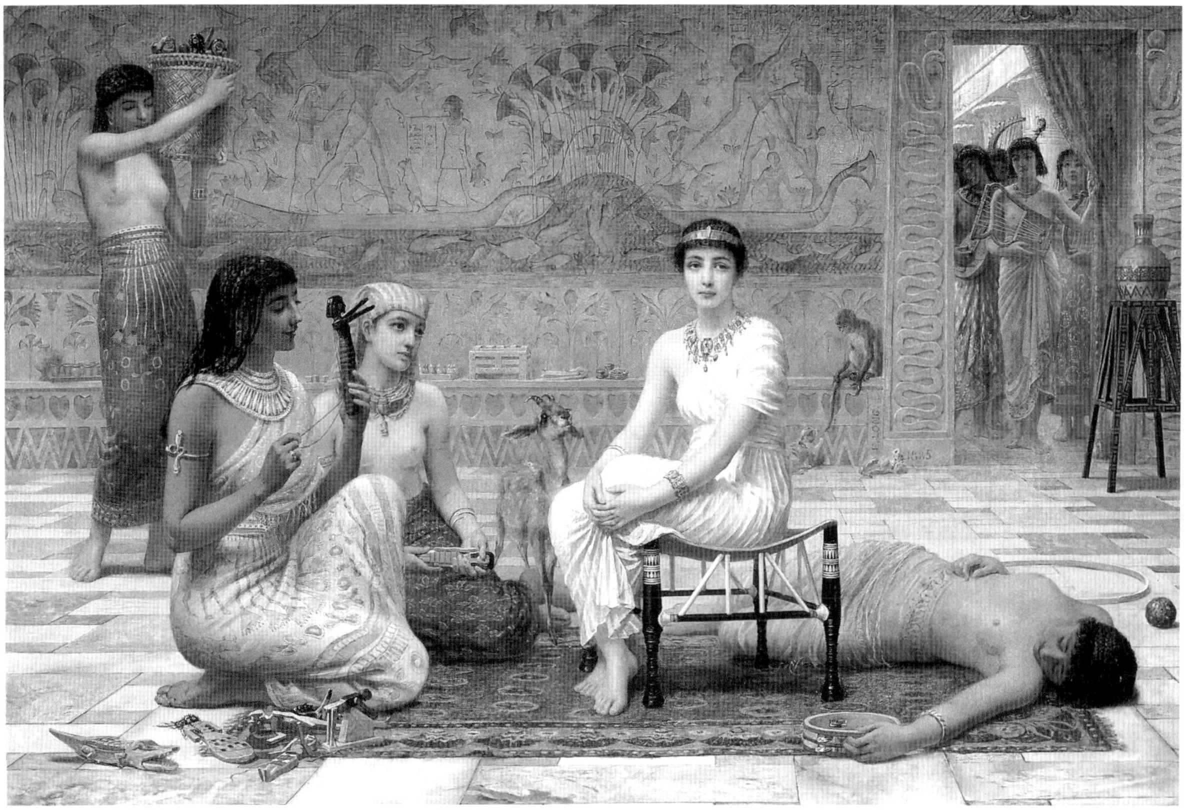

206. *Love's Labour Lost*, 1885.

> Mr. E. Long is always sentimental, and he sometimes tries to be poetical. In 'Love's Labour Lost' (226) a very smooth and fair princess, evidently in Egypt, sits in a chair we have seen in the British Museum. It is incomparably the best painted portion of the picture. She seems to be bored by the attentions of certain damsels, the confused condition of whose anatomy may account for their conduct. She is 'distraite', as well she may be, and the musicians standing in the doorway cannot comfort her. This is a boneless design, without fibre or thought of any kind. A superficial archaeology, a smooth, neat, but unsound mode of painting, prettily harmonized colours, and a sort of vacuous elegance distinguish one of the dullest pictures in the Academy. Mr. Long, besides exhibiting in Bond Street and elsewhere, has sent six pictures, most of them of a considerable size, to Burlington House this year.[3]

1. The name of Long's eldest son is mistakenly transcribed in Chapel 1982, p. 109, as Maurice Stelair.
2. Clayton, p. 180.
3. Ath., 16 May 1885, p. 636.

PROVENANCE Thomas Agnew and Sons purchased from the artist 31 March 1885 as *An Egyptian Princess 'Love's Labour Lost'*; sold to J. Reiseach 28 May 1889 for £1,550 and two paintings; Julian Hartnoll, London in 1977; sold at Christie's on 3 June 1994 for £120,000; sold at Christie's New York in 1995 to the Dahesh Museum.

EXHIBITIONS RA 1885 (226); 'Eastern Encounters: Painters of the Nineteenth Century', Fine Art Society, London, 1978 (112); 'Spring '84', The Fine Art Society, London (17); 'Picturing the Middle East', Dahesh Museum, New York, 1995–96 (36).

LITERATURE *Academy Notes* 1885, p. 9; *Apollo*, no. 105 (June 1977), p. 117 (ill.); Ath., 16 May 1885, p. 636; *Burlington Magazine*, no. 120 (August 1978), p. 548, p. 549 (ill.); Chester 1908, p. 341 (ill.); Clayton 1982, p. 180; *Magazine of Art*, 1885, p. 350; Quick 1931, p. 23 (ill.), p. 45; Walkely 1994, p. 109.

COLLECTION Dahesh Museum, New York.

207. Gunga

1885; unknown size; oil on canvas.

EXHIBITIONS RA 1885 (100).

208. Phyllis

c. 1885; 50 × 37", 127 × 94 cm; oil on canvas.

This was painted during Long's time at Fitzjohn's Avenue. The copyright was bought by Arthur Tooth & Sons.

PROVENANCE Sold in 1889 for 490 guineas.

209. The Search for Beauty (Zeuxis at Crotona)

1885; 60 × 96", 152.4 × 243.8 cm; oil on canvas; signed and dated.

The first of two companion paintings depicting Zeuxis at Crotona. Both of the pictures are of identical size, both were commissioned by Fairless and Beeforth for the Lawrence Gallery where they were first exhibited in 1885. The paintings depict two scenes from the story of Zeuxis's painting of Helen for the temple of Hera at Crotona. Long took the subject directly from the writings of Cicero and Pliny the Younger:

> The citizens of Croton, realising that Heaven had blessed them with a prosperity such as even the Gods might envy, were desirous of showing their gratitude by an offering to their Protectress Hera, that should not be unworthy of the acceptance of a Goddess. They accordingly proposed to embellish her temple with beautiful paintings, and for that purpose engaged the services of Zeuxis, of Heraclea, who gave them several fine specimens of his art. But there was one picture that he painted for them of Helen, in which he aimed to express the perfection of female beauty. To obtain models for this he asked the authorities what beautiful maidens the city could grant for him to paint from? They replied by conducting the artist into the Gymnasium, where they showed him several boys of surpassing beauty, saying, as he marvelled at their grace of limb and form, 'These are the brothers of our maidens, you can imagine what their sisters are like from them'. 'Then pray show me the most beautiful of your maidens,' answered Zeuxis, 'that my work may be a true impression of nature, for unless mirrored from life art is inanimate and dumb'. Accordingly a decree was passed commanding the attendance of all the maidens of the city in a place convenient for the inspection of the artist, who thereupon

> selected five. For he knew that he could find no single form possessing all the characteristics of perfect beauty, which impartial Nature distributes among her children, accompanying each charm with a defect, that she may not be at a loss what to give the rest by lavishing all she has to afford one.[1]

In these two paintings Long comes closest to being the Victorian Olympian to which he aspired in many of his works. In *The Search for Beauty*, Long depicts Zeuxis making his initial choice against the setting of the atrium of the temple. The magazine *Society* found the work:

> Eminently natural in grouping, and charming in the grace of the figures draped, nude, or semi-nude, sitting or standing about in various attitudes, Mr. Long has built up a delightful scheme of colour in his contrasts of cool marble and glowing flesh, in the dark Tyrian purple of the himation or toga verilis of Zeuxis, with its delicate gold embroidery, and the soft shimmer of the silken pepli, pink, golden, and white, worn by the victorious or vanquished virgins. The hale hearty look of the elder man and the matured manly beauty of the artist come in strong relief with the svelte and lissom figures of the springtime grace of the girls; and Mr. Long's known mastery of technique and texture has rarely been shown to fuller advantage.[2]

1. Cicero, *de Inventione*, II: i–iii, quoted in LG 1885.
2. Mahlstick, *Society*, 1885, quoted in LG 1885.

PROVENANCE Purchased from the artist by Fairless and Beeforth of the Lawrence Gallery in 1885; sold in 1915 for £189 10s; bought by Leytonstone Hospital in 1954 for £18; sold at Christie's on 24 June 1988 for £40,000.

EXHIBITIONS LG 1885–89.

LITERATURE *Apollo*, no. 128 (September 1988), p. 63 (ill.); *Belfast News Letter*, 1885, quoted in LG 1885; *Daily News*, 1885, quoted in LG 1885; *Edinburgh Daily Review*, 1885, quoted in LG 1885; LG 1885, pp. 27–34; *Magazine of Art*, 1885, p. xxii; *Society*, 1885, quoted in LG 1885; Reitlinger 1961; *The Standard*, 1885; Walkely 1994, p. 109; *Waltham Forest Guardian*, 4 Aug, 1989; *The World*, 1885, quoted in LG 1885.

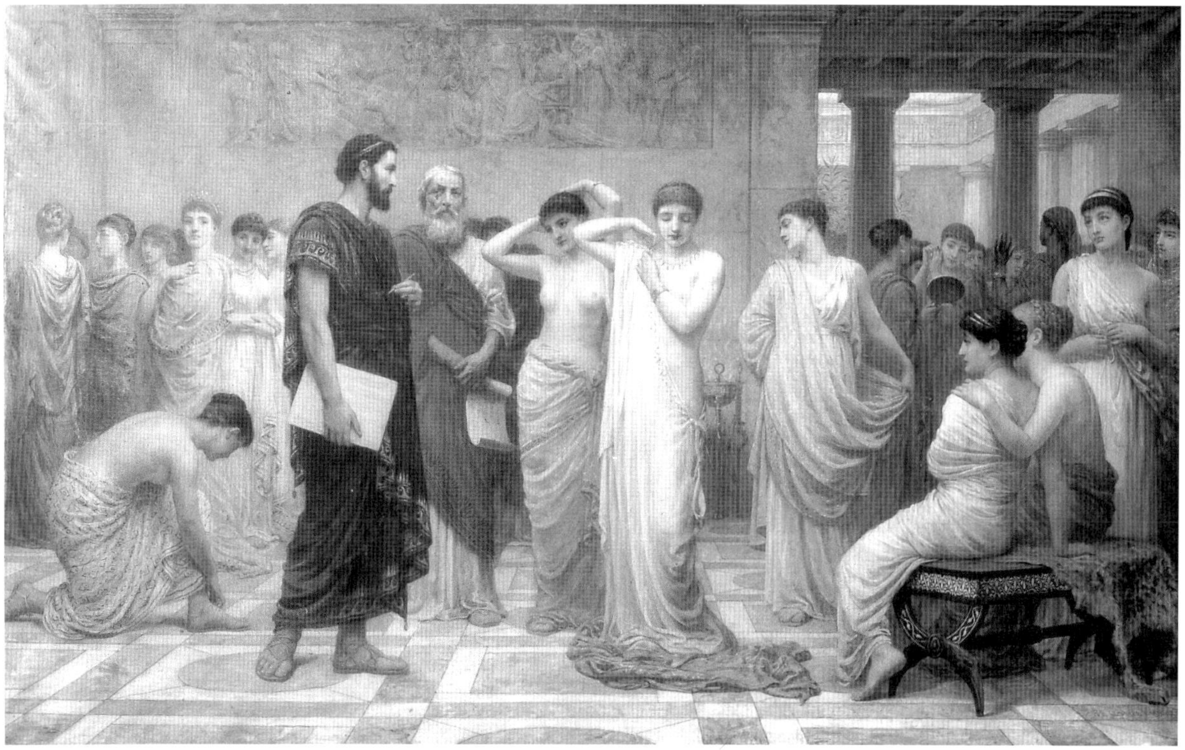

209. *The Search for Beauty (Zeuxis at Crotona)*, 1885.
CHRISTIE'S IMAGES

210. The Chosen Five (Zeuxis at Crotona)

1885; 60 × 96", 152.4 × 243.8 cm; oil on canvas; signed and dated on Zeuxis's footstool.

The second of two companion paintings depicting Zeuxis at Crotona. It was exhibited with *The Search for Beauty* at the Lawrence Gallery in 1885. Long took the subject directly from the writings of Cicero and Pliny the Younger:

> Zeuxis is allowed in addition to the super-eminent power he displayed in the delineation of the face and limbs, to have been possessed of such delicate taste, that, when he had undertaken to paint a picture for the citizens of Agrigentum, to be presents by the town to their temple of Hera, he was admitted to see their maidens nude, from whom he chose five, that he might render in his work the most admirable beauties of each.[1]

In *The Chosen Five*, Long shows Zeuxis at work in his studio taking the most admirable features of each to produce the classical ideal of Helen. The main model is raising her arms above her head in an evocative classical pose. The poses of all the models have a statuesque quality and the particular features that expressed Long's own personal ideal of beauty. The *Standard* commented of the work:

> But the second picture has the interest of Zeuxis buckling seriously to the task, minutely observant, as only the trained eye can manage to be, of every excellent or characteristic contour, and the steadiness of the model is well expressed, and the pose of the girl who looks on from behind, and leans back, half reclining as she looks, has a singular grace and charm. The painting, too, is of brilliant and solid quality. There is a large public whom these canvases may rightly fascinate.[2]

1. Pliny the Younger, *Epistles* 35, 9, and 36, quoted in LG 1885.
2. *The Standard*, 1885, quoted in LG 1885.

PROVENANCE Purchased from the artist by Fairless and Beeforth of the Lawrence Gallery in 1885; bought by Sir Merton Russell-Cotes.

EXHIBITIONS LG 1885–89.

LITERATURE *Belfast News Letter*, 1885; *Bulletin (R-C)*, vol. II, no. 2 (June 1923), p. 22 (ill.); *Daily News*, 1885, quoted in LG 1885; *Edinburgh Daily Review*, 1885, quoted in LG 1885; William Gaunt, 'An Edwardian Bequest' *Architectural Review*, no. 119 (March 1956), p. 171 (ill.); Kestner 1989, pp. 230–31, p. 258 (ill.); LG 1885, pp. 27–34; *Magazine of Art*, 1885, p. xxii; Quick 1931, p. 6, p. 39 (ill.), p. 45; *Home and Abroad*, pp. 709 and 711; *Society*, 1885, quoted in LG 1885; *The Standard*, 1885, quoted in LG 1885; Walkely 1994, p. 109; *The World*, 1885, quoted in LG 1885.

COLLECTION Russell-Cotes Art Gallery and Museum, Bournemouth.

211. Mrs Chamberlain Starkie

1885; unknown size; oil on canvas.

A presentation portrait of Mrs Chamberlain Starkie exhibited at the 1885 Royal Academy Exhibition.

EXHIBITIONS RA 1885 (1147).

LITERATURE Quick 1931, p. 43.

212. Miss Fleetwood Wilson

1885; unknown size; oil on canvas.

A portrait of Miss Fleetwood Wilson exhibited at the 1885 Royal Academy Exhibition.

EXHIBITIONS RA 1885 (655).

LITERATURE Quick 1931, p. 43.

213. Jephthah's Vow: The Return

1886; 89½ × 135", 227.4 × 343 cm; oil on canvas; signed and dated on chariot lower left.

Long painted a trilogy of paintings based upon the story of Jephthah's vow between 1885 and 1886. The source for the paintings are Judges, xi: 30–40. The paintings were commissioned by the fine art publishers Fairless and Beeforth (establishers of the Doré and Lawrence Gallery). In their scale and subject they

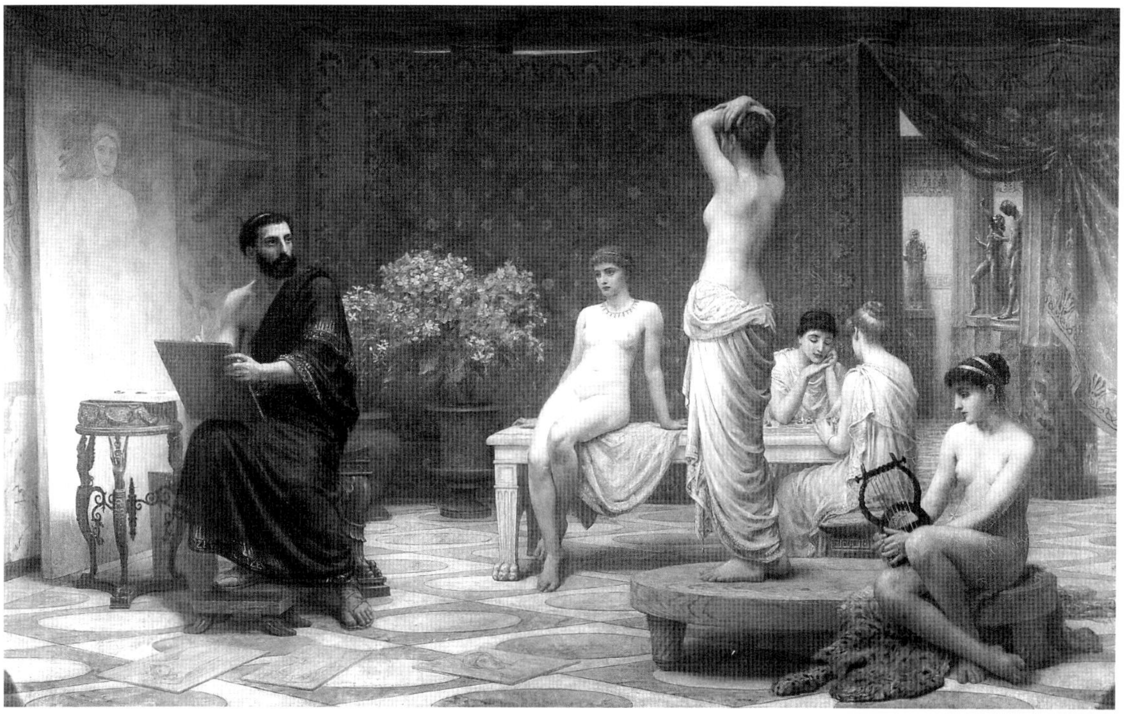

210. *The Chosen Five (Zeuxis at Crotona)*, 1885.
RUSSELL-COTES MUSEUM AND ART GALLERY, PHOTOGRAPH JAMES HOWE

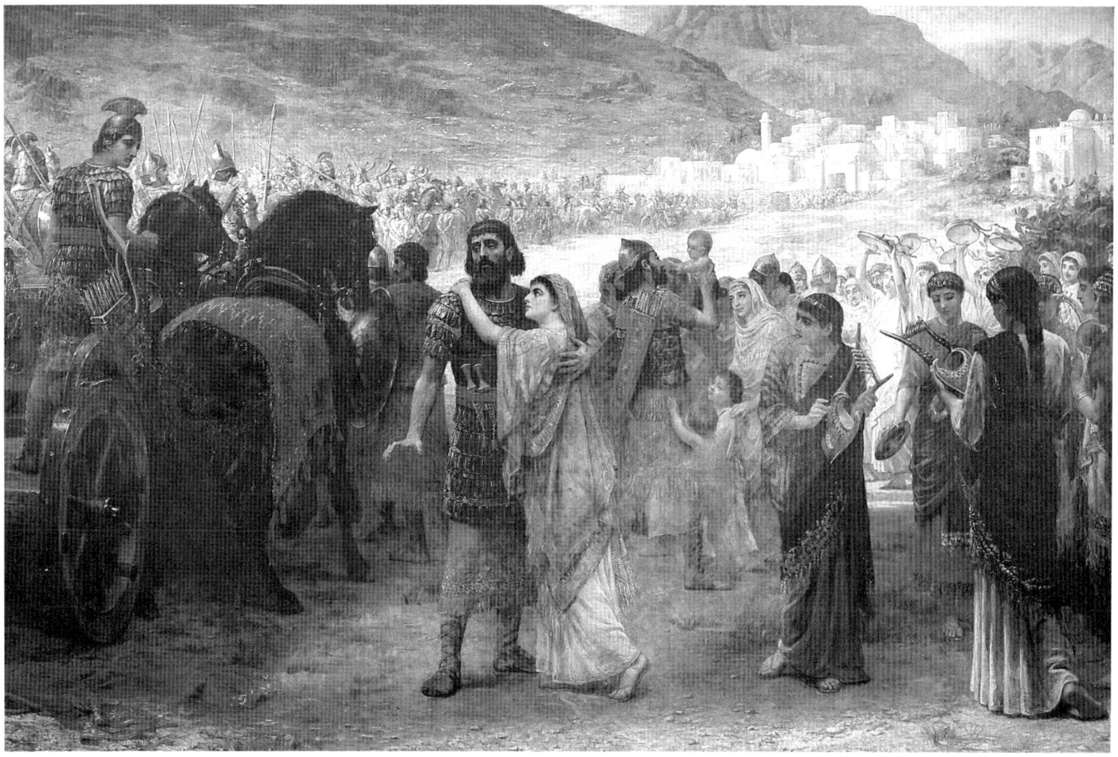

213. *Jephthah's Vow: The Return*, 1886.
RUSSELL-COTES MUSEUM AND ART GALLERY, PHOTOGRAPH JAMES HOWE

clearly fit into the mantle of Doré and were soon after completion engraved for an eager public. Long began exhibiting at the Lawrence Gallery in January 1884 in the place of Gustave Doré who died in 1883. This trilogy of paintings were first exhibited there in 1886. Remaining in the ownership of Fairless and Beeforth for the next ten years they were exhibited at the Doré Gallery (renamed in 1892 as the Gallery of Sacred Art) as *The Story of Jephthah.*

The works resemble the more conventional biblical scenes and lack the creative imagination of *Anno Domini.* The first scene, the last to be completed of the scene is based upon the following verses:

> And Jephthah came to Mizpeh unto his house, and, behold, his daughter came out to meet him with timbrels and with dances: and she was his only child; beside her he had neither son nor daughter. And it came to pass, when he saw her, that he rent his clothes, and said, Alas, my daughter! thou hast brought me very low, and thou art one of them that trouble me: for I have opened my mouth unto the LORD, and I cannot go back.[1]

Pentimenti are visible on the right arm of Jephthah and the chariot where Long has modified the painting from the positions indicated in the sketch.

1. Judges, XI: 34–35.

PROVENANCE Commissioned by Fairless and Beeforth; bought by Sir Merton Russell-Cotes before 1920; Russell-Cotes Art Gallery and Museum.

EXHIBITIONS LG 1886–9; Doré Gallery, 35 New Bond Street, London, 1890–92; as *The Story of Jephthah* at the Gallery of Sacred Art, 35 New Bond Street, London, 1892–96.

LITERATURE *The Times*, 13 December 1892. *Bulletin (R-C)*, vol. v, no. 3 (September 1926), p. 31 (ill.); Quick 1931, p. 5, p. 35 (detail ill.), p. 38 (ill.), p. 44; *Home and Abroad*, pp. 709–11; William Gaunt, 'An Edwardian Bequest', *Architectural Review*, no. 119 (March 1956), p. 173 (ill.).

COLLECTION Russell-Cotes Art Gallery and Museum, Bournemouth.

213.1 Jephthah's Vow: The Return *(sketch)*

c. 1886; 32 × 48″, 81 × 122 cm; oil on canvas; signed with monogram.

A study for the completed painting at the Russell-Cotes Art Gallery and Museum. It appears from the pentimenti on the completed version that this was the version that Long sketched in and then subsequently changed. The notable changes from this sketch in the finished version are the resolving of the chariot which is more convincingly placed and the more natural positioning of the figure of Jephthah.

PROVENANCE Sold at Christie's on 12 July 1990 for £1,200.

214. Jephthah's Vow: In the Wilderness

1885–86; 89 × 60″, 226 × 152.4 cm; oil on canvas; signed and dated lower left.

"And she said unto her father, Let this thing be done to me: let me alone two months, that I may go up and down upon the mountains, and bewail my virginity, I and my fellows. And he said, Go. And he sent her away for two months: and she went with her companions, and bewailed her virginity upon the mountains".[1] In this scene Long overtly emphasises the Christian element of the Old Testament story. Jephthah's daughter is dressed in white and is the lightest part of the picture which reflects her purity. She looks heavenwards as her companions cast their eyes downwards, as doves hover to the left of the painting.

1. Judges, XI: 37–38.

PROVENANCE Commissioned by Fairless and Beeforth; bought by Sir Merton Russell-Cotes before 1920; Russell-Cotes Art Gallery and Museum.

EXHIBITIONS LG 1886–89; Doré Gallery, 35 New Bond Street, London, 1890–92; as *The Story of Jephthah* at the Gallery of Sacred Art, 35 New Bond Street, London, 1892–96.

LITERATURE *Bulletin (R-C)*, vol. v, no. 3 (September 1926), p. 31 (ill.); William Gaunt, 'An Edwardian Bequest', *Architectural Review*, no. 119 (March 1956), p. 173; Quick 1931, p. 5, p. 42 (ill.), p. 44; *Home and Abroad*, pp. 709–11; *The Times*, 13 December 1892.

COLLECTION Russell-Cotes Art Gallery and Museum, Bournemouth.

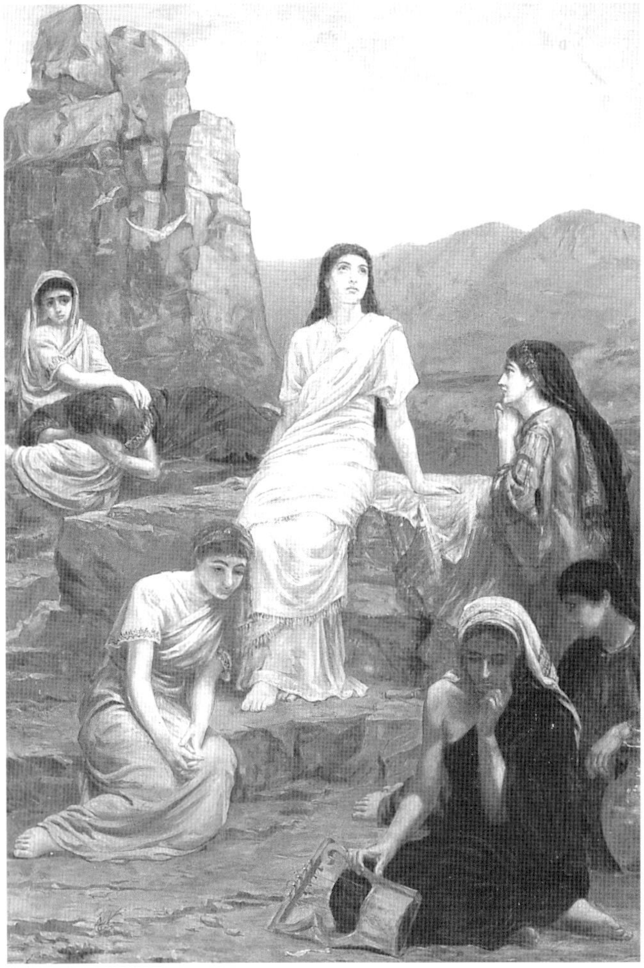

214. *Jephthah's Vow: In the Wilderness*, 1885–86.
RUSSELL-COTES MUSEUM AND ART GALLERY, PHOTOGRAPH JAMES HOWE

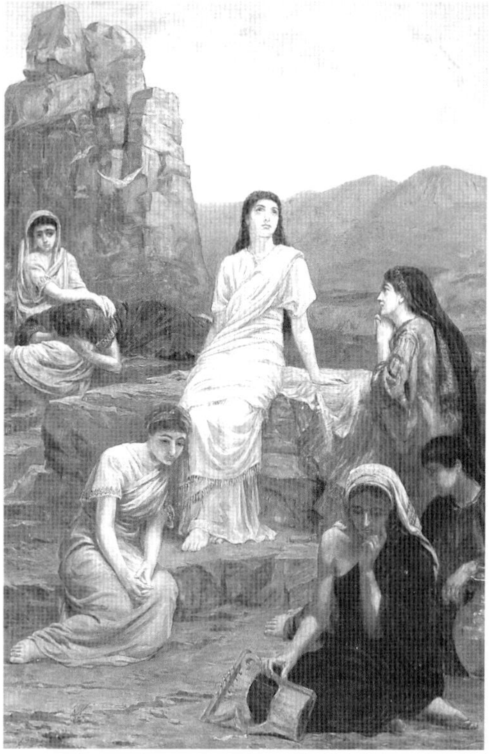

214.1. *Jephthah's Vow: In the Wilderness* (study), 1885.
RUSSELL-COTES MUSEUM AND ART GALLERY, PHOTOGRAPH JAMES HOWE

214.1 Jephthah's Vow: In the Wilderness *(study)*

1885; 21¼ × 14", 54 × 35.6 cm; oil on Academy board.

A small oil study for *Jephthah's Vow: In the Wilderness.*

PROVENANCE Sold at Sotheby's on 29 January 1974 as *O Lord how Long!*; sold at Sotheby's on 27 July 1976 for £100 as *Waiting*; The Russell-Cotes Art Gallery and Museum, Bournemouth.

COLLECTION Russell-Cotes Art Gallery and Museum, Bournemouth.

215. Jephthah's Vow: The Martyr

1885; 84 × 60", 213.3 × 152.4 cm; oil on canvas; signed and dated on pyre, left hand side.

"And it came to pass at the end of two months: that she returned unto her father, who did with her according to his vow which he had vowed: and she knew no man. And it was a custom in Israel, That the daughters of Israel went yearly to lament the daughter of Jephthah the Gileadite four days in a year"[1]. In the final scene of the story Long displays Jephthah's daughter on a funeral pyre with a burnt offering. At the top left of the painting angels can be seen awaiting her soul. The presentation of the martyr bare-breasted points to the hypocrisy of sexuality clothed in religious sentiment.

1. Judges, XI: 39–40.

PROVENANCE Commissioned by Fairless and Beeforth; bought by Sir Merton Russell-Cotes before 1920; Russell-Cotes Art Gallery and Museum, Bournemouth.

EXHIBITIONS LG 1886–9; Doré Gallery, 35 New Bond Street, London, 1890–92; as *The Story of Jephthah* at the Gallery of Sacred Art, 35 New Bond Street, London, 1892–96.

LITERATURE *Bulletin (R-C)*, vol. v, no. 3 (September 1926), p. 31 (ill.); William Gaunt, 'An Edwardian Bequest', *Architectural Review*, no. 119 (March 1956), p. 173; Quick 1931, p. 5, p. 36 (detail ill.), p. 37 (ill.), p. 44; *Home and Abroad*, pp. 709–11; *The Times*, 13 December 1892.

COLLECTION Russell-Cotes Art Gallery and Museum, Bournemouth.

216. Pharaoh's Daughter: The Finding of Moses

1886; 77½ × 109″, 197 × 277 cm; oil on canvas.

The *Finding of Moses* was a popular subject for the exploration of Egyptian themes. Frederick Goodall had painted a notable version of the subject a year before. Long's version, unusually, emphasizes the flora and fauna of Egypt which includes examples of exotic lillies and flamingoes which he had opportunity to study in his visit in 1874 and 1875. The Pharoah's daughter was painted directly from the statue of her in the British Museum. The composition shows the languid figures of the Pharoah's daughter and her servants discovering Moses in his basket, his mother can be seen hiding in the rushes overlooking the scene.

The *Athenaeum* was critical of the work and compared it to Angelica Kauffman who "herself never painted a milder or more wooden princess".[1] *The Times* also found the work artistically lacking, but felt that it would appeal to "the public, which likes a Biblical scene treated with a facile imitation of local knowledge . . . ".[2] Spielmann however, in his article on Long noted the success of the painting and parried criticism of Long's depiction of Egyptian natural history:

> The last big picture, it will be remembered was 'Pharoah's Daughter,' two years ago; and it may be mentioned that the extremely noble type of heroine's head was painted from the statue in the British Museum, though the landscape was from sketches painted on the spot. It has been pointed out as an extraordinary natural history error that Mr. Long has represented on the marble steps in the picture a flamingo picking up seed off the ground, which it could not possibly succeed in doing had it even been so unflamingo-like as to try, for this race of birds only fishes for its food in the water or the mud. But, after all, this lapsus is no worse than the little eccentricities we have lately seen from the most eminent hands, such as lizards 'basking in the moon-light and with their red spots showing!' (Of course, colour is invisible by the light of the moon); of a lion drinking like a dog, instead of like a cat – the tongue being reversed; of pelicans eating butterflies – of galloping huntsmen with their spurs upside-down – of a rainbow with its colours in reverse order – and a hundred other playful little phenomena of the artist-poet's unfettered imagination.[3]

1. Ath., 8 May 1886, p. 621.
2. *The Times*, 1 May 1886, p. 16.
3. Spielmann 1888, p. 612.

PROVENANCE By descent to Margaret Jemima Long; sold at Christie's on 1 February 1908 for £441 to Richard Quick for Bristol Art Gallery.

EXHIBITIONS RA 1886 (no. 115); exhibited at Melbourne 1888; ELG 1893–94 (4); 'The Last Moments of Raphael', Bristol City Art Gallery, 1969 (22); 'Victorian and Edwardian Paintings', Bristol City Art Gallery and Swansea Glynnrian Art Gallery, 1975; 'The Old Guard's Cheer', Bristol City Art Gallery, 1980 (48); 'Europa and the Orient 800–1900', Berlin, 1989 (175).

LITERATURE *Academy Notes* 1886; Ath., 8 May 1886, p. 621; Chester 1908, p. 348; Clayton, p. 180 (ill.); ELG, 1884, pp. 17–18; F. Grennacre, *An Anthology of Victorian and Edwardian Paintings from the Collection of the City Art Gallery, Bristol* (Bristol: Bristol City Art Gallery, 1977), p. 25; Bau Gropius, *Europa and the Orient 800–1900*, catalogue to an exhibition in Berlin, 1989, p. 469, p. 470 (ill.); de Meulenaere 1992, p. 119 (ill.), p. 138 (ill.); Quick 1931, p. 5, p. 8, p. 25 (ill.), p. 44; Spielmann 1888, p. 612; *The Times*, 1 May 1886, p. 16.

COLLECTION Bristol City Museum and Art Gallery.

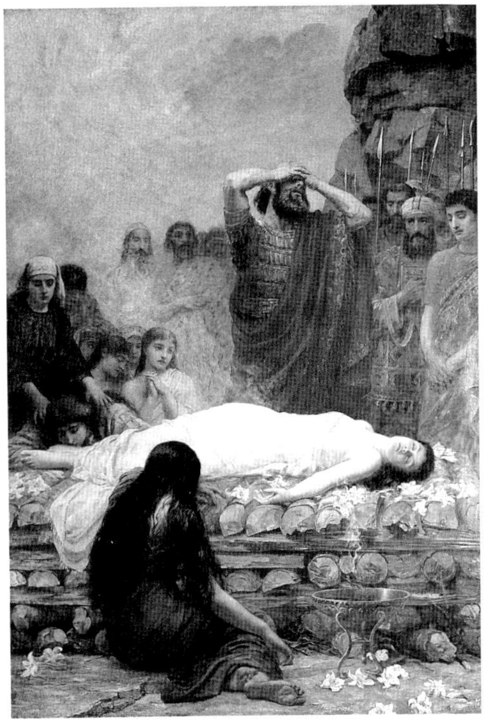

215. *Jephthah's Vow: The Martyr*, 1885.
RUSSELL-COTES ART GALLERY AND MUSEUM
PHOTOGRAPH JAMES HOWE

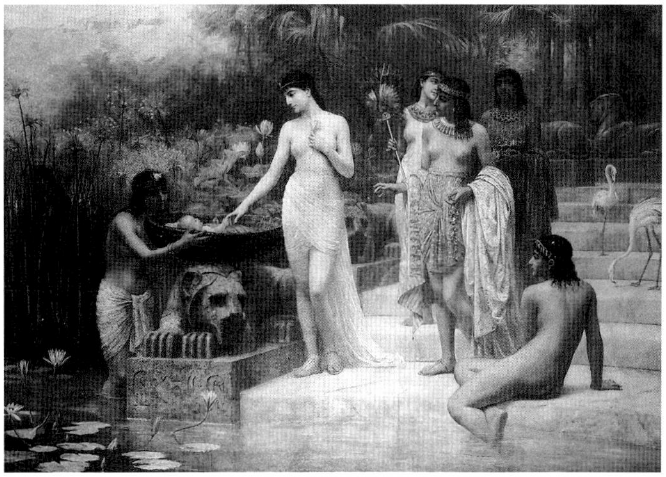

216. *Pharaoh's Daughter: The Finding of Moses*, 1886.
CITY OF BRISTOL MUSEUM & ART GALLERY

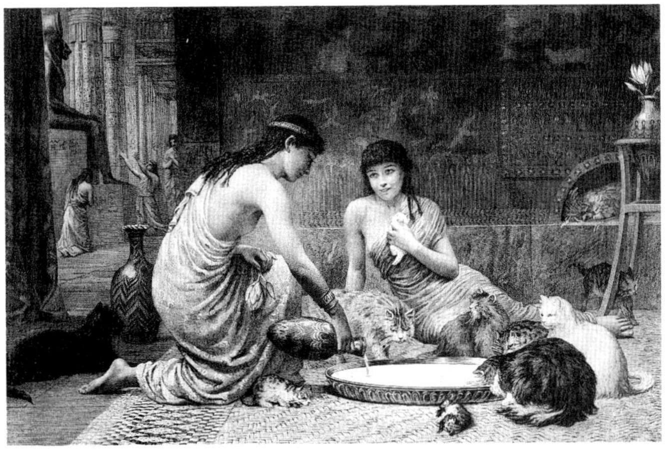

217. *Sacred to Pasht*, 1886. Etching by Achille Jacquet.
RUSSELL-COTES ART GALLERY AND MUSEUM, PHOTOGRAPH JAMES HOWE

217. Sacred to Pasht

1886; unknown size; oil on canvas.

A painting of a temple decicated to the god Pasht. In the background to the left there is a large statue of Pasht being prayed to by a group of worshippers. In the foreground two priestesses of Pasht fill a large cylindrical basin with milk for the cats which lived in the temple and were associated with the cat-headed god. To the right the familiar vase stand that appears in many of Long's pictures appears. The scene is filled with cats and kittens which prompted *The Times* to write: "What he has painted really well this year are the cats in 'Sacred to Pasht' ".[1]

1. *The Times*, 1 May 1886, p. 16.

PROVENANCE J. Griffiths Dearden Esq. of Wytham Hall, in 1888.
EXHIBITIONS RA 1886 (253).
LITERATURE *Academy Notes* 1888; Quick 1931, p. 22 (ill.), p. 45; *The Times*, 1 May 1886, p. 16.

218. An Eastern Offering

1886; 44½ × 28½", 113 × 72.4 cm; oil on canvas; signed and dated.

A three-quarter-length figure in Eastern robes and amulet casts her eyes downwards towards a tray of trinket offerings.

PROVENANCE Owned by Baroness Burdett-Coutts in 1887; sold at Christie's on 7 May 1982 for £1,200 (noted as signed and dated 1886); sold at Christie's on 26 November 1982 for £6,000 (noted as signed and dated 1880).

EXHIBITIONS Manchester Jubilee Exhibition 1887 (428).

219. The Mandolin Player and an Egyptian Girl with a Sistrum

1886; 26½ × 19½", 67.3 × 49.5 cm; oil on panel.

A pair of oil panels of musicians, one with a small mandolin and the other with an Egyptian rattle, painted in 1886.

PROVENANCE Sold at Christie's on 30 June 1933 for £33 12s; sold at Christie's on 6 June 1935.

220. A Portrait of His Eminence Cardinal Manning

1886; 50 × 40", 127 × 101.6 cm; oil on canvas; signed and dated.

A portrait of "'His Eminence Cardinal Manning,' in his scarlet robes, ermine cape, necklace and golden cross".[1] The Cardinal, initially of the Anglican Church, converted to Catholicism in 1851. Wilfred Meynell, in an article on the paintings of Cardinal Manning, wrote of an anecdote that surrounded the painting:

> Mr. Long's portrait is less good as a likeness, and is destitute of the artistic character belonging to the portraits of Watts and Legros. While sitting to Mr. Long, the Cardinal one day arrived unexpectedly, and, by some accident, went into the studio where the painter was at work on an undraped model. All the Archbishop's sympathies were with Mr. Horsley on this point, and before his stern eye the 'shilling-an-hour victim' fled in dismay. 'Poor thing' he said to the painter; 'is she one of my flock?'.[2]

1. *Academy Notes* 1887, p. 16.
2. Wilfred Meynell, 'The Portraits of Cardinal Manning', *Magazine of Art*, 1893, pp. 365–66.

PROVENANCE By descent to Mrs. Margaret Jemima Long; sold at Christie's on 1 February 1908 for £26 5s.

EXHIBITIONS RA 1887 (680); ELG 1893–94 (6).

LITERATURE *Academy Notes* 1887, p. 16; AJ, 1887, p. 278; ELG 1894, pp. 20–21; Wilfred Meynell, 'Portraits of Cardinal Manning', *Magazine of Art*, 1893, pp. 365–66; Quick 1931, p. 6, p. 43.

221. Lady Robartes

1886; unknown size; oil on canvas.

A portrait of Lady Robartes exhibited at the 1886 Royal Academy Exhibition.

EXHIBITIONS RA 1886 (422).

LITERATURE Quick 1931, p. 43.

222. Mrs Edward Maude Scott

1886; unknown size; oil on canvas.

A portrait of Mrs Edward Maude Scott exhibited at the 1886 Royal Academy Exhibition.

EXHIBITIONS RA 1886 (1026).

LITERATURE Quick 1931, p. 43.

THE DAUGHTERS OF OUR EMPIRE

A Series of Pictures by Edwin Long, R.A., exhibited at Messrs. Thomas Agnew & Sons Gallery, 39 Old Bond Street, Picadilly, W. 1887. (cat. nos. 223–242)

223. Aden

1886; 50 × 33", 127 × 83.8 cm; oil on canvas; signed with monogram and dated.

A three-quarter-length portrait depicting Aden holding a large clam shell filled with sea water and coral. She is standing against a backdrop of sea and cliffs with seagulls wheeling in the sky. She is wearing a necklace of sea-shells. The imagery is that described in the catalogue. It was exhibited with the following verse: "There lies a shell beneath the waves / In many a hollow winding wreathed, such as of old / Echoed the breath that warbling sea-maids breathed."

PROVENANCE Purchased from the artist by Thomas Agnew and Sons on 18 November 1886 for £600; sold to A. Eckersley for £1,260 on 5 July 1888; bought by Mr. Vaughan; by descent to Diane Price.

EXHIBITIONS Agnew's 1887 (12).

LITERATURE Agnew's 1887, p. 9.

224. Bethlehem

1886; 54 × 34", 137.2 × 86.3 cm; oil on canvas; signed with monogram and dated.

A three-quarter-length portrait depicting Bethlehem holding a water jug in her left hand. Since 1887 the painting has been variously described as *Water-Carrier of Bethlehem* and *The Daughter of Bethlehem.* It was exhibited with the following verse:

> Now on these steps worn smooth by countless feet,
> Young Arab maids at eve are want to meet,
> Their fair heads bearing pitchers, and the hands,
> Wreathing the well's dark sides with flowery bands.

PROVENANCE Purchased from the artist by Thomas Agnew & Sons; sold to J. E. Walker Esq; bought by Thomas Agnew and Sons on 30 June 1888 for £950; sold to J. Williamson MP on 21 July 1891 for £1,260; sold at Christie's on 28 November 1930 for 10 guineas, referred to as *A Water-Carrier of Bethlehem*; sold at Sotheby's on 26 September 1986 as *The Daughter of Bethlehem.*

EXHIBITIONS Agnew's 1887 (16).

LITERATURE Agnew's 1887, p. 11; *Daily Telegraph*, date unknown, 1908; Roberts 1897, vol. II, p. 135.

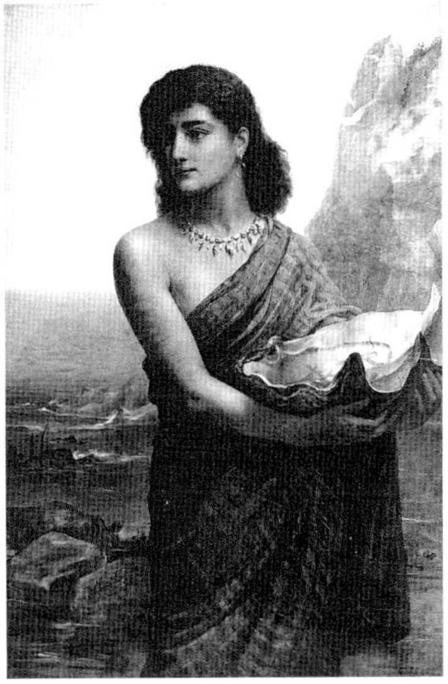

223. *Aden*, 1886.
MRS DIANE PRICE

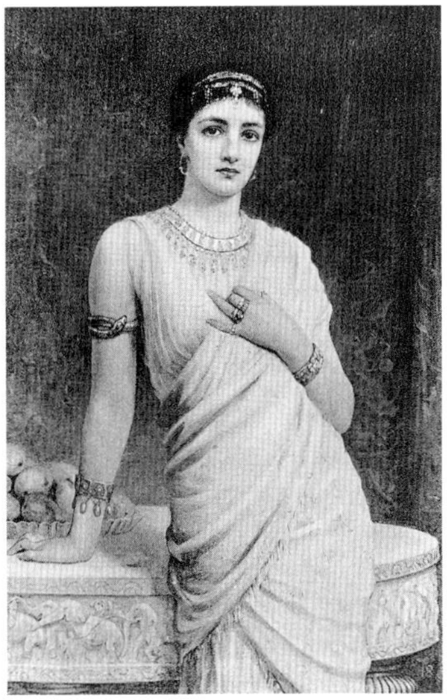

225. *India*, c. 1886.

225. India

c. 1886; c. 50 × 30", 127 × 76.2 cm; oil on canvas.

A three-quarter-length portrait of a woman in sari and jewellery leaning against a stone table with relief carvings of elephants along the rim. It was exhibited with the following verse:

> Who has not heard of the Vale of Cashmere
> With its roses the brightest that earth ever gave,
> Its temples, and grottos, and fountains as clear.
> As the love-lighted eyes that hang over their wave?

PROVENANCE Purchased from the artist by Thomas Agnew & Sons for £600; sold to W. Gillilan, 18 December 1888[?] for £1,575.
EXHIBITIONS Agnew's 1887 (11).
LITERATURE Agnew's 1887, p. 9; Chester 1908, p. 344 (ill.), p. 349; Quick 1931, p. 15 (ill.).

226. Wales

1886; 49½ × 33½", 125.8 × 85 cm; oil on canvas; signed with monogram and dated.

A three-quarter-length of a young woman in peasant attire with a basket to her left, and Welsh mountains in the background. It was exhibited with the following verse:

> I bless thee! – yet not for the beauty which dwells.
> In the heart of thy hills, on the rocks of thy shore;
> And not for the memory set deep in the dells,
> Of the bard and the hero, the mighty of yore;
> And not for the songs of those proud ages fled –
> Green land, poet land of my home and my dead!
> I bless thee for all the true bosoms that beat
> Where'er a low hamlet smiles up to they skies;
> For the cottage hearths burning the stranger to greet;
> For the soul that shines forth from the children's kind eyes
> May the blessing, like sunshine, about thee be spread,
> Green land of my childhood, my home, and my dead!.

PROVENANCE Purchased from the artist by Thomas Agnew and Sons on 27 May 1887 for £600; Charles Neck Esq.; sold at Christie's on 3 May 1890 for £425 by Agnew's as *In the Welsh Mountains*; sold at Christie's on 14 February 1986 as *A Welsh Girl.*
EXHIBITIONS Agnew's 1887 (10).
LITERATURE Agnew's 1887, p. 8; Roberts 1897, vol. II, p. 144.

227. Australia

1887; 50 × 33", 127 × 83.8 cm; oil on canvas.

Exhibited with the following verse:

> Methinks I see Australian landscapes still,
> But softer beauty sits on every hill;
> – I see bright meadows decked in livelier green,
> The yellow cornfield, and the blossomed bean;
> A hundred flocks o'er smiling pastures roam,
> And hark! the music of harvest home.

PROVENANCE Purchased from the artist by Thomas Agnew & Sons for £600 on 27 May 1887; sold to J. E. Walker on 13 May 1889 for £950; Thomas Walker Esq.; sold at Christie's on 16 May 1903 to Sampson for £120 15s.
EXHIBITIONS Agnew's 1887 (1).
LITERATURE Agnew's 1887, p. 3; *Daily Telegraph*, date unknown, 1908; Roberts 1897, vol. II, p. 135.

228. Canada

1887; 50 × 33″, 127 × 83.8 cm; oil on canvas.

Exhibited with the following verse: "Land of mighty lake and forest! / Where the winter's locks are hoarest; / Where the summer's leaf is greenest, / And the winter's bite the keenest."

PROVENANCE Purchased from the artist by Thomas Agnew and Sons on 11 February 1887 for £600; sold to S. H. Gooden on 12 May 1897; Margaret Jemima Long; sold at Christie's on 1 February 1908 for £50 8s to Mullen as *Canadian Type of Beauty.*

EXHIBITIONS Agnew's 1887 (2).

LITERATURE Agnew's 1887, p. 3.

229. Cyprus: Ancient, Love's Messenger

1887; 49½ × 33½″, 125.7 × 85.1 cm; oil on canvas; signed with monogram and dated.

A three-quarter-length portrait of 'Cyprus: Ancient' wearing a toga and holding a dove. It was exhibited with the following verse:

> In Cyprus, where I live Summer never dies
> Love's native land is. There the seas, the skies,
> Are blue and lucid as the breath and hair
> Of Beauty's Queen; whose gracious godship dwells
> In that dear island of delicious dells.

Inscribed on a label on the stretcher "One of the series of 'Beauty' pictures, commission requested by Thomas Agnew and Sons. Copyright Registered by Thomas Agnews and Sons".

PROVENANCE Purchased from the artist by Thomas Agnew and Sons for £600 on 22 February 1887; sold to George Holt on 16 July 1889 for £1050; bought by Agnew's on 19 May 1909 from E. Hadam for £65; sold to W. Low on 20 May 1909 for £470; M. J. Cederwell; Christopher Forbes; sold at Willis's Rooms on 30 May 1928 for 5 guineas as *Portrait of a Girl with a Dove*; sold at Christie's on 14 July 1972 for £157; sold at Christie's on 21 July 1978 for £1,000; sold at Sotheby's on 14 July 1983 for £4,800.

EXHIBITIONS Agnew's 1887 (14).

LITERATURE Agnew's 1887, p. 10.

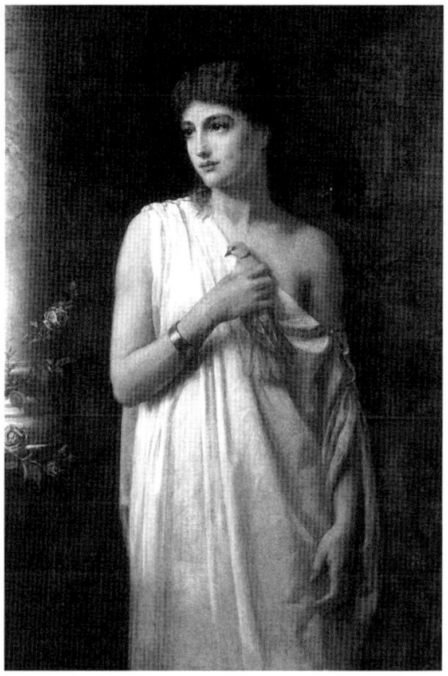

229. *Cyprus: Ancient, Love's Messenger,* 1887.
COURTESY OF SOTHEBY'S, LONDON

230. Cyprus: Modern

1887; c. 50 × 33″, 127 × 83.8 cm; oil on canvas.

This painting was exhibited with the following verse:

Know ye the land where the cypress and myrtle.
Are emblems of deeds that are done in their clime.
Cypress here, and stateliest pine,
Spire o'er the nether shades as emulons.
Of sole distinction, where all nature smiles.

PROVENANCE Purchased from the artist by Thomas Agnew and Sons on 22 February 1887; sold to Sir Henry Edwards on 31 May 1887.
EXHIBITIONS Agnew's 1887 (19).
LITERATURE Agnew's 1887, p. 13.

231. Egypt

1887; c. 50 × 33″, 127 × 83.8 cm; oil on canvas.

The painting was exhibited with the following verse:

Hail, Egypt! Land of ancient pomp and pride,
Where Beauty walks by hoary ruins' side;
Land of the pyramid and temple lone! –
Honour to Egypt – honour!
May Allah smile upon her!.

PROVENANCE Purchased from artist by Thomas Agnew and Sons for £600 on 18 March 1887; sold to V. Esthersley on 5 July 1888 for £1475.
EXHIBITIONS Agnew's 1887 (17).
LITERATURE Agnew's 1887, p. 12.

232. England: The Parson's Daughter

1887; c. 50 × 33″, 127 × 83.8 cm; oil on canvas.

The painting was exhibited with the following verse:

To comfort and to bless,
To find a balm for woe,
To tend the lone and fatherless;
Is angels' work below.

PROVENANCE Purchased from the artist by Thomas Agnew and Sons on 29 March 1887; sold to Sir H. Edwards for £1,050.
EXHIBITIONS Agnew's 1887 (4).
LITERATURE Agnew's 1887, p. 5.

233. England: The Violet

1887; c. 49½ × 33½″, 127 × 84.5 cm; oil on canvas.

A three-quarter-length portrait of England in a meadow leaning against a wooden fence and holding a posy of violets. She is wearing a white dress and her straw hat hangs on the fence. It was exhibited with the following verse: "Violets dim, / But sweeter than the lids of Juno's eyes, / Or Cythera's breath."

PROVENANCE Purchased from the artist by Thomas Agnew and Sons on 18 March 1887 for £600; sold to Colonel E. L. Levita on 14 May 1897; Christie's; bought bt Agnew's from Christie's for £42 on 2 March 1910; sold to Colonel Sevita on 6 March 1910 for £42.
EXHIBITIONS Agnew's 1887 (5).
LITERATURE Agnew's 1887, p. 5; Chester 1908, p. 343 (ill.).

234. England: The Rose

1887; c. 50 × 33", 127 × 83.8 cm; oil on canvas; signed and dated.

Also known as *Rose of England and Portrait of Princess Victoria.* Although part of the series 'Daughters of Our Empire', this is a portrait of Princess May of Teck (later Queen Mary). The Rothschild family gave the painting to the Queen Mother as a silver wedding gift in 1891. It was mentioned in the *Strand Magazine* of 1893, "On the walls [White Lodge] are some good portraits . . . the Princess May of Teck, by Long – a silver wedding gift – being chief of them".[1] It is a three-quarter-length portrait of the Princess May of Teck in a white dress against a plain background surrounded by and wearing a large number of variously coloured roses. It was exhibited with the following verse:

From town to town, from tower to tower,
The red rose is a gladsome flower;
She lifts her head for endless spring
And everlasting blossoming.
Both roses flourish red and white,
In love and sisterly delight
The two that were at strife, are blended,
And all troubles now are ended.

1. *Strand Magazine,* (date unknown) 1893, p. 237.

PROVENANCE Purchased from the artist by Thomas Agnew and Sons on 27 May 1887 for £600; sold to Leopold de Rothschild on 13 June 1891 for £650; gift to the Queen's mother in 1891.
EXHIBITIONS Agnew's 1887 (6); ELG 1893–94 (18).
LITERATURE Agnew's 1887, p. 6; Chester 1908, p. 342 (ill.); ELG 1894, p. 23; Quick 1931, front plate (ill.), pp. 6–7; *Strand Magazine,* date unknown, 1893, p. 237; Walkely 1994, p. 109.
COLLECTION Petersham Lodge (Queen Mary's Governess's Holiday Home) in 1936.

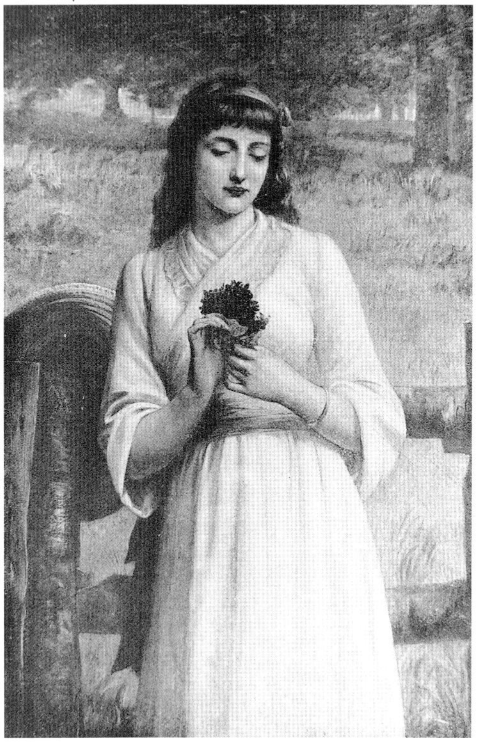

233. *England: The Violet,* 1887.

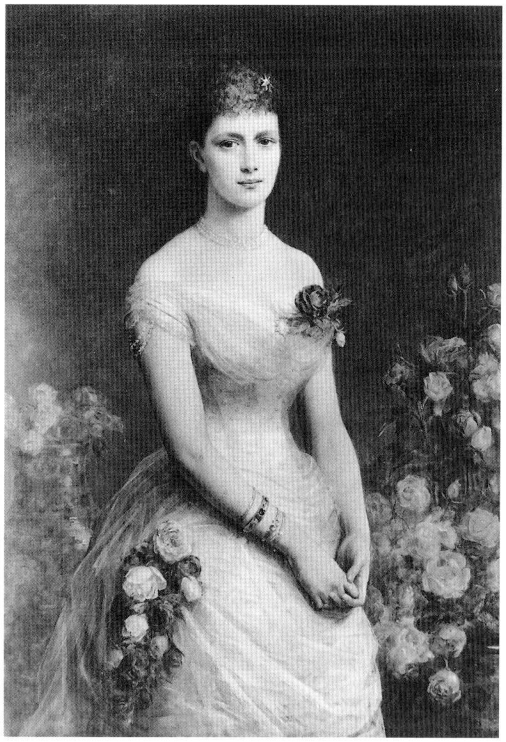

234. *England: The Rose,* 1887.

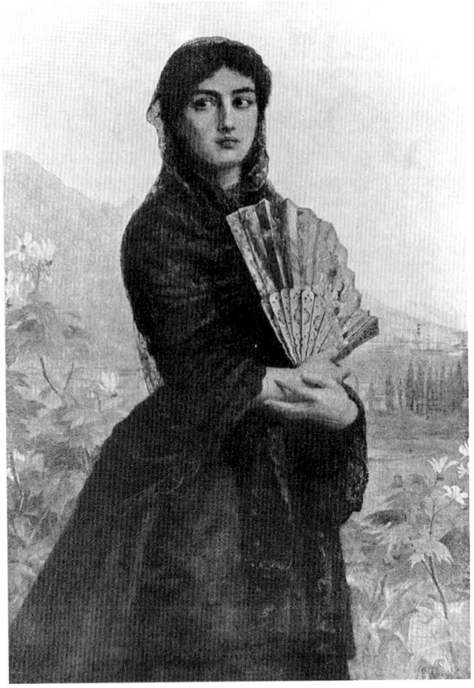

237. *Gibraltar*, 1887.

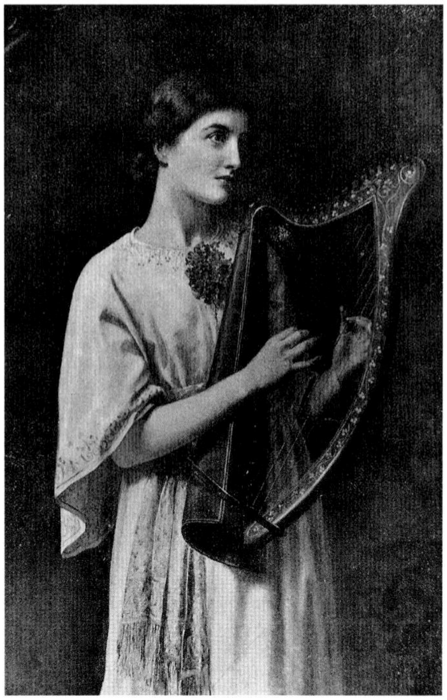

238. *Ireland*, 1887.

235. England: The Primrose

1887; c. 50 × 33", 127 × 83.8 cm; oil on canvas.

England: The Primrose was exhibited with the following verse: "Primrose, first-born child of Ver, / Merry springtime's harbinger".

PROVENANCE Purchased from the artist by Thomas Agnew and Sons on 18 March 1887 for £600; sold to Lanier on 7 June 1889 for £945.
EXHIBITIONS Agnew's 1887 (7).
LITERATURE Agnew's 1887, p. 6.

236. England: The Little Sister of the Poor

1887; c. 50 × 33", 127 × 83.8 cm; oil on canvas.

The painting was exhibited with the following verse: "In faith and hope the world will disagree, / But all mankind's concern is charity".

PROVENANCE Purchased from the artist by Thomas Agnew and Son on 18 March, 1887 for £600.
EXHIBITIONS Agnew's 1887 (9).
LITERATURE Agnew's 1887, p. 7.

237. Gibraltar

1887; c. 50 × 33", 127 × 83.8 cm; oil on canvas.

A three-quarter-length portrait of a woman in a mantilla and holding a fan. The background of Gibraltar shows its rock and cypress trees. It was exhibited with the following verse: "High on the rock that fronts the sea / Stands alone our fortress key, / Lady of the Southern main".

PROVENANCE Purchased from the artist by Thomas Agnew and Sons on 11 February 1887 for £600; sold to J. Reiseach on 20 June 1888 for £650.
EXHIBITIONS Agnew's 1887 (13).
LITERATURE Agnew's 1887, p. 10; Chester 1908, p. 347 (ill.).

238. Ireland

1887; c. 50 × 33", 127 × 83.8 cm; oil on canvas.

A three-quarter-length portrait of a woman in Celtic revival robes and playing an Irish harp. The painting was exhibited with the following verse:

> What harp shall sigh o'er Freedom's grave? Oh, Erin! thine! –
> Dear harp of my country! in darkness I found thee,
> The cold chains of silence had hung o'er thee long,
> When proudly, my own Island harp, I unbound thee,
> And gave all thy chords to light, freedom and song!
> The warm lay of love and the light note of gladness
> Have weakened thy fondest, thy liveliest thrill;
> but so oft has thou echoed the deep sigh of sadness,
> That even in thy mirth will steal from thee still.

PROVENANCE Purchased from the artist by Thomas Agnew and Sons on 27 May 1887 for £600; sold to James Reckitt on 25 July 1887 for £750.
EXHIBITIONS Agnew's 1887 (3).
LITERATURE Agnew's 1887, p. 3; Chester 1908, p. 346 (ill.).

239. Jamaica

1887; 36 × 28¼", 91.4 × 71.4 cm; oil on canvas; signed with monogram.

A half-length seated portrait of Jamaica against, the setting of a sugar cane plantation. It was exhibited with the following verse: "Freedom has a thousand charms to show / That slaves, however contented, never knows". Writing on an old label on the stretcher: "Jamaica / by / E. Long R.A. / One of the series of "Beauty" pictures / Copyright reserved by Thomas Agnew".

PROVENANCE Purchased from the artist by Thomas Agnew and Sons on 22 February 1887 for £600; sold for £747 10s; sold at Sotheby's on 28 September 1988 for £6,500; sold at auction on 4 May 1989 for £6,000; sold at Christie's on 4 November 1994 for £18,000.
EXHIBITIONS Agnew's 1887 (18).
LITERATURE Agnew's 1887, p. 13.

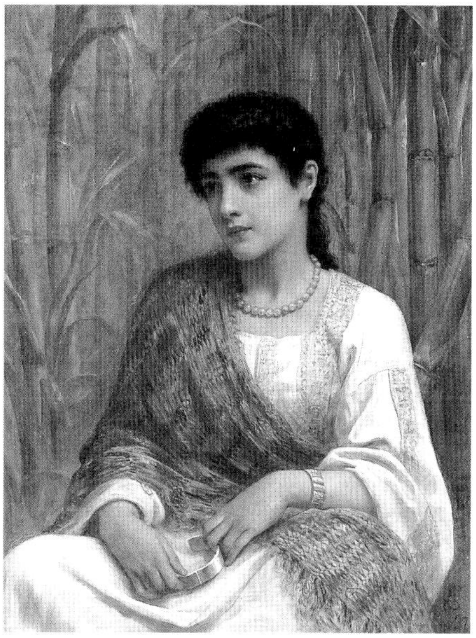

239. *Jamaica*, 1887.
COURTESY OF SOTHEBY'S, LONDON

240. Malta

1887; c. 50 × 33", 127 × 83.8 cm; oil on canvas.

Exhibited with the following verse: "For half her days were passed at church, the other / Between her tutors, confessor and mother".

PROVENANCE Purchased from the artist by Thomas Agnew and Sons on 11 February 1887 for £600; sold to H. Illingworth on 25 January 1889 for £1050.
EXHIBITIONS Agnew's 1887 (20).
LITERATURE Agnew's 1887, p. 13.

241. Scotland 'Rose Bradivous Zaine'

1887; c. 50 × 33", 127 × 83.8 cm; oil on canvas.

Exhibited with the following verse:

Rose Bradivous Zaine
Oh! had each set of ancient times
Been, Jeannine Scott, as thou art,
The bravest heart in English ground
Had yielded like a coward!

PROVENANCE Purchased from the artist by Thomas Agnew and Sons on 31 May 1887 for £600.
EXHIBITIONS Agnew's 1887 (9).
LITERATURE Agnew's 1887, p. 7.

242. Trinidad

1887; 35½ × 27½", 90 × 70 cm; oil on canvas; signed with monogram dated lower right.

A young woman dressed in black sits inside a Christian church, in the background is an altar with a vase of flowers and a Pieta sculpture group; she holds in her lap what appear to be rosary beads; behind her and above the artist's monogram is the Judaic symbol of the Star of David. It was exhibited with the following verse:

Oh! Thou who dry'st the mourner's tear
How dark the world would be,
If, when deceived and wounded here,
We could not fly to Thee.

PROVENANCE Purchased from the artist by Thomas Agnew and Sons on 11 February 1887 for £600; sold to H. W. Wright on 15 December 1887; sold in 1900 for 190 guineas; presented to Bury Art Gallery and Museum in 1901 by James Kenyon.
EXHIBITIONS Agnew's 1887 (15).
LITERATURE Agnew's 1887, p. 11.
COLLECTION Bury Art Gallery and Museum.

243. The Earring

1887; 46¾ × 35", 118.8 × 89 cm; oil on canvas; signed and dated.

PROVENANCE Rt. Hon. Lord Cheylesmore; sold at Christie's on 7 May 1892 for £399.

244. A Love Feast

1887; unknown size; oil on canvas.

The subject for *A Love Feast* is Cardinal Wiseman's novel *Fabiola, or the Church of the Catacombs* (1855)[1] which aimed to "introduce us to some view of the morals and opinions of the pagan world, as a contrast to those of Christians".[2] Its full Royal Academy title indicates the section of the novel it depicts *A Love Feast. Syra the slave sharing her meal with Caecilia, the blind beggar girl.* It was exhibited alongside *Callista* at the 1887 exhibition at Burlington House and shares its similarity of theme, the exploration through fiction of the relations between the early Christians and the pagan world. *Academy Notes* described the painting as "the subject taken from Cardinal Wiseman's 'Fabiola,' in which Syra the slave shares her meal of pomegranates and lentils with the blind-girl Caecilia, as they sit together on the marble pavement of Fabiola's house".[3]

1. Nicholas Patrick Stephen Wiseman, Cardinal, Archbishop of Westminster.
2. Introduction to Cardinal Wiseman, *Fabiola, or the Church of the Catacombs* (London, 1855).
3. *Academy Notes* 1887, p. 3.

EXHIBITIONS RA 1887 (3).
LITERATURE *Academy Notes* 1887, p. 3; Chester 1908, p. 350; *Magazine of Art*, 1887, p. 275; Quick 1931, p. 7, p. 45.

245. Callista the Image Maker

1887; 33 × 44½", 84 × 113 cm; oil on canvas; signed and dated with monogram on label on reverse.

The subject for the painting is a novel by Cardinal John Henry Newman (1801–90) titled *Callista, a sketch of the third century*. Published in 1856 its aim was to "attempt to imagine and express . . . the mutual feelings and mutual relations of Christians and Heathens . . . ".[1] The narrative is set in third-century Sicca, Carthage, and tells of Callista, a maker of religious imagery, whose destiny leads her to become a Christian martyr. The painting depicts Callista and Aristo at work, Callista in the foreground modelling a cupid from life, from a small boy seated on a low table with a miniature bow and arrow. A variety of idols are displayed around the room. The setting is described by Newman in *Callista*:

> He has reached the house, or rather the floor, to which he has been making his way. It is at the back of the city, where the rock is steep; and it looks out upon the mountain range to the north. Its inmates, Aristo and Callista, are engaged in their ordinary work of moulding or carving, painting or gilding the various articles which the temples or the private shrines of the established religion required.[2]

Long's fascination with the early Christian martyrs was already made clear in paintings like *Diana or Christ?* (1881) and the fictional accounts of these by writers like Newman and Wiseman[3] particularly captured Long's imagination. The scene depicted, like the later *Alethe* (1889), shows no real indication of the main protagonists' forthcoming martyrdom. In works such as the *Gods and their Makers* (1878) Long made no overt reference to his own Christian morality. Paintings like *Callista* allowed him to show the same interest in the exoticism and charm of the 'false' idolaters with only a covert Christian message.

1. Newman, introduction to *Callista* (dated 13 September 1855, published 1856).
2. Newman, *Callista* (London: Burn & Oates and Co., 1856, repr. 1879), p. 115.
3. *Fabiola*, by Cardinal Wiseman (see cat. no. 244).

PROVENANCE Sold at Christie's on 18 October 1974 for £315; sold at Christie's on 27 March 1975 for £840.
EXHIBITIONS RA 1887 (132).
LITERATURE *Academy Notes* 1887, p. 7, p. 36 (ill.); AJ, 1887, p. 279; Kestner 1989, p. 229; *Magazine of Art*, 1887, p. 275; Quick 1931, p. 7, p. 28 (ill.), p. 45.

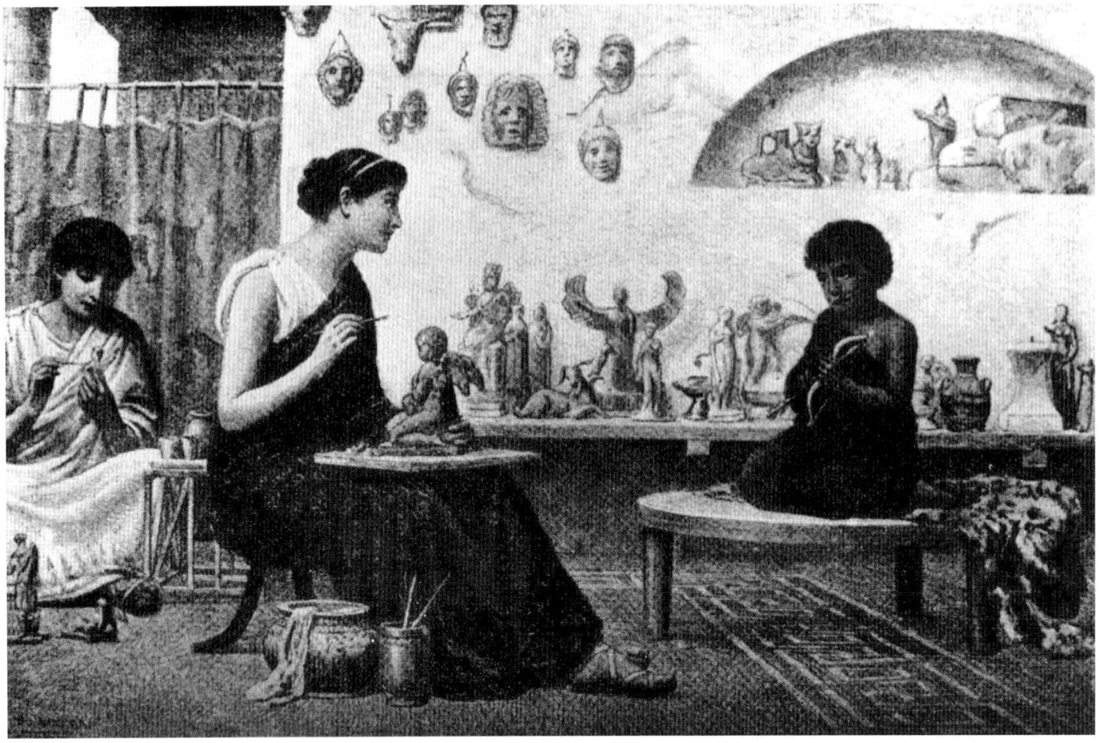

245. *Callista the Image Maker*, 1887.

246. Princess Helen Randir Singh

1887; 12½ × 10″, 32 × 25.5 cm; oil on canvas; signed with monogram and dated on reverse.

A small portrait of Helen Randir Singh. On the reverse is a label which reads: "Scene at Caanporthala? painted by Edwin Long R.A., 1887".

PROVENANCE Graves gift to Sheffield 1935–43; Graves Art Gallery, Sheffield.
COLLECTION Graves Art Gallery, Sheffield.

247. Sir Edmund Henderson K.C.B. (1)

1887; unknown size; oil on canvas.

The first of two portraits painted by Long of Sir Edmund Henderson KCB. The painting was commissioned as a retirement presentation in 1887 for Sir Edmund after his service as Commissioner of Metropolitan Police. "At a meeting at Grosvenor House, Henderson was presented with a painting by Edwin Long, R.A., and a purse of 1,000".[1]

1. *Dictionary of National Biography* (1921 edn.).

EXHIBITIONS RA 1887 (629).

248. Dora.

unknown date and size; oil on canvas.

PROVENANCE Sold at Christie's on 19 July 1890 for £50 8s.

249. Rebecca.

unknown date and size; oil on canvas.

PROVENANCE Sold at Christie's on 19 February 1898 for £28 7s to McLean.

250. **Laus Dio.**
unknown date; 30¾ × 16¾", 78.1 × 42.7 cm; oil on canvas; signed.

A small classical painting of a crowd saluting a god in the setting of a Roman arena.

PROVENANCE Sold at Sotheby's on 11 July 1978; sold at Christie's on 26 October 1979 for £380.

251. **Jessica.**
unknown date and size; oil on canvas.

EXHIBITIONS ELG 1893–94 (23).
LITERATURE ELG 1894, p. 24.

252. **Persuasion.**
unknown date and size; oil on canvas.

PROVENANCE Sold in 1883 for 280 guineas.
LITERATURE *Daily Telegraph*, date unknown, 1908.

253. **Eastern Lily.**
unknown date and size; oil on canvas.

PROVENANCE Thomas Agnew and Son; sold to J. Hemingway on 27 June 1912.

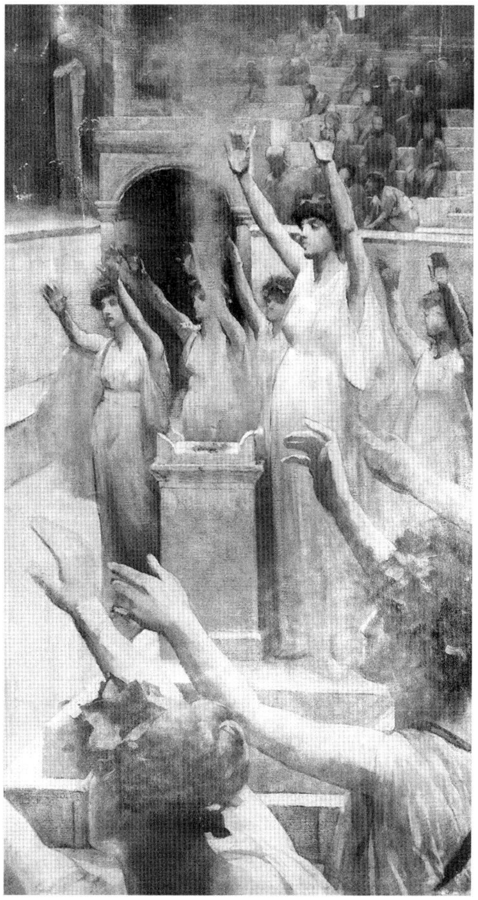

250. *Laus Dio*, unknown date.
COURTESY OF SOTHEBY'S, LONDON

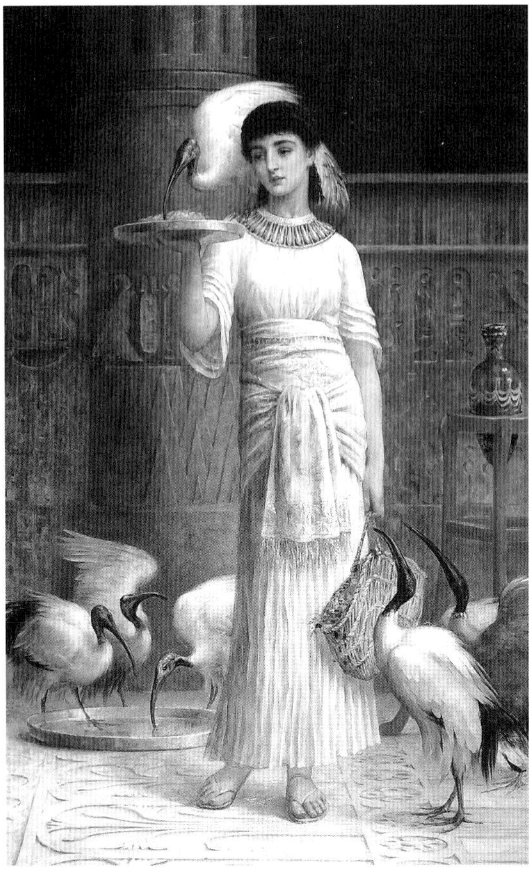

254. *Alethe, Attendant of the Sacred Ibis*, 1888.
RUSSELL-COTES ART GALLERY AND MUSEUM, PHOTOGRAPH JAMES HOWE

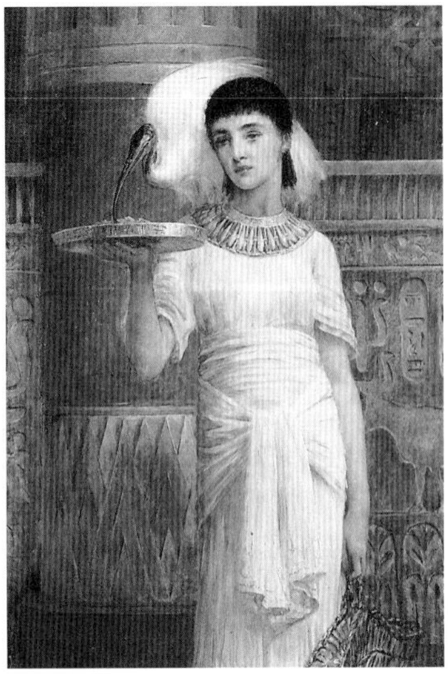

254.1. *Alethe, Attendant of the Sacred Ibis*, 1887.
KATHY & RONALD RAE

254. Alethe, Attendant of the Sacred Ibis

1888; 42 × 26″, 106.7 × 66 cm; oil on panel; signed and dated on vase stand.

Alethe, Attendant of the Sacred Ibis in the Great Temple of Isis at Memphis, circa 255 AD, is a depiction of a poem and a novel by Thomas Moore.[1] These tell of Alicphron, a young Greek philosopher who travels to Egypt in 257 to discover the secret of eternal life. He meets Alethe, a young Egyptian priestess and secret Christian, and helps her escape from her life in the service of an Egyptian god. Alethe is martyred and Alciphron is sent to the mines where he meets his untimely end.

The picture, titled by Long "circa 255 AD", depicts Alethe before her fateful meeting with Alciphron. Without the title it is impossible to guess of her Christian martyrdom from the image that Long has painted. Clearly the centre of the picture, Alethe is an exotic beauty from an ancient culture. The morality of the piece and the implied purity of beauty is alluded to through its anecdotal content. The pensive expression and facial features of Alethe is typical of Long's work as are the religious overtones. According to the *Egyptomania* catalogue of 1994 the work is riddled with archaeological inaccuracies, despite Long's reputation for accuracy. "An imprecise setting, the Neo-Byzantine pavement, and above all the so-called 'Priestess of Isis', who, with her winged companions, has clearly come to the wrong temple: she would be more at home as a priestess of Thoth. The costume is equally as implausible: the sash knotted at the waist could have been worn by any elegant, late nineteenth-century lady".[2]

Although beautifully painted with clarity, subtle colour, detail and fine composition, Long fails to explore his subject as fully as he does with many other of his other early Christian martyrs. It was not mentioned in the main journals of the period on its exhibition at the Royal Academy, with the exception of the *Athenaeum* which was scathing in its review:

> Mr. E. Long's picture of 'Alethe, Attendant of the Sacred Ibis' (66) is a fit illustration to Thomas Moore's trivial romance 'Alciphron,' and in some respects, in spite of its lack of a virile taste and style, recalls to mind a well-known picture by Mr. Poynter, which showed how the sacred birds of Isis were fed – a picture, by the way, in which the subject proper could hardly be said to count for much in comparison with technical successes to which Mr. Long has not yet succeeded in attaining. Alethe, who seems to have been studied from a damsel whom Mr. Long has painted so often that she has become almost imbecile, has an ibis on her shoulder, and is surrounded by ibises who do not even walk with energy. Apart from its prettiness, which offends one's sense of the fitness of things, this feeble virgin is much marred by paint; but even the weakness of the design, the inanity of the action and expression, and the paint, will not explain why the young lady's limbs do not show through her dress.[3]

1. Thomas Moore's poem 'Alciphron' formed the basis for the novel later published in 1839, and his novel *The Epicurean* was published in 1827. A French translation of *The Epicurean* appeared in 1865 which was illustrated by Gustave Doré, an artist for whom Long held great admiration.
2. *Egyptomania, Egypt in Western Art, 1730–1930*, catalogue to an exhibition at Paris, Ottawa and Vienna, 1994, p. 493.
3. Ath., 18 May 1889, p. 637. The review refers to Sir Edward John Poynter's painting *Feeding the sacred Ibis in the Halls of Karnak*, 1871, 92.6 × 69.2 cm.

PROVENANCE A G Kurtz; sold at Christie's on 23 May 1891 for £735; sold at Christie's on 30 November 1928 for £42; bought by the Russell-Cotes Art Gallery and Museum in 1929.

EXHIBITIONS RA 1889 (66); 'Egyptomania, Egypt in Western Art, 1730–1930', Paris, Ottawa and Vienna, 1994 (336); 'Iside, Il Mito Il Mistero La Magia', Palazzo Reale, Milan, 1977 (x.25); Art Treasures of England, RA 1898 (184).

LITERATURE *Academy Notes* 1889, p. vi, p. 7 (ill.); *Art Treasures of England, The Regional Collections*, catalogue to an exhibition at the Royal Academy, London (London: Merrell Holberton, 1988, p. 250 (ill.); Ath., 18 May 1889, p. 637; Chester 1908, p. 332 (ill.); Clayton, p. 180 (ill.); *Daily Telegraph*, date unknown, 1908; *Egyptomania, Egypt in Western Art, 1730–1930*, catalogue to an exhibition at the Louvre, Paris, and Ottawa and Vienna, 1994, p. 493 (ill.); Humbert 1989, p. 240; *Iside, Il Mito Il Mistero La Magia*, catalogue to an exhibition at Palazzo Reale, Milan (Milan: Electo Milan, 1977), p. 653 (ill.); De Meulenaere 1992, p. 109 (ill.), p. 138 (ill.); Quick 1931, p. 9 (ill.), p. 45; Roberts 1897, vol. II, p. 162.

COLLECTION Russell-Cotes Art Gallery and Museum, Bournemouth.

254.1. Alethe, Attendant of the Sacred Ibis

1887; 23½ × 16⅛", 59.7 × 42 cm; oil on panel; signed with monogram and dated.

A three-quarter-length study of Alethe titled *The Sacred Ibis* at a Christie's sale in 1911.

PROVENANCE Thomas Agnew and Sons; sold at Christie's on 19 May 1911 for £34 13s as *The Sacred Ibis*; purchased by Kathy Rae in 1982.

255. Ready for the Bath

1888; 53 × 37½", 134.5 × 95.2 cm; oil on canvas; signed with monogram twice and dated.

The full-length nude figure is typical of Long's preference for dark-featured beauties.

PROVENANCE Sold at Christie's on 22 February 1908 for £38 17s; W. S. Hoare Esq.; sold at Christie's on 20 February 1912 for 9 guineas to Sampson; sold at Sotheby's on 7 June 1985; sold at Peter Nahum at the Leicester Galleries in 1996.

256. The Crown of Justification

1888; 72 × 144", 183 × 366 cm; oil on canvas; signed with monogram and dated.

The painting's subject and source is described at length by Long in the 1888 Royal Academy catalogue:

> Among the curious customs of the Ancient Egyptians mentioned by Diodorus Siculus, that of judging the dead is especially remarkable. Before an important personage could receive the rites of honourable judgement, a trial, typical of that to which his soul would be subjected in the nether world, was conducted in the presence of his body. Forty-two assessors sat in judgement upon him, each representing one of the cardinal sins of the Egyptian moral code; accusers came forward from all parts; even from prison. The woman whose affections he had slighted or had been ruined by his love; the man whom, justly or unjustly he had wrecked with punishment or disgrace – all, however controlled by his power during life were let loose upon his corpse. If the decision of the judges was adverse, a matter of no small importance to the family of the deceased, his body was taken home in disgrace and stood in the corner of the house. If, however, the accusations were not considered of sufficient weight and the justification was accorded, the mummy was anointed with oil and crowned with a wreath of white lotus flowers. It was then placed in an ark on a boat and carried across the Sacred Lake to be deposited in the tombs opposite.[1]

The painting shows the semi-circular seated assessors considering and discussing the merits of the accusations. A central figure looking towards the assessors, points an accusation at the encased corpse. The corpse is in slight silhouette against the main entrance where light streams in and a boat can be seen awaiting the judgement. One of the dead person's family, possibly his wife, is seen clinging to the mummy case. The compositional construction of the painting is essentially theatrical, a point reinforced by Long's working method. According to Spielmann, in an interview with Long:

> The picture that is most interesting to him, because the most complicated and difficult, that he has yet painted is the one in this year's Academy – 'The Crown of Justification' – representing the trial of the dead by the living as described by Diodorus Siculus in his history of the Egyptians. To facilitate matters in this work – which has given him twelve months' hard labour – Mr. Long has modelled the whole 'mise-en-scene' as well as the 'dramatis personae' in clay or wax, clothing the latter with rags round them, or with little robes from the diligent hand of his wife. It was as he was moving these little figures about, planning their final disposition in the improvised Egyptian Court of 'post-mortem' Justice, that the writer broke in upon him, and found the painter 'par excellence' of Oriental antiquity adopting much the same device – that of dressed dolls – as was employed by the elder Dumas, and by more than one English novelist.[2]

This description is clearly illustrated in Renouard's drawing which accompanied the text "The Artist arranging wax models for the grouping of his picture 'The Crown of Justification'".[3] In the foreground a working drawing is visible and in the background is the canvas on its easel with the compostion sketched out.

The painting was well reviewed and *The Times* despite finding the subject too esoteric and obscure for its audience praised its painting:

> As to Mr. Long, no-one can say that he has not been ambitious enough in his 'Crown of Justification' (453) –

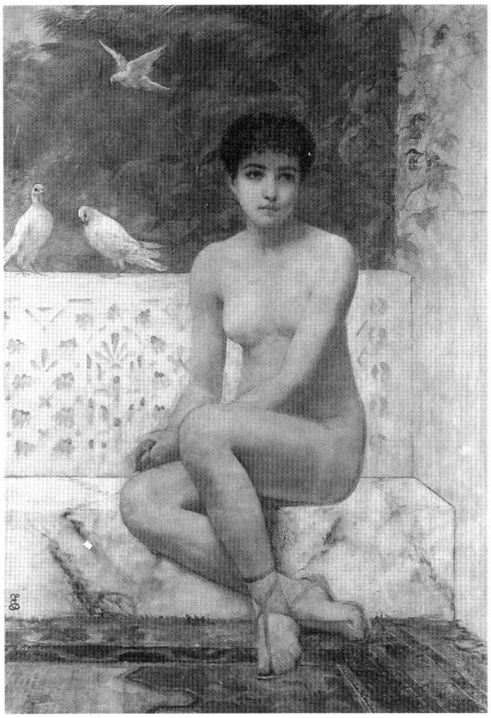

255. *Ready for the Bath*, 1888.
COURTESY OF SOTHEBY'S, LONDON

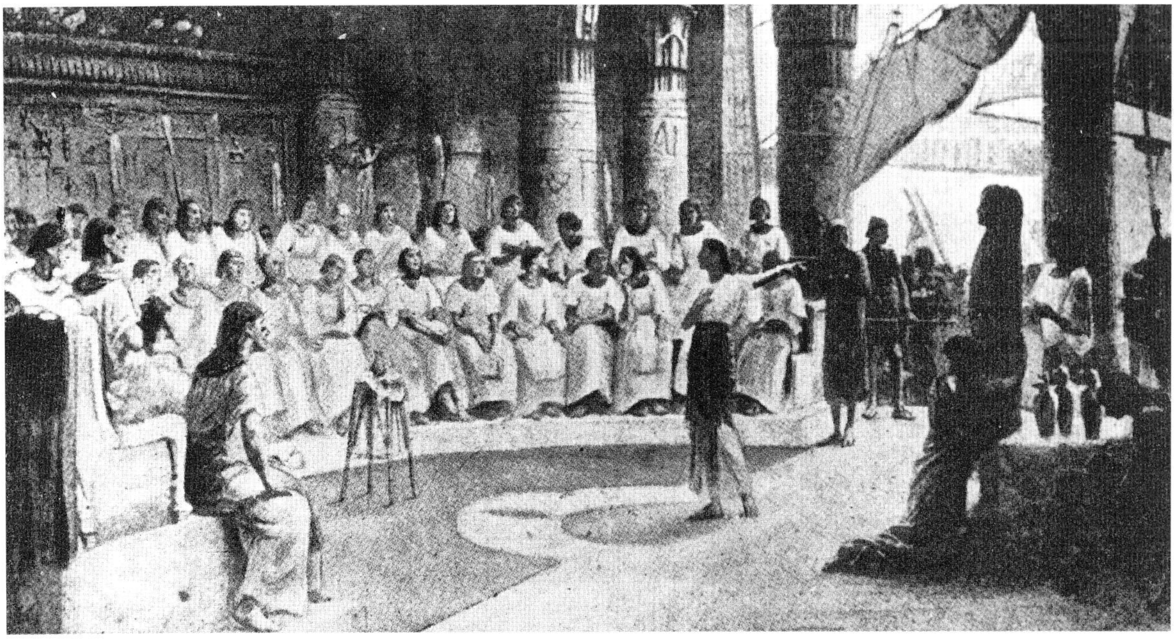

256. *The Crown of Justification*, 1888.

> the huge Egyptian picture which covers the greater part of the opposite wall. Its first fault is that it takes half a page of a catalogue to explain it; but this is the common vice of artists who go to remote lands and remote literatures for their inspiration. Leaving the details of the story to Egyptologists, we remark that a group of forty-two men in Egyptian costume are seated round a hall; a mummy is raised erect before them; near it is a woman who seems to be pleading, and another woman and children are grouped in the background. Premising that it is a fundamental mistake to devote elaborate art to the illustration of stories that have not passed into the common inheritance of the race, or, at all events, of the nation to which the artist belong, we may grant that this work of Mr. Long's shows signs of considerable care and even of thought; the faces are represented with some dramatic power and the painting of the alabaster is remarkable.[4]

The *Magazine of Art* praised its "archaeological research and detail", and its "technical difficulties of drawing and design triumphantly overcome", but found "the sentiment as dead as the mummy itself".[5] The *Athenaeum* was critical of Long's painting finding it 'silly' and superficial which it equates with femininity comparing him to Angelica Kauffman. The review seems to show little understanding of the picture's content: "There is much any lady may profitably study; the tender devotion of those who bow before the richly gilded corpse is exemplary, the departed is duly honoured, and the mourning garments and other decencies of woe could hardly be more becoming or more neatly painted".[6]

1. *Academy Notes* 1888, p. 10.
2. Spielmann 1888, p. 612.
3. Illustrated in Spielmann 1888, p. 613. Also illustrated on p. 23 above.
4. *The Times*, 16 May 1888, p. 4.
5. *Magazine of Art*, 1888, p. 271.
6. Ath., 9 June 1888, p. 732.

PROVENANCE By descent to Mrs Margaret Jemima Long; sold at Christie's on 1 February 1908 for 150 guineas to Sampson; sold at Sotheby's on 9 April 1980.
EXHIBITIONS RA 1888 (453); ELG 1893–94 (2).
LITERATURE *Academy Notes* 1888, p. 10, p. 63 (ill.); AJ, 1888, p. 218; Ath., 9 June 1888, p. 732; *Bulletin (R-C)*, vol. II, no. 2 (June 1923), p. 22; Chester 1908, p. 350; *Daily Telegraph*, date unknown, 1908; ELG 1894, pp. 15–16; *Magazine of Art*, 1888, p. 271; Quick 1931, p. 6, pp. 7–8, p. 29 (ill.), p. 31 (ill.), p. 45; Spielmann 1888, p. 612–3 (ill.); *The Times*, 16 May 1888, p. 4.

257. Katherine ('The Taming of the Shrew')

c. 1888; 26 × 20", 66 × 50.8 cm; oil on canvas; frame inscribed "Katherine the Shrew".

A head and shoulders portrait of the character Katherine from Shakespeare's *The Taming of the Shrew*. The painting was commissioned by *The Graphic* for illustration and exhibition at their gallery on Brook Street as part of a series of Shakespearean heroines. Other work included *Desdemona* by Sir Frederick Leighton, *Portia, Wife of Brutus* by Lawrence Alma-Tadema and *Jessica* by Luke Fildes. The series was a great success, so much so that Queen Victoria invited William Luson Thomas (1830–1900), managing director of *The Graphic*, to Osborne House so that she could inspect the series of twenty-one prints first hand.

PROVENANCE *The Graphic* commissioned fro the artist; sold at Christie's on 9 March 1889 (The *Graphic* Collection, 2nd sale) for 140 guineas to Arthur Tooth and Sons (without copyright).
EXHIBITIONS The Graphic Gallery, 14, 16 & 18 Brook Street, London, 1888 (20).
LITERATURE *The Graphic Gallery of Shakespeare's Heroines* (London, 1888), pp. 534–35; *The Graphic*, 20 January 1888 (supplement) (ill.).

258. Lorna Doone

c. 1888; unknown size; oil on canvas.

A full-length portrait of R. D. Blackmore's heroine in *Lorna Doone* seated on a rock in a shady glade.

PROVENANCE Thomas Agnew and Sons purchased from the artist on 30 July 1888; sold to W. C. Watson on 29 January 1889 for £900.
LITERATURE Chester 1908, p. 340 (ill.).

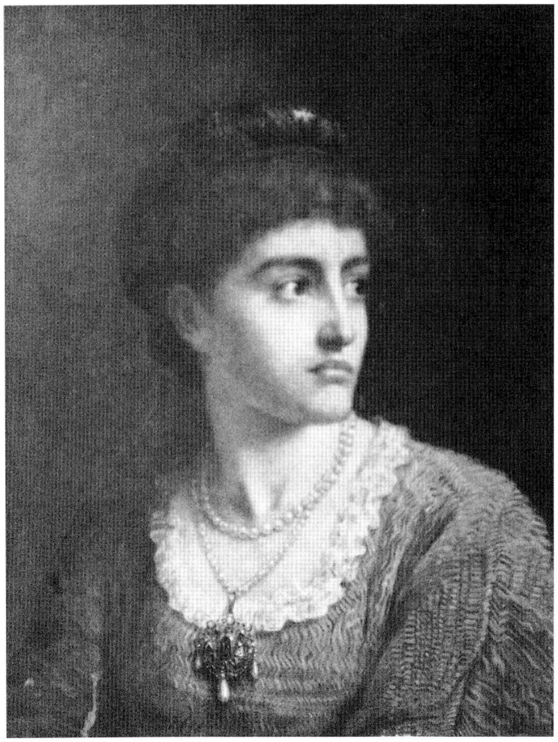

257. *Katherine ('The Taming of the Shrew'),* c. 1888.
GEORGE WELLESLEY-FRY

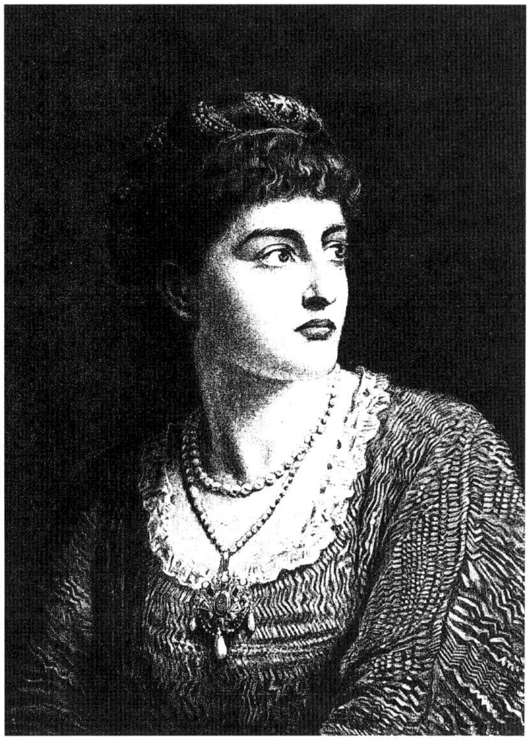

257. *Katherine ('The Taming of the Shrew'),* Engraving from *The Graphic,* 20 January 1888 (supplement)

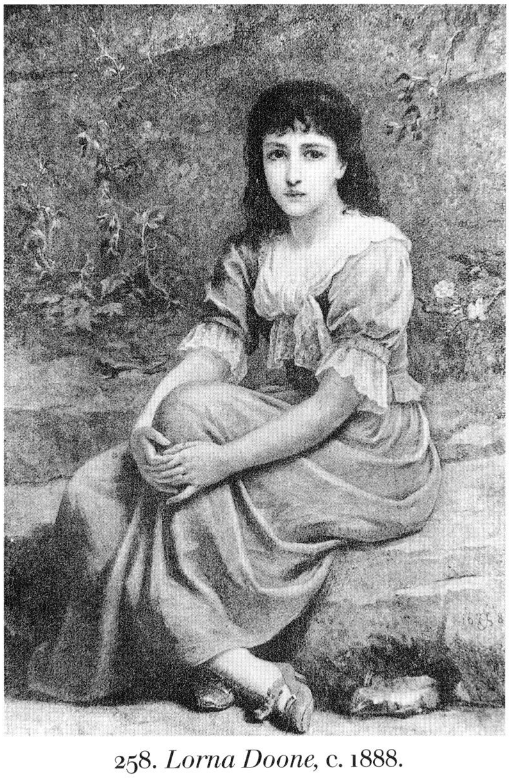

258. *Lorna Doone,* c. 1888.

259. Sir Edmund Henderson K.C.B., (2)

1888; unknown size; oil on canvas.

A second portrait by Long of Sir Edmund Henderson (1821–96). Henderson was made commissioner of the Metropolitan Police in 1869 and during his time in office substantially increased its numbers. The portrait was painted two years after his retirement in 1888. It was favourably reviewed in *The Times*: "Other pictures in this room which deserve notice are . . . Mr. Long's portrait of Sir Edmund Henderson (998)".[1] It seems unlikely that it is a copy of the 1887 version as it would not have been exhibited twice at Burlington House.

1. *The Times*, 25 May 1888, p. 4.

EXHIBITIONS RA 1888 (998).
LITERATURE Quick 1931, p. 6, p. 43; *The Times*, 25 May 1888, p. 4.

260. Lord Randolph Churchill

1888; 50½ × 40", 127.4 × 101.6 cm; oil on canvas.

A seated portrait of Lord Randolph Churchill exhibited at the 1888 Royal Academy Exhibition. The *Art Journal* found it: "A likeness, but neither the colour nor the workmanship is pleasing".[1] *The Times* was similarly critical in calling it "a sadly commonplace version of the mobile and animated presence of Lord Randolph Churchill".[2]

1. AJ, 1888, p. 183.
2. *The Times*, 16 May 1888, p. 4.

PROVENANCE Presented by J. Blundell Maples Esq., MP, to the Constitutional Club, London; bought by the National Portrait Gallery, London, from Bonham's in 1976.
EXHIBITIONS RA 1888 (184).
LITERATURE *Academy Notes* 1888; AJ, 1888, p. 183; Quick 1931, p. 6, p. 17 (ill.), p. 43; *The Times*, 16 May 1888, p. 4.
COLLECTION National Portrait Gallery, London

261. George M'Corquodale

1888; unknown size; oil on canvas.

EXHIBITIONS RA 1888 (385).
LITERATURE *Academy Notes* 1888; Quick 1931, p. 43.

262. Egyptian Fruit Seller

1889; unknown size; oil on canvas; signed and dated.

A painting of an Egyptian fruit seller painted in 1889.

PROVENANCE Sold at Christie's on 18 June 1892 for 600 guineas.

263. Preparing for the Feast of Anubis

1889; 42 × 60", 106.7 × 152.4 cm; oil on canvas; signed and dated.

Like *Sacred to Pasht*, Long chose the subject of the worship of an Egyptian zoomorphic god with its attendant associated animals. In this case he depicted the worship of Anubis, the jackal-headed god. The setting is an Egyptian interior with two figures surrounded by dogs. The male figure is seated with a group of performing dogs whilst a girl is standing holding a blue vase. The subject of the painting was elucidated in the Royal Academy catalogue:

> It was usual with the ancient Egyptians during the great festivals, for the priests to go among the people and astonish them with conjuring and necromantic tricks, in which animals played an important part. On the feast of Anubis the jackal-headed god, who presided over the scales in the final weighing of the soul, dogs and jackals, sacred to the deity, were employed: when fortune-telling, detection of crime, or messages from the dead, convinced people of the priests' supernatural power.[1]

1. 1889 RA exhibition catalogue.

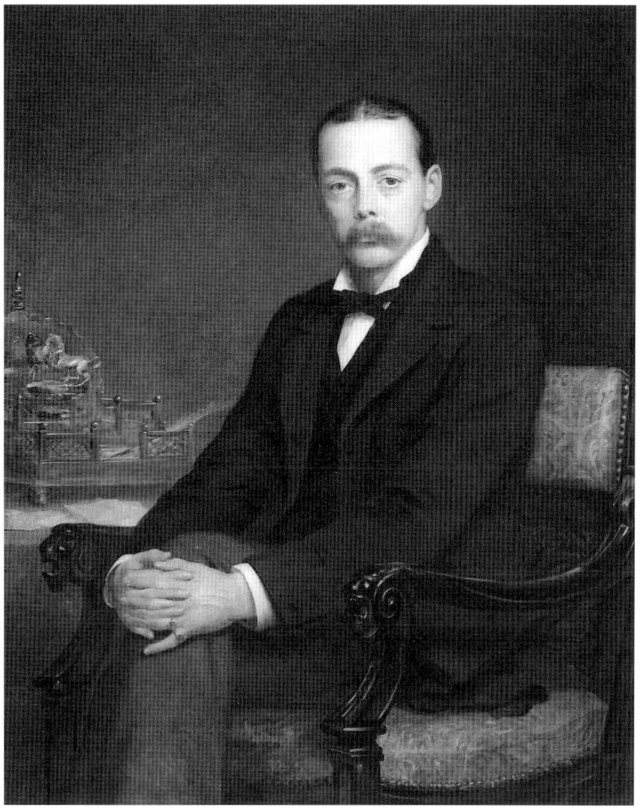

260. *Lord Randolph Churchill*, 1888.
COURTESY OF THE NATIONAL PORTRAIT GALLERY, LONDON

PROVENANCE By descent to Margaret Jemima Long; sold at Christie's on 1 February 1908 for £75 12s to W. W. Sampson; sold at Christie's on 20 November 1911 for 145 guineas to Linton.
EXHIBITIONS RA 1889 (255); ELG 1883–84 (3) as *Before the Feast of Anubis.*
LITERATURE *Academy Notes* 1889, p. x; Chester 1908, p. 350; ELG 1894, p. 17; Quick 1931, p. 45; Reitlinger 1961.

264. Propriating the Deity

1889; 58 × 38", 147.3 × 96.5 cm; oil on canvas; signed with monogram and dated.

A three-quarter-length portrait of an Eastern woman filling a large temple vase with flowers. She is dressed in colourful robes and rich jewellery. In the background to the left through the doorway a mother and daughter can be seen carrying baskets.

PROVENANCE Purchased from the artist by Thomas Agnew and Sons on 1 November 1889 for £1,260.
LITERATURE Chester 1908, p. 345 (ill.), p. 349.

265. Ruth the Gleaner

1889; 39½ × 54¼", 100 × 138 cm; oil on canvas; signed with monogram and dated.

The subject for the painting is the book of Ruth, "And she went, and came, and gleaned in the field after the reapers: and her hap was to light on part of the field belonging to Boaz . . . ".[1] It depicts Ruth in a field of wheat kneeling and looking directly at the viewer. In the background to the left, two girls who have been reaping look on and discuss her. To the right a small settlement is visible and further forward a group of men working in the field are looking up at her. The painting was given to Bristol City Art Gallery

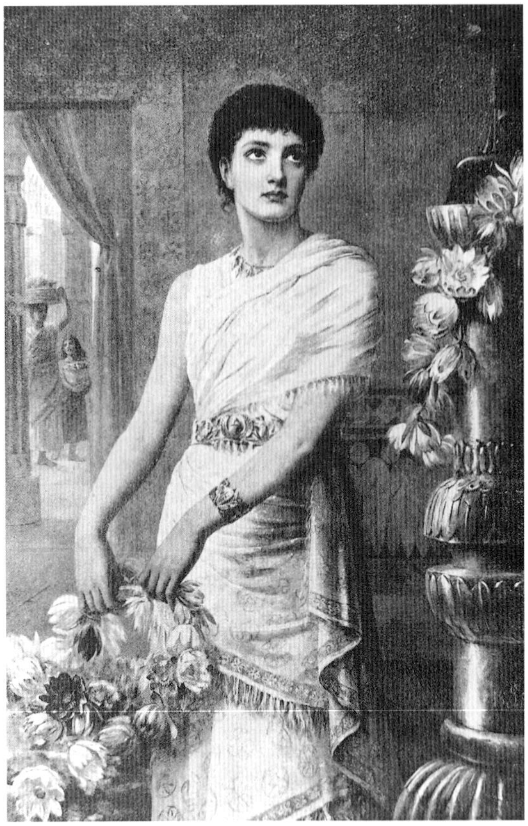

264. *Propiating the Deity*, 1889.

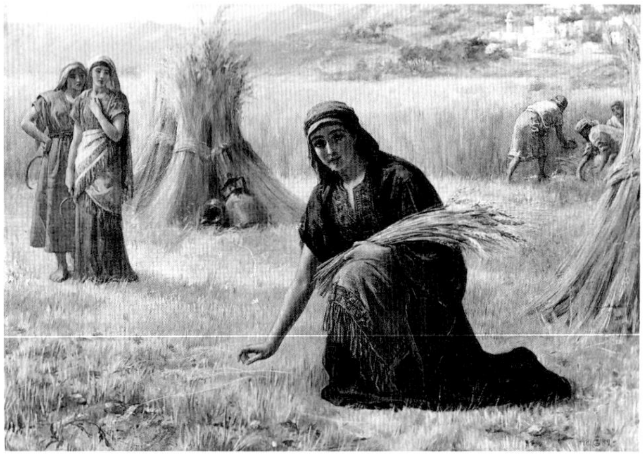

265. *Ruth the Gleaner*, 1889.

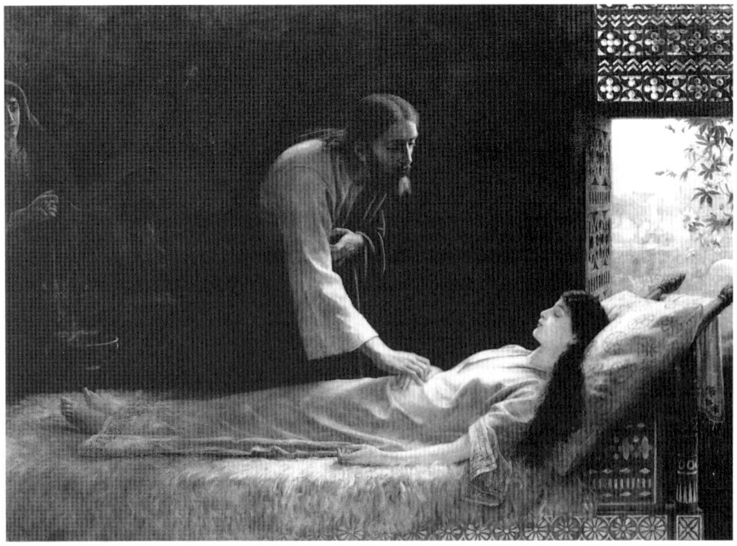

266. *Jairus' Daughter*, 1889.
VICTORIA ART GALLERY, BATH & NORTH EAST SOMERSET COUNCIL

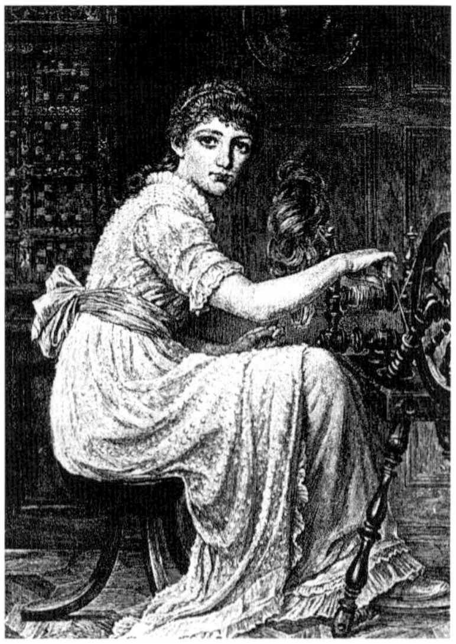

267. *The Spinster (A Simple Maiden)*, 1890.
Engraving by J. Dobie,
in the *Magazine of Art*, 1891.

in 1931 and subsequently went missing. A painting by Long entitled *In the Land of the Pharaohs* went for auction at Christie's in New York on 30 October 1985 for $1,500 (£1,049). The auction house illustration of the painting appears the same as illustrations of *Ruth the Gleaner*. Both are signed with a monogram and dated 1889, both are the same size (allowing for very slight differences in accuracy of measurement). They are clearly either the same painting, or *In the Land of the Pharaohs* is a copy of *Ruth the Gleaner*.

1. Ruth, II: 3.

PROVENANCE Sold at Frost and Reed in 1931 to W. M. Wills; W. Melville Wills presented to Bristol City Art Gallery in 1931.
LITERATURE Quick 1931, p. 24 (ill.), p. 44.
COLLECTION Registered as lost from Bristol City Art Gallery in 1978.

265.1 Portrait of Ruth

c. 1889; 20 × 16", 51 × 41 cm; oil on canvas; signed.

A portrait of Ruth and study for *Ruth the Gleaner*.

PROVENANCE Sold at Sotheby's on 8 October 1987 for £1,100.

266. Jairus' Daughter (2)

1889; 54 × 74", 137.2 × 188 cm; oil on canvas; signed with monogram and dated.

The second version of *Jairus' Daughter* by Long takes a later stage in the story than he had in the first. The painting illustrates St. Mark: "And he took the damsel by the hand, and said unto her, *Talitha cumi*; which is, being interpreted, Damsel, I say unto thee, arise".[1] The painting shows Christ leaning over Jairus' dead daughter who lies on a bed across the front of the picture. Typical for Long is the attention to detail, on the decoration on the bed and window. The light source is the open window through which we can see examples of Middle Eastern architecture. Jairus' daughter is fully illuminated by the light and Christ in half-light emphasising the softness of his figure and profile. Jairus is seen seated in the dark corner of the room. Blackburn described the painting in *Academy Notes*: "The girl is lying on a bed covered with soft white goats' skin, the pallor of her Jewish face is heightened by contrast with her jet black hair. Through the open window to the right is seen the city of Nazareth; on the left a group of father, mother and disciple, watch the progress of the miracle".[2]

1. Mark, V: 41.
2. *Academy Notes* 1889, p. xv.

PROVENANCE By descent to Mrs. Margaret Jemima Long, gift to the Victoria Art Gallery, Bath, 1900.
EXHIBITIONS RA 1889 (503); Manchester Autumn Exhibition, 1891; ELG 1893–94 (5), Bristol 1907.
LITERATURE *Academy Notes* 1889, p. xv, p. 48 (ill.); ELG 1894, pp. 19–20; *Magazine of Art*, 1892, p. vi; *Pictorial Education*, vol. v, no. 3 (1931), p. 5 (ill.); Quick 1931, p. 26 (ill.), p. 44.
COLLECTION Victoria Art Gallery, Bath.

267. The Spinster (A Simple Maiden)

1890; 49 × 35", 124.5 × 89 cm; oil on canvas; signed and dated.

This work shows an auburn-haired girl in eighteenth-century dress in a period room setting and she appears to be spinning her own hair. There is a clear fairy tale feel to the painting, reinforced by its subtitle *There was a simple maiden, long ago. The Times* found it unsatisfactory, and *Punch* wrote: "'Long Ago' LONG (Edwin RA) and more 'a go'. Instead of 'Long Ago,' which is more egotistical, why not 'Long Egit' or 'Long Fecit?'"[1] Nevertheless, the popularity of the image resulted in its reproduction in the *Magazine of Art*: "'The Spinster' was exhibited at the Academy, and was highly popular. The plate has been etched by Mr. Dobie in the manner which he has practically invented for himself".[2] When shown at the Edwin Long Gallery it was titled *A Simple Maiden*, but its subtitle was retained.

1. *Punch*, 9 May 1891, p. 227.
2. *Magazine of Art*, 1891, p. 402.

PROVENANCE Sold at Christie's on 26 May 1972 for £199 as *At the Spinning Wheel.*
EXHIBITIONS RA 1891 (5); ELG 1893–94 (9).
LITERATURE *Academy Notes* 1891, p. 1; Ath., 16 May 1891, p. 641; ELG 1894, p. 22; *Magazine of Art*, 1891, p. 402 (ill.); *Punch*, 9 May 1891, p. 227; Quick 1931, p. 45; *The Times*, 11 May 1891, p. 8.

268. The Artist's Studio

1890; 6 × 9½", 15 × 24 cm; oil on panel; signed with monogram and dated; signed and with monogram, dated and inscribed on reverse; "To my [young] friend [Wilbur, or Charles] Debenham with best wishes for his success".

The same picture appears twice at Phillips' but with different titles and slightly different inscriptions. Both note the possibility of it being a preliminary study for *The Chosen Five*, but this is impossible as it was painted in 1885. It is possible however that Long is dealing with the same subject matter, and that the artist depicted is Zeuxis.

PROVENANCE Sold at Phillips' on 20 March 1990 for £1,600 as *The Artist's Studio* and inscribed "... young friend Charles ..."; sold at Phillips' to the Christopher Wood Gallery on 14 December 1993 as *The Artist's Model* and inscribed "... friend Wilbur".

269. La Pia Dei Tolomei

1890; 59 × 32¼", 150 × 82 cm; oil on canvas; signed with monogram and dated.

A three-quarter-length portrait of Miss Calhoun as Pia Dei Tolomei of Dante's *Purgatory*: "Remember me, that am called Piety; Siena made me and Maremma undid me, As well he knows who plighted troth to me, And set his ring upon my hand to wed me".[1] The painting is described in *Academy Notes* as a "dark-robed figure, with clasped hands and dreaming eyes, whose slow martyrdom, when imprisoned by a jealous husband in a fever-stricken castle has been described by Dante".[2] She is holding rosary beads and wearing a dark dress which is decorated with the star of David and the Lamb of God. She stands against a

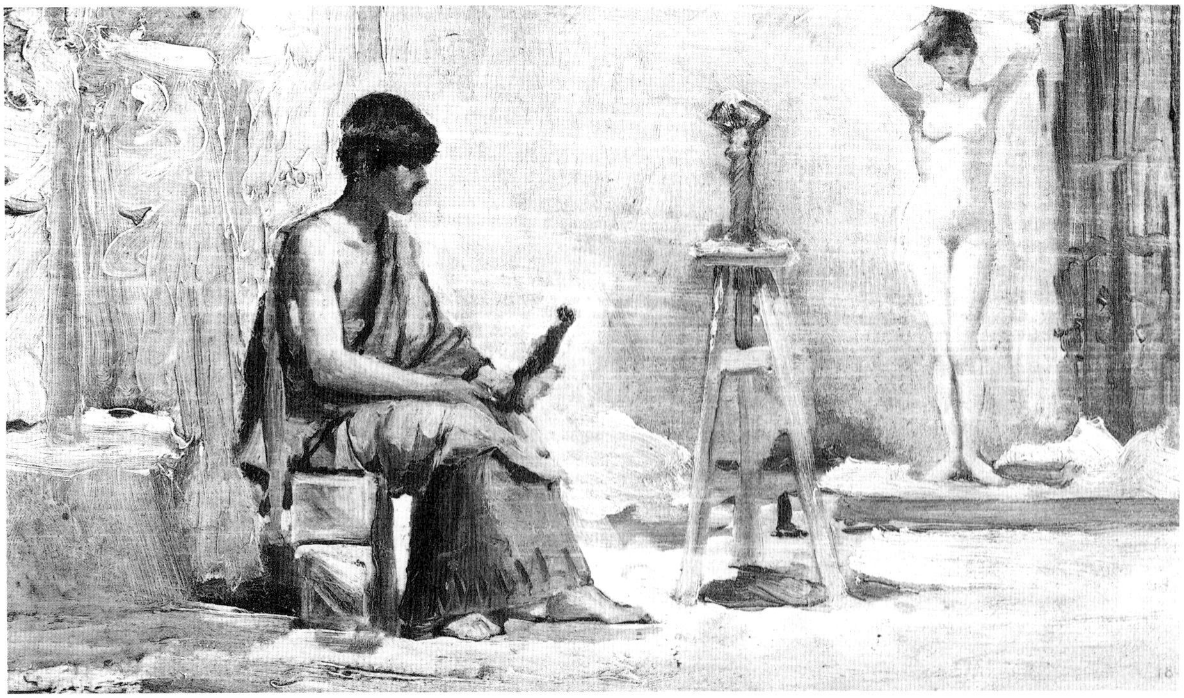

268. *The Artist's Studio*, 1890.
PHILLIPS FINE ART AUCTIONEERS, LONDON

flattened and sketched backdrop of early Italian iconic Christian images. Pia, the daughter of a Sienese family is said to have married Nello, a lord of the Castello della Pietro who murdered her. In this painting Long once more explores the subject of the impending martyrdom of innocent young women.

1. Dante Alighieri, *Purgatory*, canto v: 133–36; translated by Dorothy L. Sayers (London: Penguin, 1955), p. 107.
2. *Academy Notes* 1890, p. 6.

PROVENANCE Purchased from the artist by Thomas Agnew and Sons on 14 August 1890 for £600; sold to Henry Townsend October 1890; sold at Christie's on 25 May 1972.
EXHIBITIONS RA 1890 (26).
LITERATURE *Academy Notes* 1890, p. 6, p. 29 (ill.).

270. Colonel Sanderson, MP

1890; unknown size; oil on canvas.

A portrait of the late Colonel Sanderson MP exhibited at the 1890 Royal Academy Exhibition.

EXHIBITIONS RA 1890 (689).

271. Lady Garvagh

1890; unknown size; oil on canvas.

A portrait of Lady Garvagh exhibited at the 1890 Royal Academy Exhibition.

EXHIBITIONS RA 1890 (250).

272. Mrs M'Corquodale and Children

1890; unknown size; oil on canvas.

A portrait of Mrs M'Corquodale and her children exhibited at the 1890 Royal Academy exhibition.

EXHIBITIONS RA 1890 (486).

273. A Madonna

1891; 23½ × 19½", 60 × 49 cm; oil on canvas.

A small portrait exhibited at the Edwin Long Gallery between 1893 and 1894.

PROVENANCE By descent to Mrs Margaret Jemima Long; sold at Christie's on 1 February 1908 for 13 guineas.
EXHIBITIONS ELG 1893–94 (15).
LITERATURE ELG 1894, p. 22.

274. Before the Festival

1891; unknown size; oil on canvas.

An Egyptian nude preparing for an ancient festival. *Academy Notes* described the painting as "An Egyptian maiden, nude, fronting the spectator, fastens in her hair a flower from among some on a scarlet table at her side. Background of paintings in yellowish grey on a blue wall".[1]

1. *Academy Notes* 1891, p. 10.

EXHIBITIONS RA 1891 (249); '21st Annual Exhibition of Modern Works of Art', Walker Art Gallery, Liverpool, August 1891; ELG 1893–94 (23).
LITERATURE *Academy Notes* 1891, p. 10; ELG 1894, p. 24; *Magazine of Art*, 1892, p. i.

275. Mrs Lampson and her Children

1891; unknown size; oil on canvas.

A portrait of Mrs Lampson and her children exhibited at the 1891 Royal Academy Exhibition. *The Athenaeum* noted that: "The late Mr. Long's 'Mrs Lampson and her Children' (594), two life-size figures seated on a bench, a child looking over the back of the seat, shows more spirit than usual . . . "[1] The painting came into the news in 1892 due to a court action taken by Long's executor in Milles v. Lampson.

> In the action brought by the executor of the late Mr. Long, R.A., against Mr. Norman Lampson of Old Bond Street, to recover a thousand guineas, the price of a picture of the defendant's wife and daughter painted by Mr. Long for the defendant, no sum appears to have been agreed upon between the artist and the purchasor, and it was therefore left to the jury to assess the value of Mr. Long's work, which they did at the price claimed.[2]

1. Ath., 23 May 1891, p. 673.
2. *Magazine of Art*, 1893, p. v.

PROVENANCE Commissioned by Mr. Norman Lampson from the artist for 1,000 guineas.
EXHIBITIONS RA 1891 (594).
LITERATURE Ath., 23 May 1891, p. 673; *Magazine of Art*, 1893, p. 5; *The Times*, 1 November 1892, p. 7.

276. Angela Vanbrough

1891; 40 × 28″, 101.5 × 71 cm; oil on canvas.

A half-length portrait of Miss Angela Vanbrough playing a violin, against a background of patterned wallpaper, wearing a white dress and dark sash. *Punch* punned "No. 467. 'Angela Vanbrough' playing the fiddle; or, All alone with her Beau. EDWIN LONG RA".[1] The *Illustrated London News* singled out this portrait for praise in 1891 when they wrote: " . . . the others being figure subjects, and of these the most attractive portrait of Miss Angela Vanbrough, a youth violinist, in a white dress aond dark coloured sash".[2]

1. *Punch*, 16 May 1891, p. 238.
2. *Illustrated London News*, 1891.

EXHIBITIONS RA 1891 (467).
LITERATURE *Academy Notes* 1891, p. 14, p. 90 (ill.); *Illustrated London News*, 1891; *Punch*, 16 May 1891, p. 238.

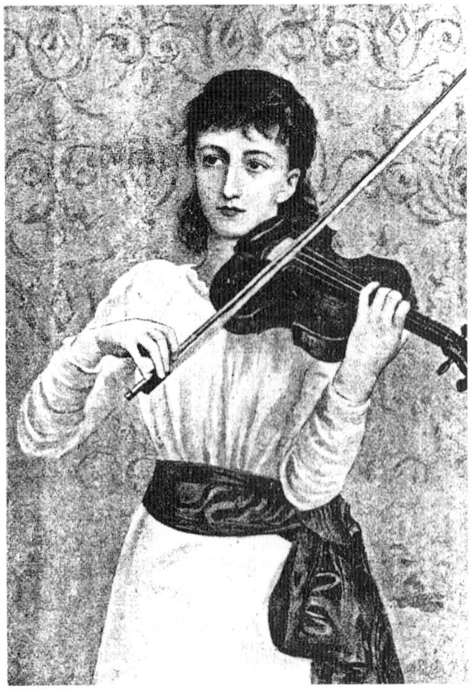

276. *Angela Vanbrough*, 1891.
In *Academy Notes*, 1891, p. 90.

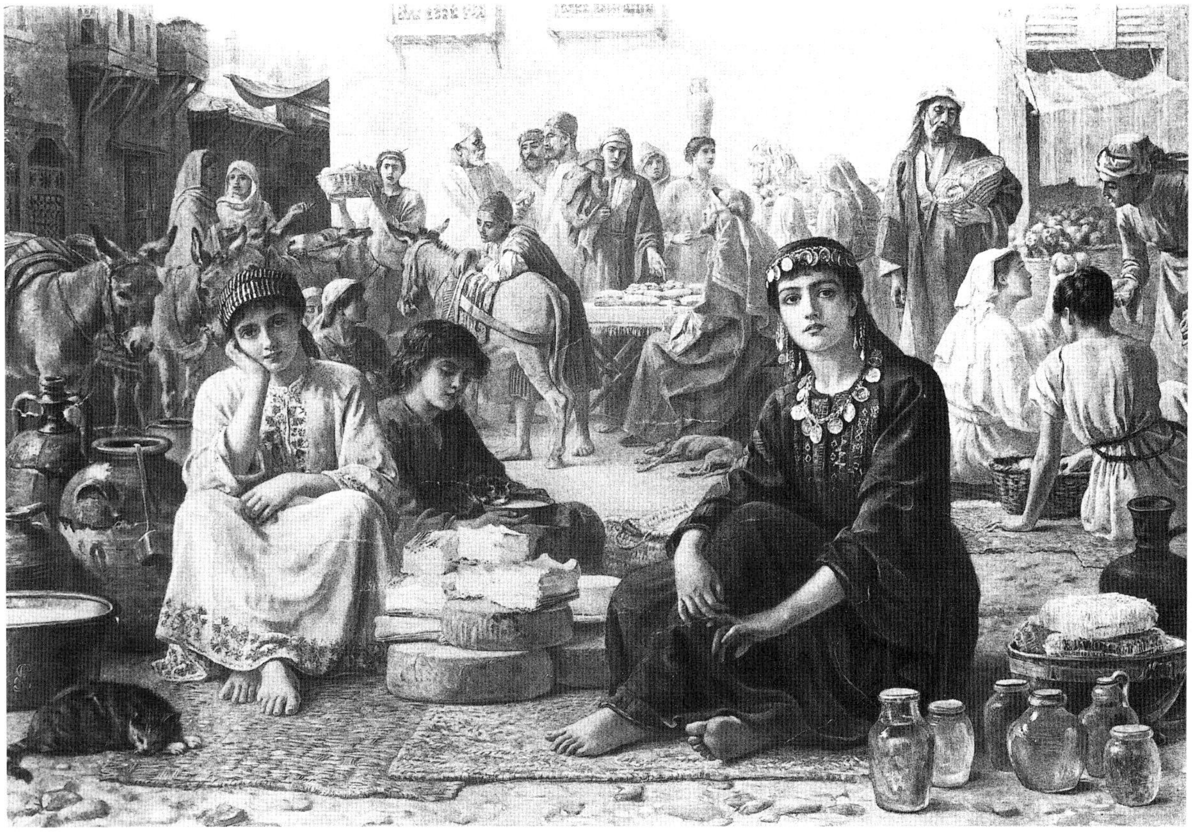

277. *The Market-Place at Nazareth*, 1891. Print.
RUSSELL-CATES ART GALLERY AND MUSEUM, PHOTOGRAPH SHAUN GARNER

277. The Market-Place at Nazareth

1891; 51 × 78″, 129.6 × 198.2 cm; oil on canvas.

Long's painting of a Nazareth Market-Place is reminiscent of many of his early Spanish market scenes. Presumably this is the reason that Messrs Frost and Reed wrongly titled it in 1929 as *The Market Place, Seville*. The scene is clearly of the Middle East and the women are in Palestinian dress. Further, Long's painting ability had significantly advanced by 1891 and the models portrayed in the work are clearly from after his Spanish period. The picture depicts two young women dressed in their traditional finery, sat on carpets looking directly at the viewer. In the background, Arabs and Jews can be seen mingling in a busy market place.

The work was exhibited in 1891 at the Doré Gallery and advertised in *The Times*: "amongst Doré's great pictures an important new work, the Market-Place at Nazareth by Edwin Long, R.A. On view Daily 10–6, 1s".[1] The picture was then exhibited at the Edwin Long Gallery where its title was altered to the *Market Women of Bethlehem*.[2]

1. *The Times*, 16 March 1891, p. 1.
2. ELG 1894, p. 22.

PROVENANCE Fairless and Beeforth; sold at Messrs Frost and Reed in 1929 as *The Market Place, Seville*. Doré Gallery, 35 New Bond Street, London, 1891; ELG 1893–94 as *Market Women of Bethlehem* (11).

LITERATURE ELG 1894, p. 22; *The Times*, 16 March 1891, p. 1.

278. The Parable of the Sower

1891; 101 × 203", 256.6 × 515.7 cm; oil on canvas.

The full title of the painting is *The Parable of the Sower, Christ Preaching on the Lake of Galilee*, and is described at length in 1894 by the Rev. Canon Farrar.[1] It is Long's largest and one of his most ambitious works, depicting the moment of the telling of the first parable. Christ is the central figure, dressed in a blue robe, preaching from a boat in an inlet of Galilee. In the background is a flat-roofed Eastern house with fishing nets out to dry, farther off Mount Hermon is visible. The background also contains the field and sower that was the inspiration for the parable about to be told. The crowd that has gathered to hear Christ includes a variety of races and nationalities including Africans, Jews, Orientals and two Roman soldiers. One of the figures is a portrait of Josef Mayer who played Christ in the 1890 Passion of Ober-Ammergau.

The painting is the epitome of Long's later ambitions as a religious painter. The description by Canon Farrar praises Long's religious convictions:

> But in the many yearly exhibitions in England, among multitudes of landscapes, portraits, and specimens of genre painting, sacred art is often entirely unrepresented, and few masterpieces of this generation are connected in any way with the faith of Christians. It is, therefore, a matter of congratulation when an artist of such eminence as Mr. Edwin Long devotes his powers to the illustration of scenes which bear on the life of the Saviour of the World.[2]

The work was painted in the last year of Long's life and is one of his last finished works. When Sir Merton Russell-Cotes visited Long at Netherhall Gardens in 1891, he saw the work in progress: "He was at work at that time on a huge canvas depicting our Saviour preaching from a boat on the Sea of Galilee".[3] Long's obvious pleasure in the painting and its religious conviction was reflected in his refusal of 5,000 guineas for it. "Long refused 5,000 gs for it, and it remained on his widow's hands. Mark the sequel. After a contest lasting exactly 35 seconds, Mr. W. W. Sampson of Air Street, lifted the prize at 125 gs".[4]

1. ELG 1894, pp. 3–15.
2. Ibid, p. 4.
3. *Home and Abroad*, p. 709.
4. *Daily Telegraph*, date unknown, 1908.

PROVENANCE By descent to Margaret Jemima Long; sold at Christie's to Mr. W. W. Sampson for £131 and 5s.
EXHIBITIONS ELG 1893–94 (1); Royal Society of Artists, Spring Exhibition, London, 1906.
LITERATURE *Bulletin (R-C)*, vol. 11, no. 2 (June 1923), pp. 22–23; *Daily Telegraph*, date unknown, 1908; ELG 1894, pp. 3–15; Quick 1931, p. 6, p. 44; *Home and Abroad*, p. 709.

279. Egyptian Girl Cutting Lotus Flowers.

unknown date and size; oil on canvas.

EXHIBITIONS ELG 1893–94 (21).
LITERATURE ELG 1894, p. 23.

280. Egyptian Princess.

unknown date. 50 × 25", 127 × 63.5 cm; oil on canvas.

PROVENANCE By descent to Margaret Jemima Long; sold at Christie's on 1 February 1908 for £30 9s.

SELECT BIBLIOGRAPHY

Anno Domini *Painted by Edwin Long R.A.* Catalogue. London: Lawrence Gallery, 1884.

Anno Domini *Painted by Edwin Long R.A., also* Zeuxis at Crotona . . . *etc.* Catalogue. London: Lawrence Gallery, 1885.

Archer, Frank. *An Actor's Notebooks.* London: Stanley Paul & Co., 1912.

Bills, Mark. 'Edwin Longsden Long, R.A.', *Antique Collecting* (November 1996), pp. 4–9.

Bulletin of the Russell-Cotes Art Gallery & Museum vol. II, no. 2 (June 1923), pp. 16–23.

———, vol. V, no. 3 (September 1926), pp. 30–31.

———, vol. IX, no. 3 (September 1930), p. 29.

———, vol. XI, no. 2 (June 1932), p. 18, p. 20.

———, vol. XI, no. 3 (September 1932), pp. 30–32.

Catalogue of Pictures. Egham, London: Royal Holloway College, 1896.

Chapel, Jeannie. *Victorian Taste: The Complete Catalogue of Paintings in the Royal Holloway College.* London: Royal Holloway College, 1982.

Chester, Austin. 'The Art of Edwin Long, R.A.' *Windsor Magazine* (February 1908), pp. 332–350.

Clayton, Peter A. *The Rediscovery of Ancient Egypt.* London: Thames and Hudson, 1982.

Curl, James Stevens. *The Egyptian Revival.* London: Allen and Unwin, 1982.

Daughters of Our Empire by Edwin Long R.A. Catalogue. London: Agnew's, 1887.

De Meulenaere, Herman. *Ancient Egypt in Nineteenth Century Painting.* Belgium: Berko, 1992.

Descriptive Catalogue of the Pictures of the Late Edwin Long, R.A. Catalogue for Edwin Long Gallery. London: Doherty & Co., 1894.

Ditchfield, P. H. *The City Companies of London.* London: J. M. Dent & Co., 1904.

Egyptomania, Egypt in Western Art, 1730–1930. Catalogue to exhibition organised by the Louvre, and shown in Paris, Ottawa, and Vienna, 1994.

Gaunt, William. 'An Edwardian Bequest'. *Architectural Review*, no. 119 (March 1956), pp. 170–174.

Hawthorne, Julian. *Shapes that Pass.* London: John Murray, 1928.

Humbert, Jean-Marcel. *L'Égyptomanie dans l'art occidental.* Paris: ACR édition, 1989.

Kestner, Joseph A. *Mythology and Misogyny.* Wisconsin and London: University of Wisconsin Press, 1989.

Members and Associates of the Royal Academy of Arts, 1891, photographed in their studios. London: National Portrait Gallery, 1892.

Olding, Simon, and Shaun Garner. *So Fair a House.* Bournemouth: Russell-Cotes Art Gallery and Museum, 1997.

Ormond, Richard. *Early Victorian Portraits.* 2 vols. London: HMSO, 1973.

Quick, Richard. *The Life and Works of Edwin Long R.A.* The Russell-Cotes Art Gallery and Museum: Bournemouth, 1931.

Reitlinger, Gerald. *The Economics of Taste.* Vol. 1., *The Rise and Fall of Picture Prices, 1760–1960.* 3 vols. London: Barrie and Rockliff, 1961.

Ruskin, John. *Academy Notes, 1875.* London: George Allen, 1902.

Russell-Cotes, Sir Merton. *Home and Abroad.* 2 vols. Bournemouth: privately printed, 1921.

Spielmann, M. H. 'Painters in their Studios, II.– Mr. Edwin Long R.A'. *The Graphic* (9 June 1888), pp. 612–14.

Walkley, Giles. *Artists' Houses in London 1764–1914.* Aldershot: Scolar Press, 1994.

White, Gleeson. *The Master Painters of Britain.* Birmingham: Combridge, 1910.

Wood, Christopher. *Olympian Dreamers, Victorian Classical Painters.* London: Constable, 1983.

INDEX OF NAMES AND WORKS

Page numbers in **bold** refer to the main reference to a work in the catalogue section. Where a work is illustrated in the catalogue section, the page number is followed by "(ill.)". An asterisk means that the work is reproduced in colour.

INDEX OF NAMES AND WORKS

INDEX OF NAMES AND WORKS

INDEX OF NAMES AND WORKS

INDEX OF NAMES AND WORKS

INDEX OF NAMES AND WORKS

INDEX OF NAMES AND WORKS